Transactions of the Royal Historical Society

SIXTH SERIES

I

LONDON 1991

British Library Cataloguing in Publication Data

Transactions of the Royal Historical Society.
— 6th Series, vol. 1 (1991)
1. History—Periodicals
I. Royal Historical Society
905   D1
ISBN 0-86193-134-3

Made and printed in Great Britain by Butler & Tanner Ltd, Frome and London

CONTENTS

TRANSACTIONS OF THE
ROYAL HISTORICAL SOCIETY
PRESIDENTIAL ADDRESS
By F. M. L. Thompson

ENGLISH LANDED SOCIETY IN THE TWENTIETH CENTURY
II NEW POOR AND NEW RICH

READ 16 NOVEMBER 1990

THE notion that the great leviathans of wealth, who had for so long been accustomed to taking first place in a nation of snobs which contrived simultaneously to accept, admire, envy, and criticise their opulence, might actually become impoverished first began to gain some currency in the 1890s. True, this had been anticipated by a few specially pessimistic and debt-ridden landowners in the immediate anxieties aroused by the Repeal of the Corn Laws. Lord Monson, who had inherited from a cousin estates liberally furnished with dowagers and other inescapable expenses, and who was in despair at the tendency of income to fall while outgoings remained fixed, exploded to his son in 1851: 'What an infernal bore is landed property. No certain income can be reckoned upon. I hope your future wife will have Consols or some such ballast, I think it is worth half as much again as land.' A similar but more sober banker's view had been put by Evelyn Denison, a classic gentlemanly capitalist, in 1847 when he announced his intention to sell much of his land 'not because I am of the class of encumbered landlords, for I have luckily extricated myself from that, but because I do not think it worth while to keep a security paying 2 per cent, when I can get an equally good one paying 5'.[1]

In practice, as long as landed estates yielded some positive return, an income large enough to cover outgoings, keep up a position, and keep the creditors happy, great landowners did not have much

---

[1] Lincoln Record Office, Monson MS, 25/10/3/1, no. 19, 22 Nov. 1851; Sheffield Public Library, Wentworth Woodhouse MS, G 20, J. E. Denison to Lord Fitzwilliam, 18 Aug. 1847. Quoted in F. M. L. Thompson, *English Landed Society in the Nineteenth Century* (1963), 290.

inclination to behave as economic men making accountants' nice calculations about the best way to arrange their investments. The panic over the effects of Repeal, such as it was, soon passed. It is true that the spectacular land sales by the Duke of Buckingham in the 1840s, culminating in the grand spectacle of the sale of the contents of Stowe in 1848, sent shock waves through the entire landed order, and were a powerful stimulus to a vogue for prudence and caution in financial affairs, as were the equally well publicised troubles of the Duke of Beaufort or the Earl of Mornington.[2] Such troubles, however, were palpably the result of individual mismanagement, self-indulgence, and eccentricity on the grand scale, and had very little to do with corn laws, the price of wheat, or the level of agricultural rents, although the conjuncture of uncertainty over the immediate future of rents with the collapse of mighty figures with supposedly mighty fortunes undoubtedly added to the sense of drama as the whole of Society journeyed out to the viewing days at Stowe. But then, basking in the agricultural prosperity of the 1850s and 1860s, the jittery nerves were forgotten. When prominent figures like the Duke of Newcastle or the Earl of Winchilsea were in severe financial difficulties in the late 1860s, forcing them into land sales and to the edge of bankruptcy, there was no sense of a general crisis of the landed order, and so the reporting was tucked away in the reports of bankruptcy court proceedings and there was no *frisson* in high society.[3] It is useful to remember, however, that a certain amount of failure, impoverishment, or disgrace was normal among the ranks of the landowners, and that it attracted wide notice only when individual instances happened to coincide with general adverse or ominous trends in land values.

By the 1890s a general gloom of this kind had set in, and was to prove so persistent that it is generally held to herald the beginning of the complete collapse of the British aristocracy. Oscar Wilde's rediscovery, in 1895, of the sentiments expressed by Monson a generation earlier is the most well-known announcement of the impending demise of the world as the patricians had known it. Lady Bracknell's

---

[2] *The Times*, 14 Aug. 1848, leader on the disgrace of the Duke of Buckingham 'who has struck a heavy blow at the whole order to which he unfortunately belongs'. *Annual Register*, 1848, 125–9. See also D. and E. Spring, 'The Fall of the Grenvilles, 1844–8,' *Huntington Library Quarterly*, XIX (1956); F. M. L. Thompson, 'The End of a Great Estate,' *Economic History Review*, 2nd ser. VIII (1955).

[3] For the Duke of Newcastle, *The Times*, bankruptcy reports, 3 June 1869, 11, to 27 Jan. 1871, 11; the Duke, with heavy racing debts, eventually paid 5*s.* in the £ to his creditors. For the Earl of Winchilsea, *The Times*, bankruptcy reports, 6 Oct. 1870, 11, to 30 June 1871, 10; the Earl tried to sell the Hatton Collection to the British Museum, which he said 'have been buried for the last 200 years and have been of no use to anyone', but the B.M. offered only £1,800, against his asking price of £10,000.

aphorism is much more memorable than any amount of rent statistics or royal commission reports: 'What between the duties expected of one during one's lifetime, and the duties exacted from one after one's death, land has ceased to be either a profit or a pleasure. It gives one a position, and prevents one from keeping it up. That's all that can be said about land.'[4] This was a clever dramatist's instant response to Harcourt's death duties, imposed the previous year, only a shade less instant than that of *Punch* which within weeks of the 1894 Budget ran a cartoon on the 'Depressed Dukes' in which the Duke of Devonshire says: 'If this Budget passes I don't know how I'm going to keep up Chatsworth', and the Duke of Westminster replies: 'If you come to that, we may consider ourselves lucky if we can keep a tomb over our heads.'[5]

It has always been the habit of the very rich to imagine that they are about to become short of money. A hundred years later these particular dukes still have rather ample roofs over their heads and broad acres under their feet, and are not short of tombs. Imposed at a time when agriculture had been in a bad way for more than a decade and land values had been slipping rather steeply, the psychological impact of the death duties was certainly sharp, and the shiver of apprehension they sent through the propertied classes was understandable. All the same, their real impact was not ruinous, and they were intended, as is so often the case with new forms of taxation, to pay for a rearmament programme, in this instance Spencer's policy of building a whole new battleship fleet (the *Magnificent* class, the first ships mounting cordite-using big guns, which remained the technical masters of the seas until the invention of the Dreadnought in 1906), and were not conceived as an instrument of any social policy of discrimination against inherited wealth or promotion of greater equality.[6] The maximum rate of Harcourt's duties was in fact 8 per cent on estates valued at £1 million or more, and this rate, as indeed the whole scheme of consolidating the previous scattered and complicated group of inheritance taxes into a single set of death duties, was the brainchild of Alfred Milner, at that time chairman of the Board of Inland Revenue, who was keen on efficiency but even more keen on preserving the existing social order and its basis in private property, through enlightened imperialism, the elimination of waste, and the spread of property ownership.[7] Milner was the last man to seek to deal a death blow to the territorial system, although he did

[4] Oscar Wilde, *The Importance of Being Earnest* (1895).
[5] *Punch*, 30 June 1894, reproduced in D. Cannadine, *The Decline and Fall of the British Aristocracy* (1990), 96.
[6] R. C. K. Ensor, *England, 1870–1914* (Oxford, 1936), 288–9.
[7] A. Offer, *Property and Politics, 1870–1914* (Cambridge, 1981), 205—7. Milner had a mistress, which gave him some kind of interest in the taxation of illegitimate children.

not look kindly on effete or incompetent aristocrats. It was even possible to make a case for death duties at reasonable rates as a positively beneficial instrument for goading slothful and ineffective landowners into self-preservation through the discipline of prudent and careful management of their affairs, for it was calculated that people with a normal life span could comfortably save, through life insurance or other means, sufficient to discharge at death a tax of eight to ten per cent of the capital value of their estates without their heirs needing to touch the capital at all.

In any case, it was not as if there was anything revolutionary, in 1894, about levying taxes on inherited wealth. Death duties were an integral part of the structure of medieval tenures, going under the names of reliefs and heriots, but even if Victorian property owners may well have retained no memory of these they still had personal experience of an array of inheritance taxes which were strictly administered and scrupulously collected. On occasion, indeed, where a succession was contingent upon some event other than the death of the testator, such as the subsequent death of a brother or sister who was the intervening inheritor, the duty might not become payable until fifty or sixty years after the initial death from which it stemmed, so that ledgers opened by the Inland Revenue in the 1870s were sometimes still active in the 1920s and 1930s, collecting duties at the rates that had been in force in the 1870s.[8] The duties involved were not large, but in some circumstances they could be more than trivial; moreover, neither the rates nor the scope of the duties were immutable, and Victorians were reasonably accustomed to accepting changes without their occasioning vociferous protests. The oldest duty was the probate duty, levied on the value of personalty only. Until 1880 this was arranged in a series of tax bands at mildly progressive rates, levelling out as a tax of $1\frac{1}{2}$ per cent on all estates in personalty valued at over $£\frac{1}{2}$ million; from 1880 probate duty was raised to a flat rate of 3 per cent on all estates over £1,000 in value. Landed estates were not liable to probate duty, but from 1853 they were subjected to legacy and succession duties. These duties varied according to the degree of consanguinity of the successor to the deceased, and in the most common case where property passed to direct lineal descendants, either the children or the grandchildren, the one per cent duty was indeed insignificant. But in the not uncommon instances of inheritance

---

[8] B. English, 'Probate Valuations and the Death Duty Registers,' *Bulletin of the Institute of Historical Research*, LVII (1984), 80–91, and J. M. Collinge, '"Probate Valuations and the Death Duty Registers," Some Comments,' *Historical Research*, LX (1987), 240–5. Thus, P.R.O. IR 26/3228, ff. 518–22, opened in 1880 to account for the estate of John Michael Williams of Caerhays Castle, Burncoose, Cornwall, copper magnate, was still active in 1946, recording the deaths of his daughters.

by brothers or sisters, or nephews or nieces, duties of three or five per cent were payable; while levels which the complainants of the 1890s considered penal had long been exceeded for successors who were 'strangers in blood to the deceased'. These had to pay ten per cent, and the Inland Revenue held illegitimate children to be 'strangers' for this purpose. That may have been a proper fiscal penalty for moral delinquency and for endangering the true course of primogeniture in the inheritance of landed estates, but it was still a penalty that a few were willing to pay.[9]

Changes in these duty rates were not frequent, but were not unknown. Thus, in 1889 Goschen increased all the rates of succession duty by one per cent, again as part of a budget to pay for a battleship programme. And in 1881 there was an interesting although fiscally unproductive attempt to levy a tax on voluntary gifts and gifts *inter vivos,* which in the nature of things escaped liability to probate or legacy duties. This, known as the Account Duty because it was payable by stamp on the account of gifts delivered by the donor to the Inland Revenue, depended entirely on self-declaration by donors which it was impossible to police, and was apparently actually paid by no more than a tiny handful of exceptionally conscientious benefactors, among them the Duke of Bedford.[10] It is likely that the great majority of the landed classes were paying no more than two or three per cent in duty on the value of their inheritances, although a minority were already paying double or treble that. In one sense, therefore, the 1894 budget was a rude shock, multiplying the normal rate of death duties by three or four times (but actually reducing the rate for illegitimate heirs). In another sense, however, it was hardly a thunderbolt, since the principle of death duties and of periodical changes in them and increases in their rates had long been familiar. It was naturally possible in 1894 to take the view that the new duties were relatively innocuous in themselves but were a sinister thin end of the wedge since they created a machinery that might be used in the future for really hurtful turns of the screw. It was logically no more sensible to take such a view in 1894 than it was in 1853, 1881, or 1889, when no such views were articulated. The difference was that the 1894 budget was carried by a radical Chancellor, and the image of the radical wing of the Liberal party was anti-landlord and anti-aristocratic.

[9] The rates of the duties are most easily accessible in the annual editions of *Whitaker's Almanack*; it is interesting that all these duties were collectively described as 'the death duties' in the annual reports of the Commissioners of the Inland Revenue for many years before 1894.

[10] Finance Act, 1881, 44 Vict. cap. 12, sec. 38; and see *25th Report of the Commissioners of Inland Revenue*, P.P. 1882, XXI, 39. A second attempt to impose a tax on gifts *inter vivos* was made in 1910: Offer, *Property and Politics,* 111.

The cause of the panic in the 1890s and the source of Lady Bracknell's disenchantment with the attractions of landed property were thus essentially rooted in party politics. It was not the act so much as the author of the act which created the alarm. It was a pattern that was to be repeated. To put it in another way, it is not the dog's teeth, but the dog's bark, which the landed classes and the propertied classes have always found most terrifying. When government returned to the safe hands of the Hotel Cecil in 1895, and the country was ruled for the next eleven years by probably the most aristocratic cabinets it has ever known, the nervousness vanished, as it had done before in the 1850s. The Tory governments did remarkably little even to try to alter the objective circumstances of agricultural landowners or farmers, of low rents and low incomes and rural depopulation, mindful of the fact that although they were a party of country gentlemen they actually depended on suburbia and cheap bread for their votes. Not only did these governments neglect agriculture, something noticed by no more than a handful of dedicated or cranky Tory agriculturalists like the Earl of Onslow, Charles Bathurst, and Henry Chaplin, but they also omitted to repeal Harcourt's death duties, thus deliberately keeping in being the very machinery whose future operations they had professed to dread.[11] Despite this, the landowners survived, they paid their taxes, they experienced as a body no more than a normal rate of wastage or turnover through property sales or family failure, and they did not appear to be suffering from impoverishment.

All this changed yet again after 1906, and especially after the dog with the most frightening bark of all, Lloyd George, arrived in the Treasury. A rottweiler before his time, Lloyd George first of all baited the wealthy and particularly the landed classes with the land taxes, increased death duties, and supertax of his 1909 Budget (occasioned principally by the success of the Tory-inspired popular campaign for an accelerated Dreadnought building programme), and when they reacted by denouncing the proposed new taxes as plundering the rich, he deftly converted his budget into an instrument of social reform and class war and went for the jugular vein in the Limehouse and Newcastle speeches, claiming that 'a fully-equipped duke costs as much to keep up as two Dreadnoughts, and dukes are just as great a terror and they last longer,' and that the House of Lords consisted of 'five hundred men, ordinary men, chosen accidentally from among the unemployed.'[12] The anger of the propertied interests was unbounded,

[11] M. Fforde, *Conservatism and Collectivism, 1886–1914* (Edinburgh, 1990), 86–7.
[12] Speech at Newcastle, 9 Oct. 1909, quoted in E. Halevy, *A History of the English People in the Nineteenth Century*, VI, *The Rule of Democracy* (1932, English translation 1961 edn.), 298.

and fierce resistance was mounted by the Lords, by individual land-owners, by the Central Land Association, by the Agricultural Organ-ization Society, by the organs of the property professions, and by the Budget Protest league, all of whom had ready access to the press. Their rhetoric was fully the equal of Lloyd George's in hyperbole if not in popular appeal. A spate of speeches denounced the taxes as vicious and vindictive, aimed at the destruction of a class. The dukes excelled themselves: Beaufort wanted 'to see Winston Churchill and Lloyd George in the middle of twenty couple of dog hounds'; Rutland dismissed the Liberals as a set of 'piratical tatterdemalions'; Somerset announced that he would be obliged to discharge his estate staff and reduce his subscriptions to charities because of the Budget; and Buccleuch followed suit by publicly refusing a guinea to a Dum-friesshire football club for the same reason. Matters were not improved by the renegade Lord Rosebery defending the dukes as 'a poor but honest class'.[13]

All this fuss and hullabaloo might well lead one to suppose that the landlord class was on the brink of ruin, staring poverty in the face, and unable to make ends meet should the new taxes be imposed. In due course, a year late, the 1909 Budget was passed, and the House of Lords had its wings clipped. Landowners did not like this, but they were not ruined. The much-feared land taxes collapsed under the intricacy of their own machinery, and never produced any net revenue for the state. Even the great land valuation which had to precede the calculation and collection of these taxes, which was more feared as an engine of extortion that could be used by future governments than were the immediate taxes themselves, and which was slowly and painfully completed only in the middle of the War, was never put to any use at all, constructive or destructive, until it was made available to historians in the 1980s.[14] It is true that there was a growing volume of land sales between 1909 and the outbreak of the War, some of them dramatically large like the sale of the whole of the Duke of Bedford's 18,800 acre Thorney estate in Cambridgeshire. The great majority of these, however, were defensive sales designed to strengthen finances through restructured portfolios, or political sales designed to supply ammunition for Conservative propaganda; very few were forced sales by owners unable to meet their obligations and within sight of bank-ruptcy.

[13] Roy Jenkins, *Mr Balfour's Poodle* (1968 edn.), 88–90.
[14] The land clauses of the 1909–10 Finance Act were repealed in 1920. The historians' guide to the land valuation records is B. Short and M. Reed, *Landownership and Society in Edwardian England and Wales: The Finance (1909–10) Act Records* (University of Sussex, 1987).

The political motive is, indeed, the key to the landowners' cries of distress, in 1909 as in 1894. What in fact they were trying to do was to defend their political position, not their estates. Their political position meant their influence in the House of Commons, in local constituency associations, and in local government, and the powers of the House of Lords, but it also meant maintaining the Union with Ireland, restricting the extension of the power of the state and bureaucracy, resisting the inroads of collectivism and socialism, and containing democracy to prevent the poor plundering the rich.[15] This did, of course, also mean that defence of their political position was indirectly and in the long run the same thing as defence of their wealth against the threat of ultimate erosion. But whatever the rhetoric said, immediate expropriation and impoverishment were not in prospect. They talked a great deal about reversing 'a tendency towards establishing a bureaucratic system in this country' with all the new administrative authorities 'which are to oust our Law Courts [and] are given vast powers, powers which enable them, if they so will, positively to ruin the people who come under their jurisdiction.' They proclaimed that the bureaucratic-statist measures of the Liberals threatened their own ruin, and that of the whole economy. What they really wanted to preserve was the 'easy-going extravagance, the fox-hunting, the huge slaughter of pheasants, the 60-horse-power motors, the incessant golf of pre-War days' which one of their M.P.s, Lord Henry Cavendish-Bentinck, recalled in 1918: a condition somewhat removed from penury or its near approach.[16]

What emerges from this analysis is that the landed interest had not been 'crying wolf' in the fifty years or so before 1914, when they spoke about the erosion of their power and influence. By the end of the First World War the power was all but gone, and although a ceremonial governing elite survived, with fluctuating fortunes, at least until the end of the Second world War, there was never any chance of reviving or restoring aristocratic prestige however much governments might be dominated by other propertied interests. What also emerges is that the great landowners had been 'crying wolf', loudly if not continuously, when they paraded their impending financial ruin. When that ruin really arrived, as many thought it did with the great sales of 1919–21, the continuing steady break-up of estates in the interwar years, and the abandonment and destruction of country houses, they made no great public outcry. To be sure, there were plenty of individual complaints and much breast-beating by the losers who were selling up, there was a good deal of sermonising about ancestral homes

---

[15] See Fforde, *Conservatism and Collectivism*, 23–41 for a recent restatement.
[16] Fforde, *Conservatism and Collectivism,* 107 (Lansdowne), and 151 (Bentinck).

and the loss of heritage in the property press, and a few comments, surprisingly untriumphalist, by the political heirs of the land taxers that their objectives of demolishing the extreme concentration of landownership were being achieved without any need for the taxes. But of anything like the chorus of anger, fear, and outrage of the prewar years, or even of 1894, there was no sign. Even *Punch* was too busy with a completely different vein of aristocratic comment, lampooning Lloyd George's sales of honours and ridiculing the anachronistic overloading of Bonar Law's 1922 Cabinet with second-rate landed grandees, to think of re-running cartoons on depressed dukes.

There were many reasons for this silence: the war, its disproportionately high officer casualties and hence landed family casualties, its high taxation, and its cumulative sapping of aristocratic morale; the Fourth Reform Act of 1918 which profoundly altered the rules of the political game and put the management of constituencies and of political parties firmly into the hands of the professionals; the Liberal split and the rise of Labour, which concentrated business and general propertied interests into one anti-socialist camp and left but little room for landowners; and the expansion of the sphere of government into health, housing, unemployment, trade and industry, and economic policy generally, which proved irreversible and which gave a strong fillip to the tendency for the conduct of politics and the exercise of effective power to be taken over by businessmen and professional politicians. All this amounts to saying that the patricians had ceased to be a ruling elite. It had happened very suddenly; it had happened because the necessities and casualties of war magnified and accelerated the tendencies visible in the previous half century; and it had happened with the connivance of the patricians' political spokesmen, who had eagerly joined Lloyd George's Coalition Government. By the 1920s the dethronement of the landowners as a governing elite was an accomplished fact, and they accepted it with reasonably good grace, sometimes regretting and criticising the follies of their successors in power but not attempting to reverse the verdict. By 1990 it seemed entirely natural for the Duke of Devonshire to explain that 'If you have a title like mine, then you aren't taken seriously. How could I have been given a post talking about unemployment or health or social services, when everyone knows I've got all my millions here at Chatsworth? If you are as privileged as I am, and you have the material good fortune that you see all around you, then you must realize that the price you pay for that is that you cannot have influence.'[17]

There in a nutshell is the twentieth-century history of one section

---

[17] J. Paxman, *Friends in High Places* (1990), 29.

of the landed class: wealth and privilege without power or influence, and more than that, resignation to the reversal of all previous history in which power and influence had been the prerogative especially of landed wealth, and unabashed acceptance of the doctrine that had been carefully concealed by the Victorians, that great wealth does not carry with it great public responsibilities and duties. There is also here a clue to another and more material reason for the silence of the landed order in the 1920s: the 8th Duke of Devonshire whom *Punch* depicted in 1894 as not knowing how he was going to keep up Chatsworth, is represented in 1990 by the 11th Duke, who is keeping up Chatsworth and some 26,000 acres in fine style, although admittedly quite a lot of acres and a few pictures and drawings have been shed in the interval.[18] In short, the apparent evidence of financial disaster and looming poverty provided by the great land sales, the demolition of most of the great town mansions, or the abandonment of country houses, was not necessarily a sign of ruin. If a class of poor nobles and impoverished gentry had arisen in the 1920s it might not have had the opportunity to mobilise itself as an effective political force or even as a group with political nuisance value, in the manner of the poor nobles in nineteenth-century Russia or the poor gentry in nineteenth-century Hungary; but it would certainly have made itself heard and felt in some way. The potential for such a class was considerable, given the social cohesion of its likely members, even if not numerically large. There may have been no more than some 5,000 heads of landed families; but in the traditional system younger sons, nephews, and many cousins looked to the head of the family and the family name for support and patronage in careers in the army, the church, the land professions, or the public service, while the women in similar degree expected the family connection to be reflected in marriage. Those who would have been upset and deranged by any general impoverishment of the landed order might well have numbered 50,000 or more, and given their degree of inter-marriage and inter-relationship they could have been organized without difficulty.

This was not a dog which did not bark in the night. It was a dog which never existed, and that for a simple reason. Not only was impoverishment verging on destitution extremely rare among the landed classes, but also it was not the common experience for landed families to part with all their land and to sever completely their

---

[18] 'Britain's Rich: The Top 200', *Sunday Times*, 2 April 1989, 46, credits Devonshire with 70,000 acres in Derbyshire, Yorkshire, and Sussex. Paxman, *High Places*, 29, states that 'Chatsworth alone runs to 26,000 acres.' In 1883 Devonshire owned 120,000 acres in Derbyshire, Yorkshire, and Sussex, and overall 198,000 acres which included 60,000 acres in Ireland.

traditional roots in the country. In his recent book, *The Decline and Fall of the British Aristocracy*, David Cannadine chronicles in rich and colourful detail many of the largest and most striking sales of great estates which took place between the early twentieth century and the 1930s. From that account 92 individual sellers can be identified, many of them disposing of estates even larger and more renowned than Bedford's Thorney estate. Two-thirds of them, however, had direct descendants still living in the traditional family seat and still owning sizeable estates in the 1980s.[19] A different sample, composed of 500 separate estate sales which were reported in the *Estates Gazette* between 1919 and 1970 and covering the lesser gentry as well as the patricians, tells a slightly different story: 113 individual sellers can be identified, many families being involved in more than one sale, and 40 per cent of them were represented by landed survivors in the 1980s. The basic message, however, is much the same. Among the sellers with peerages or baronetcies the survival rate was about 60 per cent; the big casualties, where the family disappeared from the land although not necessarily from some public prominence, were among the gentry, where scarcely one-third of the sellers survived.[20] Even so, some of the casualties among the list drawn from Cannadine might more accurately be classified as walking wounded. Thus the title of Lord Ashburnham became extinct in 1924, after he had sold off all the family's Welsh estates, but his daughter remained in the family seat of Ashburnham Place in Sussex long enough to cause a scandal among preservationists and architectural historians when the house was partially demolished in 1959 (providentially bits were saved and incorporated into Hinton Ampner in Hampshire, which the future 8th Lord Sherborne was just then rebuilding after a disastrous fire).[21] Lord Kensington sold much of the family's Pembrokeshire estate in 1920, and his eldest son, the 7th baron, took himself off to Rhodesia; but in the 1960s a younger son was living at Broad Haven in the heart of the family's traditional territory and the Kensington Estate Company was managing the estate. The Duke of Montrose sold a large part of the family's Lanarkshire estate in 1928, and his son, the 7th Duke, became a farmer in Rhodesia and one of Ian Smith's more notoriously extreme ministers; but the Marquess of Graham, the heir to the dukedom, was ensconced in the seat of Auchmar, near Glasgow,

---

[19] Cannadine, *Decline and Fall*, 103–12, 125–38.

[20] The sample, covering all sales reported in the *Estates Gazette* in which the vendor is identified (including sales by corporate owners), was drawn by my research assistant, Dr Andrew Rowley; without his resourceful, painstaking, and patient help it would have been impossible to write this paper.

[21] J. M. Robinson, *The Latest Country Houses* (1984), 79. R. Strong, M. Binney, and J. Harris, *The Destruction of the Country House, 1875–1975* (1974), plate 113, and 190.

in the 1980s. While the 8th Lord Somers continued his career as a music teacher after succeeding to the title in 1953, becoming professor of Composition and theory at the Royal College of Music between 1967 and 1977, living like any mere academic at 35 Links Road, Epsom, he inherited the title only because his father had unexpectedly succeeded his own nephew; he himself was indeed without land, but although parts of the family estate in Worcestershire and Herefordshire had been sold during the First World War, the widow of the 6th Lord, who had made those sales, continued to live in the family seat of Eastnor Castle, near Ledbury, into the 1950s.[22]

What is the explanation? Many of those who sold off large chunks of land and yet remained landed did so because they realised that it no longer made sense to hold all their assets in one stock, land. It had not made financial sense for a long time, as Evelyn Denison's comments in 1847 had shown; after 1918 it no longer made social or political sense. It was that, quite as much as the goads of debt and taxation, which liberated aristocracy and gentry to consider themselves simply as rational investors and rentiers, free to liberate themselves from their lands which had become surplus to social needs. Rational self-interest dictated the diversification of portfolios, and investment in stocks and shares, in home banks and industries as well as in imperial and overseas companies, which had previously only been made out of savings from current income by the wealthiest patricians, and which became a normal feature of capital restructuring in the interwar years. Hence, perhaps, the penchant of aristocratic sons for making a career on the Stock Exchange, which became one of the most acceptably gentlemanly professions. As a result many families, making the switch from a security yielding at most two per cent net before tax, to investments with double or treble the rate of return, were presumably more comfortably off without their lands, and that was probably so even when part of the sale proceeds had been swallowed up in paying off accumulated debts and death duties.

Others, and these were the non-survivors, were not so fortunate. They were the victims of an unhappy succession of deaths in the family—and the demographic lottery of longevity or early death played a significant role in landed fortunes—or they failed to listen to accountants' advice on the setting up of private estate companies or the construction of elaborate webs of beneficial trusts to replace the old family settlements. Mainly, however, they were the twentieth-century successors of the profligates, the wastrels, and the incompetents who had been around in landed circles in all earlier centuries, somewhat more numerous than the Ailesburys, Buckinghams, or New-

---

[22] *Burke's Peerage and Baronetage* (1949 edn.); *Who's Who* (1980 edn.).

castles of the nineteenth century, but not dramatically so. Debts had piled up to unsupportable levels, incurred for all manner of reasons from the long accumulation of family charges to horse-racing or to gambling on shaky or crooked ventures in the City in the hope of hitting the jackpot, and expenditure had not been curtailed. A death and its duties might in such cases often be the last straw which broke up the estate for good; although it should be remembered that estates were taxed on their net worth, after deducting outstanding debts. It is true that the interwar years, with depressed farming and depressed agricultural rents, were a particularly bad time for heavily indebted estates to survive. Nevertheless, gross financial mismanagement seems to have been the root cause for the complete disappearance of such as the Dukes of Leeds, Manchester, or St Albans from the scene, mismanagement dating well back into the nineteenth century.[23] Insofar as that was the case it was nothing new, just part of the process of normal wastage.

In any case, those who were forced to sell up everything were rarely put out onto the street with nothing but the clothes they stood up in. There was usually enough capital left to live in a villa in the Channel Islands or the south of France, or to start again in Rhodesia, Kenya, Canada, Australia, or New Zealand. The export of the aristocratic way of life and its re-creation in Kenya was, indeed, one of the memorable features of the 1930s and 1940s. The planter society of Happy Valley showed to what extremes of promiscuity, adultery, hedonism, idleness, and prejudice members of the old nobility like Carbery, Delamare, Erroll, or Finch-Hatton could go once they were freed from the restraint of having to keep up appearances in England.[24] On a more sober, and undoubtedly more typical, note, sales even of modest gentry estates generally left enough to support the seller in fairly comfortable retirement and to pay for the expected, that is public school, education of the children. That, and the family name, were sufficient to give the sons ready entry into the gentlemanly professions: a small sample of twenty gentry families which had sold their estates before 1937 yields two sons who were diplomats, one becoming an ambassador; one lieutenant-colonel; one senior India Office official; one barrister; one doctor; one stockbroker; and only one businessman, the chairman of Amalgamated Metal and a director of Sun Life.[25] An estate agent is missing from this list, although it became a popular gentlemanly occupation: the well-connected became land agents, surrogate landowners managing agricultural

[23] Cannadine, *Decline and Fall*, 403; Thompson, *English Landed Society*, 319–20.
[24] J. Fox, *White Mischief* (1984), 52–68.
[25] *Burke's Landed Gentry* (1937 edn.), first 20 'former gentry' under letter 'S'.

estates, and the less well-connected entered the upper end of the house market, dealing in country properties and fine town houses and conserving some sort of tenuous link with their landed gentry backgrounds.

In this analysis there are some new dispossessed, but no new poor. In 1984 Monson and Scott wrote a book called *The Nouveaux Pauvres: A Guide to Downward Nobility*, but however colourful (and partially inaccurate) their list of this species, it is a strikingly small one. It runs:

> The 9th Earl of Buckinghamshire, who died in 1983, ended his career as a municipal gardener in Southend. The present Earl of Breadalbane lives in a bed-sitting room in Finchley, while the Earl of Effingham ... lives in the Cromwell Road. The Earl of Munster had to be carried to the Lords to get his attendance allowance until the day of his death, since it was his only source of income, as he had been too poor to pay his national insurance. Earl Nelson is a police constable. Lord Northesk is a jewelsmith in the Isle of Man. The Countess of Mar is a saleswoman for British Telecom. Lord Simon Conyngham is an assistant in a delicatessen. Lord Teviot is a bus conductor. Lord Kingsale, the premier baron of Ireland, is a silage-pit builder in the west country, having previously been a bingo caller in Stourbridge, a lorry driver, and a safari keeper at Woburn. Lord Grey—the direct descendant of the Reform Act Prime Minister and the Governor-General of Canada—lives on a house boat and has been the director of a chain of sex shops.[26]

That is eleven people, and eleven people do not constitute a class, especially if we eliminate Lord Grey, because he inherited the title without inheriting the estate; Lord Teviot, because that is a peerage of a cadet branch of the Marquess of Lothian's family, and was never landed, while on inheriting the title the present Teviot gave up being a bus conductor and became a record agent working in the P.R.O.; and the Countess of Mar, because she says being a salesgirl was just for youthful experience, not for the money.[27] A great many others, from the ranks of those who still retain landed estates as well as from former landed families, work for their livings, more or less in a 9 to 5 kind of way, in a fashion quite unknown to their predecessors, for whom 'work' meant the supervision of agents or the performance of political and administrative duties.

The gainful employment of the late twentieth-century aristocracy

---

[26] N. Monson and D. Scott, *The Nouveaux Pauvres: A Guide to Downward Nobility* (1984), cited by Cannadine, *Decline and Fall*, 660.

[27] *Sunday Times*, 2 Sept. 1990, for angry comments by some aristocrats, new and old, on pre-publication copies of Cannadine, *Decline and Fall*.

includes a great range of occupations: there are engineers, pho-
tographers, film producers, television promoters, shopkeepers, dairy-
men, and journalists, for example, as well as the highly traditional
army officers, civil servants, diplomats, and lawyers, and the nearly
traditional stockbrokers. But the two most favoured fields of employment are on the land, as farmers, and in the City, as directors.
The one signifies the transformation of landownership from a status
category into a business, and was signalled by the name-change of the
Central Land Association, set up in 1907 to be the political arm of all
the land interests, into the Country Landowners Association following
the advice of one of the founders, Charles Bathurst, 1st Lord Bledisloe,
in 1922, that landowners ought to devote themselves to their estates
and give up trying to influence public affairs. That was perhaps the
moment when the aristocracy and gentry consciously moved 'from
being a governing elite to being an agricultural profession'.[28] The
other signifies a significant shift in the terms on which the age-old
dialogue and merger between the old landed elite and the new rich
takes place, a shift which has brought old families into the City on a
scale only dimly foreshadowed in the 1890s, has all but stopped the
social climbers among the new rich from trying or even wishing to
joing the old elite via the old route of land purchase, but has if
anything stimulated the most entrepreneurial wing of the new rich to
develop and gratify an appetite for country estates and sporting
properties. It is a shift which has so blurred the distinctions between
the most successful upper-middle class businessmen and the most
business-minded landowners that some sociologists now call the
governing elite 'the business class', a small group of the powerful
drawn from both sources.[29]

The old theory was that new money constantly flowed into land,
largely replacing old families who dropped out for one reason or
another, in a continual ebb and flow which only slowly affected
the overall balance of landownership. The theory was confidently
reasserted by Hugh Montgomery-Massingberd, a Lincolnshire land-
owner and editor of *Burke's Landed Gentry*, in 1972, when he stated that
'of the families included in 1863 at least 50 per cent had disappeared
by the 1914 edition.'[30] That is an almost incredibly high rate of
turnover, and many historians of landed society, not least Lawrence
Stone, Bill Rubinstein, or John Beckett, would be startled or even
upset by the thought that it was the pre-1914 norm for half the body

---

[28] The striking and illuminating phrase is that of Fforde, *Conservatism and Collectivism*, 167.
[29] J. Scott, *The Upper Classes: Property and Privilege in Britain* (1982), 123.
[30] *Burke's Landed Gentry* (1972 edn.), editorial preface, III, ix.

of landed gentry to vanish and be replaced by newcomers every fifty years. Yet a cursory check on the ownership of ten country houses within a five mile radius of St Albans confirms that such a turnover was within the bounds of possibility: in 1912 only three of these houses were in the hands of the same owners or families as in 1890, and they were the houses of the old nobility and gentry, Lord Verulam, Lord Cavan, and the Cherry-Garrards. The others housed, temporarily, such newcomers as Lord Grimthorpe, lawyer, banker, and church restorer; Sir John Blundell Maple, upholsterer and furniture store-keeper; and John Barnato Joel, South African diamond dealer. Maple was an M.P., Grimthorpe was in the Lords, and all were J.P.s.[31] The inward flow was made up of two streams. One came from new money made in business, in banking, in commerce, in industry, or in the professions; the other came from the junior branches of the established landed order itself, from younger sons or cadet branches constantly throwing up individuals who either inherited estates from distant relatives, or managed to purchase estates with the proceeds of for-tunate marriages or the accumulations from successful careers.

Prior to the First World War, perhaps prior to the 1890s, the second stream was probably larger than the first. It then began to dwindle, as land on its own ceased to be adequate for the support of social position, and dried up altogether after the War. The first stream remained and has continued to flow. This continued movement of new money into land is an essential part of the explanation of the survival of landownership and the system of estates and tenant farmers into the 1990s, although the extent to which there was any traditional movement available for continuation is, of course, a matter of some disagreement among historians. Leaving aside the question of the exact degree of the openness of the traditional landed elite to pene-tration by new men of wealth, all that needs to be said for present purposes is that in the nineteenth century, down to the mid-1890s, something like 90 per cent of the super-wealthy new men who left fortunes at death of $£\frac{1}{2}$ million and over acquired large country houses and landed estates in the range of 1,000 to 40,000 acres. The exceptions were chiefly the small number of millionaires who were unmarried, childless, or without male heirs, who therefore had no prospect of founding landed families. At lower levels of wealth, those leaving fortunes at death of between £100,000 and £500,000 in personalty, the proportion who purchased landed estates was sharply lower, perhaps no more than 15 per cent of the group. This suggests that

[31] *Kelly's Directory of Hertfordshire* (1890 and 1912 edns.). The houses checked are: Aldwickbury, Batchwood, Childwickbury, Gorhambury, Lamer House, Mackerye End, Marshallswick, Oaklands, Sandridgebury, and Wheathampstead House.

land was highly prized by Victorian businessmen but was recognised to be an expensive luxury which it was prudent not to touch unless one had ample means.[32]

The movement of new money into land slackened somewhat between the mid-1890s and 1914, and it slackened in a significant way. The social climbers, intent on palming themselves off as real landed aristocrats, tended to drop out of the race or content themselves simply with large country houses divorced from any surrounding estates. Those who were left in the race were increasingly those who liked to have country houses and country estates for hunting, shooting, and landlord-acting, and at the same time liked to remain powerful businessmen. Thus, between the mid-1890s and 1914 over one-third of the 100 millionaires who were new men of wealth dying in that period purchased country houses and considerable estates. They included the freshly ennobled such as Grimthorpe from banking, Armstrong from armaments, Burton from brewing, Winterstoke from cigarettes, and Swaythling from finance; and the less renowned but equally wealthy Muntz from steel pens, Strutt from cotton, Maple from furniture, Coats from sewing thread, and Tennant from chemicals; all of these were active entrepreneurs, several succeeded in founding family firms as well as landed families.[33] After 1918 purchasers of the old style, looking on land as a social elevator which would erase their vulgar origins, pretty well disappeared. What was left was a continually replenished group of purchasers who were intent on adopting, in some form, the life style and possessions of the aristocratic bourgeoisie as those had been developed by the Victorians, that is they aimed at remaining prominent businessmen as well as becoming country landowners.

The interwar period provides particularly eloquent testimony to the persistence of this behaviour, since it was a time when the outlook for farming and farm rents was generally regarded as so gloomy and uncertain that only fools or farmers themselves would dream of buying agricultural land, a time when J. M. Keynes was successfully advising his Cambridge college to unload farmland while it could and move into stocks and shares, a time when many of the traditional landowners were dong likewise.[34] Yet this was the time when William Lever, 1st

[32] F. M. L. Thompson, 'Life after Death: How Successful Nineteenth-Century Businessmen Disposed of Their Fortunes,' *Econ. Hist. Rev.* 2nd ser. XLIII (1990), 40–61.

[33] W. D. Rubinstein, 'British Millionaires, 1809–1949,' *B.I.H.R.* XLVIII (1974), 202–23, for lists of millionaires. Before 1914 *Who's Who* was a moderately good guide to landowning; after that individuals increasingly tended not to mention their landowning or the size of their estates, although a few continue to do so in the 1990s.

[34] R. F. Harrod, *The Life of John Maynard Keynes* (1951), 162, 287, 300–1, 389. It is only fair to add that Keynes was not always a seller of land at this period, and bought

Lord Leverhulme, dealt in land by the hundred thousand acres, the largest purchaser of real estate for hard cash in British history, when Weetman Pearson, 1st Viscount Cowdray, established himself as a grandee of polo in Sussex, of grouse and castles in Scotland, as well as of oilfields in Mexico, when Alfred Mond, 1st Lord Melchett and founder of I.C.I., equipped himself with a Hampshire manor, when George Lawson Johnston, 1st Lord Luke and inventor of Bovril, took over the Odell Castle estate in Bedfordshire, when George Vestey, a younger son of the Vestey meat-packing family, bought the 10,000 acre Warter Priory estate in Yorkshire, and Sir Hugo Cunliffe-Owen, creator of British American tobacco, acquired the small but prime Sunningdale estate near Ascot.[35] Perhaps as much as one-fifth of the interwar millionaires can be counted as players in the estate game and as prominent, often aggressively prominent, businessmen. It was a proportion that had sagged slightly from its pre-1914 level, when around one quarter of the super-wealthy had become aristocratic bourgeois. In the more prosperous and optimistic times since the Second World War, particularly since the 1950s, the proportion seems to have moved back to around one quarter. In our own day one half of the 200 wealthiest people in Britain represent old money, inherited wealth, and one half new money of the self-made multi-millionaires who began in a bicycle shed or corner shop. At least a quarter of these 100 new super-wealthy have already, while still in their entre-preneurial prime, purchased sizeable country properties ranging from one square mile up to 45,000 acres, the latter admittedly rather cheap Scottish acres in Glenfiddich and Balmoral country. Pride of place among today's new aristocratic bourgeois must go to Lord Sainsbury of Preston Candover, Britain's wealthiest private individual after the Duke of Westminster, largest shareholder in Britain's biggest

---

some for the College and some for himself in the trough of the most acute years of agricultural depression between 1929 and 1932.

[35] Leverhulme, *Estates Gazette*, 23 Feb. 1918, 176; 13 Sept. 1919, 357; 24 Jan. 1920, 133; and *Dictionary of Business Biography*, III, 747. Cowdray, *E.G.*, 17 Sept. 1921, 392; 21 Jan. 1922, 89. Melchett, *E.G.*, 8 June 1929, 840. Luke, *E.G.*, 21 July 1934; and *D.B.B.* III, 515. Vestey, *E.G.*, 22 Sept. 1928, 401; this estate was purchased from the dowager Lady Nunburnholme, widow of C. H. Wilson, Hull shipping magnate, who had bought the house and estate in 1878 (*D.B.B.* V, 848). Cunliffe-Owen, *E.G.*, 31 Aug. 1929, 29; and *D.B.B.* I, 868. Other purchasers of this period included: Sir William H. Aykroyd, carpet manufacturer, Kenneth Clark, sewing thread manufacturer, Sir Thomas Devitt, shipowner, Sir Arthur Du Cross, tyre manufacturer, Sir Eric Geddes, transport executive, Esmond Harmsworth, press lord, Sir Alfred Hickman, ironmaster, Sir James Hill, wool merchant, Sir Edward Iliffe, press lord, Lord Inverforth, shipowner, Sir Herbert Leon, stockbroker, Sir Alfred McAlpine, contractor, Sir Edward Mountain, insurance underwriter, Sir Mortimer Singer, sewing machine heir, Sir Herbert Smith, carpet manufacturer, Ronald Tree, journalist, Samuel James Waring, furniture retailer, and Hilda Wills, one of the cigarette family.

supermarket chain, who has put together an estate of 17,000 acres of prime land in Hampshire. But others have also laid out large sums in the purchase of landed estates, such as Anthony Bamford, the maker of JCB bulldozers, who has recently spent £12 million on the 2,500 acre Daylesford estate in Gloucestershire. And it is a sign of the times and the immense fortunes which can be made in the entertainment industry that Andrew Lloyd Webber has a 1,000 acre retreat in Hampshire, John Hall, ex-coal miner from Tyneside and leisure centre king, has the 4,500 acre Wynyard Park estate in County Durham, and Paul Macartney, pop star, is enjoying becoming a laird in the west of Scotland.[36]

The rapidly escalating land values of the 1960s and 1970s, when prices rocketed from around £100 an acre to the stratospheric regions of £2,000 or more, did indeed make land a favourite hedge against inflation and enable the wealthy to regard it once more as a sound financial investment, which in the interwar period only the most wildly imaginative gambler could have done. It is, however, most unlikely that the new rich of the late twentieth century have been buying estates as ordinary investments, although property companies may have been doing so. For one thing, estate buying has continued into the late 1980s, after land prices have turned down again and when the outlook is bearish; disinvestment has occurred, but as with Alan Bond it has been caused by the general collapse of a vast individual business empire, not by disenchantment with the landed estate. Of greater importance, these business-purchasers do not commit more than a very small fraction of their total wealth to the acquisition of their country retreats. In this they differ radically from those of their eighteenth or nineteenth century predecessors who transformed the major part of their fortunes into landed property: those were the arrivistes, now a defunct species. They do not differ at all in essentials, on the other hand, from that smaller stream of Victorians who bought or built country houses and acquired large estates, but retained the major part of their wealth in other forms, usually in their family businesses.[37]

The new rich of today who go down the country road, it seems safe to say, do so because they enjoy the new finery of country houses, manors, farms, parks, and shooting properties for weekends and holidays, for impressing business colleagues, and for indulging in hobbies and leisure activities unrelated to the serious enterprise of earning livings and getting incomes. Nevertheless, they play the game of being landowners with considerable efficiency, and model themselves on the

[36] *Sunday Times*, Britain's Rich, 1989.
[37] Thompson, 'Life after Death,' 58.

traditional modes of behaviour whether as farm landlords or sporting squires, even if for them it is a game of conspicuous consumption and not one of food or income production. One obvious effect of this conduct is to help to perpetuate the peculiar British structure of large landownership and tenanted farms, against the tide of owner-occupation and the triumph of urban middle-class values, even though the motives for desiring landed property have been turned inside out since the days when the large estate system was being developed and consolidated in the eighteenth century because it conferred political and social power. These new landowners co-exist, as they have always done, with the old families of the former landed ascendancy, and for that reason it is an unstable alliance, since the surviving old families regard their family estates as their central interests, properties which have to be made to yield an income even if that is subsidised by outside operations in the City. For the time being, however, the alliance works. The new rich continue to do their bit in shoring up the territorial system, and the former patrician elite has settled down to a low-profile existence as a formidable body of great landowners engrossed in protecting and furthering their own self-interest without all the trouble and expense of claiming to have public responsibilities and public-service duties. It is a system all the more powerful in farming policy, in planning decisions, in heritage games, and in the wealth stakes themselves because it keeps itself out of the headlines, largely hidden from the public eye.

SOCIAL MENTALITIES AND THE CASE OF MEDIEVAL SCEPTICISM

By Susan Reynolds

READ 26 JANUARY 1990

THE history of mentalities has now become so widely accepted that even British historians sometimes refer to it: one hardly needs to talk about *mentalités* any more, though the French word still sounds more modish.[1] But the subject goes back at least to Vico. Although *Weltanschauung* and *Zeitgeist* sound old hat by comparison with *mentalités* the words remind us that nineteenth-century German historians were interested in the different ways past societies may have viewed the world, while F. W. Maitland and Henry Adams are obvious examples of Anglophones who in their different ways tried to understand medieval ways of thought. In 1933 Jean Guitton, a Frenchman, it is true, but one who presumably came out of that older tradition of intellectual history against which Lucien Febvre set himself, wrote about the need to study the *mentalité* of an age and summed up what he meant by this as 'the totality of those implicit assumptions which are imposed on us by our environment and which rule our judgements.[2]

What unites all these approaches to the subject is that they have all been products of societies in which it has more often been assumed

---

[1] Among more recent discussions, which refer to earlier ones: P. Burke, 'The History of Mentalities in Great Britain', *Tijdschrift voor Geschiedenis*, xciii (1980), 529–40; G. Tellenbach, 'Mentalität', in *Ideologie und Herrschaft im Mittelalter*, ed. M. Kernes (Darmstadt, 1982); A. Burgière, 'La Notion de "Mentalités" chez Marc Bloch et Lucien Febvre', *Revue de Synthèse*, civ (1983), 333–48; D. L. d'Avray, *The Preaching of the Friars* (Oxford, 1985), 7–11, 238–40; A. Gurevich, *Categories of Medieval Culture*, trans. G. L. Campbell (1985), chap. 1; *Mentalitäten im Mittelalter*, ed. F. Graus (Vorträge und Forschungen, 35, 1987), especially the essays of F. Graus and R. Schneider; R. Chartier, *Cultural History*, trans. L. G. Cochrane (Oxford, 1988), 19–52: A. Boureau, 'Propositions pour une histoire restreinte des mentalités', *Annales E.S.C.* 44 (1989), 1491–1504. Among many people who have discussed the subject with me I should like to thank in particular the Early Medieval Seminar at the Institute of Historical Research, the Goldsmiths College Interdisc Conference 1988, Professor W. C. Jordan, and Dr. D. L. d'Avray.

[2] J. M. P. Guitton, *Le Temps et L'Éternité chez Plotin et Saint Augustin* (Paris, 1933), xii (as translated by D. L. d'Avray, 239). The rest of his discussion (xi–xxiv) is full of interest. Cf. R. G. Collingwood, *Philosophical Essays* (Oxford, 1940), ii. 21–77. L. Capéran used the word *mentalité* in *Le Problème du salut des infidèles: essai historique* (Paris, 1912), 196–7, but not, apparently, in its collective sense. For its novelty in Proust's early twentieth-century Paris: Tellenbach, 385–407, at 385.

than argued that people in different societies think differently. Since the eighteenth century, for instance, it has commonly been assumed that people in the middle ages were less critical and rational than modern people and that religious faith came naturally to them. Eighteenth- and nineteenth-century ideas of historical evolution and progress made this a reasonable assumption. The combination of Enlightenment and ethnocentricity allowed eighteenth-century Europeans to see their own society as having emerged from centuries of superstition and barbarism at the same time as they regarded the physically different 'savages' whom they were converting, conquering, or enslaving as intellectually inferior. Some notable thinkers of the time attributed cultural differences to environment rather than innate capacity, but the growth thereafter of racial and linguistic nationalism tended to stress inherent differences between peoples or races, while theories of evolution lent intellectual support to the belief that primitive people were less able to reason because they were at an earlier stage of development.[3] So long as culture was assumed to be linked to biological descent, and so long as anthropologists were not exposed to close acquaintance with savage societies, it was reasonable to interpret differences of culture as deriving from differences of innate mental capacity.[4] Even those scholars who continued to think that all mankind had the same basic mental equipment tended to agree that, since a savage was at a more primitive stage of evolution, his mental development would be 'in many respects not beyond that of a young child of a civilised race'.[5] Theoretical unity was a matter of potential, to be achieved when savages had evolved to the level of civilized men. Meanwhile, although romanticism and the Catholic revival turned the European middle ages into an Age of Faith and Chivalry rather than one of superstition and barbarism, the underlying assumption that post-medieval changes reflected general, *social* changes in ways of thought and levels of rationality still remained unchallenged.[6]

Much of the recent discussion of medieval *mentalités* seems to me to

---

[3] Though the actual word primitive is not recorded in this sense before 1903: *OED* (2nd edn 1989), xii, 484, 485.

[4] R. L. Meek, *Social Science and the Ignoble Savage* (Cambridge, 1976), M. Harris, *The Rise of Anthropological Theory* (1969); G. W. Stocking, *Race, Culture and Evolution* (1982); M. Cole and S. Scribner, *Culture and Thought* (New York, 1974), 11–33; G. Jahoda, *Psychology and Anthropology* (1982), 9–29.

[5] E. B. Tylor, quoted by Jahoda, 13; cf. Jahoda, 170 and n. 5 and, on a modern argument to the same effect, *ibid.* 223–38.

[6] A. Chandler, *A Dream of order* (1970), 1–11, 17–25, 125–34; K. Kumar, *Prophecy and Progress* (Harmondsworth, 1978), 30–4, 79–83, 95–102; J. van Engen, 'The Christian Middle Ages as an Historiographical Problem', *American Historical Review*, xci (1986), 519–52. For the application of the general evolutionary paradigm to the middle ages by an anthropologist: E. B. Tylor, *Primitive Culture* (1871), i. 138–9, ii. 450.

betray the same implicit assumptions and habits of thought—the same *mentalité* in fact—as this long tradition of evolutionary thought.[7] In doing so it begs some big questions of human culture and psychology.[8] To start with there is the question of the difference between the content of thought and the processes of thought. It is obvious that societies differ in their beliefs, traditions, values, attitudes. But does that imply a difference in the processes of thought? To put it at its crudest, are individuals in some societies less capable than individuals in other societies of criticizing and reasoning about the content of their thought? Given different premises, do different societies or cultures produce different ways of drawing, or not drawing, inferences from them? Second, there is the question of the difference between the belief system or collective representations of a society and the attitudes, thoughts, and beliefs of individuals. Belief systems are collective, while particular thought processes may be collectively fostered or inhibited, but the actual thinking is done in the minds of individuals, however much and in whatever way their thought is conditioned by their society—and I hope that that statement is not thought to proceed simply from naïve British individualism. If the first and most elementary stages of thinking are, perhaps, everywhere much the same, but some societies encourage the further development of cognitive abilities in all or most of their members better than others do, is the encouragement or stunting absolute or does it represent a tendency which some individuals may somehow resist?

Once one starts to think about the distinction between the content of thought and the processes of thought, and between collective belief systems and the beliefs and thought of individuals, the idea of mentalities becomes more problematic. In the past twenty years the nature and the very existence of differences in processes of thought between different societies or cultures has come under discussion.[9] Attention has been drawn to the unreality of contrasts between the scientific thought of modern society and the more magical or mystical or less

---

[7] Guitton, xiii, refers to 'cette "évolution" indéfinie, qui fait office à la fois de causalité et de finalité'. His own reference to categories and values as innate (p. xii) illustrates his point. For a recent explicit analogy between the thought of 'les hommes du Moyen Age' and that of 'les primitifs': J. Le Goff, *La Civilisation de l'occident médiévale* (Paris, 1977), 18–19.

[8] Though see Christina Larner, *The Thinking Peasant* (Glasgow, 1982), 75–91 *et passim*.

[9] Among other discussions: *Modes of Thought*, ed. R. Horton and R. Finnegan (1973); Cole and Scribner, *Culture and Thought; Rationality and Relativism*, ed. M. Hollis and S. Lukes (Oxford, 1982); Jahoda, 167–238; C. Geertz, 'Anti-anti-relativism', *American Anthropologist*, 86 (1984), 263–78; I. C. Jarvie, *Rationality and relativism* (1984); *Reason and Morality*, ed. J. Overing (1985); H. Gardner, *The Mind's New Science* (New York, 1987), esp. c. 8; P. K. Bock, *Rethinking Psychological Anthropology* (New York, 1988); M. Bloch, *Ritual, History and Power* (1989), 106–36.

rational thought of 'traditional', preliterate societies. 'People', to quote Gustav Jahoda, 'be they Azande or Americans, can act under the influence of their magical beliefs in some contexts and in a rational-technical manner in others.'[10] Barry Barnes points out that all paradigms involve anomalies, but that, obvious as such anomalies seem to an outsider, 'beliefs in all societies are for the most part passively accepted.'[11] Even modern western scientists, it now seems, think in paradigms most of the time. On the other hand, some older descriptions of the unquestioning acceptance of beliefs that the ethnographers found irrational and odd now look as though they were based more on ethnocentric ideology than on evidence.[12] Participant observation has made it much harder for anthropologists to dismiss the people they study as uniformly childlike, credulous, or unreasoning. There seems to be no hard evidence that scepticism is unknown even in the most untouched and traditional societies. *Some* people in such societies seem, even if only privately, to doubt or question practices which reflect generally accepted beliefs, and do so in a way that implies some kind of common-sense rationalism.

Some societies, of course, offer no opportunity to acquire particular mental equipment or develop particular kinds of thought. If you lived in the eighth century you could not become a physicist, though if you were lucky enough to be a monk with a good library, you might exercise your mathematical talents on calculations of Easter. In a society without writing, a whole range of aptitudes may be hard to develop—though writing does not always lead to much cognitive development even among the literate, and illiterate people can still make surprisingly complicated classifications and calculations.[13] Studies by cross-cultural psychologists suggest that although 'some environments "push" cognitive growth better, earlier and longer than others [what] does not seem to happen is that different cultures produce completely divergent and unrelated modes of thought.'[14] In all but the simplest societies, moreover, different categories of people pursue different occupations which tend to give or withhold opportunities to develop particular skills, habits of thought, and styles

---

[10] Jahoda, 181.

[11] B. Barnes, 'The comparison of Belief-systems: Anomaly versus Falsehood', in *Modes of Thought*, 182–98, at 188, 192.

[12] J. D. Y. Peel, 'Understanding Alien Belief-systems', *British Journal of Sociology*, xx (1969), 69–84; *Modes of Thought*, 'Introduction', 37–42; S. J. Tambiah, 'Form and Meaning of Magical Acts', in ibid., 199–229; A. Salmond, 'Maori Epistemology' in *Reason and Morality*, 240–63; Jahoda, 167–88; M. Douglas, *Implicit Meanings* (1975), 73–82.

[13] e.g. J. Goody, *Domestication of the Savage Mind* (Cambridge, 1977); W. Ong, *Orality and Literacy* (1982).

[14] P. M. Greenfield and J. S. Bruner, quoted in Cole and Scribner, 24–5.

and patterns of reasoning. In relatively large, complex, economically divided, and changing societies like those of the European middle ages, both the content and the processes of thought must have differed widely. Many peasants then were no doubt as poor at syllogisms, flexible and abstract classification, or conservation of quantity as many people in 'traditional' and preliterate societies apparently are today—and as some people in modern western societies. Other people in the middle ages were, however, very good indeed at such procedures.[15]

I have no wish to play down the importance of recognizing differences in beliefs and values and the social conditioning of ways of thinking. Even if, as an eighth-century monk, your actual mental capacity for thinking rationally and critically about what you had to think about were much the same as it would be in the twentieth, you would have been taught to be more respectful of past authorities and less inclined to try to be original than if you were a university student in the twentieth-century west. But intellectuals in the twentieth-century west are themselves conditioned by the traditional beliefs of their society and the habits of thought inculcated by their professions. If they are trained as historians they may well, for instance, take it for granted that past societies had strange mentalities, assume that those mentalities were more homogeneous than those of modern society, and unconsciously assimilate strange beliefs to strange thought processes. One manifestation of this profession *mentalité* may well be the assumption that most or all people in the middle ages were incapable of atheism or outright scepticism.

Among non-historians—including some scholars interested in religions in general—this assumption still takes the old form of seeing the middle ages as the Age of Faith.[16] Although medievalists now seldom use the expression, the idea of the Age of Faith also survives among us more or less unnoticed, rather like a shabby old chair in our mental sitting-rooms. It is rather rickety, and goodness knows where it came from, but it looks all right now that we have smartened it up with the new loose covers of heresy and 'popular religion'. All the same, the old chair is still there underneath. It is constructed out of the assumed credulity, the incapacity for atheism, of the medieval mentality. What the people who had popular religion or heresy believed may—we are now told—have been even odder than what the church taught, but

[15] A. R. Luria, *Cognitive Development: its Cultural and Social Foundations*, trans. M. Lopez-Morillas and L. Solataroff (1974); Cole and Scribner, 101–6, 148–68; Jahoda, 177, 227–38.

[16] e.g. A. Macintyre, 'Understanding religion and believing' in *Rationality*, ed. B. Wilson, (1970), 62–77, at 73.

few historians of popular religion seem to wonder whether some medieval people maybe took all religious beliefs with a pinch of salt.[17] Vast quantities of historical imagination and sympathy have been devoted to medieval religious beliefs, whether orthodox, heretical or 'popular', but very little has been given to unbelief. Some medievalists probably fear that any discussion of it would involve the historical sin of anachronism.[18] Most of those who mention unbelief do so only to dismiss it.

I offer four examples, from different kinds of books, all written quite recently by undeniably good and respected historians. First, *Le Temps des Cathédrales* (1976), in which Georges Duby described eloquently, with a wealth of splendid images and apt illustrations, a world dominated by religious values. The nature of his subject partly explains his approach: the extraordinary quality and quantity, the power and the scale, of religious art and architecture that survive from the period need some explanation. But may it not be a version of the pathetic fallacy to suppose that the power of monuments of art to impress us is a reflection of the faith of the whole society which produced them? Is it really true to say, as Duby says, that around 1000 'the sole function of what we call art—or at least, of what remains of it after a thousand years . . .—was to offer unto God the riches of the visible word . . . All great art was sacrificial.'[19] What about jewellery or crowns or armour? There was, Duby thinks, great intellectual development in the twelfth century, but, though he talks about growing secularism, disillusion with the failure of crusades, threats from heresy and from the study of Aristotle, and growing knowledge of the world outside Christendom, he discusses the possibility of unbelief (I think) only twice. The first time is when he has been talking of Frederick II and asks whether one is entitled to speak of his 'unbelief, or even scepticism'. The answer is apparently No, for, Duby says, Frederick's 'faith in Christ was unquestionable'. The other time is when he says that the fourteenth century became declericalized but not less Christian. On the contrary, society then became more Christian as the gospel was disseminated and popularized. Christianity was now fortified against uncertainties: there was more credulity and blinder faith.[20]

[17] For an illustration of views of medieval 'popular religion' as they have percolated through to non-medievalists: N. Abercrombie and others, *The Dominant Ideology Thesis* (1980), 65–70.

[18] L. Febvre, *Le Problème de l'incroyance au xvie siècle* (Paris, 1949), 6. The book's influence probably extends to those who have not read it. But cf. M. Hunter, 'The Problem of "Atheism" in early modern England', *Supra*, ser. 5, 35 (1985), 135–157.

[19] *Age of the cathedrals*, trans. E. Levieux and B. Thompson (1981), 9; French edn. (*Le Temps des Cathédrales*) Paris, 1976.

[20] *Age of the cathedrals*, 179, 221.

My second example comes from a volume of essays called *Faire Croire* published in 1981, in which J. C. Schmitt argued that belief and unbelief did not mean in the thirteenth century what we think they mean: to theologians unbelief meant wrong belief, not atheism or agnosticism.[21] Most of the other contributors to the volume also seem to take the line that *faire croire*—making people believe–was not a matter of combating scepticism but of giving instruction in better or more correct belief and behaviour. Thirdly, Frank Barlow in his life of William Rufus (1983) discussed William's apparently cynical profanity and commented that 'any suggestion that [William II] was a pagan, a rationalist, or even a sceptic is clearly absurd.'[22] Finally, Bernard Hamilton in his general survey of *Religion in the Medieval West* (1986) maintained that 'atheism in a theological sense ... seems to have been virtually non-existent', and so was agnosticism.[23] There was plenty of doubt, including about the resurrection of the body, but 'there was a universal belief in the immortality of the soul.'[24]

I could cite many other examples to show that historians of different schools take much the same line—French *Annalistes* and British empiricists, Marxists and non-Marxists, catholics, protestants, and agnostics, historians of politics, of the economy, and of culture and thought. As Guitton pointed out, the kind of assumption that disputants share is a good indicator of a prevailing mentality. But, as I have already argued, prevailing *mentalités* need not be shared by all individuals. G. C. Coulton, for instance, found several examples of medieval unbelief. His robust protestant anti-clericalism may have discouraged further exploration of the topic for a while but more recently W. L. Wakefield found people in thirteenth-century southern France who doubted or denied orthodox doctrines, not, he thought, because they were Cathars, but out of 'a certain independence of mind and native skepticism.' Alexander Murray has produced convincing evidence of impiety, doubt, and possible scepticism in Italy and France during the thirteenth and fourteenth centuries, and of outright atheism in Italy. John Edwards has produced evidence of a similar range from doubt to full denial of God from late fifteenth-century Spain.[25] I salute them all.

[21] J. C. Schmitt, 'Le bon usage du "Credo"', *Faire Croire* (Collection de l'École française de Rome, 51, 1981), 337–61.

[22] F. Barlow, *William Rufus* (1983), 113.

[23] B. Hamilton, *Religion in the Medieval West* (1986), 190.

[24] *Ibid.* 191, though he notes one case on p. 190.

[25] G. C. Coulton, 'The Plain Man's Religion in the Middle Ages' in *Ten Medieval Studies* (Cambridge, 1930), 189–200; W. L. Wakefield, 'Some unorthodox Popular Ideas of the Thirteenth Century', *Medievalia et Humanistica*, N.S. iv (1973), 25–35; A. Murray, 'Piety and Impiety in thirteenth-century Italy', *Studies in Church History*, 8 (1972), 83–106; *idem*, 'Confession as a Historical Source in the Thirteenth Century', in

What I want to do is not only to widen their arguments by producing a few bits of evidence of unbelief in other areas and times
within the middle ages but to consider the subject as an illustration
of the problems raised by the concept of social mentality. Before
turning to the evidence, however, I want to look more closely at two
traditions of writing about medieval history which have discouraged
consideration of the possibility of unbelief. The first derives from the
nature of the sources. Nearly all our information about medieval
religious belief and practice comes from the clergy whose professional
mentality made it much easier for them to attribute nonconformity
to ignorant error than to thoughtful rejection. The historical tradition
does not seem to have made enough allowance for this. Many medieval
historians still seem to assume that, whereas intellectuals may have
doubted or rejected what they were taught (though some deny even
that), peasants at any rate will believe anything if only they are taught
it properly.[26] The most charitable view I can take of this intellectual
and social snobbery is to assume that it is absorbed from the sources.
A second way in which the mentality of historians of medieval religion
still seems to reflect that of the medieval clergy is in the trickle-down
theory of Christianity:[27] that is, the assumption that true Christianity
was what the clergy taught, or failed to teach. The historian, however,
has no business with True Christianity. It is not our job to evaluate
the truth-claims of Christianity or any other religion: they are not a
matter of *historical* argument or proof. Whatever the Church or any

---

The Writing of History in the Middle Ages, ed. R. H. C. Davis and J. M. Wallace-Hadrill
(Oxford, 1981), 275–322; *idem*, 'The Epicureans', in *Intellectuals and Writers in Fourteenth-
century Europe*, ed. P. Boitani (Cambridge, 1986), 138–63; J. Edwards, 'Religious Faith
and Doubt in Late Medieval Spain: Soria c. 1450–1500', *Past & Present*, 120 (1988),
3–25. Gavin Langmuir, *History, Religion, and Antisemitism* and *Towards a Definition of
Antisemitism* (both Berkeley/Los Angeles, 1990), which appeared after my paper was
delivered, contain important discussions of the evidence of medieval religious doubt
and its nature.

[26] e.g. G. Le Bras, 'Déchristianisation: mot fallacieux', *Social Compass*, x (1963), 445–
52, at 449; J. Delumeau, *Le Catholicisme entre Luther et Voltaire* (Paris, 1971), 227–92.
For a notable exception to this kind of intellectual snobbery in the middle ages:
Reginald Pecock, *Reule of Crysten Religioun* (Early English Text Society, 171 (1927), 20,
38, 93.

[27] For discussions of dangers of 'two-tier models' of popular religion, e.g. N. Z. Davis,
'Some Tasks and Themes in the Study of Popular Religion', in *The Pursuit of Holiness*,
ed. C. Trinkaus (Leiden, 1974), 307–36 and Davis, *Society and Culture in Early Modern
France* (1975); J. C. Schmitt, ' "Religion populaire" et culture folklorique', *Annales
E.S.C.*, xxxi (1976), 941–53; P. Zambelli, 'Uno, due, tre mille Menocchio?', *Archivio
Storico Italiano*, cxxxvii (1979), 51–90 especially at 62; P. R. L. Brown, *The Cult of the
Saints* (1981), 14–20; T. F. Tentler, 'Seventeen Authors in Search of Two Religious
Cultures', *Catholic Historical Review*, 71 (1985), 248–58; Chartier, *Cultural History*, 37–
40.

particular branch of it may believe, its practices and doctrines have changed a lot through the centuries. Christianity did not just trickle down. In the middle ages some doctrines, like purgatory, only became accepted by the authorities long after they seem to have been around, in an unrationalized and inarticulate form, among the laity.[28] Some of those who were condemned as heretics seem to have had quite a close knowledge of what look like important parts of Christianity and others had just got muddled about matters like transubstantiation that were very difficult for anyone to get right—whatever right means. In my enquiry into scepticism and unbelief, therefore, I concentrate on the degree of faith, not its orthodoxy. People condemned as heretics who seem to have believed seriously in something which looks as if it could have been derived from Christianity count for me as believers, and so do lay people who indulged in ceremonies and jollifications, even at Christian feasts, that looks to us quaintly unchristian. The fact that the clergy condemned such manifestations of 'popular religion' as unchristian sorcery or paganism is irrelevant in this context. Words like superstition and sorcery belong to polemic, not to analysis: I have religion, you have superstition, he believes in magic.[29]

The mentality of the sources and the degree to which it was shared by the whole of society also need more critical consideration in face of the mass of miracle stories which have for centuries been taken as evidence of medieval credulity.[30] Most of the collections of miracle stories which were so notable a feature of the eleventh and twelfth centuries were made by monks to promote particular shrines.[31] Taking their word as evidence of general belief is like taking television commercials as evidence of the public's preferences among pet-foods. The miracle stories are full of scoffers.[32] Like people in commercials who use the wrong soap-powder, they get their come-uppance, but they would not be in the stories if such people had not existed in real life and needed to be converted. There seems to be no evidence for the curious belief that people then took marvels and prodigies 'comme une manifestation naturelle et ordinaire'.[33] The words *miraculum* and

---

[28] A. J. Gurevich, 'Popular and Scholarly Medieval Scholarly Traditions'; cf. R. W. Southern, 'Between heaven and hell', *Times Literary Supplement* (1982), 651–2.

[29] On the distinction, see e.g. Thomas, *Religion and the Decline of Magic*, 25–50, 74–7, 636–40; H. Geertz and K. Thomas, 'An Anthropology of Religion and Magic', *Journal of Interdisciplinary History*, vi (1975), 71–109; I. C. Jarvie, *Rationality and Relativism* (1984), 51.

[30] See F. Graus, *Volk Herrscher und Heiliger* (Prague, 1965), 39–59, 451–5.

[31] P. R. Morison, 'The Miraculous and French Society, *c.* 950–1100' (Oxford D.Phil. thesis, 1983), 46–50, 66–87, 171–2, 239–43.

[32] *Ibid.* 66–9.

[33] P. Rousset, 'Le Sens du merveilleux à l'Époque Féodale', *Le Moyen Age*, 62 (1956), 25–37, at 26; cf. Graus, 48; A. Gurevich, *Medieval Popular Culture*, trans. J. M. Bak and

mirum, phrases like *mirabile dictu* and *quod mirum est* belie it. Some more serious writers, moreover, who were not producing advertising copy for their own churches or writing the life of their own local saints, deplored the incredibility of some stories.[34] I see no reason to suppose that many ordinary people did not make a common-sense distinction between events that seemed to follow the natural course and those that did not, and that they took some persuading of the clergy's explanations of the latter. The commonest offences, after that of working on feast-days, for which wicked peasants were smitten by saints in French miracle stories between 950 and 1100 were blasphemy and disbelief.[35] Furthermore, if people in the middle ages liked miracle stories that need not imply that they believed them. Some people may have enjoyed the stories just as today I enjoy thrillers without expecting to find incorruptible private eyes walking the mean streets or villains coming out of horse-boxes on country lanes. Some people then may have believed every improbable story they heard, just as some people believe in every new 'miracle cure' nowadays: we need not assume that their credulity was part of some blanket *mentalité* of their age without looking at the evidence with at least as much critical attention as the more thoughtful medieval writers gave it. Miracle stories do not prove that more people in the middle ages were credulous than at any other time, though it would certainly illuminate differences in social mentalities to investigate the different things about which people in different societies are credulous and the different ways in which both the credulous and the sceptical express themselves.

Taking the word of clerical sources about the ignorance and credulity of medieval laymen is an old tradition. Another which has diverted attention from the evidence of medieval scepticism is more recent. It comes from the fashion for drawing analogies between medieval Christianity and the religions of other 'primitive' societies on the basis of rather vague ideas about *la pensée sauvage*. Fascinating and illuminating as the findings of social anthropology are, however, we need to think about the differences between religions before we comb the ethnographic literature for picturesque religious practices

---

P. A. Hollingsworth (Cambridge, 1988), 205; B. Ward, *Miracles and the Medieval Mind* (1982) 2, 33 but cf. 205. Gerald of Wales made a distinction between miracles and marvels only *seemed* contrary to nature: R. Bartlett, *Gerald of Wales* (Oxford, 1982), 105–9.

[34] Though not necessarily because they were themselves totally 'rational': R. I. Moore, 'Guibert of Nogent and his World', in *Studies in Medieval History presented to R. H. C. Davis* H. Mayr-Harting and R. I. Moore (1985), 107–18, also citing some earlier discussions.

[35] Morison, 'The Miraculous and French Society', 145–6.

to use as analogies.[36] It seems clear that there are wide variations both within and between different religions in the emphasis which they put on belief. At one end of the scale is modern western society, where religion is an optional extra for individual commitment. Anyone brought up in our society who wants to study medieval religion must therefore, as Duby has pointed out, 'make a determined effort to liberate himself from the pressure of [the] mental attitudes' induced by his own situation.[37] But what mental attitudes are appropriate? Are they those found in societies where there is no tradition of debate about religion and where there are no alternative religious options available? Although individuals in such societies may be rather more critical and sceptical about bits of their collective representations than anthropologists used to assume, and although one could perhaps infer the strength of an individual's belief from the varying assiduity with which he or she performs ceremonies, it is still fundamentally mistaken to draw analogies between the irrelevance of beliefs in the 'community religions' of such societies and the beliefs of medieval Christians.[38] That is not because it is improper to compare Christian Europe with heathen lands afar o'er which thick darkness broodeth yet. It is because any religion which has a creed that demands personal affirmation, which hunts heretics, which imposes rules of conduct which are notoriously difficult to fulfil in the conditions of everyday life, and which threatens those who fail to fulfil them with eternal damnation (or a long time in purgatory), inevitably offers choices, however little its authorities may wish it to do so.

Even in the early middle ages, when many within the nominally Christian populations of western Europe had little chance of learning about the religion they were supposed to profess, belief was not totally irrelevant. As early as the ninth century the creed was supposed to be taught to everyone in the Carolingian empire. From the eighth it was supposed, at least in England, to be taught in the vernacular when necessary.[39] From the twelfth century there was more literacy and

---

[36] On the dangers of analogies: E. P. Thompson, 'Anthropology and the Discipline of Historical Context', *Midland History*, i, no. 3 (1972), 41–55.

[37] *The Chivalrous Society* (1977), 13 (or *Annales E.S.C.*, 26 (1971), 1–13, at 12).

[38] M. Ruel, 'Christians as Believers', in *Religious Organization and Religious Experience*, ed. J. Davis (1982), 9–32; B. Wilson, *Religion in Sociological Perspective* (Oxford, 1982). For beliefs in other religions see, in addition to works cited in nn. 4, 9, 11–12, Collingwood, *Philosophical Essays*, ii. 185–227; E. Geliner, *Saints of the Atlas* (1969), 111–15; C. O. Frake, 'A structural description of Subanun "religious behavior"', in S. A. Taylor ed. *Cognitive Anthropology* (New York, 1969), 470–87; C. Geertz, *The interpretation of cultures* (1975), 87–125, 170–89; cf. idem, *Negara* (Princeton, 1980), 194–5; R. Thapar, 'Imagined Religious Communities', *Modern Asian Studies*, xxiii (1989), 209–31.

[39] *M. G. H. Capitularia Regum Francorum*, i, ed. A. Boretius (Berlin, 1883), no. 120 (c. 3); Theodulf of Orleans, 'De ordine Baptismi), c. vii: *Patrologia Latina*, ed. J. P. Migne,

more academic education, more development of doctrines and methods of argument about them, more parish churches, better educated priests, and more religious instruction for the laity. By the thirteenth century everyone was supposed to confess and take communion once a year and was supposed to be taught to repeat the creed. Even if some did so (as a contemporary preacher complained) like magpies, without knowing what they were saying,[40] the knowledge that a statement of belief, cast in the first person singular, existed, that they were meant to be able to say it, and they were not meant to say it like magpies, may have stimulated people to think about what it meant. The evidence of heresy suggests that some did just that, and it is surely not impossible that the very existence of heresy—the mere rumour of heresies—should have provoked more thoroughgoing doubts. Perhaps the clergy's increasing fear of heresy and their tendency to stress obedience to authority as a reason for belief were not the best ways of winning hearts and minds.[41] By this time, too, medieval Christendom had a well-established learned culture which combined study of an increasing number of books written by non-Christians with deep respect for the authority of the written word. Even some of the unlearned had some knowledge of the New Testament. There is a great deal about belief and unbelief in the New Testament. Belief in those circumstances cannot have been as apparently irrelevant as it is in some other religions. Many medieval peasants—even some clergy—may have lived in a state of theological innocence like Clifford Geertz's Balians or Ernest Gellner's tribesmen of the Atlas.[42] They did not need to agonize about their faith and they had not got the philosophical expertise to do so very effectively. Furthermore theirs was an authoritarian society and so any reluctance to challenge religious authority is not surprising. But that does not necessarily mean that everyone believed equally. When human beings are presented with choices they take them variously. In societies where they appear not to be making choices it may be because circumstances do not make those particular choices available. But Christianity, even medieval Christianity, tends to invite a modicum of personal

---

cv, col. 227–8; Aelfric, *Homilies*, ed. B. Thorpe (*Homilies of the Anglo-Saxon Church*, pt. 1: 1844–6), ii. 596–8; *The Homilies of Wulfstan*, ed. D. Bethurum (Oxford, 1957), 157–65, 299–302.

[40] N. Bériou, 'L'Art de Convaincre dans la Prédication de Ranulphe d'Homblières' in *Faire Croire* (Collection de l'École française de Rome, 51, 1981), 39–65, at 53.

[41] The stress on authority: 'Bériou, L'Art de Convaincre'; J.-C. Schmitt, 'Le Bon Usage du "Credo"', also in *Faire Croire*, 337–61, at 354–8; Murray, 'Religion among the Poor', 298.

[42] Geertz, *The Interpretation of Cultures*, 177 and *Negara* (Princeton, 1980), 194–5; Gellner, *Saints of the Atlas*, 114–15.

commitment and therefore lays itself open to conscious, if often unac-
knowledged, doubt.

Since most people in any society probably accept its prevailing beliefs,
and most dissidents in a persecuting society will keep their heads
down, it is not surprising that medieval references to outright unbelief
or even serious doubt about central tenets of the Christian faith are
not very common.[43] Nevertheless, I can produce a couple of cases of
outright denial of the existence of God beyond those already cited by
Wakefield, Murray, and Edwards. One woman from a village near
Montaillou in the early fourteenth century bewailed her inability to
believe in God—as well she might.[44] Thomas Walsingham says that
some people blamed the Peasants' Revolt of 1381 on the sins of lords,
some of whom were said to believe, not only that there was no life
after death, but that there was no God and that the sacrament of the
altar was nothing.[45] Doubt or denial of immortality seems to be more
often recorded than direct denial of God and may be just as serious
in its implications. 'For if the dead rise not, then is not Christ raised:
and if Christ be not raised, your faith is vain.'[46] King Amalric I of
Jerusalem told William of Tyre of what I suspect were his own
difficulties in believing in the resurrection—though, like many people
confessing to embarrassing problems, he presented them as not actually his own. William was able to set the king's mind at rest, but then
that is what one would expect in a story told by an archbishop about
himself and the king he served.[47] Also in the twelfth century, the
French monk Hélinant referred disapprovingly to those who believed
that there was no other world and no more life after death for men
than for animals.[48] Similar thorough-going denials of immortality are

[43] J. G. A. Gaskin ed. *Varieties of Unbelief* (1989) discusses the different forms of
unbelief usefully. Several of his forms can be found in the middle ages even if (p. 10)
'no significant or influential literary unbelief can be identified' then.
[44] P. Dronke, *Women writers of the middle ages* (Cambridge, 1984), 267, 271 and cf.
204–15; as Dronke points out, E. Le Roy Ladurie (*Montaillou* (Paris, 1975), 474, 491–2,
532–4) conflates Aude Faure's disbelief in God with her disbelief in transubstantiation.
Although Le Roy Ladurie discusses belief, denies the 'immense appétit du divin' which
Febvre (*Problème*, 528–35) attributed to the middle ages, and ostensibly plays down
the element of magic in medieval beliefs (*ibid.* 465–8, 579–84), the book as a whole
seems to stress what is strange and 'folklorique' about the people of Montaillou (and
their sex lives) rather than their rationality: cf. L. E. Boyle, 'Montaillou Revisited' in
Pathways to Peasants, ed. J. A. Raftis (Toronto, 1981), 119–40, at 124, 126–7.
[45] Thomas Walsingham, *Historia Anglicana* (Rolls series, 28, 1864) ii. 12. Murray,
'Epicureans', Wakefield, and Edwards all cite examples of similarly sweeping unbelief.
[46] I Corinthians, xv. 16–17.
[47] *Recueils des Historiens des Croisades: Historiens Occidentaux*, i (Paris, 1841), 887–8 (XIX.
3).
[48] Hélinant, *Les Vers de la Mort*, ed. F. Wulff and E. Walberg (Paris: Société des

said to have been common in early fourteenth-century Italy. They are mentioned in southern France in the thirteenth century, in Spain in the fifteenth, and in England, apart from the fourteenth-century rumour mentioned by Thomas Walsingham, also in the fifteenth.[49] Among other types of scepticism mentioned are assertions that the gospels were inventions like any other stories and that crops grow, not because God makes them, but because of the nature of seed and soil, helped by man's labour.[50] Transubstantiation seems to have aroused fairly widespread doubt: one thirteenth-century preacher admitted that it was hard to believe and it was obviously a stumbling block for many who were accused of heresy.[51] It may be that the importance attached to it by church officials, like their emphasis on obedience to authority, actually provoked some to doubt, and then to doubt other doctrines too.

Many more people must have suffered from doubts than ever got into trouble for denying dogma. Jean de Joinville seems to have needed fortification by his king against some kind of unbelief. St Louis' argument was a nice one: since Joinville took his mother's word about the identity of his father and believed it without question he ought also to believe on the word of the apostles all the articles of faith which he heard sung on Sunday in the creed. Strong as Louis' own faith was, moreover, he still thought that no layman ought to risk arguing with Jews: argument might shake the faith of anyone who was not a skilled theologian.[52] He was not alone in fearing conversions to Judaism: a young thirteenth-century Dominican worried whether Christians or Jews or pagans were right, while ecclesiastical legislation of the same period suggests that service in Jewish households was thought to be liable to lead simple minds astray.[53] This fear of the Jews reminds us that an alternative religion was available at least to the small part of the population that met and talked with Jews, and that, although Jews were hated and feared, their religion nonetheless apparently had attractions. Conversions from Judaism also show vari-

---

Anciens Textes Français, 1905), 32–3 (strophes xxxiv–xxxv) and cf. p. xxxiii.

[49] Wakefield, 28, 31; Murray, 'Epicureans', 143; Walsingham, *Historia Anglicana*, ii. 12; A. M. Hudson, *The Premature Reformation* (Oxford, 1988), 385; Edwards, 13–16, 21, 25.

[50] Murray, 'The Epicureans', 150; Wakefield, 27, 32.

[51] Murray, 'Piety and Impiety', 98; J. A. F. Thomson, *The Later Lollards* (Oxford, 1965), e.g. 68–9, 74, 246–7.

[52] Jean de Joinville, *Histoire de Saint Louis*, ed. N. de Wailly (Paris, 1874), 15–20.

[53] A. Murray, 'Confession as a Historical Source', 296; *Corpus Iuris Canonici*, ed. A. Friedberg (Leipzig, 1833–9), ii. col. 772–6. For the attractions of Judaism in the ninth century: C. Edwards, 'Tohuwabohu: the *Wessobrunner Gebet* and its analogues', *Medium Aevum* 53 (1984), 263–81, at 268–9.

ation in belief: some Jews were more sincerely converted than others. The degree of belief varied.

Many preachers stressed the need for faith. In the thirteenth century one of them, like King Louis, explicitly warned against wanting to enquire into its roots and make it secure by reasoning.[54] According to Innocent IV, all the laity needed to believe was that God exists and rewards the good. They should then believe the rest of the articles of faith implicitly: that is, they should believe that whatever the Catholic Church believes is true. The poorer lower clergy needed to believe just a little more, namely the real presence at the sacrament of the altar, but it seems clear that Innocent regarded implicit and uncomprehending faith as a concession and a safeguard for the supposedly simple-minded.[55] More was expected of theologians. Schmitt, in the study in *Faire Croire* that I mentioned earlier, adduces as evidence that theologians did not take unbelief seriously the way that they described those who denied the existence of God as mad.[56] If they had, one might be tempted to reply: But they would, wouldn't they? In fact, however, as his footnote says, Aquinas described unbelievers as *stulti et superbi*, which does not imply that he regarded unbelief as unenvisageable for the sane. The stupid and proud are not mad, and, like the poor, they are always with us. Medieval scholars, moreover, went to some trouble to work out theologies of the existence of God. After all, the ontological argument was actually invented at the very beginning of the great period of medieval scholarship. Although Anselm and his successors worried as much or more about the emotional commitment which ought to follow intellectual assent as about the assent itself, it is hard to see how one can rationally maintain that they were unaware of the possibility of unbelief or unworried about it. They clearly knew about unbelief and regarded it as dangerous, even before the thirteenth century brought so much more of Aristotle, as well as other classical pagans and some Jewish and Islamic philosophers, to their notice.

When people doubted or disbelieved they naturally did so on different grounds from modern agnostics or atheists. Unbelief, like belief, is socially conditioned. Medieval sceptics and atheists were moulded and conditioned both by the Christianity they questioned or denied and by the other information that was available to them.[57]

[54] Bériou, 'L'Art de Convaincre', 48.
[55] Quoted by van Engen, 'The Christian Middle Ages', n 91. Cf the different degrees of faith demanded in the fifteenth century by Reginald Pecock and the rationalizing cast of his arguments: E. F. Jacob, 'Reginald Pecock, Bishop of Chichester', *Proc. British Academy*, xxxvii (1951), 121–53.
[56] Schmitt, 'Le Bon Usage du "Credo"', 338–9.
[57] A. M. Bowes, 'Atheism in a religious Society' in *Religious Organization and Religious*

That does not make them any the less sceptical or unbelieving. If medieval people said that they, or others, did not believe in important doctrines of Christianity, then unbelief was not impossible for them even if their grounds for doubting were not the same as those of, for instance, Lucien Febvre. People who were accused of all the various types and levels of unbelief or doubt included nobles, townsmen, and peasants, as well as secular and religious clergy. Some seem to have been cynical or casual, others look more serious, but there does not seem to me to be any significant correlation between social status or formal education on the one hand and degree of rationality on the other. One Montaillou woman, when asked where she got her doubts about hell and the resurrection from, said that she got them from no one: she thought of them for herself.[58] Even medieval peasants—even peasant women—could think. It may be objected either that some of the evidence I have cited is merely hearsay or that examples from the later middle ages, particularly from Italy, reflect the growth of 'modern' attitudes. On the first point, contemporary rumours show at least that the idea of unbelief is not anachronistic. On the second, leaving aside the circularity of arguments about modernization, the evidence is best where persecution was active and records of it were preserved. Given that there was persecution, given the professional difficulties that the clergy might face if they admitted to serious doubts, it seems likely that many people who felt doubts or worse did so, as Murray puts it, 'without getting to the point of stubborn challenge to orthodoxy', continuing instead to live 'in a chronic state of double-think; the logical instability of their condition being buttressed by the fact that many other people lived in it too.'[59]

Once it is accepted that doubt and unbelief were possible in the middle ages, the much more generally accepted evidence of impiety, indifference, even of anticlericalism, may need reassessment. Clearly, none of these need imply scepticism, let alone atheism, but I do not see how we can be sure that in some cases they did not. Neither William Rufus nor Frederick II need have been an unbeliever, let alone a consistent one throughout his life, but, *pace* Barlow and Duby respectively, either may have been. Henry II of England is another possible sceptic. Although he respected goodness and holiness in one bishop at least, his warning to the pope that he would rather become a Moslem (*Noradini citius sequeretur errores et profanae religionis iniret*

Experience, 33–49. Febvre's argument in *Le Problème de l'incroyance* seems to be that sixteenth-century intellectuals had not the intellectual equipment for unbelief of twentieth-century ones.

[58] Dronke, *Women writers*, 267.

[59] A. Murray, *Reason and Society in the Middle Ages* (Oxford, 1978), 8.

consortium) than have Thomas Becket as archbishop of Canterbury any longer, however lightly made and however little he knew of Islam, suggests that he took his Christianity in a rather detached and carefree way.[60] It may be suggested that before the twelfth century most of the laity were too ignorant about Christianity to be capable of rejecting it seriously. Poor information, however, though the initiated may think it makes rejection futile, does not actually preclude rejection. Lay religion was certainly less belief-oriented before the twelfth century than later but degrees of piety may sometimes, nonetheless, have reflected degrees of faith. Some of the nobles who were condemned as enemies of the Church in the tenth and eleventh centuries may have been sceptical, as well as contemptuous, of what they knew of the Church's teaching, even if others were pious patrons of their own family monasteries and attacked rival establishments only for sound political reasons. There are several references to an opinion generally held in different parts of eleventh-century France that monasticism provided a useful refuge for the sick or disabled: knights would not become monks while they were still in good fighting trim.[61] A good many nobles who made donations to churches found them on second thoughts too costly and delayed their implementation for long periods.[62] Piety, in other words, ebbed and flowed, stronger in times of illness or crisis than when the world was comfortable. Yet this is the period of which Duby says that knights and peasants gave what they had willingly to monasteries because they feared death and judgement and which Peter Brown describes as having a 'tremendous sense of the intimacy and adjacency of the holy'.[63] I suggest that these two distinguished historians are lavishing their historical imagination on a social mentality of which the character and prevalence is yet to be fully established.

Later in the middle ages we have evidence that some people in France, for instance, did not go to church for years at a time, and that others behaved in a way that suggests that they did so chiefly in order to meet and gossip and hear the news.[64] Some historians hold that this reflects the Church's failure to get its message across,[65] but

[60] *Materials for the history of Thomas Becket* (Rolls series, 1875–85), vi. 106. Cf. other sources cited by W. L. Warren, *Henry II* (1973), 211.

[61] Customs of Cluny in *Patrologia Latina*, 149, cols. 625–6; G. Sitwell ed. *St Odo of Cluny* (1958), 9–11, 97–8; J. Armitage Robinson, *Gilbert Crispin* (Cambridge, 1911), 89, 94–5.

[62] C. B. Bouchard, *Sword, Miter, and Cloister* (1987), 227–46.

[63] G. Duby, *L'Europe au Moyen Age: Art Roman, Art Gothique* (Paris, 1979), 43; Brown, 'Society and the Supernatural', 141. Cf e.g. P. Geary, 'Humiliation of Saints', in *Saints and their Cults*, ed. S. Wilson (Cambridge, 1983), 123–40, at 133.

[64] P. Adam, *La Vie Paroissiale en France au xive Siècle* (Paris, 1964), 246–76.

[65] e.g. J. Toussaert, *Le Sentiment Religieux en Flandre à la fin du Moyen-Age* (Paris, 1960),

in view of the evidence that lay people were capable of unbelief, it is not impossible that some who gossiped or played dice in church, or never went there at all, did so because they rejected the message. Many of those who rejected church teaching were heretics rather than unbelievers but, as Hudson, as well as Edwards, Murray, and Wakefield have shown, some who were prosecuted for heresy were probably sceptics. Some look like casual cynics—what J. A. F. Thomson has called 'the loose speaker [or] the tavern unbeliever',[66] but colloquial expression of opinions, even their expression in taverns, need not invariably mean that the opinions were unconsidered or irrational. They may have arisen, as Wakefield put it, 'from the cogitation of men and women searching for explanations that accorded with the realities of the life in which they were enmeshed.'[67]

None of this is intended to deny that most people probably accepted the Church's teachings without agonizing over them. The Church was in every sense established. Its teachings, however misunderstood or adapted to secular moralities, permeated life. To judge from the doubts some of them expressed, peasants and poor townspeople some-times knew a fair amount about Christianity. We have no reason to believe that most of them were out of reach of the Church's teaching. Some were,[68] but, hard as it is to get at the views of those at the bottom of society, there is not much evidence that pagan survivals, magical beliefs, or what has been called a 'common substratem of European folk-lore'[69] formed a genuinely alternative belief-system or ideology to which peasants in general gave more adherence than they did to the Church. Beyond the conventional piety of the majority, moreover, there must have been genuine and fervent piety—perhaps as much among the laity as among the clergy. It was, by and large, the piety of lay people that covered Europe with a network of parishes and that built and embellished parish churches. Lay people found release from their sense of guilt in pilgrimages, and hope in the doctrine of purgatory which they themselves developed. They found forms of affective devotion in brotherhoods and at shrines.[70] Parish churches and local fraternities depended on the support of a wide range of

---

117–22, 158–60, 368–71, 595–604; J. Delumeau, *Le Catholicisme*, 227–55; Le Bras, 'Déchristianisation'; cf. van Engen, 'The Christian Middle Ages', 521–2.

[66] Thomson, *Later Lollards*, 241–2. For examples of accusations of heresy which may reflect scepticism, e.g. ibid 248 and Hudson, *Premature Reformation*, 165–8, 384–5.

[67] Wakefield, 33.

[68] e.g. the story of master Guncalinus: d'Avray, 40–1.

[69] The phrase comes from D. Martin, 'The Secularization Question', *Theology*, lxxvi (1973), 81–7, at 84.

[70] S. Reynolds, *Kingdoms and Communities in Western Europe* (Oxford, 1984), 67–90; G. Rosser, 'Communities of Parish and Guild in the late Middle Ages' in *Parish, Church and People* ed. S. J. Wright (1988), 29–55.

society and perhaps particularly of those who were not qualified to become monks. Monasteries, in any case, were not uniformly exclusive: their proliferation, like the creation of orders of friars, testifies to the growth of lay piety. It was laymen—and from the twelfth century generally adult laymen—who became monks or friars. Many of them did so because they were already pious and yearned to fulfil their piety in the best way they knew. Motives of course were mixed then as they always are. There could be many motives for going on pilgrimage or crusade, for founding and endowing monasteries, or even for becoming a monk, but it is not part of my argument that all or even most were worldly. Much pious behaviour must have reflected real faith.[71]

Statistics are impossible. Whether there were a dozen or a hundred humble St Louis's for every humble William Rufus is impossible to say, but at least from William's lifetime on the pressures of convention were against him and for Louis. The open expression of unbelief could be dangerous and took courage, but on the other hand faith could be difficult. Like piety it probably ebbed and flowed. It must often have been strongest in moments of crisis (no atheists in the trenches) and on deathbeds, though even respectable people on their deathbeds could express doubts about some parts of Church teaching.[72] There is, in short, considerable evidence that religion was not just a matter of social convention and ceremony, that some people believed in Christianity less than others, and that this was not simply because of ignorance or the peasantry's preference for unchristian magic. On the contrary the evidence suggests that some people found Christianity, or parts of it, hard to believe in, and that some may not have tried very hard.

If it is agreed that sceptics and unbelievers were to be found, in however small a minority, in several countries and in all the centuries for which we have remotely adequate evidence from which to detect them, then the common assumption that religious scepticism was somehow foreign to the medieval mind looks like another of those 'unexpressed and fundamental assumptions about the nature of European society' to which R. I. Moore has recently drawn attention as

[71] On noble motives for benefactions: C. B. Bouchard, *Sword, Miter, and Cloister*; E. Mason, '*Timeo Barones et Dona Ferentes*', *Studies in Church History*, 15 (1978), 61–75; J. Howe, 'The Nobility's Reform of the Medieval Church', *American Hist. Review*, xciii (1988), 317–39.

[72] *L'Histoire de Guillaume le Maréchal* (Paris, 1891–1901), lines 18495–6. There seems little evidence that William's piety was more than conventional, though see G. Duby, *William Marshal* (1986), 12–13.

being historically unfounded.[73] I submit that one thing which has helped to preserve this particular assumption, in defiance of evidence against it, is the carefree way in which the idea of social mentalities has been used. Historians may well feel that they cannot engage in arguments about differences in thought processes or evaluate the relative merits of cognitive relativism, universalism, intellectualism, symbolism, and so forth. But we need to be aware of the arguments. It is rash to base studies of mentalities on an unargued premise that people in different societies or cultures are known to have fundamentally different thought processes. They may have, but it is not established that they do. So long as we start from the assumption that strange beliefs imply strange and uncritical processes of thought, and that mentalities arise from whole societies like miasma from a swamp, we have no hope of understanding how and why people in different societies, and in different sections of different societies, really do develop different ideas and ways of thinking. It is probably a mistake to start with whole societies. It is too difficult to define their boundaries in time and space and to identify their relevant characteristics. Recent work by medievalists suggest that differences in the content and processes of thought can better be approached through seeing how particular groups of people develop quite specific elements of thought and on the methods of transmission both within the group and from it to society at large.[74]

Whatever aspect of historical mentalities is studied historical imagination will be needed. But one also needs evidence, evidence which must be critically assessed and rationally argued, whether or not it fits one's assumptions and hypotheses. Before we use our imaginations to explain a phenomenon we must try to identify the phenomenon as exactly as possible. If the religious faith and piety of the middle ages were not the product of a mentality by which 'society as a whole instinctively recoiled' from certain issues,[75] then the explanations and understanding of them need to be different. Explanations and descriptions, however, vivid and appealing, which ignore this must be wrong. In fact the more appealing and vivid they are the more they may mislead. We cannot just sail off into the wide blue yonder of explaining religious attitudes that may not have been general on the ground of mentalities that may not have been universal. The evidence of scepticism produced here is not extensive, but even one piece would be enough to falsify the hypothesis that it was foreign

---

[73] R. I. Moore, *The Formation of a Persecuting Society* (Oxford, 1987), 4.
[74] e.g. d'Avray, *Preaching of the Friars:* E. Peters, *Torture* (Oxford, 1985); R. Bartlett, *Trial by Fire and Water* (Oxford, 1986); Moore, *Formation of a Persecuting Society.*
[75] Hamilton, 196, 197.

to 'the medieval mind.' Everyone in the middle ages had rather different ideas from ours (whoever 'we' are with our supposedly rational, secular, and uniform ways of thought) about a great many topics—politics, social relations, and the world in general, as well as about God. But that need not mean that their cognitive processes, their ways of thinking, were in themselves either more uniform than ours or entirely strange to us. If they were entirely strange, how could we write about them and expound them at all? Evidence of indifference or scepticism, whether among intellectuals, nobles, or peasants, cannot be convincingly explained away on the ground of *a priori* ideas about medieval mentality that must themselves depend on the absence of evidence of indifference or scepticism. Medieval credulity, whether applauded as faith or patronized as superstition and 'popular religion', may, with good evidence and argument, become the conclusion of a discussion. It cannot be a premise. And nor can any other aspect of the 'mentality' of any society.

THE REPUTATION OF ROBERT CECIL:
LIBELS, POLITICAL OPINION AND POPULAR AWARENESS IN THE EARLY SEVENTEENTH CENTURY

By Pauline Croft

READ 2 MARCH 1990

ON 29 April 1612 the London letter writer John Chamberlain penned another of his regular epistles to his friend Sir Dudley Carleton, ambassador in Venice. For weeks a chief news item had been the declining health of the Lord Treasurer, Robert Cecil Earl of Salisbury. 'I wish I could send you better assurance' Chamberlain wrote, 'but as far as I can learn there is more cause of fear than hope'. Salisbury was journeying to Bath, where he had often sought relief before, but he had been 'very yll by the way yesterday and was almost gon once or twise'. His death was assumed to be imminent. 'He is aldredy much lamented and every man sayes what a misse there wold be of him and indeed [he] is much prayed for'. The news later in June was more of a surprise. Salisbury's passing, on the return journey from Bath, had been followed not by the expected tributes to his irreplaceability, but by a flood of 'outragious speaches'. Chamberlain reported that 'fresh libells come out every day', and on 2 July he was constrained to write that

> 'the memorie of the late Lord Treasurer growes dayly worse and worse and more libells come as yt were continually, whether yt be that practises and juglings come more and more to light, or that men love to follow the sway of the multitude: but yt is certain that they who may best maintain yt, have not forborn to say that he jugled with religion, with the King, Quene, theyre children, with nobilitie, Parlement, with frends, foes and generally with all. Some of his chaplains have ben heard to oppose themselves what they could in pulpit against these scandalous speaches but with litle fruit'.[1]

---

[1] *The Letters of John Chamberlain*, ed. N. E. McClure (2 vols., Philadelphia, 1939), i. 346–7, 350, 362, 364–5.

The libels of 1612 have often been noted in passing, but never studied in detail. They are of great historical interest, revealing much about current attitudes and demonstrating the existence of a lively and informed body of public opinion which relished political gossip and subjected famous figures to a far-from-deferential scrutiny. Moreover, although Chamberlain noted only the defamatory libels, the debate was not one-sided, for the late Lord Treasurer proved to have some vigorous and hard-hitting defenders.

There has been a danger of exaggerating the significance of the outburst against Cecil, not least because of the references in Chamberlain's famously readable letters. Another observer, the second Earl of Dorset, noted that 'when great men die, such is either their desert or the malice of the people or both together, as commonly they are ill spoken of'. Although Dorset considered the attacks on Salisbury the worst he had seen, his words are a reminder that satirical and denigratory comments were very much part of Elizabethan and Jacobean politico-literary culture. Later in 1612, within weeks of the death of the extravagantly mourned Prince Henry, 'lies and slanders' were circulating about him.[2] The 1580s and 1590s saw the rise of popular and sensational news pamphlets (associated particularly with the prolific Thomas Nashe), moralistic and topical tracts, prose fiction, and above all, satires and epigrams. So great was their ferocity that in June 1599 further publications were banned.[3] This crackdown had only a temporary effect, for epigrams, epitaphs and memorial poems were establishing themselves as standard literary forms. Between 1590 and 1620, the composition of short pieces of verse, both satirical and laudatory, on named or anonymous figures, became immensely fashionable at court, in the universities and in the taverns of London. The vogue owed much to Sir John Harington, the Queen's godson, who circulated scores of epigrams in manuscript, but there were many other writers who popularised the form in print.[4] Thomas Bastard, Samuel Rowlands, Richard West, Sir John Davies and John Davies of Hereford all published volumes of epigrams in these years, as did the parliament man John Hoskyns, who met regularly with other wits

[2] British Library, Stowe MS 172, fo. 319, 22 June 1612. Roy Strong, *Henry Prince of Wales and England's lost Renaissance* (1986), 8–9.

[3] Recent studies include Charles Nicholl, *A Cup of News: the life of Thomas Nashe* (1984), Sandra Clark, *The Elizabethan Pamphleteers: popular moralistic pamphlets 1580–1640* (1983), Paul Salzman, *English Prose Fiction 1558–1700: a critical history* (Oxford, 1985), and Raman Selden, *English Verse Satire 1590–1765* (1978). For the bishops' ban, Selden, 72.

[4] 'Epigram' with regard to verse satire describes any length of poem. John Wilcox, 'Informal publication of late 16th century verse satire', *Huntington Library Quarterly*, xiii (1) 1949–50, 191–200. *The Letters and Epigrams of Sir John Harington*, ed. N. E. McClure (Philadelphia, 1930), 44–52.

including Inigo Jones and Richard Martin at the Mermaid and Mitre taverns. From this group came the famous 'fart poem' with its vivid descriptions of members of the Commons who in 1607 had been present at an embarrassing incident. In 1609 the playwright Thomas Dekker, in his parody of contemporary manners *The Guls Hornebooke* explained how to attract attention in a tavern. 'After a turne or two in the roome, take occasion (pulling out youer gloves) to have some Epigrams, or Satyre, or Sonnet fastned in one of them that may ... offer itselfe to the gentlemen'.[5] Such items would include the libels on Cecil and other leading figures. They circulated widely, spreading from the chattering classes of the capital out into the provinces, and the commonplace books kept by innumerable gentlemen were full of them. One copied over the years between 1602 and 1630, probably in London and Wales, contains poetry and prose in Latin, English and Welsh, with items on public figures (including Cecil) and court scandals.[6] Epitaphs and libels often circulated for decades in manuscript, written out either by professional scrivenors for a fee, or passed from hand to hand for readers to copy themselves. The impact of printing has overshadowed the continued importance of manuscript circulation right up to the end of the seventeenth century. Political, educational and polemical texts, separates of parliamentary speeches, the works of Sir Robert Cotton and Sir Henry Spelman, the poetry of John Donne, all reached a wide public through manuscript rather than print. In some literary circles there was still a belief in the social and intellectual superiority of manuscript publication, but with a vast range of lesser items, 'predominantly satiric and occasionally lubricious', the need to escape censorship, or a prosecution in Star Chamber for scandalum magnatum – the libelling of great men – seems a more likely motive. Anonymity was a useful protection.[7] To this extensive genre of manuscript epigram literature belong the libels that appeared on the death of Robert Cecil.

The majority of epigrams were unflattering, and most of the great personages of the day figured in them. The accession of James I was celebrated in innumerable verses, but a more critical note was soon

---

[5] For a printed version of the fart poem and discussion of the texts, Baird W. Whitlock, *John Hoskyns, Sergeant-at-Law* (Washington D.C., 1982), 283–92. *The Non-dramatic Works of Thomas Dekker*, ed. A. B. Grosart (5 vols., 1884–6), ii. 240.

[6] Richard Roberts' commonplace book is now Bodleian Library, MS Don c 54. For a printed example, *The Doctor Farmer Chetham MS., being a commonplace book in the Chetham Library*, ed. A. B. Grosart (2 vols., Manchester, 1873).

[7] Harold Love, 'Scribal publication in 17th century England', *Transactions of the Cambridge Bibliographical Society*, ix (2) 1987, 130–54. It is notable that the manuscript satires and epigrams on the Overbury scandal openly name Robert Carr and Frances Howard, but the printed pamphlets do not. Clark, 87.

apparent. One which begins 'Listen jolly gentlemen' ridiculed the king's indolence and his 'merry boys', while a clutch of related couplets ironically acclaimed James' hunting prowess. There are verses attacking the avarice of the Scots alongside odes of thanksgiving for escape from the Gunpowder plot. The first Earl of Dorset, Salisbury's predecessor as Lord Treasurer, was lampooned after his death for taking bribes in legal cases.[8] The Earl of Northampton, 'the great archpapist, learned Curio', was depicted as converted to the Church of England not so much by the theological skills of James I, as by his 'power to say, Recant thine error, And thou shalt be a privie counsellor'. Northampton's religious ambiguity was also skewered in an epigram labelling him as 'His Majesty's earwig'. The matrimonial problems of Sir Edward Coke, 'Cocus the pleader', inspired other versifiers.[9] Leading churchmen did not escape. On Whitgift's death in 1604 a lengthy set of verses accusing him of being 'the Jesuits' hope' was pinned to the hearse itself. His successor was similarly blamed for Romish tendencies. 'Bancroft was for plays, Lean Lent and holy days' begins one libel which alleged that the archbishop kept open a back door at Lambeth for 'the Strumpet of Rome'. The extensive literature of the 1620s has recently been studied for evidence of the transmission of news and the formation of public opinion, but it should not be assumed that critical appraisal of political figures began with the Duke of Buckingham. The voluminous libels and epigrams of the later Elizabethan and Jacobean period offer a valuable and as-yet-unworked source for the political culture of the earlier years.[10]

Libels were often linked with campaigns of defamation. In the tense summer of 1585, a smear campaign against Lord Burghley insinuated that he was not committed to the protestant cause. It asserted also that 'England was become regnum Cecilianum'.[11] The attacks of 1585 set the pattern, for similar criticisms both written and spoken continued through the 1590s. As Robert Cecil joined his father on the privy council, the plausibility of a *regnum Cecilianum* increased. It became a commonplace to assert that they conspired to thwart the

[8] Bodleian, Malone MS 23, pp. 10, 19. Public Record Office, State Papers Domestic Jas. I, SP 14/69/67. Bodleian, MS Hearne's Diaries 67, pp. 28–9. Folger Shakespeare Library, Washington D.C., MS 1027.2, p. 6. Bodleian, MS Rawlinson poet 65, fo. 2. Bodleian, MS Tanner 306, fo. 422. Bodleian, MS Eng poet e 14, fo. 95v. rev. Bodleian, MS Don c 54, fo. 6v.

[9] *Doctor Farmer Chetham MS*, ii. 198. Bodleian, MS Malone 23, p. 1a.

[10] *Les reportes del cases in Camera Stellata*, ed. W. P. Baildon (1894), 223. Bodleian, MS Ashmole 1463, fo. 13. Richard Cust, 'News and Politics in early 17th century England', *Past and Present*, 112 (1986), 60–90. Thomas Cogswell, 'The Politics of Propaganda: Charles I and the people in the 1620s', *Journal of British Studies*, 29 (1990), 187–215.

[11] PRO, SP 12/180/23, 47.

careers of other men of talent, promoting only 'base penn clarkes'.[12] The second Earl of Essex was depicted as the most prominent victim of the policy of exclusion. The contrast between the Cecils, a recently-ennobled family of civil servants, and the dashing military leader was a sharp one, and followers of Essex attacked the Cecils as 'goose-quilled gents'. Members of Essex's household reviled the younger Cecil's hunchback; 'here lieth the Toad' was scrawled on the lintel of his chamber at court.[13] After Essex's abortive rising, libels about his opponents circulated in London. Sir Walter Ralegh was censured for 'bloody pride' and the avarice which led him to lay additional burdens on the Cornish tin miners. Robert Cecil was caricatured.

> Little Cecil trips up and down, He rules both court and crown
> With his brother Burghley clown, In his great fox furred gown
> With the long proclamation, He swore he saved the town
> Is it not likely![14]

Essex and his aristocratic followers deplored the absence of noble blood on the privy council, and another libel accused the Cecils of a deliberate campaign against the nobility.

> First did thy sire and now thy self by Machivillian skill
> Prevail and curb the Peers as well befits your will.

The tone is remarkably venomous, addressing Cecil as 'Proud and ambitious wretch that feedest on naught but Faction' and describing him as 'Dissembling smoothfaced dwarf ... I know your crookback's spider-shapen'.[15] In a much lengthier poem, which memorably relates the downfall of Essex in dream form, using a beast fable, Cecil featured as 'the Camel' with its hump, while Essex was 'the Hart' and Elizabeth 'the Lion'. The camel brings a poison in a glass which deceives the lion into exiling the hart.

> O that a Camel should a Lion lead ...
> Camel for burden is, and for the way,
> And not for kingdom's stern and sceptre's sway.
> By sleight get Camels sways, and Lion sleeps
> And noble Hart in dampie dungeon keeps.
> Wake noble Lion, and this Camel scorn ...

[12] *The State of England Anno Dom. 1600 by Thomas Wilson*, ed. F.J. Fisher, Camden 3rd ser., Miscellany xvi, (1936), 42.

[13] *Historical Manuscripts Commission, Salisbury*, xi, 586, xiv, 162.

[14] PRO, SP 12/278/23. I have modernised the spelling in this and other libels.

[15] Bodleian, MS Don c. 54, fo. 20. For an allegation in 1592 that Burghley deliberately suppressed the ancient nobility, British Library, Additional MS 12510, fos. 8v, 22v.

Your Grace to Ireland should the Camel send
His back will bear Tyrone and never bend.[16]

Many of the themes of the posthumous libels were present in the earlier outburst of popular verse defending Essex. Cecil's shortness of stature, his monopoly of power, his hunchback and his factious villainy became established tropes. The death of Essex was to haunt him. In 1604, Samuel Daniel's classical tragedy *Philotas* was censured by the privy council for alluding too dangerously to the late Earl, and by analogy hinting at Cecil himself in the character of the treacherous dwarf Craterus. The accusation that Cecil and his friends at court had 'plotted worthy Essex' fall' was still being repeated in 1612, with the added twist that Cecil's painful death, his 'foul loathsome end', was itself proof of 'how foully then they did offend'. Another libel referred to a 'work of darkness never to be forgotten'.[17] The allegations were testimony to the enduring fascination of the Devereux name, the chivalric values which Essex personified, and probably also the attractions of that policy of a continued war against Spain which Essex had advocated and the Cecils after 1598 deplored. The contrast between Essex and Robert Cecil epitomised the common Renaissance antithesis between the sword and the pen, the man of action and the sedentary clerk, the aristocrat and the bureaucrat. It is not surprising that it proved so enduring in popular verse. In 1612 the ten-year-old Symonds D'Ewes was struck by the hate-filled rejoicing at Salisbury's death, and in his autobiography he set down his mature opinion that it was the lasting popular affection for Essex that lay behind the libels.[18]

By 1601, when Essex went to the block, Robert Cecil had succeeded his father as secretary of state and Master of the court of Wards. The assertion that he ruled both court and crown was widely believed, although he privately described the Queen as ever more autocratic and difficult to manage in her declining years.[19] In 1603 he successfully masterminded the accession of James I, which gained him a barony as well as ensuring his retention of the Wards and the secretaryship. In 1605 he was created Earl of Salisbury, and in 1608 he succeeded

---

[16] Bodleian, MS Don c.54, fo. 19. The copyist has written the identifications in the margin.

[17] David Morse, *England's Time of Crisis: from Shakespeare to Milton* (1989), 62–7. Bodleian, MS Tanner 299, fo. 12. BL, Trumbull Misc. v, fo. 11.

[18] *The Autobiography and Correspondence of Sir Simonds D'Ewes during the reigns of James I and Charles I*, ed. J. O. Halliwell (2 vols., 1845), i. 50–51. Cecil was blamed for the death sentence. In 1615 the historian William Camden, who had attended Essex's trial, considered that 'to this day but few there are which have thought it a capital crime'. William Camden, *Annales*, translated R. Norton (1635), 542–3, 549.

[19] *Calendar of the Carew MSS 1601–3 preserved in the Archiepiscopal Library at Lambeth*, ed. J. S. Brewer and W. Bullens (1870), 157, 221, 260, 358–9. *HMC Salisbury*, xix. 21.

Dorset as Lord Treasurer, thereafter holding the three greatest offices of state in an unparallelled monopoly of power. The parlous condition of the crown's finances had already been evident to Cecil in 1601 and by 1608 urgent measures were needed. Not since Lord Treasurer Winchester under Mary had there been such activity at the Exchequer, and it is not surprising that hostility to his fiscal efforts featured prominently in the posthumous libels. Taxation was a common theme. The five parliamentary sessions of 1604 to 1610 voted in all four subsidies and seven fifteenths and tenths. Even though the subsidy was in sharp decline, each levy bringing in less than the one before, the total was still an exceptional amount for peacetime. Salisbury had warned the king that it was likely to be resented, for after the heavy tax burdens of the 1590s, expectations of relief were widespread on James' accession. Far from receiving any praise for his efforts to cope with the crown's financial crisis, Salisbury was described as

> Oppression's praiser, Taxation's raiser...
> The country's scourger, The cities' cheater
> Of many a shilling.[20]

Since the collection of subsidy money was routinely staggered to ease the impact on the subject, between 1603 and 1612 only three years were free of levies. The frequency of these demands produced a particularly popular libel which begins,

> Here lies Hobbinall, our shepherd while here
> That once in a year, our fleeces did sheer.[21]

Parliamentary taxation was not the only financial burden for which Salisbury was blamed. After the sessions of 1604 and 1610, the lack of adequate supply drove the crown to require loans on privy seals. Once again, in private Salisbury had made plain his own strong distaste for these prerogative measures, but to no avail. The loans were raised and in the public eye he was to blame.

> His care for the commons his country now feels
> With tricks and with traps and with privy seals.[22]

[20] P. Croft, *A Collection of several speeches and treatises of the late Lord Treasurer Cecil*, Camden 4th ser., Miscellany xxix (1987), 262–3, 280, 290. Bodleian, Tanner MS 299, fo. 11v.

[21] Ibid. fo. 12. Northants Record Office, Isham (Lamport) MS 4304. BL, Harleian MS 1221, fo. 74. Harleian MS 6038, fo. 18.

[22] N.R.O., Isham (Lamport) MS 4304. Croft, *A Collection*, 261, 290–1. PRO, SP 14/67/43, 22 Nov. 1611. The collection of privy seals was at the forefront of attention early in 1612. Chamberlain noted that they were 'dispersed all over' and that payments were being made by 'the meaner sort' in January, and the Venetian ambassador

England was the most lightly taxed of the three great monarchies of western Europe, but the libels illustrated the immense resistance to any fiscal levies that were not related to the visible and extraordinary needs of the realm. At heart most Jacobean Englishmen still believed as their ancestors had done, that the king should live of his own, and they assumed that the ordinary revenues allowed him to do so. The integrity of the crown's own lands was thus a symbol of the assumed financial independence of the monarchy. Although in 1608 Salisbury steered through a major new entail, attempting to protect the remaining royal patrimony from the generosity of James I, he was depicted rather as a despoiler, since his efforts at rationalisation necessitated the selling off of some of the mills and outlying smaller properties. Nor was it appreciated that he had toiled incessantly to bring some order into the chaotic administration of the crown's valuable woodlands. One libel described him as

> A statesman that did impoverish the crown
> Sold mills and lands and forests cut down.[23]

Salisbury also increased the entry fines and leases for crown lands in line with inflation, bringing in a more realistic income after years of neglect. In view of the criticisms of both parliamentary taxation and loans on privy seals, it might be expected that efforts aimed at increasing regular revenue would be welcomed as a step towards lightening the burden on the subject. Inevitably, however, the policy was unpopular with those who had benefited from the slack management of previous lord treasurers. It was perhaps a tenant of crown property who concluded one libel with the line, 'He is gone to Hell, to raise the Devil's rent'.[24] The jest once again underlined the impossible financial situation of the monarchy, when every move to increase income offended one interest group or another. The libels mirrored the trenchant but often contradictory criticisms levelled by subjects against early Stuart attempts at financial reform. There was still a belief that the problem was only superficial. As an earlier epigram by Sir John Harington put it,

---

reported in February that 'every diligence will be used in calling up the loan without delay'. Chamberlain i. 330. *Calendar of State Papers Venetian*, 1610–13, pp. 291, 294.

[23] N.R.O., Isham (Lamport) MS 4304. For Salisbury's efforts on the woods, Croft, *A Collection*, 259–60.

[24] N.R.O., Isham (Lamport) MS 4304. For Salisbury's efforts to improve the rents of crown lands, L. M. Hill, 'Sir Julius Caesar's journal of Salisbury's first two months and twenty days as lord treasurer, 1608', *Bulletin of the Institute of Historical Research*, xlv (1972), 311–27.

> England men say of late is bankrupt grown
> The effect is manifest, the cause unknown.

Harington ended with an obsequious reference to the new king:

> Can any man tell how to help this disorder
> Faith one good Stewart would put it all in order.

Significantly his poem continued to circulate in James' reign with the variant ending, 'Faith one good lord would put all in order'.[25] The simplistic notion that all that was needed was a change of personnel made it impossible to attract enough support, in the House of Commons or in the country as a whole, for the fundamental restructuring necessary to avoid a bankrupt monarchy.

Although the libels emphasise Salisbury's financial exactions, there is virtually nothing about the great contract of 1610, his major attempt at a parliamentary solution to the financial crisis. It was glanced at obliquely—

> The king's misuser, The parliament's abuser
> Hath left his plotting . . . is now a-rotting[26]

but the absence of anything more specific indicates once again that popular comprehension of complex issues was limited. It was much easier to make allegations of corruption than to address the underlying problem with a constructive remedy. Moreover, Salisbury's efforts on behalf of the royal revenues had not prevented him from amassing a substantial fortune himself. Although senior posts were salaried, they brought in a pittance, not even enough to pay the secretaries and clerks employed to assist with the workload. The Lord Treasurer was entitled to a fee of a pound a day, together with robes worth £15.7s.8d.[27] Inevitably the bulk of his income came from other sources, particularly the profits of wardships and deals with the customs farmers. There were only routine comments about wardship in the libels, indicating perhaps that their authors were not of the social rank likely to suffer from the attentions of the court of Wards.[28] However, there were sharp attacks on Salisbury's own subsidy payments, which were absurdly low. The subsidy had long since ceased to provide an equitable tax system and during the reign of Elizabeth assessments became totally unrealistic. The landed classes as a whole

[25] *Letters and Epigrams of Sir John Harrington*, 301, 'How England may be reformed'. Bodleian, Malone MS 23, p. 121.
[26] Bodleian, Tanner MS 299, fo. 11v.
[27] Cambridge University Library, MS Ee v. 24, fo. 3.
[28] BL, MS Trumbull Misc. v, fo. 11. Bodleian, MS Malone 23, p. 19.

benefited from low rates, but the richest benefited the most.[29] The disparity between Salisbury's vigorous efforts on behalf of the crown, his rapidly increasing personal wealth, and his minimal tax contribution was noted and resented. The Hobbinal libel already quoted on the subsidy continues,

> For oblation to Pan his manner was thus
> Himself gave a trifle and offered up us.
> So with his wisdom this provident swain
> Kept himself on the mountain and us on the plain.[30]

Since subsidy payments fell disproportionately on the middling and poorer sort, the spectacle of a lord treasurer as wealthy as Salisbury pressing for parliamentary supply was bound to provoke accusations of tax evasion and hypocrisy. The lightness of English taxation compared to that raised abroad, which might have been a persuasive argument in the attempt to restructure the crown's finances, was forgotten in the bitterness engendered by the inequities of a system which allowed privy councillors and members of the House of Lords to avoid paying anything like their fair share.[31]

A similarly bitter note of social criticism surfaced in the libel which begins,

> Here lies thrown for the worms to eat
> Little bossy Robin that was so great
> Not Robin Goodfellow nor Robin Hood
> But Robin th'encloser of Hatfield Wood.[32]

James I's passion for hunting had led him to covet Theobalds, the great mansion surrounded by extensive parkland which Burghley had built and bequeathed to his younger son. By way of exchange Robert Cecil received the old royal property of Hatfield, which he at once began to transform. To create what is now the New Park, he took in

---

[29] 'The richer the taxpayer, the less his true wealth was captured by the subsidy assessments'. R. Schofield, 'Taxation and the political limits of the Tudor state', *Law and Government under the Tudors: essays presented to Sir Geoffrey Elton*, eds. C. Cross, D. Loades and J. J. Scarisbrick (Cambridge, 1988), 253. Salisbury was rated at 2s. 8d. in the pound on £300 in 1606, when his income was approaching £50,000 per year. *HMC Salisbury*, xix. 272. L. Stone, *Family and Fortune: studies in aristocratic finance in the 16th and 17th centuries* (Oxford, 1973), 59–60.

[30] See above p. 49.

[31] The contrast with other European states was realised at the time. On the question of a catholic bride for Prince Henry, the Venetian ambassador reported that 'it is very openly said that if a Tuscan woman comes here she will counsel taxation'. *CSPVen., 1610–1613*, p. 396.

[32] Bodleian, MS Ashmole 1463, fo. 13. MS Ashmole 38, p. 182. Bodleian, MS Rawl. poet 1155 p. 70. Bodleian, MS Tanner 299 fos. 12–12v. Bodleian, MS Eng. poet f 10 fo. 97. N.R.O. Isham (Lamport) MS 4304.

about half of Hatfield Wood (the old Great Park), in which there were extensive common rights. Much of the woodland was then used for fuel in the great brickmaking enterprise for the house itself. Common woodland was a vital local resource, not least in providing firewood for the poor, and Cecil had already proved himself a ruthless encloser at Brigstock, his property in Northamptonshire, where a large-scale riot broke out in 1603 protesting at the sale of wood.[33] The intrusion of Cecil power into the area around Hatfield was bound to cause problems, not least because the old royal estate had been indulgently managed for generations. There are indications that Salisbury was aware of the problem and made efforts to give the commoners a reasonable deal, but the enclosing of the wood was deeply resented. A striking symbolic protest was planned for the day of his funeral, when there was a plot to lay open the newly-impaled grounds. Word leaked out and the disturbances were prevented, although later the protesters succeeded in pulling down some fences. It was noted that there were 'very few or none of the gentlemen of the country' present at the funeral service, because they had not been asked. The libels' reminder of Robert Cecil's reputation as an encloser, and the thrusting of his grand new house and park into a settled rural community, points to the simmering tensions of agrarian society in the early seventeenth century. Similar conflicts of interest between landowners and the users of land led to the Midland rising of 1607, and in 1612 riots occurred in the forest of Dean against Salisbury's close friend the Earl of Pembroke.[34]

Other matters of current controversy were also touched on. As secretary of state Salisbury was responsible for foreign policy, and some libels link diplomacy with religion.

> With tricks and deceits of leger de main
> He played like a juggler with France England and Spain
> He feigned religion and zealous affection
> Yet favoured the papists and gave priests protection.[35]

The search for suitable marriages for the two eldest royal children, Prince Henry and Princess Elizabeth, dominated the years between

---

[33] I am grateful to Mr. Robin Harcourt Williams, librarian and archivist to the Marquess of Salisbury, for information from the Hatfield Manor Papers on the concentration of commoners' rights in Hatfield Wood; there were none elsewhere in the park. For the importance of woodland in the local economy of Brigstock, P.A.H. Pettit, *The Royal Forests of Northants*, (Northants. Record Society xxiii, 1968), 171–4.

[34] Chamberlain i. 353, 365. PRO, SP 14/70/49, 14 Aug. 1612.

[35] Bodleian, MS Tanner 299, fo. 11. Huntington Library California, MS HM 198, fo. 126. The juggler simile proves that this was one of the libels seen by Chamberlain in July 1612.

1610 and 1612. Although Salisbury dutifully carried out the king's instructions to seek an Infanta for Henry, he was never convinced that a Spanish match was a real possibility. The Franco-Spanish alliance of 1611, marrying the Infanta to Louis XIII, proved him right. However, the anti-popery of the verse reflected a widespread distaste for any foreign policy which was not explicitly protestant, while the greater tolerance shown to catholics both lay and clerical after 1603 did not commend itself to those Englishmen who wished to see the recusancy laws strictly enforced. Serving James I entailed walking along a tightrope of religious and foreign policy, and such a balancing act inevitably incurred the accusation of 'juggling' levelled at Salisbury both before and after his death. To many of his countrymen he seemed uncommitted to either protestantism or the protestant cause.[36] By February 1612 there were already signs of the tension over the inescapable linkage between religion at home and diplomacy abroad which was to increase so markedly after the outbreak of the Thirty Years War. In the spring and summer of 1612, as negotiations proceeded with Tuscany and Savoy for a bride for Henry, popular and ecclesiastical hostility mounted steadily. The prince himself was opposed to a catholic match, and a major confrontation with his father was only averted by Henry's premature death. The libels testify to the depth of public unease. The outpouring of popular hostility between 1621 and 1623 as the Spanish match was revived for Prince Charles was entirely predictable after the experience of 1612.[37]

It will be apparent that the 1612 libels contained many criticisms of Robert Cecil's policies. But as Chamberlain's sense of shock testified, they went beyond political criticism. The themes which emerged most insistently and savagely were those of Salisbury's crooked back and his sexual appetites. It would be easy to dismiss these more scandalous aspects as merely the Jacobean equivalent of the gutter press, but the remorseless images of deformity and moral corruption have an importance beyond mere titillation. There was no doubt about the hunched back, for even his admirers described Robert Cecil as 'a little, crooked person'.[38] The libels were relentless.

---

[36] cf. 'Religion's scoffer' in Bodleian, MS Tanner 299, fo. 11v. For further discussion, P. Croft, 'The Religion of Robert Cecil', forthcoming in *Historical Journal*.

[37] *CSPVen., 1610–13*, pp. 270, 275, 278, 280–1, 375. PRO SP 14/71/12. The negotiations are outlined by Roy Strong, 'England and Italy: the marriage of Henry Prince of Wales', *For Veronica Wedgwood These*, eds. R. Ollard and P. Tudor-Craig (1986), 59–87.

[38] Sir Robert Naunton, *Fragmenta Regalia: or, observations on the late queen Elizabeth, her times and favourites* (1824), 137. Naunton was present at Salisbury's deathbed.

> Here lies Robert Cicil, Compos'd of back and pisle

and again

> Here lies great Salisbury though little of stature,
> A monster of mischief, ambitious of nature.[39]

Comparisons were made.

> At Hatfield near Hertford there is a coffin,
> A heart-griping harpy, of shape like a dolphin[40]

always depicted heraldically as curved. Perhaps most blunt,

> The Devil now hath fetched the ape,
> Of crooked manners, crooked shape.[41]

Damning historical parallels were drawn.

> Here lieth Robin Crooktback, unjustly reckoned
> A Richard III; he was Judas the second——
> Richard or Robin, which is the worse?
> A crooktback great in state is England's curse.[42]

Chamberlain enclosed a similar effort for Carleton to see.

> While two Great Rs both crouchback stood at the helm,
> The one spilt the blood royal, the other the realm.

Disapprovingly he endorsed it, 'Richard Duke of Gloucester, Robert earl of Salisbury, a silie vurs'. Another libel more charitably commented

> Though Crookback the vulgar did term him in sight
> There were more beside him that were not upright.[43]

These 'silly verses' made plain the public identification of Robert Cecil with Richard of Gloucester, and there is a remarkable chronological relationship between Cecil's career and the popularity of the histories of King Richard III. The depiction of Richard as 'little of stature, ill-featured of limbs, crook-backed' originated with the publication of Sir Thomas More's *Workes* in 1557, but the theme was not taken up in the popular theatre until much later. Shakespeare's play was written and first performed around 1591, the year that Cecil was

---

[39] BL, Add. MS 25348, fo. 9v. N.R.O., Isham (Lamport) MS 4304. Variants in Bodleian, Malone 23, p. 65, and Huntington, MS HM 198, f. 125v.
[40] Bodleian, MS Tanner 299, fo. 11, Bodleian, MS Firth d 7, fo. 156. Huntington, MS HM 198, fo. 126. BL, MS Egerton 2230, fo. 34.
[41] Bodleian MS Tanner 299, fo. 11.
[42] Ibid fo. 13. Bodleian, MS Malone 23, p. 10, MS Malone 26, pp. 65–6.
[43] Chamberlain i. 356. PRO, SP 14/69/67 (1).

sworn a privy councillor, and about the same time an anonymous drama, *The true tragedy of Richard III* also appeared. An unsatisfactory quarto of Shakespeare's play was published in 1597, just after Cecil had become principal secretary of state, followed by another reprint in 1598. In June 1602, a year after the Essex revolt confirmed Cecil's pre-eminence on the privy council, Ben Jonson was commissioned to write a tragedy, *Richard Crookback*. It was assumed that the theme would be popular since he was paid the unusually large advance of £10. In the same year, Shakespeare's play was reprinted and it appeared again in 1605. In the year of Salisbury's death there appeared *The tragedy of King Richard III by William Shakespeare newly augmented*, in quarto. Of all Shakespeare's plays, only *Henry IV part I* can show a longer list of early reprints; but after 1612 there was no further printing for ten years, in marked contrast to the previous run of publication.[44] The enduring fascination of the saga of Richard III may seem to need little explanation, and the popularity of chronicle plays drawn from English history was at its peak between 1590 and 1610. Nevertheless, audiences in those years were also exceptionally alert to contemporary political applications, and it seems very likely that the drama of a ruthless hunchback, a younger son with vaulting ambition, gained extra appeal from its topicality.[45] Whatever the intention of the dramatists, the frequent depictions of Richard III on stage must have reinforced the public image of Cecil as a pitiless, cunning monster. John Day, whose comedy *The Isle of Gulls* was a London sensation in the winter of 1606, also underlined the hunchback motif. Day originally depicted a hunt-loving monarch, 'King Basilius', but the too-obvious pun on the king's own *Basilicon Doron* was toned down by the nervous printer, and the character emerges as Duke Basilius. He is dominated by his adviser, the upstart dwarf Dametas, who monopolises patronage and does not permit suitors to approach the duke without bribing him first. Answering a question about the play, 'Is there any great man's life charactered in it?', the spokesman Prologue responds, 'None I protest sir; only in the shape of Dametas he expresses to the life the monstrous and deformed shape of vice'. Dametas can be seen as a composite character, incorporating all the vices found at court, but the topical reference was unmistakable.[46] The libels' emphasis on Salisbury's short stature and hunched back would appeal to a public already well accustomed to the charac-

[44] *The Riverside Shakespeare*, eds. G. Blakemore et al., (Boston, 1974), 708–9. David Riggs, *Ben Jonson: a life* (1989) 90–1.

[45] Andrew Gurr, *Playgoing in Shakespeare's London* (Cambridge, 1987), 141–7. David Bevington, *Tudor Drama and Politics* (Cambridge, Mass., 1968), 233.

[46] *The Works of John Day*, ed. A. H. Bullen (2 vols., 1881), i. 5 (each play separately paginated). A. H. Tricomi, *Anticourt Drama in England 1603–42* (Charlottesville, Virginia, 1989), 34–41.

terisation. Another literary motif is the comparison between Salisbury and a fox, an animal of legendary cunning. 'Sure I am they have earthed the fox' and variants formed the last line of several libels. Ben Jonson's *Volpone: or, the Fox* was written and performed in the winter of 1606 just after the Gunpowder plot. Literary scholars have frequently linked it with Salisbury, since at least two characters—Volpone himself and the dwarf Nano—incorporate possible references. In 1606 Salisbury was still giving Jonson occasional commissions, so the likelihood that the dramatist would deliberately offend his patron seems remote. However, Jonson's intentions and the public's reading of *Volpone* may well have varied. The frequent use of fox imagery in the posthumous libels strengthens the view that the play was seen by the theatre-going populace as referring, however obliquely, to Salisbury.[47]

The images and literary resonances in the libels are of historical interest since the seventeenth century had little hesitation in equating physical imperfection with both moral and political decay. In December 1612, Francis Bacon produced his essay 'On Deformity', one of the new ones added by him to the collection originally published in 1597. It was at once remarked that 'the world takes notice that he paints his late little cousin to the life'. To Bacon, deformity was not an outward sign but an inward cause, of a character devoid of natural affection, 'extreme bold', and industrious 'to watch and observe the weakness of others, that they may have somewhat to repay'. Furthermore, deformity could be used in rising to great place, for it 'quencheth jealousy ... it layeth their competitors and emulators asleep'. As in ancient times kings put their trust in eunuchs, so now in the deformed; and since they 'seek to free themselves from scorn, which must be either by virtue or malice ... therefore let it not be marvelled if sometimes they prove excellent persons'. The suggestion that Salisbury had risen, not through talent or desert but through exploiting others' initial refusal to take him seriously, was an insidious way of belittling his achievement, while the comparison with eunuchs underlined the theme of physical and political inadequacy. The ambiguous and faint praise at the end of the essay allowed Bacon to retain his apparent superiority. From his letters to James I, however, it is clear that he had hated his cousin, while being consumed with envy at his successs and embittered by what he saw as Salisbury's

---

[47] Bodleian, MS Tanner 299, fo. 11. Bodleian, MS Ashmole 38, p. 182. Ashmole 1463, p. 13. N.R.O., Isham (Lamport) MS 4304. Tricomi, 41. For Jonson's relations with Salisbury, Richard Dutton, *Ben Jonson* (Cambridge, 1983), 144–53. Rowlands' epitaph on Salisbury, 'In Vulponem' begins, 'The Fox is earthed now in ground' and contains the lines, 'Of whose successe-full thriving wit, Bookes have been made, and playes been writ'. *Complete Works of Samuel Rowlands*, ed. E. W. Gosse (3 vols., Glasgow, 1880), iii. 13.

withholding of patronage. The essay must have been prepared for publication just as the libels were circulating. By leading the attack on Salisbury, they emboldened Bacon to vent his bile after years of suppression.[48]

Public opinion in the early seventeenth century was not squeamish in discussing physical disability, and the same brutal frankness is apparent in the libels' treatment of sex. They unhesitatingly attributed Salisbury's death to venereal disease.

> Oh ladies ladies howl and cry, For you have lost your Salisbury
> He that of late was your protection, He is now dead by your
>   infection
> Come with your tears bedew his locks, Death killed him not
> It was the pox.[49]

Robert Cecil never re-married after the death of his wife in January 1597, but two ladies were repeatedly associated with him thereafter. One was Catherine Countess of Suffolk, wife of his longstanding friend Thomas Howard the Lord Chamberlain. Lady Suffolk served Salisbury as constant go-between with successive Spanish ambassadors, who all paid tribute to both her influence and her insatiable rapacity. Their association was common knowledge—James I made jokes about it—and Salisbury bequeathed her his best diamond ring, a stupendous gift worth around a thousand pounds. Yet he also went out of his way to pay warm tribute to Lord Suffolk, describing him as his oldest and dearest friend. The family link was cemented when the Suffolks' daughter Catherine was married in 1608 to Salisbury's heir.[50] Can the association between Salisbury and the Earl and Countess of Suffolk have been an amicable *menage à trois*? Or was Lady Suffolk not so much Robert Cecil's lover as his political confidante, one effective professional operator collaborating with another? Lady Walsingham, mistress of the robes to Anne of Denmark, kept a lower profile, but it was noticed that the marriage of Lord Cranborne to Catherine Howard took place at her court lodgings, and that Lady Suffolk was not present. In Salisbury's will Lady Walsingham was left a modest annuity and £500 made up of debt remission and repayments.[51] Whatever the truth about this curious network of relationships, the libels proffered the worst interpretations, relishing

---

[48] *Francis Bacon: The Essays*, ed. John Pitcher (1985), 191–2. *The Letters and the Life of Francis Bacon*, ed. J. Spedding (7 vols., 1857–74), iv. 313, 371.

[49] Bodleian, MS Tanner 299, fo. 11v.

[50] *Letters of King James VI and I*, ed. G.P.V. Akrigg (1984), 234. A.J. Loomie, 'Sir Robert Cecil and the Spanish Embassy', *Bull. Inst. Hist. Res.*, xlii (1969) 30–57. There are numerous versions of the will. I have used that from Hatfield House, MSS Box V/182.

[51] *HMC Salisbury*, xx. 149. Chamberlain i. 273. Hatfield MSS Box V/182.

the themes of high-class cuckoldry, adultery, and their fatal consequences.

> Twixt Suffolk and Walsingham oft he did journey
> To tilt at the one place, at th'other to tourney
> In which hot encounter he got such a blow
> That he could not be cured by Atkins or Poe.

Another ends with the same allegation.

> Let Suffolk now and Walsingham
> Leave their adulterous lives for shame
> Or else their ladyships must know
> There is no help in Dr. Poe
> For though the man be very cunning
> He cannot stay the pox from running.[52]

There are other, cruder versions. Their significance lies in what they reveal about attitudes to leading court figures. Recently, James I has benefited from much positive revaluation, but the image of his court has been less studied, with the exception of the Bedchamber. Where the question of court corruption has been raised, it is usually associated with the Overbury scandal of 1614–15 and the homosexual relationship between the king and Buckingham in later life. However, there is ample evidence for a growing distaste for the court much earlier, in the years immediately before and after 1603. Thomas Bastard's scathing epigram of 1598 on monopolies held by court figures—'courtier leather, courtier pinne, and sope, And courtier vineegar, and starche and carde'—sounded a note heard increasingly in subsequent years.[53] Instead of the misleading concept of 'court and country', literary scholars have utilised the more perceptive term 'anti-court', for much of the sharpest criticism was voiced not in the country but in London, and often by individuals with court connections. The theatre was full of comment on upper-class vice, as in plays such as Marston and Barksted's 'The Insatiate Countess' of 1610.[54] The literary evidence underlines the theme of sexual depravity as a metaphor for political corruption, seen so clearly in the libels on Robert Cecil. By 1612 public opinion was savagely attacking the king's leading minister on matters of private morality, while the two women closely associated with him, defamed as 'bawds', 'drabs' and 'lecherous wretches', were

---

[52] Bodleian, MS Tanner 299, fos. 11–12.

[53] Neil Cuddy, 'The revival of the entourage: the Bedchamber of James I', David Starkey et al., *The English Court* (1987), 173–225. *The Poems English and Latin of the Rev. Thomas Bastard M.A.*, ed. A. B. Grosart (1880), 23.

[54] Tricomi, 101. By 1631 eight English countesses were thought to merit the description.

both prominent at court. The impact must have been considerable. After three generations of protestant evangelism, many English people were increasingly godly in their moral outlook. Cecil was seen in the context of a court abhorred by all Christian people.

> Oppression, lechery, blood and pride, He lived in
> And like Herod—Died.

Conduct books for women extolling such virtues as chastity, submission and silence were achieving remarkable popularity; the limits of acceptable social behaviour for women were narrowing.[55] The endlessly repeated allegation that Salisbury died of the pox, a shameful end for a great statesman but somehow even worse when caught from women of the highest social status, illustrates that rising alienation from court life and values which can be discerned from the 1590s. It is only necessary to contrast Cecil's reputation in sexual matters with that of his straitlaced father to see how great was the change between Burghley's death in 1598 and Salisbury's in 1612.[56] Popular attitudes to leading ministers and courtiers, and ultimately by association to the king and queen themselves, were being transformed. The denigration of the court was an important aspect of the increasing failure of majesty to awe the political nation, in itself far more of a problem for the Stuart dynasty than it had ever been for the Tudors.[57]

Ironically, it is clear from the papers of his chief doctor that whatever the nature of his relationships with Lady Suffolk and Lady Walsingham, Robert Cecil did not die of the pox. Sir Theodore Mayerne was emphatic; 'nihil umquam siphillicum', he wrote. By the summer of 1611, when Salisbury consulted Mayerne, he was already seriously ill, and the evidence indicates that he was suffering from an advanced state of scurvy, together with tumours, almost certainly cancerous, in the stomach, liver and neck.[58] His physical symptoms,

[55] Bodleian, MS Tanner 299, fos. 11–12. N.R.O., Isham (Lamport) MS 4304. Alison Wall, 'Elizabethan Precept and Feminine Practice: the Thynne family of Longleat', *History*, 75, no. 243 (1990), 24–7. The Lake scandal of 1619 brought forth similar libels describing Lady Lake as 'A bitch of Court, a common stinking snake'. Bodleian, Malone MS 23, p. 5.

[56] Burghley's widely-circulated 'Advice to a son' begins, 'Son Robert, the virtuous inclination of thy matchless mother...'. *Advice to A Son: Precepts of Lord Burghley, Sir Walter Raleigh and Francis Osborne*, ed. L. B. Wright (Folger Shakespeare Library, Washington D.C., 1962), 9–13.

[57] For a discussion of other aspects of 'the problem of diminished majesty' Conrad Russell, *The Causes of the English Civil War* (Oxford, 1990), 23.

[58] Mayerne's notes of the consultation of 28 July 1611 are in his *Ephemerides* (BL, MSS Sloan 2058–76), from which an abbreviated version was printed by Sir Henry Ellis, *Original Letters Illustrative of British History* (11 vols., 1824–46), 2nd ser., iii. 246. There is a full account of Salisbury's condition, based on Mayerne's notes, together

widely known and publicly discussed, were used in the libels as metaphors of the corruption of power.

> And let all that abuse the king, Themselves to greatness so to bring
> Be forced to travel to the Bath, To purge themselves of filthy froth.[59]

The symptoms of scurvy are repellant, especially the ulcerous and weeping sores which produce a bloody fungus, the 'filthy froth', and the unbearably foetid breath. The details of Robert Cecil's death do not make for easy reading, but the libels were pitiless. Several referred to the stench of scurvy.

> This Taper, fed and nursed with court oil,
> Made great and mighty by rapine and spoil—
> Unable now to spread more light about
> Like a lamp dying, Stank and went out.[60]

The 'Fox' libels usually ended with the handy rhyme, that he 'stank while he lived and died of the pox'. In the discussion of his fatal sickness, there was also gleeful satire on eminent medical men, in whose activities there was intense public interest but little confidence. Incompetent and fraudulent doctors were a familiar joke. Few could afford the fees of court physicians, so the ineffectiveness, and worse, of the ministrations of Dr Poe and Dr Atkins, who accompanied Salisbury to Bath, occasioned some satisfaction.

> To the good of the state he was a mainstay
> Till Poe with his syringe did squirt him away.[61]

Mayerne, doctor to the royal family, was widely credited with having hastened the end of both Robert Cecil and, later, Prince Henry. The failure of 'the rare Frenchman' who 'could do him [Salisbury] no good with his baths or his plaster' was enthusiastically ridiculed. That Salisbury was suffering from scurvy was common knowledge, and Chamberlain thought it 'of easie and ordinarie cure yf yt be not too far overpast'. The confidence was misplaced; the diagnosis of scurvy, which Mayerne made with impressive accuracy, was one thing, but effective treatment was another. The relationship between scurvy and diet was not fully appreciated until 1753, and little that was done for Robert Cecil by his doctors was of much use. Most of the treatments

---

with the regimen proposed for his cure, in a document made by or for Dr. Henry Atkins, another of his medical men. Hertfordshire Record Office, MS 65440.

[59] Bodleian, MS Tanner 299, fo. 2.

[60] Ibid f. 11. Alvin Kernan, *The Cankered Muse* (New Haven, 1959), 247–9, notes that disgust at sex and emphasis on the corruptions of the flesh became an increasingly common theme in the literary satire of the early 17th century.

[61] Clark, 167–8. Huntington, MS HM 198, fo. 125v. Bodleian, MS Malone 23, p. 65, reads 'sirrop' for 'syringe'.

were positively harmful.[62] The verses revealed a widespread scepticism about contemporary professional medicine which was only too justified.

The libels preserved in the surviving manuscripts are anonymous. Can anything be said about their authorship? The much-copied 'Here lies our Hobbinal' quoted earlier was asserted by John Aubrey to be the work of Ralegh, since 'old Sir Thomas Malett, one of the judges of the king's Bench, who knew Sir Walter Ralegh ... did remember these passages'. Despite this, the editor of Ralegh's verse excluded it, as merely 'a wretched piece of scurrility'. It scarcely measures up to the poet's grander efforts, but it is by far the most consciously literary of the libels, with its deliberately Spenserian references to Hobbinal, classical images of the nymph Phyllis, the shepherd's hornpipe, and oblations to Pan. In 1612 Ralegh had been in the Tower for nine years, his alliance with Cecil long since ended. He had already written verses on court corruption, and he might well have penned a bitter epitaph in the style of his old friend Edmund Spenser. It seems cavalier to ignore the very specific attribution from old Sir Thomas Malett.[63] Apart from Ralegh, the author of only one other libel is named, 'one Hessels', a servant of the Earl of Arundel and a notorious gamester, who in 1613 'blazed abroad' a poem on Salisbury. Hessels' seven verses began rousingly—'Advance advance my evil-disposed muse'— but rapidly deteriorated into limping abuse. Although his poem caused some stir at the time, the fact that it survived in only one copy indicates that, unlike Ralegh's epigram, it lacked market appeal.[64]

Recent studies have stressed the importance of faction in the politics of the early seventeenth century, and the libels written around the time of Essex's downfall undoubtedly depicted Cecil as deeply involved in factional struggle. It might be assumed that the striving for office that took place after May 1612 would reveal something about the origins of the outburst of denigration. Were these libellous attacks orchestrated by Salisbury's political enemies? There is no evidence that this was so, and nothing links the libels with any court figure apart from Ralegh. Moreover, their lively and often scurrilous language, their general lack of much literary pretension, and the absence of elaborate classical references all suggest that they should be considered as spon-

---

[62] Bodleian, MS Tanner 299, fo. 11. Chamberlain i. 338. K. J. Carpenter, *The History of Scurvy and Vitamin C* (Cambridge, 1986), 1–17. Although 'fruits in their seasons' were allowed, Salisbury underwent purges and glisters, together with punctures to draw off the waters of the accompanying dropsy. *HMC Downshire*, iii. 266.

[63] Bodleian, MS Rawl. poet 26, fo. 78. Bodleian, MS Eng. poet e 14, fo. 79. *The Poems of Sir Walter Ralegh*, ed. A. M. C. Latham (1929), 196.

[64] BL, Trumbull MS Misc. v, fo. 11. *HMC Downshire*, iv. 20.

taneous expressions of popular culture. Mostly metropolitan, the libels orginated in the tavern world of pamphlets, epigrams and satire rather than among factious courtiers. However, once they appeared, the libels were received with great pleasure by the Earl of Northampton, who passed them on with approbation to his ally Viscount Rochester, the king's favourite. Northampton's letters to Carr contain many acid references to 'the little lord' and such was his loathing that at one one point he casually referred to Cecil as 'itself'.[65] Although it has been convincingly demonstrated that Northampton collaborated with Salisbury on political issues, the letters written after the latter's death bear out Bacon's private assessment that the two men were deeply antagonistic. Like Bacon himself, Northampton hated Salisbury but kept his animosity reined in during the Lord Treasurer's lifetime.[66] His pleasure at the circulation of the libels reveals his secret hatred, but nothing points to Northampton as the patron of their authors. The presence of the obscure libeller Hessels among Arundel's retinue might suggest a Howard network, but at least one libel assumed that another Howard, the Earl of Suffolk, would form a continuing political alliance with the second Earl of Salisbury. 'Old Sarum now is dead; young Salisbury lives' it begins, before going on to insinuate that Suffolk had overlooked his wife's behaviour in order to profit politically from the connection with Salisbury.[67] It is too simple to see the Howards as a monolith in Jacobean politics. In the public eye, Suffolk was an ally of the Earl of Salisbury, Northampton was not, and there is no suggestion of an orchestrated Howard campaign. It is also too simple to ascribe all evidence of political opinion to court faction. By the early seventeenth century, public interest in current affairs was easily sufficient to generate a multitude of spontaneous political libels.[68] There is no evidence that they were artificially concocted as weapons in a court struggle.

Such spontaneity is only partly present, however, in the literature defending Robert Cecil, for the majority of the tributes can be linked to the orchestrated campaign by his family and friends to rebut criticism. The campaign was in itself a remarkable tribute to the importance attached to a good reputation in the public eye. The spontaneous items included a ballad, price 6d., entered with striking

[65] PRO, S.P. 14/71/16. Northampton's usual description of Salisbury as 'the little lord' became 'the littel one itself' and in an extraordinary passage, writing to James I, he insinuated that Salisbury was in hell with Queen Elizabeth, 'whear he kneels befor his olde mistress by an extreeme whotte fieres side'. PRO, SP 14/71/3.

[66] Spedding, iv. 52–3. Linda Levy Peck, *Northampton* (1982).

[67] N.R.O., Isham (Lamport) MS 4296.

[68] It is noteworthy that later in 1612 there was a campaign of defamation against Northampton, who prosecuted his denigrators in Star Chamber. Chamberlain i. 396.

speed in the Stationers Register on 27 May, only three days after Salisbury's death and entitled 'Brittayne's generall teares shedd for ye greate losse it hadd by the death of the righte noble and worthy Robert Earle of Salisbury'.[69] This must have been around the time of the sermons preached in his defence by his chaplains, which Chamberlain noted on 2 July, but it is clear from another tribute that these efforts did not stem the tide of libels.

> Oh that such wisdom that could steer a State
> Should now be valued at so cheap a rate...
> Fate of our age! See how this dead man lies
> Bitten and stung by Court and City flies...
> At this great Pillar's fall when all thus laugh
> Dreads not the whole world the next epitaph?[70]

The 'flies' stung the Cecil circle into more vigorous action, for on 23 July the Stationers Register listed 'a booke called "A Remembrance of the Honours due to the lyfe and death of Robert Earl of Salisbury treasurer of England" '. This was by the Londoner Richard Johnson, who had already scored a number of literary successes including a polished lament on the death of Elizabeth. Proclaiming his 'intyre affection long borne to the honoured house of the Cecills', Johnson gave an account of Salisbury's distinguished career, 'because I see the Muses lippes lockt up', and attacked the 'ignoble spirits' whose 'scandalous speeches' were defaming him. They were 'no other but the poysonous plots and devises of rebellious papists', a shrewd appeal to English prejudice. Johnson's pamphlet, also priced at 6d, went into two editions, another measure of public interest.[71] Around the same time there appeared *The Character of Robert Earl of Salisbury Lord high treasurer of England*, the work of the dramatist Cyrill Tourneur, which circulated in manuscript, possibly to appeal to a more refined audience. Tourneur had served in the low countries under Sir Edward Cecil, a leading English captain, to whom he was distantly related; Sir Edward was married to the Lady Theodosia Cecil to whom the *Character* was dedicated. It began with a tribute to Burghley, another sign of its origins within the Cecil circle, and contained a sharp rebuke to those who jeered at Salisbury's deformity. 'Had his body been an answerable agent to his spirit, he might have made as great a Captain as he was a counsellor'. The tract's most pungent comment was that while 'every effect of graciousness' was attributed to the king, fiscal

---

[69] It could be one of those items entered, but never printed. G. B. Harrison, 'Books and Readers 1591–94', *The Library* 4th ser., viii (1927), 273–6.

[70] Chamberlain i. 365. Bodleian MS Eng. poet e 14, fos. 95v. rev.–96v. rev.

[71] For a fuller discussion of Johnson's work, Croft, *A Collection*, 250.

severity was blamed on Salisbury alone. From the number of surviving copies Tourneur's work enjoyed considerable success.[72] The efforts of Johnson and Tourneur were obviously done to commission, with the Cecil family hiring writers already well known in the literary world. The picture they painted was of a devoted counsellor, trained up by his great father, and highly esteemed by both the monarchs he had served. To counter the allegations of debauchery, they stressed his philanthropy and his edifyingly Christian deathbed; allegations of corruption were ascribed to mere envy. The most distinguished of the defenders of Salisbury, however, was not a hired litterateur but Sir Walter Cope, chamberlain of the Exchequer and servant of the Cecils for a total of thirty-eight years. Cope's *Apology*, another manuscript production, was boldly addressed to the King himself, and depicted the Lord Treasurer's tireless efforts to bring some order into the chaos inherited from Dorset in 1608. 'He lost the love of your people only for your sake and for your service', wrote Cope, pulling no punches. The *Apology* was widely read and carefully noted, though according to Northampton, it was at once rebutted by another hostile epigram.[73] The closeness of the Cecil circle in death as in life attracted satirical comment. One libel concludes

> Thus here lies his lordship interred as you see
> And no doubt but his soul is where it should be
> If pray for the dead you cannot with hope,
> Yet say Lord Have Mercy on Beeston and Cope.[74]

James did not respond to Cope's plea to come to the defence of the late Lord Treasurer, and he made some sharp criticisms of Salisbury before the meeting of the next parliament. However, the King went out of his way in November 1612 to show favour to Cope, staying with him at his house in Kensington. Although the visit was not a social success, Cope was promoted to the mastership of the Wards.[75]

---

[72] Ibid. 250–1. Tourneur's characterisation was erroneously attributed to Wotton by Logan Pearsall Smith, who printed it in *The Life and Letters of Sir Henry Wotton* (2 vols., 1907), ii. 487–9.

[73] For the *Apology* and the strong probability that Cope was responsible for other measures to defend Salisbury's reputation, Croft, *A Collection* 251–4. Sir Julius Caesar's heavily underlined copy, endorsed '1 July 1612', is BL, Lansdowne MS 151, fos. 112–23v. The mathematician and geographer Thomas Harriot, friend of Ralegh and Northumberland, copied out passages of the *Apology*. BL. Add. MS 6789, fo. 527. PRO, SP 14/70/21.

[74] Bodleian, MS Malone 23, p. 65. Huntington, MS HM 198, fo. 125v. Sir Hugh Beeston, another of the inner circle, was one of the six bannerolls at Salisbury's funeral. *HMC Salisbury*, xxi. 374.

[75] Chamberlain i. 391, 393. The King 'was quicklie wearie of Kensington because he saide the wind blew thorough the walles that he could not lie warme in his bed'.

James was not a vindictive man and one of the qualities he admired, and prided himself on, was personal loyalty. Cope's outspoken defence of his late master had not permanently alienated the king. His generous attitude may also have been influenced by the fact that one of his leading courtiers was another defender of Salisbury. In 1611, as Salisbury's ill-health worsened, William Earl of Pembroke acted as his link-man with the king, which can only mean that the Lord Treasurer trusted him implicitly. Pembroke and his brother Philip Earl of Montgomery were among the inner circle of friends who watched over Salisbury one night in February 1612 when his doctors feared he was near death, and in the last days of his life, at Bath, Salisbury expressed a wish never to be parted from Pembroke. The Earl was elevated to the privy council just as Salisbury died.[76] Pembroke came from a great literary family and was an active poet before he was burdened by court office. The epitaph he composed cannot rank as one of his best efforts, but it firmly defended Salisbury against charges of corruption and recognised that by his reform of the regulations of the court of Wards in January 1611, he had sharply restricted his own profits as Master.

> You that read in passing by, Robert Earl of Salisbury
> Know that in so short a story Thou canst never find such glory.
> All state secrets on him laid, He the staff of Treasure swayd
> Gave his Master all the gain, Of the Wards reserv'd the pain.
> Govern'd all with so clean hands, As most Malice silent stands
> And who snarl will be soon, Found dogs barking at the moon.
> This tomb hath his bones possess't
> Heaven and friends hold dear the rest.[77]

Linked with Pembroke's effort was one by a poet of far greater stature, Samuel Daniel, who had begun his career as tutor at Wilton. 'Well-languag'd Daniel' also regarded Salisbury as a patron, for in spring 1612 he had completed the first draft of *The First Part of the History of England*, originally dedicated to Salisbury. On the latter's death, with the work already in press, Daniel rapidly transferred the dedication to Robert Carr.[78] This awareness of the realities of patronage did

[76] Northampton noted the closeness of Salisbury and Pembroke. PRO, SP 14/69/56, SP 14/70/21. Chamberlain i. 324, 336, 351.

[77] The holograph poem, presumably presented by Pembroke to the second Earl of Salisbury, is Hatfield MS 140/116. Robert Kreuger, *The Poems of William Herbert third earl of Pembroke*, (unpublished Oxford B. Litt. thesis, 1961), 72. There is a copy in N.R.O. Isham (Lamport) MS 4296, and other versions are discussed by J. Pitcher, *Samuel Daniel: the Brotherton Manuscript* (Leeds texts and monographs, new ser., 7, 1981), 173–5.

[78] R. B. Gottfried, 'The Authorship of "A Breviary of the History of England"', *Studies in Philology*, 53 (1956), 172–90, proves that Daniel, not Ralegh, was the author. The

not stop Daniel from composing an epigram to accompany that by Pembroke, and his poem is the finest of the literary tributes.

If greatness wisdom policy of state
Or place or riches could preserve from Fate
Thou hadst not lost the company of men
Who wert both England's purse and England's pen.

Great little lord! who only didst inherit
Thy father's goodness honours and his spirit
But death that equals sceptres with the spade
He with thy father's bones to sleep hath laid.[79]

These tributes to Salisbury all derived from his close circle of family, friends and allies. Unlike the libels, none was anonymous and it is politically significant that Pembroke and his client Samuel Daniel were prepared to be identified publicly with the Cecil family. Richard Johnson in his tract had deplored the silence of the University of Cambridge, for outpourings of verse to great men were something of a convention in both universities. Perhaps in response, Benjamin Hinton of Trinity College produced six verses of elegy on 'poor England's silver-headed senator'.[80] Another tribute, the most curious, was a lengthy poem entitled *Les larmes funebres francoises*, by a Poitevin gentleman, the Sieur de la Faye. It is an odd mixture of English and French, with a warning at the beginning about the complexities of French pronunciation, and on the title page a verse from Revelation, 'Blessed are the dead which die in the Lord ... for they rest from their own labours and their works follow them'. The Sieur de la Faye was a protestant, since he described the English as enjoying the fruits of the Gospel, and the poem was dedicated to the second Earl of Salisbury. Perhaps they had met in France on his earlier grand tour. Although the twenty verses are laboured, *Larmes funebres* emphasised that Salisbury had a European reputation. Unfortunately although it is printed, there is no indication as to where, or how widely it circulated.[81] All in all, the defences of Robert Cecil were impressive in their range and commitment, and though they lacked the raciness of the libels, they found a receptive audience. The libellers did not have it all their own way.

---

earlier draft, seeking 'your furtherance (righte Noble Earle of Salsbury)' is BL, MS Cotton Titus iii. 33.

[79] Pitcher, 175–6. There are two further verses.

[80] *Ballads from Manuscripts*, ed. W. R. Morfill (2 vols., The Ballad Society, 1873), ii. 297–8.

[81] STC 4895.7. The only copy, bound in with other works, is at Hatfield House and I am grateful to Mr. Robin Harcourt Williams for producing it for me.

The impact of the controversy over Salisbury can be seen some months later. *Abuses Stript and Whipt*, by the poet George Wither, a professional writer who lived by his pen and aimed at an extensive audience, was entered in the Stationers' Register on 16 January 1613. His comments reflected the uncertainty left in the public mind after the campaign of libels and the counter-attack.

> For that great mighty Peere that dyed lately
> Ere-while was mighty, powerful and stately:...
> But now (alas) hee's gone; and all his Fame
> You see not able to preserve his name
> From foule Reproach...
> In spight of all his greatnesse, 'tis well knowne
> That store of Rimes and Libels now are sowne
> In his disgrace. But I hear divers say
> That they are slanders. (Then the more knaves they
> That were the Authors) but if so it be
> He were from those vile imputations free;
> If that his Vertue's paid with such a curse,
> What shall they looke for, that are tenne-times worse?

Wither tactlessly touched on a number of sensitive topics, not least the description of kings 'most bountifull to fooles', but it is significant that when he was imprisoned for his work, he blamed Northampton. The latter presumably read the last two lines as a prophecy of his own posthumous prospects. It is also notable that when Wither was in trouble again in 1621, he thanked Pembroke for interceding for him.[82]

The extent of popular political consciousness in the late sixteenth and early seventeenth centuries has been much debated in recent years. The emergence of an active public opinion formed by the circulation of literary, dramatic, religious and parliamentary material can be traced back to the controversies involving Leicester and Burghley in the 1580s. The intensive lobbying engaged in by organised puritanism, and the widespread circulation of the Marprelate tracts, accelerated the process. Elsewhere in Europe, in the low countries and in Spain, the same decade saw a very similar emergence of commentary on politics and political theory.[83] In 1612, the circulation of both the

---

[82] *Abuses Stript and Wipt* was very popular, with at least five editions in 1613. For the text quoted here, George Wither, *Juvenilia* (3 vols., printed for the Spenser Society, 1871), i. 165–7. Joan Grundy, *The Spenserian Poets* (1969), 14–5.

[83] P. Collinson, 'Puritans, men of business and Elizabethan parliaments', *Parliamentary History* 7, pt. 2, (1988) p. 211 n. 97. For the outpouring of pamphlets in the low countries between 1566 and 1588, E. H. Kossman and A. F. Mellink, *Texts Concerning the Revolt of the Netherlands* (Cambridge 1974) and for the remarkable manuscript circulation in

attacks on Cecil and the defences of him illustrates the appeal of material dealing with current affairs. Originating mostly in London, where there was already an audience avid for news and quick to pick up topical references at the theatre and in printed satire, political epigrams and tracts were quickly carried to readers in the localities, in both manuscript and print.[84] More specifically, the libels revealed the divide between those in government, aware of the pressing need for a refoundation of crown finance, and a public which saw only individual corruption and extortion. Such incomprehension makes it easier to understand the reluctance of the House of Commons to respond to schemes such as the great contract. Distrust on matters of religion and foreign policy also deepened the divide. The emphasis on Robert Cecil's hunched back evoked vivid images of political crookedness, together with historical echoes of ruthless ambition. Disapproval of his private life, and the attacks on Lady Suffolk and Lady Walsingham, both described as carriers of the pox, sprang from a a deep distaste for the court which was increasingly seen as a centre of moral decay. The appalling physical details of Salisbury's death could easily be depicted not only as retribution for a dissolute life but also as evidence of corruption in high places, combining fascination with revulsion. Cecil's role in the downfall of Essex, and his own death in 1612, produced a torrent of libelling and counter-assertion which reflected the interest of an increasingly literate society in public figures. Moreover, after the polarisation of opinion in the debate over Salisbury, it comes as no surprise that there has been little subsequent agreement on his achievements. Where the libels depicted his self-interest and corruption, his defenders contrasted his tireless and devoted labours as counsellor and minister. They prefigured exactly the opposing views of Robert Cecil arrived at by modern historians.[85] In death as in life the lord treasurer proved to be an intensely controversial figure. The extensive circulation of such differing assessments of his career not only testified to the vigour of popular political culture in the early seventeenth century, but also marked the next stage in its evolution, bridging the gap between the previous high point of public interest in the 1580s and the even more highly charged atmosphere of the 1620s.

1587–8 of dream visions highly critical of Philip II's policies, R. L. Kagan, *Lucrecia's Dreams: Politics and Prophecy in 16th century Spain* (Berkeley, 1990).

[84] Gurr, 49–79. Clark, 19.

[85] Cf. Joel Hurstfield's review of Menna Prestwich, *Cranfield: politics and profits under the early Stuarts* (Oxford, 1966), 'The Political Morality of early Stuart statesmen', *History*, 56, no. 187 (1971), 235–43.

THE DECLINE AND FALL OF SLAVERY IN NINETEENTH CENTURY BRAZIL

By Leslie Bethell

READ 20 APRIL 1990

IT is in my case a particular honour to address the Royal Historical Society. As president of the Society for four years in the 1960s, Professor R. A. Humphreys, the first holder of the Chair of Latin American History in the University of London which I have been privileged to hold since 1986 (and, incidentally, my teacher both as an undergraduate and as a postgraduate student), gave a series of distinguished presidential addresses on aspects of British and United States policy towards Latin America, and Anglo-American rivalries in Latin America, during the nineteenth century.[1] But it seems that I am the first historian of Latin America to present a paper to the Society on a specifically Latin American theme.

By way of explanation of why I have chosen as my subject The Decline and Fall of Slavery in Brazil (apart from my desire to find a theme or topic in Latin American history of broad, general interest to the Society) let me be self-indulgently autobiographical. Almost exactly twenty years ago in the Preface to my book on the abolition of the slave trade to Brazil during the first half of the nineteenth century I wrote,

> In this book I have confined my attention to the abolition of the Brazilian slave trade. It is my present intention to write a second volume on the struggle for the abolition of slavery in Brazil in the second half of the nineteenth century.[2]

In the event my attention was diverted to other projects, in particular the editing of *The Cambridge History of Latin America* (which turned out to be a life sentence—or at least a sentence to fifteen years hard labour). My research interests moved more towards the political and social history of Latin America in the middle decades of the twentieth

---

[1] R. A. Humphreys, 'Anglo-American Rivalries and Spanish American Emancipation', *supra* 5th Series, xvi (1966), 131–56; 'Anglo-American Rivalries and the Venezuela Crisis of 1895', *supra*, 5th Series, xvii (1967), 131–64; 'Anglo-American Rivalries in Central America', *supra*, 5th Series xviii (1968), 174–208—all three essays reprinted in *Tradition and Revolt in Latin America* (1969).

[2] Leslie Bethell, *The Abolition of the Brazilian Slave Trade. Britain, Brazil and the Slave Trade Question, 1807–1869* (Cambridge, 1970), xii.

century. I have, however, maintained throughout these years a strong interest in both the problem of slavery and the problem of abolition in the Americas, and especially in Brazil. The invitation to address the Royal Historical Society coincided with the centenary of the abolition of slavery in Brazil in 1888. It therefore seemed appropriate to offer the Society some reflections on this question.

During the past twenty years historians have given a great deal of increasingly sophisticated attention to the rich and complex history of African slavery in Brazil—in all periods (from its beginnings early in the sixteenth century to its termination at the end of the nineteenth century), in all regions (from Maranhão in the North to Rio Grande do Sul in the South but especially the North-East and the Centre-South) and in all its various socio-economic manifestations. There has been a tendency to concentrate, in Brazil as in the United States, on such topics as slave fertility and mortality, the slave family, the slave community, slave culture and religion, slave resistance and rebellion. (As Stuart Schwartz, a US historian of slavery in colonial Bahia, once remarked after reading Kátia de Queirós Mattoso's *Être un esclave au Brésil*—a work which it should be said he greatly admired—historians of slavery sometimes give the impression that slaves did everything except work!)[3] This new research on Brazilian slavery has enriched the study of comparative slave systems in the Americas, comparisons between African slavery in the Americas from the sixteenth to the nineteenth century and slavery in other places and other times, and comparisons between slavery and other forms of forced labour.

Although some interesting new work has appeared on miscegenation, manumission and the role of free people of colour in Brazilian slave society from the sixteenth to the nineteenth century, there has been much less advance in the study of the transition from slave to free labour in Brazil during the second half of the nineteenth century and, surprisingly, almost nothing new on the abolition of slavery. The centenary of abolition in Brazil which, since it was the last slave emancipation, marked the definitive extinction of black slavery in the Americas (more than 350 years after the first introduction by Europeans of African slaves—as the solution to the problem of labour, especially plantation labour, in those areas of the New World without settled indigenous populations—and more than 100 years after the first attempts to bring slavery to an end) produced more literature on

[3] Kátia M. de Queirós Mattoso, *Être un esclave au Brésil, XVIe–XIXe siècles* (Paris, 1979); Eng. trans. *To be a Slave in Brazil, 1550–1888* (New Brunswick, NJ, 1986), with a foreword by Stuart Schwartz. For a survey of recent research, see Stuart B. Schwartz, 'Recent Trends in the Study of Slavery in Brazil', *Luso-Brazilian Review* XXV, no. 1 (1988), 1–25.

slavery than on abolition. The most recent general account—Robert Conrad's, *The Destruction of Brazilian Slavery*—was published as long ago as 1972,[4] soon after my own study of the abolition of the Brazilian slave trade (and another reason—or was it an excuse?—for not proceeding at that time to the promised second volume on the abolition of slavery).

An ambitious attempt to tell the whole story of, and to offer explanations for, the abolition of slavery throughout the Americas—the first since the outstanding contribution of David Brion Davis[5]—is currently being made by Robin Blackburn. The first of two projected volumes on abolition has recently been published.[6] It begins at the end of the eighteenth century with the American Revolution, the French Revolution and the French revolutionary wars, the Industrial Revolution and Britain's official conversion to anti-slavery—and ends with the European revolutions of 1848. By 1848 the slave trade to the United States, to the British colonies in the Caribbean, to the newly independent Spanish American republics and to the French and other European colonies in the Caribbean had been brought to an end. And slavery had been abolished and the slaves emancipated in Saint-Domingue, most of the Spanish American republics, the British and French islands in the Caribbean and the northern United States.

Nevertheless, in 1848 the African slave trade (although now universally illegal) continued on a significant scale—in fact on a larger scale than in the late eighteenth century when the first steps had been taken to abolish it. It was, however, now restricted to two major destinations: the independent Empire of Brazil and the Spanish colony of Cuba. The slave trade to Brazil was not finally abolished until 1850–1, that to Cuba until 1865. Moreover, slavery still persisted, indeed flourished, in Brazil and Cuba and in the United States (although confined, of course, by this time to the South). Indeed, as a result of the expansion of the frontier in all these remaining slave states during the first half of the nineteenth century, slavery existed over a larger area geographically than at any time in its history. And more Africans and Afro-Americans, some six million, were held in captivity; that is to say, more than twice as many as at the time of the 'first emancipation' in Haiti in 1793. There were in the middle of the nineteenth century 300–400,000 slaves in Cuba (compared with under

---

[4] Robert Conrad, *The Destruction of Brazilian Slavery, 1850–1888* (Berkeley, 1972). See also Emília Viotti da Costa, *Da Senzala à Colônia* (São Paulo, 1966; 2nd ed., 1982), which remains by far the best overview by a Brazilian scholar.

[5] See, in particular, David Brion Davis, *The Problem of Slavery in the Age of Revolution, 1770–1823* (Ithaca, 1975). Also *Slavery and Human Progress* (Oxford, 1984), Part Three, Abolishing Slavery and Civilizing the World.

[6] Robin Blackburn, *The Overthrow of Colonial Slavery, 1776–1848* (1988).

200,000 in 1800), between 2 and $2\frac{1}{2}$ million in Brazil (compared with under 1 million in 1800 and $1-1\frac{1}{2}$ million at the time of independence in 1822) and over 3 million in the United States (compared with half a million at the time of independence in 1776 and under 1 million in 1800). Slavery was not abolished in the United States until 1862 during the Civil War—when it was at its peak. It was finally abolished in Cuba in 1880–6 and in Brazil in 1888—in each case after protracted decline.

Slavery in Brazil was most certainly not an institution in decline in 1848. Nor was it doomed inevitably to wither away—at least in the short and even medium term. On the contrary, Brazil's slave population which had grown steadily throughout the first half of the nineteenth century, as we have seen, was still growing. Although the free population had grown faster it represented even now between a quarter and a third of the total population of 7–8 million. And, in contrast to the United States, slavery could be found in all regions of the country. It was, of course, heavily concentrated in large scale, export-oriented plantation agriculture (*grande lavoura de exportação*), the most dynamic sector of the Brazilian economy: above all, coffee (which had joined sugar in the nineteenth century as, in Sidney Mintz's term, a 'proletarian necessity' and which had risen from under 20% of Brazil's exports in the early 1820s to around 50% in the late 1840s), in the Vale do Rio Paraíba in the provinces of Rio de Janeiro, Minas Gerais and São Paulo in the Centre-South; sugar, principally in Bahia and Pernambuco in the North-East but also in Rio de Janeiro and São Paulo; cotton, in Pernambuco and in Maranhão; and tobacco and cacao, in Bahia. But slavery was also a mainstay of commercial agriculture, both large and small scale, and of stockraising, for the expanding domestic market. Inland transportation was largely in the hands of muleteers (*tropeiros*), who were predominantly slaves. Slaves were used extensively in subsistence agriculture.[7] Finally, they were employed in Brazil's cities as domestic servants, porters, dockers, artisans, builders, even prostitutes and, most remarkably, beggars. Rio de Janeiro (where 40–50% of the population of 200,000 were slaves) was much more obviously a slave city in the middle of the nineteenth century than, say, Havana or New Orleans.[8]

[7] See, for example, on the province of Minas Gerais, Amilcar Martins Filho and Roberto B. Martins, 'Slavery in a Non-export Economy: Nineteenth Century Minas Gerais Revisited', *Hispanic American Historical Review* 63/3 (1983) and, on the province of Rio de Janeiro, Hebe Maria Mattos de Castro, *Ao Sul da História. Lavradores Pobres na Crise do Trabalho Escravo* (São Paulo, 1987) and 'Beyond Masters and Slaves: Subsistence Agriculture as Survival Strategy in Brazil during the Second Half of the Nineteenth Century', *Hispanic American Historical Review* 68/3 (1988).

[8] On slavery in the city of Rio de Janeiro in the nineteenth century, see Mary C. Karasch, *Slave Life in Rio de Janeiro, 1808–1850* (Princeton, 1987), and Luis Carlos

This extensive and expanding system of slave labour in Brazil was underpinned by a flourishing transatlantic slave trade. Over one million slaves had been imported into Brazil since the slave trade to British colonies in the Caribbean and to the United States ended at the beginning of the century. Over half a million had been imported (all of them illegally) since 1831. In 1848 the slave trade to Brazil actually reached a peak of 60,000 in a single year.[9]

There were no signs of a weakening of the Brazilian slave owners' commitment to slavery in the middle of the nineteenth century. And we have seen that slave ownership in Brazil was unusually widespread; a considerable proportion of the free population, half of it itself black or mulatto, owned at least one or two slaves. The big slave owners were not consciously turning to free labour from preference, nor yet from necessity since slaves were in plentiful supply. And they had no difficulty justifying slavery. Ideological rationalisations, and especially those founded in racism, were perhaps weaker in Brazil than in, for example, the American South. But economic imperatives were even stronger. How was a free labour market to be organised in conditions of an open frontier and free, unoccupied or only nominally appropriated land, especially in the coffee zones of the Centre-South? With access to land, a good deal of spatial mobility and therefore alternative survival strategies, why would small producers (*sitiantes* and *lavradores*), tenants and squatters of various kinds (principally *agregados* and *moradores*), or rural labourers and peasants (*camaradas* and *caipiras independentes*) sell their labour and submit themselves to the harsh discipline of plantation agriculture which had always been served by and associated with slave labour?

Nor was there yet any significant abolitionist opinion in Brazil. Individual voices (though precious few) had been raised denouncing slavery on the grounds of its injustice and its supposed economic inefficiency since the end of the eighteenth century. Most notably, José Bonifácio de Andrada e Silva, the father of Brazilian independence from Portugal in 1822, in his *Representação* to the Constituent Assembly in 1823 had called not only for an end to the slave trade but also for the gradual emancipation of the slaves. But political and economic realities were such that no change was forthcoming. With

Soares, Urban Slavery in Nineteenth Century Rio de Janeiro, unpublished PhD thesis, University of London, 1988.

[9] Philip D. Curtin, *The Atlantic Slave Trade. A Census* (Madison, 1969), chapter 8, remains the best study of the dimensions of the nineteenth century slave trade. For estimates of the illegal slave trade to Brazil after 1831, see Bethell, *Abolition*, Appendix, 388–395 and David Eltis, 'The Nineteenth-Century Transatlantic Slave Trade: An Annual Time Series of Imports into the Americas Broken Down by Region', *Hispanic American Historical Review* 67/1 (1987).

independence slavery in Brazil had become a national issue; as such it was an even more intractable problem than it was as a colonial issue (however important) for Portugal. Moreover, independence had been achieved in the form of a conservative revolution (or counter revolution) in which the dominant Brazilian landed (and slave owning) class succeeded in maintaining existing economic and social structures, and especially slavery, in the transition from Portuguese colony to independent Empire under Pedro I (1822–31). The unity and stability of the new state had been threatened during the predominantly liberal Regency in the 1830s. But a conservative restoration had been carried out during the 1840s under the young Pedro II. (1848 in fact witnessed the defeat of the last of a series of provincial rebellions—the *praieira* of Pernambuco—against the central imperial government in Rio de Janeiro.) The twin pillars of the 'Second Empire' (1840–89) were the imperial bureaucrats and the landowners, especially the coffee *fazendeiros* of Rio de Janeiro province. The former, though to some extent, of course, autonomous, were closely linked to and dependent on the latter, who had a strong interest in the survival of slavery.

The greatest potential threat to slavery in Brazil in the middle of the 19th century was external in the form of unrelenting pressure from Britain to end the transatlantic slave trade. Brazil had already been obliged in 1826 to sign an anti-slave trade treaty with Britain and to introduce legislation (the law of 7 November 1831) making the importation of slaves illegal. But this had been simply *para inglês ver*. As Brazilian demand for slaves continued to expand with the growth of the coffee sector, itself a response to growing European and North American demand for coffee, Brazilian governments proved unwilling and unable to enforce the law of 1831. Britain's anti-slave trade efforts—diplomatic, naval and, within Brazil, a 'hearts and minds' campaign to win over domestic opinion which included a small abolitionist press financed by the British legation in Rio—had some success despite limited powers and resources. The issue of the slave trade, and by extension slavery, was at least kept on the Brazilian agenda. The year, 1848, however, witnessed the first signs that British pressure might soon in fact be eased or even withdrawn. As the Brazilian slave trade reached its highest level doubts began to surface in Britain about the efficacy of the anti-slave trade measures being adopted and even about the possibility of ever being able to bring the struggle to a successful conclusion.

The trade in slaves from Africa to Brazil which had been pursued entirely legally for three hundred years and illegally, despite all Britain's efforts, for twenty years came to a sudden, dramatic and permanent end in 1850–1. The Brazilian government claimed it could no longer resist 'the pressure of the ideas of the age in which we live'.[10] More to the point, it could not resist an intensification of British naval pressure designed to force it to act. The alternative to acquiescence in Britain's demand that it should finally take the necessary steps to bring the illegal slave trade to an end was at best an endless series of violent conflicts with the British navy and disruption of Brazil's coastal trade, at worst total economic blockade and even war with Britain (at a time when Brazil was already at war with Argentina in the Río de la Plata). The new Brazilian Empire was faced, it seemed, with a major threat to its sovereignty, its hard won unity and stability and its economic prosperity. As it happened, probably for the first time since independence, British pressure was brought to bear on a government which as a result of the political changes, administrative centralisation and economic growth of the 1840s had the legitimacy and the resources to attempt to take action against the slave trade. A new anti-slave trade law (4 September 1850) was enacted and effectively enforced by provincial presidents, chiefs of police and local magistrates. Only 3,278 slaves were imported into Brazil in 1851, less than 1,000 in 1852. The last known attempt to land slaves in Brazil occurred in 1855.

The Brazilian government was able to enact and enforce its anti-slave trade measures because there was surprisingly little resistance from the dominant land and slave owning class—in Parliament or in the country. This acceptance, albeit reluctant, of the inevitable was facilitated by the glut of slaves on the market at the time (the result of the massive imports in the late forties which had triggered the British naval action of 1850). Some feared the 'Africanisation' of Brazil and the increased danger of slave revolt. Many anticipated an increase in the value of their 'property' as slave prices rose (they in fact doubled between 1852 and 1854). There was also every reason to believe, on the evidence of the past, that the total ban on slave imports would not prove permanent. When demand resurfaced the transatlantic trade would be reopened (here the slaveowners were wrong) or replaced by an interprovincial trade especially from the North-East to the Centre-South (here they were correct). Moreover, the 1850 law was carefully framed so that it was directed at slave traffickers and speculators (the majority of whom were foreign, above all Portuguese, and thus the object of easily aroused nationalism) not the *fazendeiros* who purchased illegally imported slaves. At the same time the pill was sweetened by new legislation (1850) regularising land titles and attempting to control access to land, offers of improvements in trans-

[10] Paulino José Soares de Sousa, Brazilian Foreign Minister, quoted in Bethell, *Abolition*, 362.

portation (the early 1850s witnessed Brazil's first, government-guaranteed railway construction) and some encouragement for the first attempts being made at the time to attract European, especially Swiss and German, 'colonos' (sharecroppers but, in effect, indentured labourers) to Brazil. Finally, and most importantly, no threat was posed by the law of 1850 to slavery itself. Existing slave property, including slaves illegally imported since 1831, remained untouched. A bill for the liberation of children born to slave mothers introduced into the Chamber of Deputies in 1850 by deputy Silva Guimarães was rejected—without discussion. When it was reintroduced in 1852 it was supported only by its author and one other member.[11]

The suppression of the Brazilian slave trade in 1850–1, that is to say, the cutting off of the external supply of slaves to Brazil, even when it proved effective and permanent, need not necessarily have undermined the slave system in Brazil. (In the United States the slave population had grown three or four times since the ending of the slave trade.) In fact it proved to be a decisive blow to slavery. The reason was the failure of the Brazilian slave system, which had never been self perpetuating and had come to rely on a massive annual injection of new slaves from Africa, to reproduce itself even though the demand for slaves soon intensified and prices rose steeply. Birth rates remained low (in part because of the sex ratio within the slave population, itself a reflection of recent dependence on the trade); mortality rates remained high (in part because of ill treatment but more because of Brazil's disease and nutritional environment); rates of manumission (and rates of escape) also remained high. The end of the regular and massive importation of slaves from Africa brought therefore the beginnings of the quantitative decline of the Brazilian slave population. By 1866–7 when Agostinho Marques Perdigão Malheiro published his great study *A Escravidão no Brasil: ensaio histórico, jurídico e social*, it had fallen from 2–2½ million to 1,700,000 (which now, because of a steady increase in the free population during these two decades, represented only 15–20% of the population).[12]

Not only did the Brazilian slave population begin to shrink after

[11] José Murilo de Carvalho. *Teatro de Sombras. A Política Imperial* (São Paulo, 1988), 61.

[12] For a quantitative analysis of the decline of the total slave population in Brazil between the suppression of the slave trade (1850) and the final abolition of slavery (1888), and other demographic issues, see, in particular, Robert W. Slenes, The demography and economics of Brazilian slavery, 1850–88, unpublished PhD thesis, Stanford University, 1977; T. Merrick and Douglas H. Graham, *Population and Economic Development in Brazil, 1800 to the Present* (Baltimore, 1979), Chapter IV 'Slaves and Slavery in the Demographic History of Nineteenth Century Brazil'; and *Estudos Econômicos* Vol. 17, No. 2 (1988), special issue.

1850 but it was also relocated. In the first place, it became more heavily concentrated in the coffee areas of the Centre-South. Just as the illegal transatlantic slave trade in the 1830s and 1840s had been largely directed at the coastline 100 miles north and 100 miles south of Rio de Janeiro (and the coffee plantations inland), so in the 1850s and 1860s an interprovincial slave trade developed from the provinces of the North and North-East, 'the new African coast', to the Centre-South. By 1870 almost two-thirds of Brazil's slave population could be found in three provinces, Rio de Janeiro, Minas Gerais and São Paulo, 'as provincias negreiras da nação'. Furthermore, within the Centre-South itself there was a significant movement of slaves from the cities to the countryside (the slave population of Rio de Janeiro, for example, almost disappeared and was replaced by Portuguese immigrants), from subsistence and non-export agriculture to plantation agriculture, and from declining to expanding coffee areas. Railway development released slaves from muleteering, and technological changes in the coffee industry itself released slaves from processes like hulling, shelling, separating and sorting for labour in the fields. Free (or at least non-slave) labour thus began to replace slave labour in the North and North-East (although large concentrations of slaves still existed on some sugar plantations), in the urban areas, in the non-export economy, and even, in an auxiliary role, in the coffee zone.

Even so, slavery in Brazil in 1870 could hardly be said to be reaching the end of its natural life. Brazil's first national census in 1872 indicated that there were still 1,500,000 slaves (more than at the time of independence) in a country with a population of ten million. Slavery was still to be found in all regions of the country, in both urban and rural areas, in both export and non-export agriculture. In the most economically dynamic region of the country, that is to say, the coffee producing Centre-South whose centre of gravity had begun to move from the Paraíba valley to the north and west of São Paulo province and which produced 70 per cent of Brazil's exports, slavery was actually stronger than twenty years before, despite the rising cost of slave labour and the beginnings of a problem of slave supply. The most progressive coffee *fazendeiros*, that is to say, the most capitalist in attitudes to land, credit, investment in machinery and transport continued to find slavery a highly profitable form of labour. Few hesitated to purchase slaves. There was no attempt at a significant mobilisation of free and freed labour in non-export and subsistence agriculture which now represented over 80% of the rural labour force in the country as a whole (compared with less than 50% in 1822), no major substitution of free for slave labour in the core activities of the coffee plantations. Nor was there any significant attempt to attract

European immigrants to Brazil on a large scale for coffee plantation labour. The experiments made in the late 1840s and early 1850s with European contract labour had proved a resounding failure. At this stage coffee planters had more interest in Chinese than in European labour, although in the end the few attempts made to replace slaves with coolies were unsuccessful. Finally, it is striking how little significant anti-slavery opinion existed in Brazil. Intellectuals, the press, Parliament had been largely silent on the issue of slavery in the 1850s and early 1860s. Only during the Paraguayan War (1865–1870) was there the beginnings of a change in the intellectual climate (as well as some signs of early abolitionist activity and of increased restlessness in the slave population itself)—none of which survived the end of the War and a modest legislative victory over slavery in 1871.

Under *A Lei do Ventre Livre* (28 September 1871) children born to slave women were henceforth to be legally free. Following the abolition of the external supply twenty years earlier, Brazil had now abolished the internal supply of slaves. The clock was set ticking on the end of slavery which was now inevitable, although not necessarily until the death of the youngest slave in Brazil. The Law of 1871 also liberated state owned slaves, codified the right of slaves to purchase their own freedom, established an Emancipation Fund to facilitate manumission by individual initiative and declared the need for a register (*matricula*) of all Brazil's existing slaves.

Unlike the 1850 anti-slave trade law which, as we have seen, was almost entirely the result of external (British) pressure, the 1871 law of free birth had its origins in domestic pressures. More research needs to be done on the politics of abolition in the late 1860s if the passage of Brazil's free birth legislation is to be properly explained. One thing is quite clear: the initiative was taken at the highest level— by the Emperor himself. See, for example, his *Fala* (Speech from the Throne) in 1867 and the various anti-slavery projects put before the Council of State in 1866, 1867 and 1868. A relatively liberal 'Victorian' statesman (in reality as well as certainly in appearance and demeanour), well-travelled and well-informed about the world, Dom Pedro responded positively to international humanitarian pressures; he had come to believe that slavery in Brazil could no longer be justified. More important, he also believed that the decline of slavery since 1850 was irreversible and that it should be deliberately accelerated and, at the same time, controlled (to ensure the minimum of economic and social dislocation). Moreover, at a time when Brazil, along with Argentina and Uruguay (both of which had long since abolished slavery), was engaged in a protracted and bloody war against the López dictatorship in Paraguay slaves were potentially a dangerous 'internal enemy'. Slaves who fought in the Brazilian army during the Paraguayan War were freed. But further steps were deemed inappropriate until the end of the War, by which time, interestingly, the commander of the Brazilian troops, the Conde d'Eu (the Emperor's son-in-law), had successfully promoted the emancipation of the slaves in Paraguay.

In March 1871 the Emperor invited the Visconde do Rio Branco to form a Conservative administration which was willing to bring a bill of free birth before Parliament. The bill was supported by some prominent Conservatives, some prominent Liberals, representatives of the provinces of the North and North-East which despite the shift in the economic and demographic centre of gravity towards the Centre-South in the middle decades of the nineteenth century had a preponderant voice in both the Chamber of Deputies and the Senate and which were by now the least committed to slavery, and those won over to the 'Crown interest' by various forms of patronage (including the liberal conferment of aristocratic titles). The free birth bill nevertheless represented a major clash of interest between the state and the most dynamic sector of the dominant landowning class, the *barões do café* (especially in the province of Rio de Janeiro). It was not possible to avoid a lengthy and passionate parliamentary battle—perhaps the most important in the history of the Empire and one which put a severe strain on the political system—before the bill was passed by 65 votes to 45 in the Chamber and 33 to 7 in the Senate.[13]

Once passed the law of free birth, like the anti-slave trade law twenty years earlier, was generally accepted by the slave owning classes throughout the country. There was not a hint of disobedience or armed resistance, no threat of secession. At least, it could be argued, slavery had survived; perhaps its final collapse had even been postponed. Incipient abolitionism had been headed off, and potentially rebellious slaves offered some hope for the future. As in 1850 the new legislation in no way interfered with existing property. Moreover, children born of slave mothers (*ingênuos*), though nominally free, remained with, and worked for, their owners until they were twenty-one (unless the owners preferred to hand them over to the state at eight in return for indemnification—which few did). The Emancipation Fund was modest in scale and slow to be established. For example, the first quota was not distributed in the *município* of Rio Claro (São Paulo province) until 1877.[14] In the 10–15 years after 1871

[13] The Chamber of Deputies was elected, indirectly, on an extremely narrow franchise primarily determined by property and income. Senators were appointed by the Emperor for life.
[14] See Warren Dean, *Rio Claro. A Brazilian Plantation System, 1820–1920* (Stanford, 1976), 129.

more slaves were *alforriado* (freed) and thus became *libertos* by private act (often in return for *prestação de serviços*, a commitment to work for the former master for a specific period) and self purchase than by means of the Emancipation Fund. And twice as many slaves died as were manumitted.[15] Thus, as many planters had anticipated, the law of 1871 had little immediate, direct effect on the institution of slavery.

During the 1870s the Brazilian slave population and thus the supply of slave labour to the economy continued to decline (albeit still relatively slowly). Its regional (and sectoral) concentration was further accentuated. In the main coffee areas in São Paulo province the slave population actually increased slightly. As Brazil's population grew (from 10 million to almost 12 million) the balance between slave and free labour shifted even more towards the latter in the economy as a whole, including by now the coffee sector itself where although slave labour still predominated, especially in the fields, *libertos* (with and without long-term contracts), *ingênuos*, European immigrants and Brazilian wage labourers could also be found. There was, however, relatively little serious public discussion of the problem of slavery in Brazil, of the inexorable process of transition from a predominantly slave to a predominantly free labour system, or of the broader issue of how in the longer term to provide plantation agriculture with a permanent supply of free labour. Only at the end of the decade was a first attempt made under *A Lei de Locação de Serviços* (15 March 1879) to structure a 'free labour market' by outlawing vagrancy, regulating the various experiments with long-term employment contracts (most commonly three years for Europeans, five years for free Brazilians and seven years for *libertos*), and controlling 'free' labourers by punishing breaches of contract and collective resistance to conditions of work, especially strikes.[16] It is not clear, however, whether the law had much practical application.

In the early 1880s, twenty years after the emancipation of the slaves in the United States and with the Spanish government having taken the first steps to end slavery in Cuba, there were still $1\frac{1}{4}$ million slaves in Brazil—almost certainly more than there had been in 1800. Regional variations in the size and economic importance of the slave population were, however, even more evident than they had been 10–15 years earlier. Seventy per cent or more of Brazil's slaves were concentrated in Rio de Janeiro, Minas Gerais and São Paulo. In fewer than half of Brazil's provinces (compared with two thirds in 1874)

---

[15] Carvalho, *Teatro de Sombras*, 72; Mattoso, *To be a Slave in Brazil*, 157.

[16] See Maria Lúcia Lamounier, *Da Escravidão ao Trabalho Livre* (*A Lei de Locação de Serviços de 1879*) (Campinas, SP, 1988) and Ademir Gebara, *O mercado de trabalho livre no Brasil* (1871–1888) (São Paulo, 1986).

were more than ten per cent of the population slaves. In more than a quarter (mostly in the North, the South and the West) slaves constituted less than five per cent of the population. This was the level at which in North America the northern states of the Union had opted for emancipation almost a hundred years earlier. As Adam Smith said of the Quakers in Pennsylvania, '[Their] resolution . . . to set at liberty all their negro slaves may satisfy us that their number is not very great'.[17] And in Brazil in 1884 the slaves were indeed emancipated first in Ceará, then in Amazonas and finally, in a more limited sense (since a form of apprenticeship was instituted) in Rio Grande do Sul.

In the North-East, especially in Pernambuco, where the sugar based economy stagnated, a number of sugar planters retained hundreds, even in some cases thousands, of slaves. And the inter-provincial slave trade which had constituted, above all, a steady outflow of slaves from the North-East to the Centre-South had been prohibited in 1880–1. But the region as a whole where two-thirds of Brazil's slave population was located in 1822 had by now fewer slaves than, for example, the province of Minas Gerais. There had been little recent investment in slaves; the existing slave population, unable to renew itself, was ageing fast; and there was an adequate supply of alternative 'free' labour. The North-East was more densely populated than the Centre-South, access to land was more restricted and society was more traditional, highly stratified and stable. In short, as we saw as early as 1871, while not actively promoting its final collapse, the bulk of the dominant class in the North East no longer regarded the survival of the slave system as a matter of life and death.

In contrast, in the Centre-South in the older region of coffee production—the Paraíba Valley in the provinces of Rio de Janeiro, Minas Gerais and São Paulo—which was in economic decline the dominant class clung desperately to slavery. Many landowners had invested recently and heavily in slaves (through purchase at high prices and through maintenance); their slaves were younger than those in the Northeast and potentially mobile (that is to say, given the opportunity ready to move to new areas of coffee production in São Paulo); no adequate, cheap alternative free labour force was readily available; plantation society was of more recent origin and therefore less well established than in the North-East and in danger of collapse if the slaves were emancipated. The most die-hard slavocrats could be found in this region, and especially in the province of Rio de Janeiro.

On the new, expanding coffee frontier in the interior of São Paulo province the problem was more complex. *Fazendeiros* there, producing

---

[17] David Eltis reminds us of this in *Economic Growth and the Ending of the Transatlantic Slave Trade* (Oxford, 1987), 235.

coffee for a buoyant world market, found themselves in an unprecedented situation: for the first time in the history of Brazil slavery could no longer supply the labour needs of the most dynamic sector of the economy. The slave system was evidently in decline, doomed to come to an end. Slaves were increasingly difficult to obtain, increasingly expensive to buy and maintain, and a poor long-term investment. Clearly an alternative would soon have to be found. The so-called 'progressive' planters of the North and West of São Paulo province were thus by no means as committed to slavery as the planters of the Paraíba valley. It is, however, a mistake to think of them as necessarily opponents of slavery. Free Brazilians were still not considered suitable for, nor were they apparently willing to engage in, disciplined labour on coffee plantations. And the coffee sector of São Paulo was not yet attracting European immigrants in sufficient numbers and on the necessary terms to satisfy its labour requirements. At least in the short-term, slavery continued to provide the most profitable and for most planters the preferred system of labour.

In the early 1880s a new factor came into play: abolitionism.[18] In September 1880 the Brazilian Anti-Slavery Society was formed. Its best known spokesman, in and out of Parliament, was Joaquim Nabuco from a *pernambucano* landed family with a strong presence in Brazilian political life. (As Minister of Justice in the 1850s his father, José Tomás Nabuco de Araújo, had been largely responsible for the effective enforcement of the anti-slave trade measures and in the late 1860s had supported free birth legislation.) But blacks and mulattos (notably José do Patrocínio, Luiz Gama, André Rebouças) were also prominent among the leaders of a variety of abolitionist societies which now appeared. Support for abolition came from some progressive *fazendeiros* but mainly from the growing, predominantly white or mulatto, commercial and professional urban middle sectors, which were themselves a reflection of the economic and social changes brought about by export led growth since the middle decades of the century, and also from poor free blacks and mulattos and from freedmen.

The emergence, albeit belated, of an abolitionist ideology and an abolitionist movement in Brazil can no doubt be explained in part by what John Stuart Mill called 'the spread of moral convictions'. But, as earlier in Britain and North America, abolitionism was concerned

---

[18] The classic work on early abolitionism in Brazil, written and published in London in 1883, is Joaquim Nabuco, *O Abolicionismo* (Eng. trans. by Robert Edgar Conrad, *Abolitionism: The Brazilian Anti-Slavery Struggle*, Urbana, Ill., 1977). On the abolitionist movement of the 1880s as a whole, see Evaristo de Morais, *A Campanha Abolicionista* (Rio de Janeiro, 1924), Conrad, *Destruction of Brazilian Slavery*, especially Chapters 9 & 12, and the various writings of Emília Viotti da Costa.

not only with natural justice and human rights but also—perhaps in this case more—with economic progress, capitalist development, the freeing of capital immobilised in slavery, the supposed greater productivity and profitability of free over slave labour, wages and consumption. And there was a political dimension. The abolitionist campaign (public meetings, use of the press, petitions, etc.) represented the highest level of urban middle class and, to a lesser extent, popular political mobilisation thus far in the history of Brazil; and it was directed at the economic, social—and political—power of the landed oligarchy.

Nevertheless, the anti-slavery movement in Brazil was relatively weak—not least because unlike many earlier movements in other countries it had no roots in an anti-slave trade campaign. There were also some deep social (and racial) ambiguities, conflicts and divisions within the movement. It was at this early stage largely moderate, both in methods and in aims. Abolitionists petitioned Parliament and brought cases of illegally held slaves before the courts rather than appealed directly to the slave population. Gradual emancipation rather than immediate abolition was sought since the latter, it was often pointed out even by (white) abolitionist leaders, threatened society with the sudden invasion of a million *bárbaros*. Abolition in Brazil in the early 1880s played only a minor role in bringing closer the end of slavery. It reinforced the determination of the Emperor to keep the abolition of slavery on the political agenda, just as successive British governments had kept the abolition of the slave trade on the political agenda in the 1830s and 1840s, even though he did not himself have the power to enact it. And it helped undermine the defence of slavery by those politicians and *fazendeiros* not yet convinced of the virtues and practicality of free labour.

In the early 1880s no government and no political party was prepared to assume responsibility for pushing a bill for the immediate or even gradual abolition of slavery through Parliament. In July 1884 a Liberal prime minister, Manuel Pinto de Souza Dantas, introduced a modest bill to emancipate, without compensation, slaves who had reached the age of 60—and at the same time to reinforce the Emancipation Fund. It represented the first direct challenge in Brazil to slaveowners' rights to existing slave property.[19] The Liberals had a majority in the Chamber (65 to 46), but only 52 deputies (including some Conservatives) voted for the bill. Fifty-five voted against, and

[19] The bill had more serious implications than might appear at first sight since in the slave registrations after 1871 many slaveowners had exaggerated the ages of their African born slaves in an attempt to establish that they had been legally imported before the law of 1831.

the Souza Dantas government fell on the issue. The bill was rein-troduced by a Conservative government led by the Barão de Cotegipe the following year and passed in September 1885. However, as a form of compensation to their owners, slaves over 60 were obliged to serve for a further three years—or until they reached the age of 65—before manumission (and then to remain, in employment, in the same *município* for a further five years). No-one looked to the Cotegipe administration to take any further steps towards slave emancipation.

Thus slavery in Brazil might even now have been expected to endure for another five or ten years. There were still around a million slaves in Brazil in 1885 and, although the institution's natural decline was clearly accelerating (the number of slaves had been almost halved in less than a decade) three quarters of a million in March 1887. Then came a sudden collapse. There were only between a quarter and a half a million slaves in Brazil (a mere 3–4% of the population) a year later when slavery was finally abolished.

Two principal factors explain the collapse of the slave system in Brazil in the final months of 1887 and the early part of 1888. In the first place, the slaves themselves voted with their feet and fled the plantations in considerable numbers. Slave resistance and rebellion were, of course, endemic in Brazil as they had been in other slave societies. Slave flight and the establishment of *quilombos* (communities of runaway slaves) had been a particular feature of slavery in Brazil. But mass desertion in the scale of 1887–8, sometimes accompanied by violence, often non-violent, was unprecedented. It was caused by growing frustration at the failure of the Brazilian authorities to bring the long drawn out process of transition from slave to free labour to a conclusion (and perhaps—though this requires further research—by the fact that the opportunities for manumission for those remaining in bondage were actually diminishing or thought likely to further diminish).

The 1887–8 exodus of slaves from the plantations was encouraged—at times incited—by radical abolitionists led by Antônio Bento who, also frustrated by lack of progress on the abolition question, were for the first time in the short history of the Brazilian abolitionist movement prepared to take direct, illegal action to subvert the slave system. They preached a clear, redemptionist message and created a national network of transportation and of protection (principally in urban sanctuaries) for fugitive slaves. The action taken by the slaves was facilitated by the fact that from October 1887 the Brazilian army was no longer willing to defend slavery, either by coercing slaves into remaining on the plantation or by rounding up fugitive slaves. This important development was part of a deepening general crisis in civil-military relations (the Empire would be overthrown and a Republic established by a military coup in November 1889). It was also a reflection of the army's assessment of the realities of the situation, and of the penetration of abolitionist as well as republican ideas in military circles.

There is a second reason why the Brazilian slave system began rapidly to disintegrate in 1887–8: as slaves began to revolt and flee (and as slave prices collapsed) slaveowners—in São Paulo, Rio de Janeiro and Pernambuco, for example—began voluntarily to liberate their slaves, sometimes unconditionally but more often in return for labour contracts of one, two or three years. Some owners no doubt were caught up in the excitement of events; some were influenced by the Church which for the first time openly favoured abolition. But most were simply attempting to bring what was happening all around them under some sort of control and prevent the total disorganisation of labour on the plantations.

It was the recognition that slavery in Brazil was rapidly approaching its final stage, together with exaggerated fears that this might be accompanied by social upheaval, an *onda negra* (black wave or tide) overwhelming the whites, even a Haiti-style bloodbath, that finally persuaded many powerful slaveowners and their representatives in Parliament that abolition could and should no longer be avoided.[20] One other factor determined what proved to be the crucial break in the ranks of the defenders of slavery. The *fazendeiros* of the West of São Paulo province, who faced a labour crisis during a major upswing in the coffee cycle, secured at this critical juncture a plentiful, cheap alternative to slaves (the *elemento servil*)—not, significantly, free Brazilian wage labourers (the *elemento nacional*) but immigrants from Italy.

The provincial government of São Paulo, which had come increasingly under the influence of Western interests, had earlier in the decade taken the decision to subsidise the transportation of Italian immigrants. The Sociedade Promotora da Imigração was created in July 1886 and immediately initiated promotional activities in Italy. Annual arrivals of European immigrants in São Paulo had averaged under 6,000 in the five years 1882–6. In 1886 only 9,500 of the 33,000 immigrants to Brazil went to São Paulo province. In 1887, however, 32,000 of 55,000 and in 1888 92,000 of 133,000 were destined for São Paulo; most were Italians, most had been recruited to work—for extremely low wages—on the coffee plantations. In the decade following the abolition of slavery three quarters of a million European immigrants (the overwhelming majority Italian) arrived in São Paulo,

---

[20] On the subject of white fears of an *onda negra*, see in particular Célia Maria Marinho de Azevedo, *Onda negra, medo branco. O negro no imaginário das elites—seculo XIX* (Rio de Janeiro, 1987).

80% of them subsidised by the State.[21] Thus Italian immigration was both a response to the final collapse of slavery and one of the causes of its final abolition.

In March 1888 the Conservative government of João Alfredo Correia de Oliveira (in which Antônio Prado, the leading spokesman for the coffee interests of São Paulo, had a prominent role) proposed the immediate and unconditional abolition of slavery and the emancipation of Brazil's remaining slaves. There would be no indemnification for slaveowners (although it could be argued that subsidised immigration was an indirect form of compensation, at least for the slaveowners of São Paulo). An abolition bill passed through Parliament in less than a week. The vote was 83–9 in the Chamber and 43–6 in the Senate. Only a handful of prominent Conservatives (including Cotegipe) and, above all, the representatives of the old coffee regions of Rio de Janeiro province opposed the bill. The *Lei Aurea* was signed by the Princess Regent Isabel on 13 May. The slaves emancipated, between a quarter and half a million of them, were absorbed into the large free black and mulatto population that already existed at the bottom of Brazilian society where, sad to say, it has for the most part remained during the 100 years since the abolition of slavery in Brazil.

---

[21] Thomas H. Holloway, *Immigrants on the Land. Coffee and Society in São Paulo, 1886–1934* (Chapel Hill, 1980), 39–40.

MARSILIUS OF PADUA AND THE CASE FOR THE ROYAL ECCLESIASTICAL SUPREMACY[1]

The Alexander Prize Essay

By Shelley Lockwood

READ 18 MAY 1990

Nowe as touchynge the translacyon of Marsilius out of laten and in teachynge hym to speake englysshe,... whether it be done so well as it myght or shulde have ben, I woll not saye, but I hertely pray the gentle reader to take it in good parte and to correcte and amende it where nede is.[2]

TAKING William Marshall[3] at his word, a comparison of his *Defence of Peace* of 1535 with the Latin *editio princeps* of the *Defensor Pacis*, printed in Basle in 1522,[4] reveals that there is much need for 'correction'; or rather, it reveals that Marshall had himself corrected and amended the original to suit his own purposes. What those purposes were, the nature of the amendments and their consequences for our understanding of the royal ecclesiastical supremacy will be the subject of this essay.

Marshall's most glaring omissions have long been noted[5] and he himself admits, 'in the translacyon of this boke dyverse thynges ben omited and lefte out as maters not so moche profytable, as long

[1] A. Gewirth, *Marsilius of Padua: The Defender of Peace*, vol. I *Marsilius of Padua and Medieval Political Philosophy* (New York, 1951).

[2] William Marshall, *The defence of peace lately translated out of laten in to englysshe*, (R. Wyer, 1535), STC 17817, fol. 1. It was, however, written by April 1533 [*LP* VII.422 and 423].

[3] William Marshall was clerk to Richard Broke, Chief Baron of the exchequer in 1531. He was acquainted with Thomas More who tried to get him office at court [*LP* IV.3.App. 133]. He apparently obtained his licence for printing books through his connections with the Boleyn family, *DNB* XXXVI, 25; G. R. Elton, 'An early Tudor Poor Law' in *Studies in Tudor and Stuart Politics and Government*, 2 vols, (Cambridge, 1974) II, 151–3.

[4] Marshall almost certainly used this edition since he includes its preface by Licentius Evangelus (the pseudonym of the Protestant Valention Curio) and he follows the textual peculiarities of the *editio princeps*. The *editio princeps* was printed as *Opus insigne cui titulum fecit auctor defensorem pacis*... It is collated in ed. C. W. Previte-Orton, *The Defensor Pacis of Marsilius of Padua* (Cambridge, 1928).

[5] C. W. Previte-Orton, *Defensor Pacis*, (Cambridge, 1928) xl n1; Pierre Janelle, *L'Angleterre Catholique à la veille du schisme*, (Paris, 1935) 252–6; G. R. Elton, 'The Political Creed of Thomas Cromwell' in *Studies* II, (Cambridge, 1974) 215–35.

and tedyous . . .'.[6] Closer examination, however, reveals many more omissions, additions and manipulations of meaning than Marshall confessed to, or indeed than have hitherto been remarked upon. These omissions are revealing because of the distortion they produce and as indications both of the intentions of the author and of what was considered appropriate for public consumption—Chapuys remarked that the *Defensor Pacis* was now translated so that all could see and hear it.[7]

Marshall's work was clearly printed as part of the anti-papal propaganda campaign organised by Thomas Cromwell to give theoretical justification for Henry's policies.[8] There is no evidence, however, that Cromwell instructed Marshall on how to translate the work. Rather, it appears that Marshall made the translation and then applied to Cromwell for financial assistance in getting it printed and distributed.[9] Apart from these transactions with Cromwell, information concerning William Marshall is sparse and consists mainly of what can be culled from his literary works. He had perhaps been trained as a lawyer and had held government office.[10] His works include a translation of Valla's *De falso credita et ementita Constantini Donatione*,[11] *A treatyse declaryng and showyng that images are not to be sufherd in churches*,[12] and *A prymer in Englysshe . . . for all people that understande not the Laten tongue*.[13] This Primer reveals Marshall to be a follower of Luther,[14] and the Lutheran

---

[6] Marshall, fol. 1v.

[7] ed. J. S. Brewer, J. Gairdner and R. H. Brodie, *Letters and Papers, Foreign and Domstic, of the reign of Henry VIII* 36 vols (London 1862–1932) [*LP*] VII.14.

[8] G. R. Elton, *Policy and Police: The Enforcement of the Reformation in the Age of Thomas Cromwell* (Cambridge, 1972) 180–98, *Reform and Renewal: Thomas Cromwell and the Common Weal* (Cambridge, 1973) 57–65, *Reform and Reformation: England 1509–1558* (1977) 195–7; Fox and Guy, *Reassessing the Henrician Age: Humanism, Politics and Reform 1500–1550* (Oxford 1986) cc. 3, 5, 7.

[9] *LP*.VII.422, 423; XI.1355. G. R. Elton, *Reform and Renewal* 62 n79 *Policy and Police* 186 n2.

[10] *LP*.VII.722 where a Mr. Marshall is described as a gentleman 'learned in the temporall law' and see n3.

[11] *A Treatyse of the donation gyuen unto Syluester pope of Rhome*, (Thomas Godfray, 1534) STC 5641. This is an accurate translation of Ulrich von Hutten's 1517 *editio princeps*.

[12] (T. Godfrey, 1535) STC 24238, translated by Marshall from Bedrote's Latin translation of Bucer's *Das einigerlei Bild*.

[13] (J. Bydell, 1534) STC 15986. Other works are *A Worke entytled of ye olde god and the newe*, Joachim von Watt (J. Bydell, 1534) STC 25127, *An exposition after the maner of a contemplacion upon the li psalme called Miserere mei Deus*, (J. Bydell, 1534) STC 21789.3, *A lytle treatise on the forme of confession*, (J. Bydell, ?1535) STC 10498, *Paraphrase of Erasmi upon ye Epistle of Paul unto Titus*, (J. Bydell, ?1535) STC 10503.5 and *The boke of the discrepcyon of the images of a very chrysten bysshop*, (R. Wyer, ?1536) STC 16963.

[14] C. C. Butterworth, *The English Primers 1529–45*, (Philadelphia, 1953), 52–62 and Appendix 1(A) 'Martin Luther and the Marshall Primers' 279–85 in which Butterworth states that Marshall was 'clearly a staunch Lutheran' as his primer contains numerous passages from Luther's works.

aspects of Marshall's thought will become especially important when we come to look at the marginal notes and glosses in Discourse II of the *Defence of Peace*. It was either as a result of the Primer or perhaps his iconoclastic work, that Marshall was mentioned as a heretic in the articles of the Pilgrimage of Grace.[15] Finally, he managed to distribute twenty-four copies of his work to the Charterhouse monks; all were swiftly returned except one which was later burned.[16]

Since, as Marshall was using Marsilius' text as a prism through which to refract his own ideas, any attempt to assess the influence of Marsilius' original ideas in the context of the royal supremacy in England would be superfluous. What must concern us is not so much Marsilius' thought as how and to what end Marshall manipulated and applied it. How did Marshall make a case for the royal ecclesiastical supremacy from Marsilius' theory of popular sovereignty? It is precisely because Marshall's 'translation' entailed the manipulation of a conflicting set of ideas that makes it peculiarly revealing and helpful in understanding what was at issue in the 1530s.

For the purposes of the case for the royal supremacy it was essential to regain the obedience of all the king's subjects and to incorporate ecclesiastical jurisdiction into the king's exercise of *imperium*. Steven Haas has demonstrated the early appearance of what were to be the key issues concerning Henry's break with Rome through his examination of the *Disputatio inter clericem et militem* (Berthelet, 1531)— another example of an old anti-papal work being adapted to current situations for specific purposes. Haas has convincingly demonstrated the greater use of the original work to lessen papal jurisdiction in England and enhance the royal prerogative by bolstering the notion of the God-given royal *imperium* of an anointed king.[17] The term *imperium* was also being flaunted by others, in particular, Polydore Vergil.[18]

Clear evidence of Henry's own awareness of the definition of his status as king is found in his redrafting of the coronation oath. He changed his promise to maintain the rights and liberties of the holy church so that he only maintained those of the church *of* England 'not preiudicyall to hys jurysdyccion and dignitie ryall', and he promised only to keep 'approvyd' customs 'lawfull and not preiudiciall to his crowne or imperial jurisdiction'.[19] These changes together with

[15] *LP*.IX. 506–7.

[16] *LP*.VIII.600 and IX.523; G. R. Elton, *Policy and Police*, 210 n.2.

[17] Steven Haas, 'The *Disputatio inter clericem et militem*: was Berthelet's 1531 edition the first Henrician polemic of Thomas Cromwell?' in *Moreana* XIV (1977) 65–72.

[18] Richard Koebner, '"The Imperial Crown of This Realm". Henry VIII, Constantine the Great and Polydore Vergil' in *Bulletin of the Institute of Historical Research* XXVI (1953) 29–52.

[19] BL Cotton MS Tiberius E VIII fol.100 and in ed. L. Wickham-Legg, *English Coronation Records* (Westminster, 1901) facing 241.

the famous preamble to the Act of Appeals (1533)—'this Realme of Englond is an Impire'[20]—demonstrate the importance of the claims to territorial sovereignty by appealing to the notion of *imperium*. Henry's concern was for a new definition of his sovereignty, a new definition of his exercise, as Supreme Head, of *imperium* over 'all maner of folke reseauntes or Subjectes within this his realm'.[21] He wanted to exercise the powers of the king as emperor in his own kingdom and Cromwell, too, was anxious that theoretical justification of that position be put forth. This involved defining the king's jurisdiction in law and it is the problem of the scope of this jurisdiction which provides one of the major tensions between the needs of the royal ecclesiastical supremacy and the argument provided by Marsilius' *Defensor Pacis*. Marshall needed to resolve the incompatibility between the universal concept of the 'universitas civium' and the territorially limited notion of 'the realm of England'.

It was the Reformation Acts of Parliament that both anchored Henry's sovereignty territorially and defined it in law[22] and this is a measure of the growing importance of Parliament and its role in the governing of the realm. The question of the extent to which Parliament shared in the *imperium* is therefore of great constitutional significance, second only to the delineation of *regnum* and *sacerdotium* under royal jurisdiction. Marshall's 'translation' also contrives to reflect this aspect of the Henrician Reformation. Given the obvious discrepancies between Marsilius' argument and Marshall's requirements, why did Marshall choose a work so apparently unsuited to his task? His own answer is that his 'translation' was 'to help further and profyte the chrysten common weale ... namely and pryncypally in those busy-nesses and troubles whereby it is and before this time hath ben uniustly molested, vexed and troubled by the spyrytuall and ecclesyastycall tyraunt.'[23] Marshall's concept of the common weal is that of an ordered hierarchical society in which ruler, officers and people must play their own part within limits set by the law.[24] Any threat to that unity leads to sedition and the breakdown of civil society. For Marshall, as of course for Marsilius, the major threat to the peace and unity of the common weal was 'the great dragon, and olde serpente antychryste of Rome'[25] who set up an alternative focus for allegiance.

The anti-papal polemic was thus the most obviously useful aspect

---

[20] Act in Restraint of Appeals to Rome (1533: 24 Henry VIII, c.12) in G. R. Elton, *The Tudor Constitution* 2nd ed. (Cambridge, 1982) no.177, 353–8.

[21] Act of Appeals 24 HVIII c.12.

[22] G. R. Elton, *Tudor Constitution* for texts and analysis.

[23] Marshall, fol.140v.

[24] Marshall, fol.140.

[25] Marshall, fol.114v marginal note to II.xxvi.

of Marsilius' text. But Marshall also recounts that it was 'in the defence of the moste juste cause of whole imperyall maiesty'[26] that Marsilius compiled his book and he exhorts the reader 'dylygentlye to tourne ouer and to laboure this worke ... [for] thou shalte fynde in it the Image of these our tymes most perfytly and clerlye expressed and set out'.[27] As we shall see, it was in fact Marshall's ingenuity which contrived much of the clarity of this image and likeness. But clearly the defence of (Henry's) imperial majesty was no small part of the purpose of Marshall's 'translation'. *Imperium* was to Marshall, as it was to Marsilius, supreme coercive jurisdiction; he translates 'merum imperium' as 'mere empyre'[28] and 'imperium spirituale' as 'spyrytuall empyre and rule'.[29] This is, of course, distinct from the Holy Roman Empire; England was an Empire not because it was the same as the Empire—after all, the Emperor was elected[30]—but because its ruler exercised *imperium*.[31]

Definition of the relationship between ruler and ruled hinges on the law, its formulation, enforcement and the punishment of transgression of it, and it is on the concept of law that Marsilius' doctrine depends. It was Marshall's task to harness the force of Marsilius' arguments whilst turning them to serve his own ends. How did he do it? The first Discourse of *Defensor Pacis* deals with the origins of civil communities, the best form of government and the functions of the different parts of the community. Its conclusions rely almost entirely on a reading of Aristotle and manipulations and omissions are therefore to be expected since the stress placed on consent and representation was too extreme to be acceptable in England. The translation is remarkably faithful to the original[32] until chapter IX—on the methods of instituting a

---

[26] Marshall, fol.2.

[27] Marshall, 'peroracyon'.

[28] II.iv.12. This retains the sense of the Roman law term as 'mere' meant 'sole' or 'absolute'.

[29] II.v.8, Marshall, fol.59.

[30] This causes particular problems for Marshall in Discourse II.

[31] The concept of 'empire' was particularly useful in propaganda terms as its traditional emotive appeal belied the fundamental shift in its meaning; whereas early notions of empire were perceived within, and therefore as compatible with the universal concept of Christendom with the Pope as head under Christ, later, 'empire' was used to proclaim England's independence from Rome. Valla's *Confutation* of the Donation of Constantine meant that the independence of the Emperor was available as a precedent for the claims to independence of other holders of temporal jurisdictions. It is no surprise, then, when we recall that it was Marshall who produced the first English edition of Valla's work.

[32] Despite the lack of significant changes of meaning, these first chapters contain valuable insights into the problems facing English translators. For instance, terms such as 'civitas' and 'politia' are problematical. At one point Marshall adds, 'regnum may be Englysshed a realme or kyngdom and civitas a cytie' [I.ii, fol.11], this leads him to

monarchy.[33] Its conclusion that election is absolutely the better method of establishing governments[34] was simply incompatible with existing theory and practice in England and was therefore omitted. So too is the fact that it is the consent of the subjects which is the distinguishing criterion between temperate and diseased government, along with all accompanying arguments.[35] For Marshall, consent must not be seen as a positive right which gives the subject sway over government.

The title of chapter XVI is changed from whether it is better to have an elective or a hereditary monarchy where even the monarchy which is continued by succession is elected,[36] to a straightforward assertion that hereditary succession is best.[37] The chapter is reduced to a quarter of its original length and the introductory passage in the original which poses the question as to whether a single elected ruler should be chosen for his lifetime only or with all his posterity,[38] is replaced with

> That it is most conuenyent and profytable for the common weale to have a prynce or gouernoure whiche shall enioye the crowne by successyon of blode with all his posteryte and offsprynge and not by eleccyon as themperour is chosen by electours is proved by ix [*sic*] stronge and inuincyble reasons.[39]

Here Marshall cleverly manipulates the scholastic method for his own ends; by retaining the eleven reasons given in the original as to why hereditary monarchy might be preferable and then omitting the rest of the chapter in which these reasons are refuted, he affirms the principle of hereditary succession and eliminates election as the best method of establishing each successive ruler thereby inverting the conclusions of the original. Also, in chapter XII, the statement that things established by election derive authority from that alone is

---

translate 'vicus seu vicina' with 'called in the laten tonge vicus or vicina in Englysshe a strete' [I.iii, fol.12v], a street being the smaller component of an English city. But he later has 'called in the laten civitas in the englysshe a cytie or a commune weale' [I.iii,. fol.13]. 'Politia' is sometimes 'comen welthe' [I.ix, fol.24], sometimes 'ciuile gouernaunce' [I.ii, fol.11]. Marsilius is himself rather vague on these terms.

[33] I.ix, ed. Previte-Orton, *Defensor Pacis* 29–36 (henceforth P-O), Gewirth 29–34.

[34] I.ix, para.11, P–O 36, Gewirth 34.

[35] I.ix, para.5, P–O 33, Gewirth 31–2. Also omitted: I.ix, part of para.5 to para 11.

[36] I.xvi, P–O 75, Gewirth 68.

[37] 'That it is most expedyent to the commune weale to have onely one certayne man to be prynce of governoure hym selfe with all his posteryte which they call communlye the successyon of kyndred or blode' Marshall fol.35v.

[38] I.xvi,1, P–O 75, Gewirth 68.

[39] Marshall, fol.36.

omitted.[40] These changes and omissions necessitated the elimination of two of Marsilius' conclusions: that an elective ruler depends entirely upon the *universitas* which has the authority to elect and needs no other confirmation, and that the election of any elected ruler, especially one with coercive force, depends upon the expressed will of the 'legislator' alone.[41] The legitimacy of the ruler depended, for Marshall, on birth, not election, and arguments based on the principle of election are systematically excised from Dictio I

The principle of representation, however, was not wholly eradicated, as there existed in the framework around which Marshall was moulding Marsilius' ideas a representative body of the realm—Parliament. It is in chapter XII[42]—a crucial chapter in the development of Marsilius' doctrine—that Marshall makes his significant changes. This chapter concerns the 'legislator humanus' or the 'demonstrable efficient cause of human laws' which for Marsilius is

> populum seu civium universitatem, aut eius valentiorem partem per suam electionem seu voluntatem in generali civium congregatione per sermonem expressam[43]

Marshall's translation of this definition might at first appear faithful to the original but it contains a significant addition:

> the lawemaker or cheyfe and propre cause effectyue of the lawe is the people or the hole multytyde of cytezens inhabytauntes or elles the byggest parte of the sayde multytude, by theyr eleccyon or wyll by wordes expressed in the generall congregacyon *parlymente* or assemble of the communes.[44]

Marshall has here effectively institutionalised the people's expressed will in Parliament, the representative body of the realm. Marsilius' doctrine has now been made compatible with English constitutional practice. Also inserted in this passage is the word 'inhabitants' which assigns an implicit territorial limit to citizenship and therefore to the exercise of the powers involved in law-making.[45] This territorial element is almost entirely lacking in Marsilius' work[46] and it reminds

---

[40] I.xii,3, P–O 50. Also the section immediately following on the ceremonies connected with election is omitted.

[41] III.ii, Nos 9 and 10, P–O 494–5, see Appendix.

[42] I.xii, P–O 48–54, Gewirth 44–9.

[43] I.xii,3, P–O 49, Gewirth 45.

[44] Marshall, fol.27v–28.

[45] Cf. above at n21.

[46] See W. Ullmann, 'Personality and Territoriality in the *Defensor Pacis*. The Problem of Political Humanism' in *Medioevo: Rivista di storia della filosofia medievale*, VI (1980) 397–410.

us again of the tension betwen the universalistic notions of the *Defensor Pacis* and Marshall's need to confine his doctrine to the realm of England.

The key point is, however, the inclusion of the word 'parlyment' and it is a point made abundantly clear throughout the chapter by means of various changes and additions:

> the humayne auctoryte of makynge lawes appertayn to the hole multytude of cytezens or communers or else to the bygger parte of them assembled in the parlyment'[47]

replaces

> Legum lationis auctoritatem humanam ad solam civium univ- ersitatem aut eius valentiorem parem pertinere,[48]

and 'legum approbationem, interpretationem, suspensionem ... ad solius legislatoris auctoritatem tantummodo pertinere'[49] is changed to 'the approbacyon ... of the lawe ... doth appertayne and belonge to the auctoryte of the lawemaker or parlyment'.[50] The marginal glosses add yet more weight; beside Marsilius' notion that all the citizens should judge the law,[51] Marshall adds, 'in all this longe tale he speaketh not of the rascall multytude but of the parlyment'.[52]

Thus far the argument would appear to be for the legislative supremacy of Parliament with the interests of the *utilitas publica* being served by the citizen representatives in Parliament who make the law. Marsilius' 'valentior pars' represents the 'universitas civium' as Marshall's 'parlyamente' represents the people of England.[53] Marshall does not, however, want to give Parliament the same powers as Marsilius' 'legislator'. And to this end, there are two further deletions from this crucial chapter which alter the whole perspective and set the tone for the remainder of the work. Firstly, Marshall omits

> The power to cause the laws to be observed [*potestas observationis legum*] belongs only to those men to whom belongs coercive force over the transgressors [*potentia transgressorum coactiva*] of the laws. But these men are the whole body of citizens or the weightier part

[47] Marshall, fol.28.
[48] I.xii,5, P–O 46, Gewirth 46.
[49] I.xii,9, P–O 53–4, Gewirth 49.
[50] Marshall, fol.29.
[51] I.xii,5, P–O 51.
[52] Marshall, fol.28v.
[53] For Marsilius' doctrine of representation, J. Quillet, *La Philosophie Politique de Marsile de Padoue*, (Paris, 1970), ch.VIII. For England, J. G. Edwards 'The *Plena Potestas* of English Parliamentary Representatives' in *Oxford Essays in Medieval History Presented to H. E. Salter*, (Oxford, 1934), ch.VI, 141–54.

thereof. Therefore, to them alone belongs the authority to make the laws.[54]

By eradicating this section, Marshall delineates the extent of his accommodation of Marsilius' doctrine; he refuses to give the people, or as he would say, Parliament, coercive force over the transgressors of the laws. Parliament participates in the making of law and in that respect is included in Marshall's definition of 'lawemaker'—Marsilius' 'legislator humanus'—but Marshall will not allow Parliament any coercive power. Therefore Parliament is not equivalent to Marsilius' 'legislator humanus' which does have supreme coercive jurisdiction.

From this point onwards, the terminology of the two works causes confusion since the terms used are often identical but their meaning has been completely altered. Marsilius' 'legislator humanus', in so far as it exercises coercive jurisdiction, becomes Marshall's 'prynce', 'kyng' or 'gouernoure'. For Marsilius, whose ruler—'pars principans'—was an executive of the 'universitas civium', this would have been a nonsense, since for him whoever had the power to the make the law had the power to punish transgressors of that law.

The second important deletion, concerning the authority of the 'legislator humanus' is the following passage:

> 'the authority to approve or disapprove rests with those who have the primary authority to elect, or with those to whom they have granted this authority of election. For otherwise, if the part could dissolve by its own authority what had been established by the whole, the part would be greater than the whole, or at least equal to it.'[55]

Here, Marshall denies Parliament the sole authority to 'approve or disapprove'; Parliament must not have full legislative autonomy, it acts as executor of the king's will. It is summoned by the king's will in order to pass law for the governance of his realm. This is demonstrated in chapter XV with reference to the establishment of civil offices which for Marsilius belongs to the 'legislator humanus'; Marshall adds 'The lawemaker or unyversal multitude in the parlyment assembled by the prynces commandment for the same purpose'.[56] Marshall toes the conventional line skilfully: Parliament is inserted as the general assembly of the citizens, but Marshall thereby turns Marsilius' doctrine on its head. Although, in constitutional terms, Parliament may be said to represent the people, its very existence depended on the king's will and its function was to serve that will.

---

[54] I.xii,6, P–O 52.
[55] I.xii,9, Gewirth 49, P–O 54.
[56] Marshall, fol.34v–35.

The right of veto and to amend law lay ultimately with the king, as did the right to call and dissolve Parliament; in England the part was greater than the whole.[57] Supreme coercive jurisdiction is given to the king, not to the people, nor to Parliament.

This fundamental point is reiterated in Marshall's conclusions: he replaces 'Legislatorem humanum solam civium universitatem esse aut valentiorem illius partem'[58] with 'That there is none other humayne or worldly maker of lawes but onely the prynce or his perlyament or (where it is so used) hole unyversyte and congregacyon of cytezens or elles the bygger and more parte thereof'.[59] And, 'In humanis legibus solum legislatorem vel illius auctoritate alterum dispensare posset'[60] becomes 'That in the lawes of man onely the prynce or else some other man by his auctoryte, may dispence'.[61] All authority is in the hands of the ruler, he may delegate it to others to act on his behalf and he may call a Parliament for the making of law. Clearly, therefore, he is not Marsilius' 'pars principans', the executive officer acting for the citizens, but rather the 'legislator humanus' who holds supreme coercive jurisdiction. Marshall does, however, admit that this might not always be the case outside England. Just as he is prepared to admit that the emperor is elected whilst stressing the hereditary nature of kingship in England, so he allows for a more popular form of government somewhere other than England—'(where it is so used)'.[62]

The nature of kingship is elaborated in chapter XV, the title of which is changed so that a discussion of what might be the best method of establishing the government and the other civil offices[63] becomes an assertion that 'the prynce in a communyte and Kyndome is as the herte in a sensible creature and without a kyng or prynce no communyte or kyngdome can stand, and partly of a prynces duetye'.[64] Almost all of the first five paragraphs are then omitted as they concern the authority of the ruler—'pars principans'—as derived from his election by the whole body of the citizens;[65] the 'pars principans' is the secondary, instrumental cause of the civil community: it has 'coactiva potestas instrumentalis'[66] but the 'legislator' is the primary

---

[57] This is an inversion of what Marsilius was saying, see text at n55.
[58] III.ii, conc.6, P–O 494, Gewirth 427.
[59] Marshall, conc.4.
[60] Marsilius, conc.8, Gewirth 427.
[61] Marshall, conc.6.
[62] Marshall, conc.4.
[63] I.xv, P–O 66.
[64] Marsall, fol.34.
[65] Later references in Discourse II back to this crucial chapter concerning election also had to be painstakingly omitted. eg. II.v,3, P–O 146, Gewith 129; II.vi,12, P–O 170, Gerwirth 149.
[66] I.xv,7, P–O 71.

cause and it grants ('concedit') that authority to the 'pars principans' to act as executor of legal provisions.

Marshall retains the instrumental power but increases it by attributing it to the king who is now both Marsilius' 'legislator humanus' and his 'pars principans'. For example, concerning appointment to civil offices, beside Marsilius' declaration that the authority for this belongs to the 'legislator', Marshall adds,

> he meaneth here of such offyces as the prynce or kyng wyll have instytuted by acte of perlyament else all other offyces and degres it lyeth in the kynges absolute power to appointe at all tymes.[67]

Marshall's prince may use Parliament but he retains the absolute power to do without it. The sovereignty of law as the embodiment of popular consent is crushed under the absolute claims to sovereignty of the king. This theme is further strengthened in chapter XVII, the title of which is changed from the general statement that the supreme government of a city or kingdom should be one in number,[68] to 'it is necessarye that there bee but one prynce, kynge or head gouernoure in a cyuyle communyte, unto whom all other heddes and offycers must be obedyent and subiectes'.[69] Marshall is able to shape this chapter so that emphasis is placed on the fact that the plurality of men in the civil community are conjoined in a unity of order because they all owe obedience to the king. This has important implications for the second Discourse and is clearly vital to Marshall's case for the royal supremacy, since Marsilius includes the priesthood in the 'universitas' and therefore, for Marshall, the unity of the clergy in England will derive not from their allegiance to the Pope but from their being subjects of the king. Discourse II is punctuated with reminders of this; for example the marginal glosses—'who soever resysteth the power of a kyng or hed prynce is of the devyll...'[70] and 'of true obedyence towarde kynges and prynces which the bysshop of rome with his churche yet never taughte'.[71]

Chapter XVIII, which deals with the correction of the ruler when he transgresses the law is, not surprisingly, omitted: 'The xviii chapytre we have lefte out all together as nothynge appertaynynge to this realme of Englande'.[72] Since Marshall had already given sole coercive power to punish transgression of the law to the king, there exists no mechanism for curbing and punishing him. For Marshall, the king

---

[67] Marshall, fol.35.
[68] I.xvii., P–O 89.
[69] Marshall, fol.37.
[70] Marshall, fol.111.
[71] Marshall, fol.110v.
[72] Marshall, fol.40.

can do no wrong since he is like the heart in an animal which always does naturally that which is appropriate and never the contrary.[73] But Marsilius maintained the necessity for correction:

> since the ruler is a human being, he has understanding and appetite, which can receive other forms, like false opinion or perverted desire or both, as a result of which he comes to do the contraries of the things determined by the law. Because of these actions, the ruler is rendered measurable by someone else who had the authority to measure or regulate him, or his unlawful actions, in accordance with the law. For otherwise every government would become despotic...[74]

Marsilius uses the 'legislator' to correct the 'pars principans'; but for Marshall, the 'legislator' and the 'pars principans' are one and the same thing.

In his 'fyrste dyccyon' Marshall succeeded in manipulating the text in such a way that its political radicalism was defused. Marsilius' theory of the whole body of citizens as holder of supreme authority was replaced by hereditary monarchy ruling by means of the law. Law for Marsilius was a 'praeceptum coactivum', useless unless observed and enforced. But whereas Marsilius gave supreme coercive and legislative power to the whole body of the citizens, Marshall placed coercive power firmly in the hands of an hereditary king who could delegate it to his officers.[75]

Marshall transformed Marsilius' 'pars principans' into 'prynce or soueraygne', but whereas the 'pars principans' rules 'by the authority of the legislator',[76] Marshall eliminated this and attributed all the authority and powers of the legislator to his 'prynce'. The translation might at first seem valid—'pars principans' becomes 'sovereign'—but the content of the term has changed completely. Parliament participated in the creation of law, and therefore features in one of Marshall's conclusions[77] when it is included in the definition of the term 'lawemaker', but it is not mentioned in the remainder since they pertain to the holding of supreme coercive jurisdiction which is the king's. However, by inserting Parliament, Marshall had not only

---

[73] Marshall retains the analogy of the heart which Marsilius took from Aristotle, *De partibus animalium* III.4.665a 29 ff. I.xv,5, P–O 69. By seizing upon Marsilius' use of a biological analogy and using it as the title of his revised chapter on the ruler, Marshall not only conventionalises the concept of kingship but also the terms in which it is discussed, that is, he returns to the familiar body politic imagery, abandoning the more abstract and legal terminology of the 'universitas' and its parts.

[74] I.xviii,3, P–O 97, Gewirth 87–8.

[75] See Marshall, conc.8. For all references to conclusions, see Appendix.

[76] 'Auctoritate legislatoris', Marsilius, conc.15, compare with Marshall, conc.10.

[77] Marshall, conc.4.

taught Marsilius to speak English, he had brought him into line with accepted constitutional practice.

The final chapter of Discourse I introduces the main polemical element in the work which becomes evident once the assertions made in Discourse I are applied to the church and to ecclesiastical jurisdiction in Discourse II. The Papacy is marked out as the chief cause of intranquillity, to which Marshall adds 'the bysshops of Rome with theyr desyryng of domynyon hath ben the causers of dyscorde and warres',[78] and the task at hand is made clear—to 'oppresse the usurped powre of the man of Rome'.[79]

Marshall is forced to make it clear in Discourse II that whilst the original work concerned the Empire and emperor, he is applying the arguments to England. The anti-papal argument hinges on the fact that the Pope was interfering in the Empire, usurping power. Marshall needed to retain these sections of the work whilst stressing that the king in England was facing similar problems. Marshall's work therefore becomes more explicitly comparative.[80] Now, given that Marshall effectively eliminated popular will or the consent of the people as being the origin of coercive political power and attributed it instead to the king, the theory being applied in the second Discourse is that of a divinely-ordained, hereditary monarch. Having stifled popular will and representation, Marshall lays greater stress on the other two major themes of the *Defensor Pacis*—the necessity of unity and coercive power for government, and the vital importance of peace and tranquillity for the smooth running of the perfect civil community. The latter is ensured by the former. But whereas in Marsilius it is the will or consent of the 'universitas civium' which legitimises the principle of coercion and unity in government, with Marshall, the voluntarist aspect is replaced by the notion of the christian prince who will, by dint of the divine character of his authority, always work for the common good.

In the second Discourse, the object of attack is the 'plenitudo potestatis' of the Pope, since it is seen as the greatest impediment to the rightful functioning of the civil community. The Pope was preventing the Emperor from acting as sole representative of the 'universitas civium/fidelis' and therefore was undermining the unity of Christendom. Thus it is increasingly the Emperor who is set up to

---

[78] Marshall, fol.42v.

[79] Marshall, fol.43.

[80] The increasing number and nature of the marginal glosses reflect this; for instance, where it is stated that all bishops must be appointed with the consent of the emperor [II.xxv,9, P–O 388–9, Gewirth 337], Marshall adds 'This he meaneth of bysshops within the emperours dominion for els the emperour hathe nought to do in the leccyon of bisshops in Englande'.

counter the universalistic claims of the Papacy. This makes Marshall's task relatively simple since, by omitting the fact of the Emperor's authority deriving from his election by the people, he can attribute all the power and authority of the 'supreme human faithful legislator' to the king of 'chrysten prynce'[81] whose only source of power is God.

There is, however, a problem to be overcome as it would be impossible for Marshall entirely to omit the election of the Emperor and the nature of his office and still retain the full force of the anti-papal character of the work. The argument against the Pope was precisely that he was impeding the proper functioning of the Empire and emperor by interfering in imperial elections and trying to keep the imperial office vacant for as long as possible. In chapter XXVI— 'How the Bishop of Rome has used this plenary power and primacy particularly with regard to the Roman ruler and Empire'[82]—the coronation of the Emperor by the Pope is explained as a mere mark of respect not a bestowal of authority:

> But who will say that such coronation gives any greater authority to the Roman pontiff over the Roman ruler than to the archbishop of Rheims over the king of the Franks? For such solemnities do not bestow authority; they only signify that authority is had or that it has been bestowed.[83]

The Pope's arrogation of authority in claiming to bestow and confirm the Emperor's power is the prime target of attack, and Marsilius focuses on the election, inauguration and 'coronacion' (as Marshall inserts[84]) of the Emperor. Marshall has to retain these passages but he minimises the damage to his own doctrine firstly by replacing the 'legislator' with the 'wyll of the electours' as that upon which the 'effect' of the election depends,[85] and secondly by means of an admonitory marginal gloss. At the point in the text where Marsilius describes the custom of having the Pope place the crown on the Emperor's head, Marshall adds,

---

[81] Particularly instructive is the translation of II.vi,13—that 'it pertains to the whole body of the faithful to *appoint* a judge'—as that it belongs to 'the hole congregacyon of faythful beleuynge people ... to *haue* a superyoure heed'. In Discourse II, as Marsilius' 'universitas civium' becomes 'universitas fidelis', Marshall begins to translate it as 'hygher powers', 'hygher powers or theyr deputees', 'superyoure powers' or 'superyoure or soueragyne' [see particularly II.vi.]. Also, as 'legislator humanus' becomes 'legislator humanus fidelis', so Marshall's 'prynce' becomes 'chrysten' or 'chrystened' [eg. in II.xvi.]. Thus Marshall generalises Marsilius' examples to include all temporal 'powers'.

[82] II.xxvi, Gewirth, 344.

[83] II.xxvi,.4, P–O 399–400, Gewirth, 346.

[84] Marshall, fol.107v.

[85] II.xxvi,5, P–O 401. Marshall, fol.108.

Let al kynges by this take hede how they suffre the bysshops to exercyse any ceremonyes about or upon them, yea or bysshop upon bysshop undre what coloure of holyness so ever it be, for in conclusyon an other daye yf they maye come a lofte, they wyll challenge therby a certayne relygyon necessarye holyness and a love of God.'[86]

Here Marshall warns kings not to let bishops consecrate them or each other in case there may come a time when the bishops will be in a superior position and will be able to exploit their power of consecration to claim that they confer royal office, just as the Popes have done with the Emperor. This is a clear warning of the dangers of *iure divino* episcopacy and is entirely consistent with what is known of Marshall's Lutheranism.[87]

Marshall clearly wants to claim supreme temporal and ecclesiastical jurisdiction for the king; the church is to be brought under royal authority. This is, of course, the doctrine of the royal ecclesiastical supremacy. Marshall thus concludes

that it appertayneth onely to prynces to iudge the persones which are to be promoted to ecclesyastycall ordres, and also to iudge the suffycyencye habylyte of any such persone by coactyue iudgement and that without the auctoryte of prynces it is not lawful for any bysshop or preests to promote any man to any such ordres.[88]

Here again Marshall has replaced Marsilius' 'legislator fidelis' with 'prynce'.

In his polemic against the Pope, Marshall was able to make stronger claims than Marsilius by using his own translation of Valla's *Confutation* of the Donation of Constantine,[89] to which he refers the reader in the *Defence of Peace*;

If thou wylt se the truthe of this gyfte rede the boke entytled the gyfte of Constantyne the emperour and thou shalt there se manyfestly that it was but forged of the bysshoppes of Rome.[90]

---

[86] Marshall, fol.107v.

[87] The distinction is being drawn between the *potestas jurisdictionis* and the *potestas ordinis* with a warning against allowing bishops to lay claim to the latter. For Marshall's Lutheranism see above n14.

[88] Marshall, conc.15. Compare with Marsilius, conc.21. Appendix.

[89] *A Treatyse of the donation gyuen unto Syluester pope of Rhome*, (Thomas Godfray, 1534) STC 5641. In a letter to Cromwell in April 1534 [*LP*.VIII.423], Marshall wrote of his book: 'I think there was none ever better set forth for the defacing of the Pope of Rome'.

[90] Marshall, fol.94, beside II.xviii,7, P–O 309.

Where Marsilius could only express doubts—'quidam dicunt'[91]—
Marshall was able to deny the validity of the Donation and other
extracts from the Pseudo-Isidorian decretals.[92] Many of the references
to Constantine in the *Defensor Pacis* are in fact omitted[93] but some
remain to bolster the supreme power of the Emperor over and against
the claims of the Papacy. For example, Constantine is remembered
as the first Roman ruler to allow Christian believers to assemble in
public—it was by his authority that the first General Councils were
held. Marshall exploits this by once more eliminating the popular
representative element and exchanging 'legislator' for the 'prynce'
who gives coercive sanction to the regulations enacted by the General
Councils.

The whole question of the authority and calling of General Councils
was much debated in England at this time. Indeed, Chapuys reported
that it was 'celle du monde que trouble plus ledict roy'.[94] Nicholson
has shown why the doctrine of conciliarism would be attractive to
some of the Henrician reformers; apart from being a treasure-trove of
anti-papal propaganda, it undermined papal supremacy on the
premiss of episcopal equality and replaced the Pope with the General
Council as the final place of authority and appeal.[95] Professor Sawada
has examined many of the written results of this enthusiasm for
conciliar theory in the 1530s and has concluded that from Henry's
Sententia de Concilio, to the *Treatyse concernynge generall councilles*, there was
an increasing emphasis on the extended scope of the king's jurisdiction,
strongly pressing the claims of *regnum* over *sacerdotium*.[96] The Pope's
claim to be infallible head of the Church is denounced and instead of
General Council of the Church is to be summoned by Christian
rulers. These ideas are reflected in a judgement of the Convocation of
Canterbury in 1536:

> Neither the bishop of Rome nor any one prince ... may by his own
> authority call ... or summon a General Council without the express
> consent and agreement of the residue of Christian princes and
> especially such as have within their own realms and seignories

[91] I.xix,8, P–O 105.

[92] Beside II.xxviii,19, P–O 451: 'I thynke this to be a loud lye forged in the name of
Constantyne as was the gyfte called the donacyon or gyfte of Constantyne', Marshall,
fol. 124v; and beside II.xii,8, where Marsilius refers to Constantine's gift to Sylvester,
Marshall adds, 'That coulde not the emperour do iustly'.

[93] See below n102.

[94] *Calendar of State Papers (Spanish)*, V.2.no.223.

[95] G. Nicholson, 'The Nature and Function of Historical Argument in the Historical
Reformation', Cambridge Univ. Ph.D. thesis, 1977, chap. I, especially on the writings
of Nicholas of Cusa.

[96] P.A. Sawada, 'Two Anonymous Tudor treatises on the General Council' in *Journal
of Ecclesiastical History* vol.XII (1961) 197–214.

'Imperium merum' that is to say such as have the whole entire supreme government and authority over all their subjects without knowledge or recognising of any other supreme power or authority.[97]

The authority of the General Council consists in the supreme power of the rulers who convoke it—they must hold *imperium* over the subjects within their realms—but the origin of that authority is not discussed. John Guy has noted that Christopher St. German compromised the populist element in his *Dialogue* (1530)[98] by substituting 'christian rulers' for 'faithful legislator' as having authority to summon and assemble General Councils and enforce their decisions, following news of the abortive Council of Mantua.[99] Marshall, writing at the latest in the Spring of 1533, prefigures these conclusions despite the fact that he was not under the immediate pressure of the calling of the Councils of Mantua and Vicenza.

The only reference to General Councils retained in Marshall's conclusions is contained in his twenty-fifth; 'that it appertayneth and belongeth onely to the prynces and gouernours in the communytes of chrysten people to gather by coactyue power a generall counceyll of preestes and bysshoppes and of other chrysten men'.[100] Once again, coercive power can, for Marshall, only belong to his king, prince or governor; the original 'faithful legislator or the ruler by its authority'[101] becomes 'prynces or gouernours' who, in view of what has been established above, do not derive their power from the people. This inclusion of the power to call a General Council is a consequence of the transferal of supreme coercive jurisdiction from Marsilius' *universitas civium* to Marshall's king. Whilst Marshall retains the calling of the Council of Nicaea by Constantine (as a useful precedent for other holders of *imperium*) and admits of the existence of General Councils, he entirely omits Marsilius' discussion of their authority and purpose.[102] Marsilius declares that authority to define meaning in Scripture

---

[97] 'Judgement of the convocation of Canterbury 1536', D. Wilkins, *Concilia Magnae Britanniae et Hiberniae*, 4 vols (1737), iii 808–9.

[98] Christopher St. German, *Dialogue in English betwixt a Doctor of Divinity and a Student of the laws of England* (London, 1530) STC 21561. Ed. for Selden Soc. by T. F. T. Plucknett and J. L. Barton (1974).

[99] J. A. Guy, *Christopher St. German on Chancery and Statute* (Selden Soc. Supp., 1985) 14.

[100] Marshall, conc.25.

[101] Marsilius, conc.33, Gewirth 430.

[102] The sections omitted are II.xviii,8, II.xx, II.xxi and III.iii. There are also numerous references throughout II which are systematically eradicated (as were those concerning election in I), eg. xix,1, 3 and 6, xxvii,9 and xxviii parts of (xxi) and (xxii).

belongs to the General Council,[103] that only the faithful human legislator can call a General Council[104] and that all decrees concerning
the church are to be binding only if they are by the authority of the
General Council or the faithful human legislator.[105] Also, it pertains
to the faithful human legislator to appoint to offices[106] and to distribute
ecclesiastical goods and benefices.[107] Marshall attributes all but one
of these powers to the king, the exception being the interpretation of
Scripture which is omitted altogether. For Marshall, Scripture stands
on its own authority, a conclusion entirely consonant with his known
Lutheran beliefs. There then follows an outburst of Protestant zeal
against the papists when Marshall explains

> The xx, xxi and xxii chapytres be lefte out as not of moche value
> and to auoyde the offence of some spyrytuall persones that beare
> peper in theyr noses and that iudge euery truthe to be spoken of
> malyce.[108]

The first two of these omitted chapters[109] are a detailed elaboration
of Marsilius' doctrine of representation—every province elects faithful
men to represent them and these assemble where it is most convenient
for the majority. The General Council thus formed is given supreme
power to determine interpretation of scripture, appoint to benefices
and so on. Marshall would not countenance giving these powers to
an elected, representative body; they could only belong to the king
who might then delegate them.

The third of the deleted chapters discusses the expediency of having
a bishop (with no coercive power) to be 'ceterarum caput et prin-
cipalior'.[110] Marsilius is anxious only to give an honorary headship
which must not be allowed to develop into a claim of *plenitudo potestatis*.
This chapter could not be assimilated into Marshall's account; firstly,
because it reaffirmed the authority of the General Council as representative of the faithful through a process of election, and secondly,
because it accorded one bishop supremacy over the others, albeit a

---

[103] Marsilius, conc.2. Marshall omits this, see Appendix.
[104] Marsilius, conc.33.
[105] Marsilius, conc.36.
[106] Marsilius, conc.21 and 23.
[107] Marsilius, concs.27 and 28.
[108] Marshall, fol. 95v.
[109] II.xx, 'To whom belongs or has belonged the authority to define or determine
doubtful sentences of the holy Scripture' [Gewirth 279]. II.xxi, 'To whom belongs or
has belonged the coercive authority to assemble a General Council of priests, bishops,
and other believers...' [Gewirth 287].
[110] II.xxii, 'In what sense the Roman bishop and his church are the head and leader
of the others; and by what authority this headship belongs to them' [Gewirth 299].

limited one. For Marshall, the only head of the church apart from Christ was the king in his own realm.

Marsilius' conciliarism is therefore greatly misrepresented in Marshall's translation; General Councils can only be called by 'chrysten rulers', they are representative bodies brought into existence by the power of the secular ruler, as is the Parliament in England. For the most part, Marshall avoids discussion concerning the General Council, that is, he deletes the discussion, since General Councils pertain rather to the universal church than to the emergent church of England. Marshall is almost exclusively concerned with England, only straying to the Empire, Emperor and General Councils where they are essential to retaining the anti-papal polemic.

Further, whilst for Marsilius the hope for unity and peace is the Emperor and the impediment the Pope, for Marshall all hope is vested in the king as supreme head of the church and of the realm of England. Therefore the immediate threat within the realm is that posed by a *iure divino* episcopacy and their clergy who owe allegiance other than to the king. As Marshall comments, 'The emperours ar vexed of the byshop of rome and so be all other kynges of theyr bysshops and clergye'.[111] Where Marsilius rails against the Pope's practice of absolution, Marshall adds, 'to absolue the subiecte from the othe and bonde of his allegeaunce is manyfest heresy' and 'Absolucion from synne and payne to all that wyll be traytours to theyr prynces'.[112] He uses Thomas Becket as the prime example of such treachery.[113] Marshall, in particular as a Lutheran, appears very anxious to settle the matter of the allegiance of the bishops and their clergy, hence the lengthy marginal glosses in chapter XVII on the authority to appoint bishops and other ministers of the church:[114]

> It were a wyse way now also one bysshop to be electe by an other yf man myght be sure that the bysshops were all of the apostles complexion but because there is a great doubte in that, thanked be to god a more wyse and sure way is found that the eleccyon and all together belongeth to the kyngs moste gracyous hyghenes[115]

---

[111] Marshall, fol.111v, marginal note to II.xxvi.

[112] Marginal notes to II.v,8 and II.xxvi.

[113] Beside II.viii: 'Preestes oughte to be punysshed by the secular iudge and yet Thomas of Caunterbury wolde not haue it so' [Marshall, fol.68v.]. And beside the statement that priests refuse to be subject to rulers and that they even claim to be superior to them in coercive jurisdiction [II.ix,8]: 'As obstynat Thomas of Caunterbury otherwyse called Thomas Beket' [Marshall, fol.71v]. Becket experienced a general reversal of favour under Henry VIII.

[114] II.xvii, P–O 288.

[115] Marshall, fol.91v.

but

It were to moche tedyous for the kyngs grace to be troubled his owne persone with the eleccion of every simple preeste ... and therefore his grace may commyt the offyce to them that ben undernethe hym which yf they wolde be neglegent and uncircumspecte in the leccyon of them, yet ought not the bysshop hastely to put his handes upon but shew the kyng thereof, in whom is the onely remedy.[116]

Once again, the king, as holder of supreme coercive jurisdiction over both civil and ecclesiastical matters, provides the solution to the problem of divided allegiance and divided authority; it is the king *in his own realm* who is the sole focus of obedience and power—the defender of peace.

Marshall's conclusions are a succinct expression of his doctrine; as revealing in their omissions as their distortion. Only thirty of the original forty-two remain. All references to General Councils, to election and to the 'episcopus Romanus' are removed.[117] He will allow no interpretation of Scripture, either by the prince or the General Council.[118] He omits all discussion of the status of supreme poverty, not only in the conclusions but in a substantial part of the second Discourse as well.[119] He retains the equality of all bishops thereby denying the supremacy of the Pope[120] and, with Marsilius, denies priests or bishops any coercive jurisdiction over clergy or laymen.[121]

There is only one mention of Parliament when it is included in Marshall's definition of 'lawemaker'[122] but in all other cases Marshall refers only to the king since it is supreme *coercive* power that is being delineated. Marsilius' 'legislator humanus' or 'legislator fidelis' is replaced variously by 'prynce' or 'prynces',[123] 'kyng or prynce',[124]

---

[116] Marshall, fol.91v.

[117] Marsilius' conclusions 12, 36, 9, 10, 18, 26, 32, 35, 26 and 41 are omitted.

[118] Marsilius' conclusion 1–5, Marshall's 1–3.

[119] The omitted conclusion is Marsilius 38. Also, in Marshall's words, 'The xiii and xiiii chapytres ben omyted as contaynynge no matter moche necessarye' (fol.82). These long chapters explain the virtues of voluntary poverty by means of copious Biblical quotations pointing to the conclusion that Christ and the apostles lived in this state of meritorious poverty whilst on earth. I think it would be to overstate the case to claim any direct connection between these omissions and the dissolution of the monasteries. Contemporary opinion may well have been the reason, but it is perhaps most likely that lengthy elaboration of the religious orders would rankle considerably with Marshall as they were an example of that mediation between God and man so odious to followers of Luther.

[120] Marshall, conc.12. Marsilius, conc.17.

[121] Marshall, conc.9. Marsilius, conc.14.

[122] Marshall, conc.4. Marsilius, conc.6.

[123] Marshall, concs.5, 6, 13, 14, 15, 17, 22, 26. Marsilius' 7, 8, 19, 20, 21, 23, 29, 34.

[124] Marshall, concs.20 and 24. Marsilius' 27 and 31.

'prynce or gouernoure',[125] 'gouernoure or soveraygne',[126] 'hed gouernoure',[127] or 'hym that is gouernoure'.[128]

It is evident that Marshall has attributed the supreme coercive jurisdiction that Marsilius ascribed to the 'universitas civium', to the prince alone and can therefore invest him with the functions exercised by different elements in the Marsilian 'universitas'. The consequent powers accorded to the king by Marshall are therefore remarkably comprehensive, particularly with regard to ecclesiastical matters. As well as the powers already discussed, he has the authority to legitimate bastards,[129] to allocate the number of churches, priests and other ministering officers,[130] to grant vowsons to colleges or religions,[131] and to command fasts and prohibitions;[132] all of which Marsilius attributes to the 'legislator'. More significantly, the king may 'use the temporalles of the churche or clergye outher whole or in parte of them for the publyke or commune utylyte or defence of the common weale'[133] and can 'dispose all temporalles which are ordayned for charytable causes'[134]—again only Marsilius' 'legislator' has these powers. Also, 'it appertayneth onely to the auctoryte of the gouernoure or soveraygne to iudge by coactyue iudgement heretykes and all trespasers and malefactors'.[135] The king's temporal powers are also extensive: he alone has coercive force over transgressors of the law,[136] he can 'dyspence with the matrymones forbydden by the lawe of man',[137] can loose people bound by obligations or oaths,[138] forbid certain crafts and the teaching of certain disciplines and grant licences to teach.[139] But, whilst the king has supreme control over the subjects, both lay and clerical, within his realm, he has no spiritual powers, nor may he dispense divine law.[140] He therefore resembles, not surprisingly at Marshall's hands, the Lutheran 'godly prince'.[141]

[125] Marshall, concs.25 and 27. Marsilius' 33 and 37.
[126] Marshall, concs.21 and 23. Marsilius' 28 and 30.
[127] Marshall, conc.19. Marsilius' 25.
[128] Marshall, concs.26 and 29. Marsilius' 34 and 40.
[129] Marshall, conc.14. Marsilius, conc.20.
[130] Marshall, conc.16. Marsilius, conc.22.
[131] Marshall, conc.22. Marsilius, conc.29.
[132] Marshall, conc.26. Marsilius, conc.34.
[133] Marshall, conc.20. Marsilius, conc.27.
[134] Marshall, conc.21. Marsilius, conc.28.
[135] Marshall, conc.23. Marsilius, conc.30.
[136] Marshall, concs.4 and 6. Marsilius' 6 and 8.
[137] Marshall, conc.13. Marsilius, conc. 19.
[138] Marshall, conc.24. Marsilius, conc.31.
[139] Marshall, conc.19. Marsilius, conc.25.
[140] Marshall, conc.3. Marsilius, conc.5.
[141] On the 'godly prince' see J. N. Figgis, *Political Thought from Gerson to Grotius 1414–1625*, (New York, 1960) 84 and Quentin Skinner, *Foundations*, II 12–19.

The changes and omissions made are thus largely the result of the clash between a divinely-ordained hereditary monarchy and Marsilius' 'pars principans' as executive of and elected by the 'universitas civium' or 'legislator humanus'. The clash is explicit in Marsilius' thirteenth conclusion – that no ruler has full power over the acts of others without the determination of the mortal legislator[142]—and therefore Marshall omits it. The origin of the ruler's authority is thus one of the major disparities between Marsilius' and Marshall's work, and this is the fundamental reason why the *Defence of Peace* should *not*, *pace* Nicholson,[143] be seen as an example of the 'ascending' theory of government in the 1530s.

The other major disparity is the intended scope of the work. The king has supreme coercive jurisdiction both ecclesiastical and temporal *within his realm*; he receives both his power and his kingdom from God. The scope of the monarchs' exercise of sovereignty is territorially limited, his subjects are the inhabitants of his realm. These issues are not dealt with by Marsilius; he is countering the universal claims of the Pope with the universal claims to supreme coercive jurisdiction of the Emperor.

Henry wanted to exercise *merum imperium* in his kingdom, to have supreme control over all the inhabitants of his realm, lay and clerical. Marshall saw in Marsilius' work the potential to substantiate a case for the royal ecclesiastical supremacy and to go further, that is, to satisfy his own desire to see a Lutheran solution to the king's 'great matter'. It is a credit to his analytical skills and his ingenuity that he was able to see the use of Marsilius' work for his and the government's purposes. He was able to exploit Marsilius' largely Aristotelian philosophy and terminology by altering it at a key point[144] in the development of Marsilius' argument, bringing it into line with English constitutional practice. He stressed the hereditary, *Dei gratia* nature of the monarchy in England, and governance by law made in Parliament for the good of the common weal. Parliament was not, however, a check on the king's will, but an emanation of it. His conclusions were certainly radical; and this, together with the length and repetitiveness of the work, may account for the poor sales figures which so distressed him. It was an extreme work published at a delicate stage of the Henrician Reformation; yet many of its conclusions prefigure the legislation of the Reformation Parliament. Marshall's translation and adaptation reveal a thorough understanding

---

[142] Marsilius' conc.13. See Appendix.
[143] Nicholson, 'Historical Argument' 217.
[144] I.xii, P–O 48–54.

of the premisses behind the royal ecclesiastical supremacy—he did not deserve to be remaindered.

APPENDIX: A COMPARISON OF THE CONCLUSIONS OF MARSILIUS OF PADUA AND WILLIAM MARSHALL

Marsilius'	*Marshall's*
1 Solam Divinam seu Canonicam Scripturam, et ad ipsam per necessitatem sequentem quamcumque, ipsiusque interpretationem ex communi concilio fidelium factam veram esse, ad aeternam beatitudinem consequendam necesse credere, si alicui debite proponatur. Huius siquidem certitudo est et sumi potest XIX Secundae, ex 2 in 5	1 That there is no Scripture, whiche of necessyte, we ar bounden to beleve to be undoubtedly true save onely the dyuyne or canonycall Scripture or what soever other scrypture it be, whiche necessarylye foloweth of the same.
2 Legis Divinae dubias diffinire sententias, in hiis praesertim qui Christianae fidei vocantur articuli, reliquisque credendis de necessitate salutis, solum generale concilium fidelium aut illius valentiorem multitudinem sive partem determinare debere, nullumque aliud partiale collegium aut personam singularem cuiuscumque conditionis existat iam dictae determinationis auctoritatem habere. Huius autem certitudo habetur XX Secundae, ex 4 in 13	*Omitted*
3 Ad observanda praecepta Divinae Legis, poena vel supplicio temporali nemo Evangelica Scriptura compelli praecipitur: IX Secundae, ex 3 in 10	*Omitted*
4 Solius Evangelicae Legis praecepta vel ad ipsa per necessitatem sequentia, et quae secundum rectam rationem fieri aut omitti convenit, propter aeternam salutem necesse servari; Antiquae vero Legis nequaquam omnia: IX Secundae, ex 10 in finem	2 That onely the preceptes of God in the newe lawe, or elles such as necessaryle foloweth of them or such thynges whiche accordyng to ryght reason are conuenyent to be done or lefte undone, are nedfullye for the obtaynynge of euerlastyng saluacyon to be observed and kepte but not all the preceptes of the olde lawe.
5 In divinis seu Evangelicae Legis praeceptis aut prohibitis neminem mortalem dispensare posse; permissa vero prohibere, obligando ad culpam aut poenam pro statu praesentis saeculi vel venturi, solum posse generale concilium aut fidelem legislatorem	3 That in the preceptes or prohybycyons of the newe lawe: no mortal man may dyspense

Marsilius'	*Marshall's*
humanum, nullumque aliud partiale collegium vel singularem personam cuiuscumque conditionis existat: XII Primae, 9, et IX Secundae, 1, et XXI Secundae, 8	
6 Legislatorem humanum solam civium universitatem esse aut valentiorem illius partem: XII et XIII Primae	4 That there is none other humayne or worldly maker of lawes, but onely the prynce or his perlyamente or (where it is so used) hole unyuersyte and congregacyon of Cytezenes or elles the bygger and more parte therof
7 Decretales vel decreta Romanorum aut aliorum quorumlibet pontificum, communiter aut divisim absque concessione legislatoris humani constituta, neminem obligare poena vel supplicio temporali: XII Primae, et XXVIII Secundae, 29	5 That the Decretalles or Decrees of the Popes of Rome or of any other bysshopes which ben constytuted or made by them, ioyntly or severally, without the graunte of prynces do oblygate or bynde no man to any payne temporall or punysshement of this worlde. This is declared of certaynte in the xii of the fyrst and xxviii chapytre of the second dyccyon.
8 In humanis legibus solum legislatorem vel illius auctoritate alterum dispensare posse: XII Primae, 9	6 That in the lawes of man onely the prynce or els some other man by his auctoryte, may dyspence. This is proved in the xii chapytre of the fyrste dyccyon
9 Principatum electum aut alterum qualecumque officium a sola electione auctoritatem habentis ad illam, nullaque alia confirmatione seu approbatione pendere: XII Primae, 9, et XXVI Secundae, ex 4 in 7	*Omitted*
10 Cuiuslibet principatus aut alterius officii per electionem instituendi, praecipue vim coactivam habentis, electionem a solius legislatoris expressa voluntate pendere: XII Primae et XV Primae, ex 2 in 4	*Omitted*
11 Solum unum numero supremum principatum esse debere in civitate vel regno: XVII Primae	7 That theyr ought to be but onely one chiefe soueraygne in a realme, this is euydently proved in xii chapytre of the fyrste dyccyon[145]
12 Personas et ipsarum qualitatem ac numerum ad officia civitatis, sic quoque civilia omnia determinare, ad principantis fidelis auctoritatem secundum leges aut probatas consuetudines tantummodo pertinere: XII Primae et XV, 4 et 10	8 That it belongeth onely to the auctoryte of the kynge accordyng to the lawes or approved customes: to determyn the persones and the qualyte and nombre of them, which shalbe offycers of the realme and also to determyne al cyuyll maters by them selves or theyr deputyes

Marsilius'

Marshall's

13 Nullum principantem, eoque minus collegium partiale vel singularem personam cuiuscumque conditionis existat, alienorum actuum monasticorum aut civilium absque mortalis legislatoris determinatione imperii plenitudinem seu potestatis habere: XI Primae et XXIII Secundae, ex 3 in 5

Omitted

14 Principatum seu iurisdictionem coactivam supra quemquam clericum aut laicum, etiam si haereticus extet, episcopum vel sacerdotem inquantum huiusmodi nullam habere: XV Primae, ex 2 in 4, IV, V, et IX Secundae, ac X, 7

9 That no bysshop or preeste in that he is suche one hathe any soveraygnte or coactyue iurysdyccion over any clarke or laye man, althoughe he ben a heretyke. This is euydentlye proved in the XV chapytre of the fyrste dyccion, in the iv, the v the ix and x chapytres of the seconde dyccion

15 Super omnem singularem personam mortalem cuiuscumque conditionis existat, atque collegium laicorum aut clericorum, auctoritate legislatoris solummodo principantem iurisdictionem, tam realem quam personalem, coactivam habere: XV et XVII Primae, IV, V, ac VIII Secundae

10 That onely the prynce or soueraygne hathe iurysdyccyon coactyue bothe reall and personall upon every partyculer or syngular mortall person of what so ever condycion or estate he be and also upon every partyculer colledge or companye of layeman and clarkes

16 Excommunicare quemquam absque fidelis legislatoris auctoritate ulli episcopo vel sacerdoti aut ipsorum collegio non licere: VI Secundae, ex 11 in 14, et XXI Secundae, 9

11 That it is not lawfull for any bysshop or preeste or for any colledge or company of them to excommunycate any man or to interdycte or forbyd the dyuyne seruyce to be done this is proved in the vi chapytre of the seconde dyccyon

17 Omnes episcopos aequalis auctoritatis esse immediate per Christum, neque secundum Legem Divinam convinci posse, in spiritualibus aut temporalibus praeesse invicem vel subesse: XV et XVI Secundae

12 That all bysshops are egall in the auctoryte whiche they have immedyately by Chryste and that it can not be proved accordynge to the lawe of god that one of them oughte to be above or under an other in spyrytuall or temporall thynges this is euydentlye proved in the xv and xvi chapytres of the seconde dyccyon

18 Auctoritate divina, legislatoris humani fidelis interveniente consensu seu concessione, sic alios episcopos communiter aut divisim excommunicare posse Romanum episcopum et in ipsum auctoritatem aliam exercere, quemadmodum econverso: VI Secundae, ex 11 in 14, XV et XVI Secundae

Omitted

Marsilius'

19 Coniugia seu matrimonia Divina Lege prohibita per mortalem neminem dispensari posse, humana vero lege prohibita ad solius legislatoris vel per ipsum principantis auctoritatem pertinere: XII Primae, 9, et XXI Secundae, 8

20 Natos, non ex legitimo thoro seu matrimonio, legitimos facere sic, ut hereditarie succedere possint aliaque suscipere civilia et ecclesiastica officia et beneficia, ad solum fidelem legislatorem noscitur pertinere: ubi supra immediate

21 Ad ecclesiasticos ordines promovendos ipsorumque sufficientiam iudicare iudicio coactivo ad solum legislatorem fidelem spectare, ac sine ipsius auctoritate quemquam promovere ad haec cuiquam sacerdoti vel episcopo non licere: XV Primae, 2, 3, 4, et XVII Secundae, ex 8 in 16

22 Numerum ecclesiarum sive templorum ac in ipsis ministrare debentium sacerdotum, diaconorum, et reliquorum officialium ad solum principantem secundum leges fidelium pertinet mensurare: ubi supra immediate

23 Ecclesiastica officia separabilia solius fidelis legislatoris auctoritate debere conferri et similiter auferri posse, sic quoque beneficia et propter pias causas reliqua constituta: XV Primae, 2, et 4, et XVII Secundae, ex 16 in 18, et XXI Secundae, ex 11 in 15

24 Notarios aut alios officiales publicos civiles statuere ad nullum episcopum

Marshall's

13 That the contractes of matrymonye or wedlocke prohybyted and forbydden in the lawe of god, can not be dyspensed by any mortall man and that to dyspence with the matrymonyes forbydden by the lawe of man dothe belonge onely to the auctoryte of the prynce. This is euydentlye proved in xii chapytre of the fyrste dyccyon

14 To legytymate basterdes and those that be begoten out of wedlock so that they maye succede by inherytaunce and recyue or take cyuyle or ecclesyastycall offices and benefyces belongeth onely to the prynce of a realme. This is proved by the same places whiche were rehersed in the last conclusyon afore this

15 That it appertayneth onely to the prynces to iudge the persones whiche are to be promoted to ecclesyastycall ordres and also to iudge the suffycyencye habylyte of any such persone by coactyue iudgement. And that without the auctoryte of prynces it is not lawfull for any bysshop or preeste to promote any man to any such ordres this is proved in the xv chapytre of the fyrste dyccyon and in the xvii of the seconde

16 That it belongeth onely to hym that is cheyfe gouernoure or soueraygne accordynge to the lawes of chrysten men to measure or set the nombre of churches or temples and of the preests, deacons and other offycers wiche oughte to mynystre in the same. The certaynte of this conclusyon is had in the places last rehersed

17 That the ecclesyastycall offyces whiche we have called separable or accydentall with benefyces and other thynges ordayned for godly and charytable causes ought to be given and lykewyse maye be taken awaye onely by the auctoryte of prynces. This is proved in the xv of the fyrste and xvii of the seconde

18 That to ordayne or make notaryes or other publyke and commune cyuyle

Marsilius'

pertinere inquantum huiusmodi, communiter aut divisim: XV Primae, 2, 3, et 10, et XXI Secundae, 15

Marshall's

officers doth appertayne to no bysshop in that he is such one neyther ioyntly with an other neyther seuerally. This is proved in the xv of the fyrste parte

25 Docendi aut operandi publice secundum artem aut disciplinam aliquam neminem episcopum, communiter aut divisim, inquantum huiusmodi, licentiam concedere posse; sed hoc ad legislatorem saltem fidelem aut eius auctoritate principantem tantummodo pertinere: ubi supra immediate

19 That no bysshop in that he is such one maye graunt either ioyntly or severally lycense to teache or worke or practyse openly in any art or dysyplyne but that to graunte these lycencyes appertayneth onely to prynces or to hym that is hed gouernoure this is proved in the places last rehersed

26 Promotos ad diaconatum, aut sacerdotium, reliquosque Deo irrevocabiliter consecratos in ecclesiasticis officiis et beneficiis, ceteris non sic consecratis debere praeferri: XIV Secundae, ex 6 in 8

Omitted

27 Ecclesiasticis temporalibus, expleta sacerdotum et aliorum Evangelii ministrorum (et hiis quae ad cultum divinum pertinent) ac impotentum pauperum necessitate, licite ac secundum Legem Divinam pro communibus seu publicis utilitatibus aut defensionibus uti posse legislatorem simpliciter et in parte: XV Primae, 10 et XVII Secundae, 16, et XXI, 14

20 That the kyng or prynce maye lawfully and agreably to the lawe of god use the temporalles of the churche or clergye either in the hole or in parte of them for the publyke or commune utylyte or defence of the commen weale, after that the necessyte of the preestes and other mynysters of the gospell and of those thyngs whiche appertayneth to the worshippynge and seruyce of god and of the impotent poore folke[146] is suffycyentlye prouyded for and satysfyed this is proved in the xv of the fyrste and in the xvii of the seconde dyccyon

28 Cuncta temporalia quae ad pias causas seu misericordiae opera statuta sunt, ut quae testamentis legantur pro ultramarino transitu ad resistendum infidelibus, aut pro captivorum ab ipsis redemptione, vel pauperum impotentum sustentatione, ceterisque similibus, ad solum principantem secundum legislatoris determinationem ac legantis vel aliter largientis intentionem disponere pertinet: ubi supra immediate

21 That it belongeth onely to the cheyfe gouernoure or soueraygne to dyspose all temporalles which are ordayned for charytable causes and to almone dedes and the workes of pytye. As for example such thynges whiche are bequeste in testamentes for the meyntenaunce of souldyers agaynst infydeles or for the raunsomynge of prysoners beynge in theyr handes, or for the sustenacyen and releve of impotent poore folke and suche other lyke thynges and that to hym onely it appertayneth to ordre the sayd thynges accordynge to the determinacion intencyon and mynde of the testator or otherwyse gyuer this is

Marsilius'

Marshall's
proved in the places last rehersed

29 Collegii cuiuscumque vel religionis vacationem concedere, ipsamque approbare vel instituere ad auctoritatem pertinet solius legislatoris fidelis: XV Primae, 2, 3, 4, et 10, et XVII Secundae, ex 8 in 16, et XXI Secundae, 8 et 15

22 That it appertayneth onely to the auctoryte of prynces to graunt the vowson of what soever colledge or relygyon and the same to approve and to alowe or els to reprove and disalow this is proved in the xv of the fyrste, in the viii, the x of the seconde dyccyon

30 Haereticos, omnesque delinquentes, et arcendos poena vel supplicio temporali iudicare iudicio coactivo, poenasque personales infligere, ac reales exigere, ipsasque applicare ad solius principantis auctoritatem pertinet secundum determinationem legislatoris humani: XV Primae, ex 6 in 9, et VIII Secundae, 2 et 3, et X Secundae

23 That it appertayneth onely to the auctoryte of the gouernoure or soueraygne to iudge by coatyue iudgement heretykes and all trespasers and malefactors and those whiche are to be ponysshed by temporall payne or ponysshement and to inflycte and enioyne paynes personall and reall and the same paynes reall to applye unto what use they lyst. This is proved in the xv of the fyrst in the viii the x of the seconde

31 Neminem subditum et per iuramentum licitum alteri obligatum, absque causa rationabili per fidelem legislatorem tertiae significationis iudico iudicanda, per episcopum aut presbyterum aliquem solvi posse huiusque oppositum adversari sanae doctrinae: VI et VII Secundae et XXVI Secundae, ex 13 in 16

24 That no subiecte or person, whiche is oblygated and bounde to another by lawefull othe maye be losed from the sayde bonde by any bysshop or preeste with out reasonable cause whiche is to be iudged (by the iudgement in his thyrde sygnyfycacyon) of the prynce or kynge and that the contrarye of this conclusyon is agaynst all true and ryghte doctryne this is proved in the vi the vii and xxvi of the seconde dyccyon

32 Episcopum aut ecclesiam aliquam metropolitanam simpliciter omnium statuere atque privare seu deponere ab huiusmodi officio ad solum generale concilium fidelium omnium pertinere: XXII Secundae, ex 9 in 12

Omitted

33 Generale concilium aut partiale sacerdotum et episcoporum ac reliquorum fidelium per coactivam potestatem congregare, ad fidelem legislatorem aut eius auctoritate principantem in communitatibus fidelium tantummodo pertinere, nec in aliter congregato determinata vim aut robur habere, ad observationem quoque neminem obligare temporali aut spirituali poena vel culpa:XV Primae, 2, 3, et 4, et XVII Primae, et VIII Secundae, ex 6 in finem, et XXI

25 That is appertayneth and belongeth onely to the prynces and gouernours in the communytes of chrysten people to gather by coactyue power a generall counceyll or elles a partyculer counceyll of preestes and bysshopes and of other chrysten men

Marsilius'
Secundae, ex 2 in 8

Marshall's

34 Ieiunia et aliquorum ciborum prohibitiones solius generalis concilii fidelium seu fidelis legislatoris auctoritate fieri debere; opera quoque mechanicarum artium ac doctrinas disciplinarum, quae Lege Divina nulla dierum exerceri prohibita fuerint, solum praedictum concilium seu legislatorem praedictum interdicere posse; ad observationem quoque talium arcere poena vel supplicio temporali solum legislatorem fidelem aut eius auctoritate principantem: XV Primae, 2, 3, 4, et 8, et XXI Secundae, 8

26 That the commaundynge of fastes and the prohybycyon and forbyddynges of certayne meates oughte onely to be made by the auctoryte of prynces. And that onely the aforesayde prynces maye enterdycte or forbydde the workynge and exercysynge of handcraftes or the teachyng of disiplynes whiche are not prohybyted by the lawe of god, to be exercysed and used in al maner of dayes and that it appertayneth onely to hym that is governoure to constrayne man to the obseruyng and kepynge of the same commaundementes prohibycyons by temporall payne or ponysshement

35 Canonizari aut tamquam sanctum adorari quempiam per solum generale concilium status et ordinari debere: XXI Secundae, 8

Omitted

36 Episcopis aut presbyteris aliisque templorum ministris si uxores interdicere convenit, reliqua quoque cira ecclesiasticum ritum, per generale solum fidelium concilium id statui et ordinari, ac solum eum, collegium aut personam, in hoc cum praedictis dispensare posse cui data fuerit eius auctoritas per concilium supradictum: ubi supra immediate

Omitted

37 A iudicio coactivo episcopo vel sacerdoti concesso semper ad legislatorem contendentem liceat appellare vel ad eius auctoritate principantem: XV Primae, 2 et 3, et XXII Secundae, 11

27 That it maye be lawfull alwayes for hym that is a suter or stryueth in the lawe: to appele from the coactyue iudgement whiche hathe ben graunted to any bysshoppe or preeste: to hym that is prynce or governour

38 Perfectionem evangelicam summae paupertatis servare debentem nihil immobilium in sua potestate habere posse absque determinato proposito quodlibet tale habitum vendendi, cum primum potuerit, pretiumque pauperibus tribuendi; mobilis autem aut immobilis rei nullius habere dominium seu potestatem, cum proposito scilicet vendicandi eam coram iudice coactivo ad auferente vel auferre volente: XIII Secundae, 22 et 30, et XIV, 14

Omitted

39 Episcopis reliquisque ministris evan-

28 That a multytude or synguler person

Marsilius'

gelicis quae ad alimentum et teg-
mentum necessaria fuerint, saltem
cotidiana vice, cui ministrant Evan-
gelium, multitudo vel persona singu-
laris secundum Legem Divinam et
suam possibilitatem exhibere tenetur,
decimas vero vel alterum quid aliud,
si superfuerit dictorum ministrorum
necessitati supplendae, nequaquam:
XIV Secundae, ex 6 in 11

Marshall's

to whom the gospell is mynystered is
bounde accordynge to the lawe of god
and after theyr or hys habylyte to
exhibyte and gyve to the bysshops and
other evangelycall mynystres those
thynges whiche shallbe necessarye and
nedefull to theyr nourysshement and
clothynge at the leastwyse theyr dayly
foode necessarye to the sustenacyan of
theyr lyfe. But in no wyse tyethes or
any other thynge yf it shall be super-
fluouse and more than shall be neces-
sarelye requyred to the supplyenge of
the nedes of the sayde mynystres

40 Legislatorem fidelem aut eius auctoritate principantem in subiecta sibi
provincia compellere posse tam episcopos quam reliquos evangelicos mini-
stros, quibus de sufficientia victus et
tegmenti provisum est, ad divina
officia celebranda et sacramenta
ecclesiastica ministranda: XV Primae,
2, 3, et 4, et VIII Secundae, ex 6 in
finem, et XVII Secundae, 12

29 That the faythfull lawemaker or he
that is gouernoure, by the auctoryte
of the sayde lawe maker maye in the
prouynce subiecte to hym compell as
well bysshoppes as other evangelycall
mynystres for whose foode and clothynge it is suffycyentlye prouyded to
celebrate deuyne seruyce and to
mynystre the sacramentes of the
churche this is proved in the XV of
the fyrste and in the vii of the seconde

41 Episcopum Romanum et alium
quemlibet ecclesiasticum seu templi
ministrum secundum Legem Divinam
per solum fidelem legislatorem aut
eius auctoritate principantem vel
fidelium generale concilium ad offi-
cium ecclesiasticum separabile pro-
moveri debere, ab eodem quoque
suspendi atque privari exigente
delicto: XV Primae, 2, 3, 4, et 10, et
XVII Secundae, ex 8 in 16, et XXII
Secundae, ex 9 in 13

Omitted

42 Possent autem aliae quamplures et
utiles conclusiones ex prioribus
dictionibus per necessitatem inferri;
quas tamen deduximus, contenti
sumus, quoniam ad praedictam
pestem cum ipsius causa succidendam
facilem atque sufficientem praebent
ingressum, et propter abbreviationem
sermonis

30 Other conclusyons bothe verye many
in nombre and also verye profytable
myght be inferred whiche by necessyte
foloweth of the determynacyons made
in the two fyrste dyccyons or partes.
But yet that notwithstandynge at this
tyme we wyll holde us contented with
these whiche we have all redy
deduced. For as moche as they do gyue
easye and suffycyent entraunce and
occasyon to the reder to geather and
inferre other suche lyke mo, and be
suffycyent also to the cuttynge awaye

Marsilius'	*Marshall's*
	of the aforesayde great myscheyfe otherwyse called the bysshoppe of Rome and also the cause thereof

[145] Note Marshall refers back to the crucial chapter in which supreme coercive jurisdiction is given to the king, where Marsilius does not.

[146] The distinction between the 'impotent deserving poor' and idle vagabonds was made in the Poor Laws from the 1530's onwards.

THE CONTINUITY OF THE ENGLISH REVOLUTION

The Prothero Lecture

By Lord Dacre of Glanton

READ 4 JULY 1990

IN our history, the twenty years from 1640 to 1660 are, at first sight, years of desperate, even meaningless change. It is difficult to keep pace with those crowded events or to see any continuity in them. At the time, men struggled from day to day and then sank under the tide. Even Oliver Cromwell, the one man who managed, with great agility, but spluttering all the time, to ride the waves, constantly lamented his inability to control them. When all was over, men looked back on the whole experience with disgust. It was a period of 'blood and confusion' from which no one had gained anything except the salutary but costly lesson of disillusion. How different from the Glorious Revolution of 1688: that straightforward aristocratic revolt against a king who had so considerately simplified the issues, and ensured a quick neat result, by seeking to convert the nation, like himself, to Catholicism!

It is the function of historians, happily separated from such distant events, to see past the details which it is also their function to reconstruct, and so to extract their significance. But do we in fact do any better than contemporaries? Are we not ourselves, unless we are the driest of antiquaries, parties in the struggle: royalists and parliamentarians, presbyterians and independents, levellers and anabaptists, successively hoisting and submerging each other in the same turbid steam? In the nineteenth century most historians were political historians, and they saw the revolution of the 1640s as a series of broken political experiments, convulsive stages in the struggle for parliamentary sovereignty. But then, by a happy coincidence, just about the time when the Labour Party was stealing the lead from Whigs and Liberals, that interpretation lost favour. Social equality, not parliamentary power then became the real purpose of the revolution, and the Levellers replaced the parliament-men as its heroes in the pantheon of Progress. But not for long; for soon, in the tense 1930s, when the Communists claimed the leadership of 'progressive' forces, 'radical puritanism' became the intellectual force of the revolution, Fifth Monarchists stirred again, and the voice of the Digger was heard in the land.

How recent those days are, and yet how remote they now seem! For now our history has been revised again. Toryism, a new kind of toryism, has emerged: not the old patrician toryism of Clarendon, or the revised consensus toryism of Namier, but an uncompromising populist, rather aggressive variant of it—the toryism of Peter Heylyn perhaps (who was a very learned man). Since 1980, we are told—I wonder why that date—all previous interpretations have been superseded: Lilburne, Winstanley and Hannah Trapnel have followed Pym, Hampden and Cromwell into the voracious historical dustbin, and the revolutions of 1641 and 1688 are alike dismissed as 'petulant outbursts', diconcerting, but not diverting, the smooth and stately operations of the English *ancien regime*.[1] To the Whigs, the consistent purpose of the revolution was political. To the socialists it was social. To the neo-tories it had no purpose at all: in fact it hardly happened.

In the face of these changing fashions, and this convenient but chastening synchrony of historical with political philosophy, some humility is in order. For if we all date, who can claim exemption from a universal law? Indeed, a recent reviewer of some writing of mine has made the point rather sharply. I am 'anachronistic', out of date, he says, and the proof is in my very language: do I not, like the Gladstonian Liberal S. R. Gardiner and the modern Marxist Dr Hill, refer to 'the Puritan Revolution'?

Well, of course, I do. Hang it all, one has to call it something, and I am not sure what the approved term now is. Perhaps we have gone back to Clarendon's 'Rebellion' (I was once declared 'anachronistic' for using that term: one is driven from pillar to post), or to that anodyne lawyerly archaism 'the Interregnum'. However, I am not much concerned with these semantic niceties. Words, says Hobbes, are wise men's counters but the money of fools. If you find me referring, in this lecture, to the Puritan Revolution of the 1640s or the Glorious Revolution of 1688, I ask you to believe that these conventional tokens claim no purchasing power. I do not regard the one as inherently puritan or the other as particularly glorious, though I confess that I think Puritanism was not entirely absent from the former and that the latter was, on the whole, in its time, a good thing.

With these cautious and protective provisos, recognising the danger as well as the advantage of afterknowledge, I turn to that most controversial era of our history and ask myself what continuity, if any, there was in those revolutions; and what most impresses me is the tenacity, over two or more generations, of those who, for all their

---

[1] The phrase in quotation marks is from J. C. D. Clark, *Revolution and Rebellion* (Cambridge, 1986) p. 130. I hope I have not misrepresented the argument of this lively and stimulating book.

differences and tergiversations (which are the normal incidents of politics, especially revolutionary politics), opposed and finally broke the Stuart monarchy. Men—especially conservative, traditionalist men of property—do not engage in revolution lightly, and persevere in it through changing times, merely through self-interest or inability to extricate themselves from the mess they have made. To suppose this is to trivialise both their aims and the risks that they took. For after all, the men who mounted the first great attack in 1640, and who never thought that they would find themselves challenging royal sovereignty, far less fighting a civil war with all its consequences, nevertheless, when faced with these consequences, refused to change course. In spite of everything, they persevered in a stubborn, costly and dangerous resistance, first to their legitimate king, then to all the alternative forms of government set up by the army which they had created to defeat him, until they, or their sons and successors, acquiesced, on conditions, in a system which seemed to secure their original aims; and when they found that it did not, and that the Crown, in spite of its previous experience, was resuming its former policy, then, in spite of their previous experience, and the reaction to it, and all their no doubt genuine disclaimers and promises, they did it again. This does not suggest mere 'petulance' or private interest or even mere 'high politics'. It argues a consistent purpose, or at least a consistent fear.

What then was this purpose, this fear? Obviously we must begin with the organisers of opposition: 'the great contrivers', as Clarendon called them, the men who, in the last years of the personal government of Charles I, at high risk and by intense machiavellian preparation, forced the King to face a parliament in which they had ensured their own predominance and were ready to seize the initiative. The skill with which they had secured this advantage, and the energy, determination and speed with which they exploited it to incapacitate the royal ministers is astonishing. How different from the noisy extemporised, bungled impeachment of the Duke of Buckingham fourteen years earlier! This time nothing seemed extemporised, all had been planned. Thorough met Thorough, head on, and took it by surprise. The personal rule of Charles I was to be not merely replaced but destroyed; and the measures for its destruction quickly followed: radical, rationally planned and forcefully executed.

On this they would never weaken. Whatever else was negotiable in the long struggle which followed, this was not. Tory historians, beginning with Clarendon, have argued that the initial differences were relatively slight, that the King was merely seeking to repair the old Tudor system, and that it was only by a succession of 'untoward accidents' and misunderstandings that the original rift was widened into the chasm which ultimately engulfed them all. But this is surely to overlook an important factor which Clarendon found it convenient to play down: the absolute, unremitting hatred, or rather fear, of Strafford and Laud. It was a fear born of the conviction that the government which these two men in particular represented and sustained was, if not a 'tyranny', at least the first stage of a process leading to 'tyranny'—that is, not to tyranny in the classical or propagandist sense, but to a legally institutionalised authoritarian monarchy on the continental model.

It has often been argued, and now it has become fashionable again to argue, that the struggle was over religion. But how are we to disentangle religion from politics in a revolution? Religion may form the outlook of an individual. It may serve as an ideological intoxicant for a crowd. But in high politics it is a variable. In 1640 the attack was on high Anglican episcopacy; in 1688 the high Anglican bishops were on the other side. The constant was 'absolutism'—whether of King or Protector, whether Anglican, Puritan or Catholic. Neither Anglicanism nor Puritanism nor Catholicism was objectionable *per se*: in spite of all the rhetoric, Roman Catholics suffered little persecution except when a scare was deliberately raised—and it was raised always for political purposes. They enjoyed a particularly comfortable time under the Cromwellian Protectorate. We may say that the issues were religious if we like, but what do we then mean by religion? Is it a difference of religion that troubles Ulster today? The change of Popery served to whip up popular hatred against Laud, but when he was brought to trial before his peers the accusation was political, of seeking to support absolutism. The peers who condemned him would be happy to settle for episcopacy; but it must be non-Laudian episcopacy, 'moderate episcopacy', severed from absolutism in the state.

Were their fears justified? Well, perhaps it is not for us to say. They were there; we were not. They had observed the signs, both at home and abroad. Particularly, perhaps, abroad, for there the consequences were spelt out, the comparison was clear. There they had seen how, in precisely those years, Richelieu had crushed the Protestant nobility of France and built up, at its expense, a royal absolutism sustained by a centralised national 'Gallican' Church. Sir Thomas Roe saw Laud as the Richelieu of England,[2] and Land in 1639, took special steps to recommend to his clergy the example of Richelieu's 'patriarchate'.[3] His enemies could see his drift. 'Better a Pope at Rome than a Patriarch at Lambeth', they retorted: a Patriarch sustaining royal absolutism, as in France.

[2] Roe to Queen of Bohemia. *Calendar of State Papers* (*Domestic*), 1635, 9.
[3] I have dealt with this episode in *Catholics, Anglicans and Puritans* (1987) 100–1.

An authoritarian state on the continental model, that was what the aristocratic leaders of opposition foresaw and feared. It might not exist, but they believed that it was coming, and must be stopped. The particular charges which they made in their campaign of resistance were pretexts: devices to enlist or retain necessary support. The charge of Popery was mere propaganda, as many of them knew and admitted. The grievance of ship-money was trivial and tactical. When that stage was past, and its passions cooled, ship-money would be extolled, in a Cromwellian parliament, as a model of equity.[4] Objections to the liturgy were equally tactical. Most of the Parliamentary leaders used the Prayer Book in their chapels; some of them patronised 'Arminian' clergy;[5] and who cared about the susceptibilities of the noisy preachers supported, for their own purposes, by 'our brethren of Scotland'? All these were pretexts, to be discarded after use. But opposition to a restoration of royal authority as exercised in the 1630s, or of an Anglican Church on the Laudian model, was constant. To prevent such restoration they would not shrink from extreme measures: mendacious propaganda, judicial murder, mob violence, intimidation, vandalism, civil war. It is difficult to refute the statement of Lord Saye and Sele, 'Old Subtlety', the mastermind (as some thought— and think) behind the Parliament, that 'it was not for a Service Book or for abolishing episcopacy that this war was made' but because the King had set out 'to destroy the Parliament of England, that is the government of England, in the very root and foundation thereof'.[6] Or, as it was put in more general terms by James Harrington, the only reasons why the people of England blew up their King was 'that their Kings did not first blow them up'.[7]

But if this was the compelling fear which united the opponents of Charles I and caused them to mobilise against him those other forces which in the end submerged them, what was their positive policy? The men who went to such lengths to change the form and course of government cannot have been without plans for its future exercise. If we look beyond immediate tactics and immediate responses to changing circumstances, we should be able to discern something of those

---

[4] *The Diary of Thomas Burton Esq.* ed. J. T. Rutt (1828) II 214, 218–9, 227–31.

[5] The Earls of Pembroke, Leicester and Northumberland insisted on pressing for the inclusion of the 'Arminian' Henry Hammond in the Assembly of Divines (*Commons Journals* II 595; *Lords Journals* V 84, 95–7). Northumberland's father had greatly valued Richard Montagu, Augustine Lindsell, and others whom Montagu regarded as 'honest men' (e.g. Francis Burgoyne). See *The Correspondence of John Cosin DD* (Surtees Society, 1868) I 68, 73n.

[6] (Viscount Saye and Sele) *Vindiciae Veritatis* (1654) 33.

[7] James Harrington, *Oceana* in *Works*, ed. J. Toland (1700), 129–30.

plans. I believe that we can do this, and that the plans were both political and social, but that the unexpected course of events caused them to diverge, with significant results in both political and social history.

Publicly, from the start, the men who forced the King to call the Long Parliament demanded a return to the system of government, which they idealised, of Queen Elizabeth. Many of them were themselves old Elizabethans with family traditions of public service and honour in Tudor times, and they looked back with nostalgia to Elizabethan precedents in foreign policy, religion and war. The Stuart Kings, they believed, had betrayed the Elizabethan inheritance, particularly—if a date is to be chosen—since 1612, with the death first of Robert Cecil, Earl of Salisbury, the last political link with Elizabeth, and then of Prince Henry, the white hope of the future. It was then that the cult of Queen Elizabeth took off—the annual celebration of her accession day, the painting of her tomb, and so on, all very distressing to King James; from that time that the lament for the good old days, now past, is heard from men like Camden, Sir Robert Cotton, and Fulke Greville. By the 1630s the nostalgia was undisguised and royalists had to take note of it. 'I am neither unmindful of nor ungrateful for the happy times of Queen Elizabeth', protested Clarendon, but still, the 1630s were just as happy, if not happier[8]; and Charles I, under pressure in 1641, would assure his critics that he had no other ambition than to restore all things to the state they were in in the time of Queen Elizabeth.

What did that mean? To the parliamentary leaders it meant government not of course by Parliament but by a Privy Council of which they would be members, managing co-operative parliaments when necessary and exercising lay control over an established Protestant episcopal Church. However, in order to sustain that happy system, certain reforms would be necessary. Such reforms had been proposed by Salisbury, but they had not been carried out. In particular, there was Salisbury's plan to rationalise the finances of the Crown so as to remove the grievances of the gentry: a plan made possible by his combination of the two great financial offices of state as Lord Treasurer and Master of the Wards. Had he succeeded, the oppressive feudal dues—wardship, purveyance, forest fines—would have been abolished and the royal revenue settled on impositions on expanding trade. In fact he had failed, as Lionel Cranfield after him had failed, and the feudal dues, instead of being abolished were exacted in the 1630s more efficiently than ever, so helping to finance the personal government of Charles I but at the expense (as Clarendon put it) of

---

[8] Clarendon, *History of The Rebellion* ed. W. D. Macray (Oxford, 1888) I, 93.

leaving 'all the rich families of England, of noblemen and gentlemen exceedingly incensed and even indevoted to the Crown.'[9]

From the surviving papers of the Earl of Bedford, the political leader of the reformers, it seems that he intended, once installed as Lord Treasurer, with his ally Lord Saye and Sele as Master of the Wards and his client John Pym, who was 'wholly devoted' to him, as Chancellor of the Exchequer, to resume the old policy of Salisbury: a policy in which Pym had been active as an official. In his commonplace books Bedford copied out and annotated some of Salisbury's plans; he set out a scheme for new inpositions on trade, to be sanctioned by Parliament; there is a 'project upon the Wards', a 'scheme for raising money for the King by freeing lands from wardship'; he discussed ways and means of rationalising Crown lands and royal forests with the great financier and customs farmer John Harrison; he planned a complete rationalisation of the expenses of the Crown,; and 'to my knowledge', says Clarendon, 'he had it in mind to endeavour the setting up the excise of England as the only natural means to advance the King's profit'.[10]

In the hopeful days before the execution of Strafford, all seemed set to ensure a quiet transition to a new government which would seek to carry out this programme. It was to be an inside job, fixed perhaps through the Queen. Outsiders were unaware of it. They could not understand why, after Strafford and Laud had been imprisoned and Lord Keeper Finch and Secretary Windebank had fled abroad, two of the most important ministers of the old regime, Juxon and Cottington, Lord Treasurer and Master of the Wards, one a Laudian bishop the other a 'popish Lord', were unmolested. Scotch Baillie hoped to see Cottington at least following Strafford on the route to Tower Hill.[11] Insiders knew better. They understood the mechanics of policy. The rhetoric against Laudian bishops and popish Lords was tactical only. Juxon and Cottington had made a private treaty: their security was guaranteed in return for a quiet surrender of the offices essential to the new programme.

A restoration of aristocratic government, a Privy Council working with parliament, a rationalisation of Crown finance, abolition of feudal dues—such was the form of government which would have replaced the personal rule of Charles I—had Charles I been willing to renounce it. No doubt there were contradictions in it which time

---

[9] Clarendon *op. cit.* I, 199.

[10] Bedford's notes of his projects are among the MSS of the Duke of Bedford at Woburn, by whose courtesy I have seen them. His discussions with Sir John Harrison are recorded in British Library, Stowe MS 326 fos. 71–7.

[11] *Letters and Papers of Robert Baillie*, ed. D. Laing (Edinburgh 1841–2) I. 186.

would have brought out. However Charles I was not willing and time was not granted. Within a few weeks, Strafford's death had made the King irreconcilable; Bedford was dead too; and a new train of events made all such projects, for the time, chimerical. Of Bedford's policy only fragments would be realised, not by royal government but by parliamentary ordinance, and for a very different purpose: the excise, introduced by Pym to finance war against the Crown, the abolition of the feudal dues in 1645.

But if the form of government was indefinitely postponed, what of its content, its policy? Here too the lineaments had been adumbrated in the 1630s. The same men who pressed for a return to Elizabethan forms of government called also for an (equally idealised) Elizabethan policy. It was an aggressive Protestant policy: England was once again to lead Protestant Europe, to intervene in the Thirty Years War, to strike Spain in the West Indies.[12] But it was also a policy of social reform: a policy which looked back to the 'Commonwealth men' of the mid 16th century and their Elizabethan successors—reform of the Church, reform of the law, reform of education. Though Protestant ideals, these were not necessarily puritan and they were certainly not revolutionary. Many of them had been advocated by Bacon, whose works were now widely published. It was only the polarisation of the 1630s which wedded them to 'puritan', or at least anti-Laudian, ideas and even to millenarianism, which also could be discovered in—or read into—Bacon's works.[13]

In fact, for convenience, we can call the social programme of the reformers of 1640 Baconian as the political problem can be called Cecilian. How such ideas were sharpened and given detail and amalgamated within an ideological context by Protestant refugees from the Thirty Years War has been set out, with great erudition, by Mr Charles Webster.[14] Here I need only say that the amalgam, which included simplification of law, re-allocation of Church property, extension of popular education, reform of universities, diffusion of useful knowledge, Protestant union, became the property of those who challenged the very different social ideals of the Caroline court and

[12] One of the 'extravagant particulars' referred by the House of Commons to its standing committee for the recess in the autumn of 1641 was the setting up of a West India Company on the Dutch model (*Commons Journals* II 288; Clarendon *op. cit.* I 386–7). The Dutch Calvinist scholar Johannes de Laet, who was a governor of the Dutch West India Company, was called in to give advice but found the proposals very amateur. See his letters to Sir William Boswell in the Boswell MSS (British Library, Addit. MS. 6395 fos. 120, 126, 131), and cf. the Grand Remonstrance, 3rd grievance.

[13] Bacon's supposed millenarianism was found in his *Novum Organum* and *New Atlantis*, and was explicitly cited by the millenarian prolocutor of the Westminster Assembly in his opening address.

[14] Charles Webster, *The Great Instauration* (1975).

the Laudian Church. Its patrons, in those years, define themselves: old Elizabethan churchmen like Archbishops Abbot and Ussher; opposition magnates like the Earls of Bedford and Warwick; parliamentary activists like Bedford's two clients John Pym and Oliver St John; advocates of intervention in Europe like Sir Thomas Roe and the whole interest of the exiled Palatine family; anti-Laudian bishops like Davenant and Morton; but not a single Laudian. Its grandest clerical patron was Laud's great enemy, the slippery Bishop Williams, now at last (it seemed) caught and lodged in the Tower. He had been Bacon's executor and, as Lord Keeper, his successor in office: a founder of libraries, a patron of scholars and scholarship, foreign Protestants, educationalists, 'puritan' ministers and 'all good causes', but, as one of his more cautious clerical *proteges* added, 'how far to trust him, I know not'.[15] On the whole, most people found it wise not to trust him too far.

When the Long Parliament met, Laud was sent to the Tower and Williams came out of it. Soon he was in command, regular in the House of Lords, constant on its committees,[16] chairman of two committees to reform the Church, eager to undo the work of the hated Archbishop, advising the King to let Strafford die, soon to be rewarded with the archbishopric of York. Meanwhile an assembly of clergy was nominated to meet and re-define doctrine and foreign advisers were summoned to be the architects of Baconian reform. When the great Czech reformer, philosopher, teacher J. A. Comenius, a professed admirer of Bacon, responded to the call and arrived in London, he was welcomed by the new intellectual establishment and invited to dinner by Bishop Williams. He too believed that a new government was round the corner, which would carry out all these reforms.

Of course it did not last. The Irish rebellion changed everything. By the end of the year, Archbishop Williams was back in the Tower. His committees had ceased to meet. The assembly of clergy had not begun. In Church and society, as in politics and government, projects of reform were suspended. Nothing had been achieved. Irish rebellion had started the slide into civil war.

History is often at the mercy of accident. It is often linked to individual lives. If the smallpox—that terrible new disease of the century—had carried off Strafford instead of Bedford, or had taken Charles I as it would afterwards, at an equally critical moment, take his son-in-law William II of Orange, who can say what would have

---

[15] William Welles to John Dury, 20 Sept. 1930, cited in G. H. Turnbull, *Hartlib, Dury and Comenius* (1947) 136.
[16] The Lords' Journals show that Williams was one of the most active of peers in committee—far more than any other bishop.

happened? As it was, the moment was lost. But whereas the programme of political reform had foundered indefinitely, the ideal of
social reform which had been envisaged in 1640, and for which the
ground had been prepared, was not forgotten. In all the succeeding
years of civil war and revolution, we see it regularly re-emerging as
the consistent aspiration of the parliamentary leaders. Inevitably, in
those years of turmoil and frustration, circumstances changed, tempers
worsened, resources shrank, and as each attempt at settlement failed,
a fresh price had to be paid in order to satisfy creditors, preserve
alliances and keep further revolution at bay. The Anglican liturgy
would be sacrificed to the Scots, Church lands sold to pay the army,
Ireland pawned to war financiers, 'images' abandoned to the mob.
But in spite of this the basic aims remained constant: parliaments
'freely' elected; an established protestant Church without coercive
powers, erastian and, to some extent, tolerant; reform of the law;
reform of education. In proposed treaties with the King, in composition with royalists, in regulations for the sale of Church lands, and
in specific ordinances throughout the period of war, these aims are
re-asserted or implemented; and after 1649, under changing forms of
government, the same course is pursued. For forms of government in
themselves, it is repeatedly said, are indifferent: the King's head was
not cut off because he was King, nor the Lords abolished because
Lords, nor the Long Parliament expelled because a Parliament, but
because they had 'betrayed their trust'. And that trust was social as
well as political.

It was a zigzag course. Take reform of parliament—freedom of
election, equality of representation. Though the electoral patronage
of great lords had been used to create the Long Parliament (how else
were Pym and St John elected?), such patronage worked both ways,
and from the beginning it was attacked. In challenged elections,
the committee of privileges decided, almost always, in favour of the
candidate supported by the wider franchise. In December 1641 Oliver
Cromwell, as yet a mere backbencher, moved that letters of commendation be altogether disallowed. In the 'recruiter elections of 1645
they were explicitly forbidden: even the Earl of Warwick, the great
patron of Puritan gentry and Puritan ministers, was not permitted to
recommend his son. At the same time projects of a new general
franchise were being canvassed and hitherto unrepresented areas, like
the county palatine of Durham, demanded representation. In 1653
these projects were realised. County Durham was represented in the
Barebones Parliament, and the new Protectoral constitution provided
for a completely new system. The franchise was lowered, the borough
seats were slashed, the rotten boroughs disappeared, the independent
county seats were multiplied. New industrial towns—Manchester,

Leeds, Bradford, were separately represented. It was the first and only systematic reform of the electoral system until 1832.

Or take the reform of the Church. The national assembly elected in 1641 had not then met, but by the end of the war its surviving non-royalist members composed the Westminster Assembly. Bishop Williams' committees had been overtaken by events, but their proposals re-surfaced during the civil war. In the sequestration of lands, provision was regularly made for the augmentation of livings. The corporation of Feoffees for Impropriations, an institution designed for that purpose in the 1630s, was freed in 1645 from the judgement given against it in Laudian times, and encouraged to resume its work. A series of ordinances provided for the better maintenance of ministers. Commissions for the propagation of the Gospel were set up. When the radical attack on tithes had been beaten off, the Protector put out his ordinance setting up Triers and Ejectors. The radicals screamed that this was worse than the old High Commission; but if we look at the lists, we find that this only means that the few radical agitators had been dropped from the old commissions. It was of this settlement that the 'Presbyterian' Baxter would afterwards write, 'I bless God who gave me, even under a usurper whom I opposed, such liberty and advantages to preach his Gospel with success which I cannot have under a King to whom I have sworn and performed true subjection and obedience',[17] and under it that many Anglican clergy— to the dismay of the Laudian stalwarts—were tempted to join the new non-episcopal establishment.[18]

Then there was reform of the law, long ago advocated by Bacon.[19] That cause too was damaged by radical advocacy. But the Long Parliament, the Rump, and the Cromwellians did not abandon it. The Rump passed laws in favour of poor debtors and for the Englishing of legal proceedings. Once the radical distractions were over, Cromwell returned to the problem. In his first nine months as Protector he produced the ordinance for the reform of Chancery: a measure which had been advocated by Bacon himself as head of that court. In his second parliament, he demanded reform of the criminal law. It was a reform that would be made effective only in the nineteenth century by Sir Robert Peel. The legal reforms of the Rump, having been reversed in 1660, would similarly be made effective in the nineteenth century.

Finally there is reform of education. Bacon, who thought that in

[17] *The Autobiography of Richard Baxter* (Everyman edition) 71, 80.
[18] The correspondence of Henry Hammond and Gilbert Sheldon in British Library, Harleian MS 6942 shows the concern of the orthodox at these developments.
[19] For Bacon's plans of law reform see C. R. Niehaus, 'The issue of Law Reform in the Puritan Revolution'. (Ph.D. thesis, Harvard 1957).

his time, 'of grammar schools there are too many',[20] had advocated a multiplication of elementary schools, the creation of local universities, and the reception of 'the new philosophy' in the universities. His disciples preached these doctrines in the 1630s and patronised the 'Baconian' educational reforms, Samuel Hartlib, John Dury, and, when he came to England in 1641, Comenius. In 1642, on the outbreak of civil war, Comenius left in despair, but Hartlib and Dury remained as the advocates of educational (and other) reform, pensioned by the Parliament. From 1646 onwards there was a continuous expansion of elementary schools.[21] At the same time Oxford and Cambridge were 'reformed' and the demands for local universities were repeated. Under the Protectorate both processes were continued. Oxford had become the centre of the new Baconian science, the nucleus of the future Royal Society. Cromwell, in his last year, realised the dream of the Long Parliament, the project of the Rump, and founded Durham College—its professors all drawn from the Hartlib circle.[22] His son Henry, as Lord Deputy in Ireland, planned a similar college in Dublin as a rival to Trinity College—as Durham College had been seen as a rival to Oxford and Cambridge. By then it was too late. Durham College died with its creator; the new college at Dublin was never born. Both were ultimately realised, in a different form, in the nineteenth century: Durham University in 1832, University College, Dublin, in 1851.

What for convenience we may call the Baconian reforms of 1641–59 were at best tentative and fragmentary. Always they were at the mercy of more immediate, more pressing problems: problems first of war, then of the defence of the stabilisation of the republic. Some of them, perhaps were unpractical. But we may still ask what would have happened if they had been given a chance: if the Cromwell dynasty had taken root and become, like the equally usurping Tudor dynasty, an established monarchy. This evidently was the hope of 'the Kingship party', the men who, from 1656, sought to demilitarise and legitimise the *de facto* monarchy of Cromwell and place it on the old civilian base, with two houses of Parliament and an established erastian Church. If they had succeeded, Cromwell would, in many ways, have forestalled William of Orange. Indeed, in some ways he did forestall him in the conquest of Ireland, union with Scotland, the return of England as a military power to Europe. In that case the decisive breach with the past would have been political; for how could such a new monarchy have resumed the broken thread of traditional politics with a legitimate Pretender waiting in the wings? To a dynasty founded in regicide, Carlism would have been a more serious threat

[20] Bacon, *Works*, ed. J. A. Spedding, (1857–74) xi.252.
[21] W. A. L. Vincent, *The State and School Education 1640–1660* (1950).
[22] Webster, *op. cit.* 232–42, Appendix II.

than Jacobitism after 1688. However, the new monarchy would presumably have retained and continued some at least of the social reforms which were the substance and justification of the revolution. The political breach would have been matched by social continuity: a breach with the past, continuity with the future.

In fact, since the Protectorate failed, the formula was reversed. In 1660 the revolution was rejected and political continuity with the monarchical past was restored—restored with lawyerly precision, from the moment of its breakdown in 1641: that is, from and including the reforms of the aristocratic 'great contrivers' which Charles I had accepted on paper but not, perhaps, in his heart. By this strictly legal formula the whole period from 1641 to 1660 was defined as an aberration: the parliamentary bills to which the King had formally assented were accepted as valid; the parliamentary ordinances automatically lapsed. So the prerogative courts remained abolished, ship-money and forest fines remained condemned, the triennial act remained in force. Even those parts of Bedford's programme which had not the benefit of statute were rescued from the ruined heap of ordinances and legitimised: the excise, the abolition of the feudal dues, were re-enacted by statute. So the aristocratic leaders who had lost control in the 1640s, who had stood aloof during the military usurpation, who had refused to countenance Cromwell's House of Lords, now returned to resume political life where they had left off, on their own terms.

However, they returned with a difference. In the 1630s they had patronised a social programme with a long pedigree behind it. Now they did not. That programme, which originally was neither puritan nor revolutionary, but which had been polarised by the struggle of parties, was now fatally compromised by its association with regicide, revolution and military rule. A few piecemeal reforms of the 1650s were indeed adopted after 1660. County Durham, in 1663, recovered its parliamentary franchise (the old unreconstructed Laudian Bishop Cosin resisting to the end), though Manchester, Leeds and Bradford did not. Some law-proceedings were Englished. But systematic parliamentary reform (already jettisoned with its constitutional warrant, the Instrument of Government of the First Protectorate), like systematic law reform, redistribution of Church lands, reform of the universities, new universities, had to wait till the 19th century. How appropriate that the tireless prophet and formulator of such reform, Samuel Hartlib, disappeared from the historical record after his death in 1662 until the mid nineteenth century and that his massive archive should have lain hidden till our own time![23]

[23] Hartlib emerged from his long obscurity, thanks to the dedication to him of Milton's treatise *Of Education*, in D. Masson, *Life of John Milton* (1859–94). His papers, last recorded in 1667, were rediscovered in a solicitor's office in Chester in 1945.

History does not stop, and from the new base, established in 1660, politics continued as before. The chastening memory of the recent past, a new generation, a new climate of opinion, brought a change of attitude. But before long the old tensions returned. On one side was the renewed drive of the Crown towards a legally institutionalised 'absolutism', on a continental model, supported by an established, hierarchical national church; on the other the determination of the aristocracy, animated by half-feudal, half-whiggish doctrines, to resist and contain that drive. Often, on this side as on that, the families are the same: the heirs or successors of Bedford, Essex, Leicester, Northumberland,[24] Argyll against the sons of Charles I with their new courtier nobility. Sometimes a single life, like that of Shaftesbury, links the two movements. The appeal, on both sides, was to the same arguments: Filmer, who had written during the first revolution, provided reasons against the second; Whigs drew on republican, John Locke on Leveller precursors.[25] The methods were the same too: conspiracy abroad (in Holland this time, not Scotland), alleged Popish plots (though this time more plausible), unscrupulously exaggerated and exploited parliamentary and municipal manipulation.

Once again what must strike us is surely the tenacity of the opposition. They took the same risks and showed the same resolution in resistance, the penalties for which, after all, were not slight: indeed they were now far greater than before. To forget that is to trivialise a great struggle. And now, as then, they drew strength from the European context within which that struggle was fought. Then it was the early Habsburg triumphs of the Thirty Years War and Richelieu's reduction of the Huguenot (and not only the Huguenot) nobility of France; now it was the conquests of Louis XIV and the mounting pressure leading to the wholesale expulsion of the Huguenots. And once again it was a damned close-run thing. Charles I, in 1640, had all the advantages of law and possession: what a huge effort had been necessary to mobilise resistance to him! Politically, James II's position was better: no Scottish war drained his strength and forced his hand. If only he had not madly tried to shift his ideological base from the national Anglican to the anti-national Catholic Church, perhaps he would have succeeded where his father had failed. At least he would not have collapsed so quickly.

Perhaps then we would have had another civil war, in which the

---

[24] The Percy earldom of Northumberland was extinct in 1670, but the family tradition was very consciously maintained by the last Earl's grandson, the Whig martyr Algernon Sidney (see Jonathan Scott, *Algernon Sidney and the English Republic 1623–1677* (Cambridge 1988).

[25] Locke's real radicalism and its relation to Leveller ideas is well brought out by Richard Ashcraft, *Locke's Two Treatises of Government* (Princeton 1989).

political and social radicalism which had been defeated in 1660 would
have had a second chance. Certainly its advocates were prepared to
take that chance: better prepared than fifty years earlier. For this time
men were ideologically better prepared: they thought in terms of
revolution, even political assassination; then they had waited till events
forced them to think. Now the men controlled the events. They were
also served by luck: the luck that James II, who had an army, lost his
nerve, while Charles I, who had no army, kept his. Hence the 'glory'
of their revolution which, by its speedy success, confirmed the political
achievements of 1641 and 1660 and stopped social revolt before it
could begin. This time, control never left their hands: the coalition of
1688–9 did not split as that of 1640–1 had split—as it would have
been split but for the popish folly. When the old revolutionary
Edmund Ludlow came from Switzerland to London to play his part,
he was promptly sent back again; the radical heirs of the Levellers
found no point of entry into the fray; if William III was another
Cromwell, he was a more acceptable Cromwell, with a presumptive
title and without a radical past.

The classical Whig historians of the last century, looking back from
a time of Liberal triumph, saw the revolutions of the seventeenth
century as stages in the battle for parliamentary sovereignty and the
supremacy in Parliament of the House of Commons. They had some
contemporary warrants for such an interpretation, and certainly the
process led, or pointed, in that direction. But it is a mistake to deduce
intentions from results,[26] and very few wars end by achieving the
purposes for which they were begun. Carlyle, who created the public
image of Cromwell as a living historical figure, dramatised his hero's
failure as the beginning of nearly two centuries of torpor and
stagnation. Perhaps his grotesque personalisation contains a glimmer
of truth. Looking back from the revolutionary 1840s, he was aware,
as few of his contemporaries were, of the social dimension of revolution,
whether English or French. Perhaps these two interpretations, both
now unfashionable, are not incompatible with each other, or even, if
suitably qualified, with historical truth.

---

[26] As is elegantly shown in J. S. A. Adamson, 'Eminent Victorian, S. R. Gardiner
and the Liberal Hero', *Historical Journal* (1990).

CHRISTIAN LIFE IN THE LATER MIDDLE AGES:
PRAYERS

By John Bossy

READ 15 SEPTEMBER 1990

IN 1945, which is beginning to seem a long time ago, Dom Gregory Dix published *The Shape of the Liturgy*. In the last two chapters of the book he expressed a view about the devotional and liturgical practice of the late Middle Ages which will provide a convenient starting-point for my subject. He said that the trouble about the medieval Mass was its separation of the 'corporate offering' assumed to have occurred in the primitive liturgy from the 'priesthood of the priest'; the notion of worship it expressed, like the doctrine of the eucharist it exemplified, was 'inorganic'. The effect of this was to let in, especially during the fifteenth century, non-liturgical, individualist forms of devotion which were unparticipatory and obsessed with historical facts about the life of Christ, notably with the facts of his Passion. 'The quiet of low mass afforded the devout an excellent opportunity for using mentally the vernacular prayers which they substituted for the Latin text of the liturgy as their personal worship ... The old corporate worship of the Eucharist is declining into a mere focus for the subjective devotion of each separate worshipper in the isolation of his own mind.' Liturgical doing had subsided into inactive seeing and hearing, on the way to being engulfed in a miasma of private thinking and feeling. The Protestant reform of the liturgy amounted to pickling this pre-Reformation devotional tradition while dropping the ritual performance to which it had been loosely attached.[1]

Dix was not talking about all prayers, but I think he was offering by implication a history of prayers in the late Middle Ages. His description, besides being a fairly standard kind of liturgical scholar's view, falls into a familiar class of historical or sociological lines which state that at some time we were all one, and somehow or other, as by Italian despotism, the Reformation, bureaucracy, the rise of capitalism or the advent of Mrs Thatcher, became separated out into atomic individuals. Speaking as one who has not been immune from such lines, I should like to approach the subject as empirically as I

[1] Gregory Dix, *The Shape of the Liturgy* (1945), esp. 594–608. If we may judge by C. Jones, G. Wainwright and E. Yarnold, *The Study of Liturgy* (1978), 36 f, most of these views still flourish.

can. Empiricism seems to call for two modifications to Dix's description, one of language and one of substance. I am fairly sure that the words 'corporate' and 'organic' should not be used in connection with prayers, and shall use instead a distinction between social prayers and devotional prayers. Social prayers are, as I use the word, mainly something to do with one's relation to one's neighbour; devotional prayers more directly to do with one's relation to God or to other objects of religion. The modification of substance arises from Dix's not having talked about one principal area of the subject. Although a monk, he did not find it necessary to discuss the monastic input to late medieval devotion. I presume that he had in mind, particularly in his final point about the Reformation, the passage from the monastic breviary, via the attempted reform of Cardinal Quiñones, to Cranmer.[2] But he did not talk about the influence of the monastic office in the lay prayer-books, books of hours and primers, about which it is now possible to say a good deal. When I have said something about these, I shall take up Dix's narrower subject, and talk about prayers at Mass; to start with, I shall say a very little about 'popular' prayers.

The Church had two prayers, both entirely scriptural, which everybody was supposed to know by heart: the *Paternoster* and the *Ave*. One was, broadly speaking, a social prayer, the other a devotional one. In the last of the homilies of his *Festial*, John Mirk expounded the petitions of the Lord's Prayer as seven prayers against the seven deadly sins. 'Our Father ... hallowed be thy name' was a prayer against pride: to live in peace and charity as brothers and sisters of one another and of Christ, and to pray for the conversion of disbelievers and idolators. The next two petitions were against covetousness, ambition, envy and disobedience; the last four, against sloth, wrath, gluttony and lechery, and in general against the Fiend and his vehicles of temptation. Mirk thought that people should say the *Paternoster* in English, and implied that they said or should say grace before and after meat.[3] He said almost nothing in his sermon on the *Ave*, except that it was a very devout prayer, that it should be said in English, and that one said devoutly was better than a hundred. This was a very proper piece of advice in the age of the prayer-bead. As Jan Rhodes has explained, it was scarcely before 1500 that the popular-meditative 'Rosary', or something like it, began to appear in England; it needed the Elizabethan mission, and in particular Henry Garnet, to

[2] Jones *et al.*, *The Study of Liturgy*, 383 f.
[3] *Mirk's Festiall: a Collection of Homilies*, ed. T. Erbe, i (E[arly] E[nglish] T[ext] S[ociety], extra series 96; 1905), 282–288.

turn it into the powerful instrument of thoughtful devotion, instruction and Catholic solidarity which it became. Surprisingly (to me) for his fourteenth-century date, Mirk included the name Jesus in the *Ave*, but not of course the formal prayer ('... now and at the hour of our death') which was added in the sixteenth century: the *Ave* was still, properly speaking, not a prayer but a salutation.[4]

One of the more widely practised forms of multiple repetition of the *Ave*, which eventually formed the framework of the Rosary—one hundred and fifty *Aves* divided into fifteen 'decades' each preceded by a *Paternoster* and followed by a doxology—was known as the *Lady Psalter*. As the number 150 implies, being the number of the psalms, this was an attempt to enable the unlettered to do something on the model of the monastic liturgy, and therefore to feel themselves in some way united with the efforts of the professional pray-ers.[5] For the more or less lettered this function was performed, between the middle of the fourteenth century and the middle of the sixteenth, by the Book of Hours, or Primer. This extremely interesting *genre* is now getting something like its due: the efforts of the founding fathers, Bishop and Littlehales, have been seconded by the art historians, and now by the work, on France, of the young American scholar Virginia Reinburg and, on England, of Eamon Duffy. I am greatly indebted to both of them, and especially to Dr Reinburg.[6]

Now, sitting as it were in my Elizabethan closet with my finger in the *Primer, or Office of the Blessed Virgin Mary, in Latin and English*, done by the Anglo-Netherlander Richard Verstegan and published in Antwerp in 1599, I can see this extremely solid volume of 586 pages, not to mention an appendix of another hundred, as the outcome of three centuries of a remarkable history.[7] The history transcends the passage from script to print, and from Latin to the vernacular; it

---

[4] *Ibid.*, 299–300; Jan Rhodes, 'The Rosary in Sixteenth-Century England', *Mount Carmel*, xxxi no. 4 (1983), 180–191; xxxii no. 1 (1984), 4–17.

[5] *Ibid.*, 185.

[6] *The Prymer or Lay Folk's Prayer Book* [1420–30], ed. H. Littlehales (E.E.T.S., nos. 105, 109; 1895, 1897; repr. as 1 vol., Milwood, N.Y., 1973): the introduction to vol ii contains, at xi–xxxviii, Edmund Bishop's 'On the Origins of the Primer'. Littlehales had published another version, of c. 1400, in *The Prymer or Prayer-Book of the Lay People in the Middle Ages*, i (1891). (I describe the other as *Primer II*) Virginia Reinburg, 'Popular Prayers in Late Mediaeval and Renaissance France' (Princeton University Ph.D. thesis, 1985; University Microfilms Inc., Ann Arbor, Mich., 1985, and due to appear in print shortly), 25-172. Roger S. Wieck, *Time Sanctified: the Book of Hours in Mediaeval Art and Life* (New York, 1988), with piece by Reinburg 39–44. Eamon Duffy, 'Prayer, Magic and Orthodoxy in late mediaeval Devotion', unpublished paper. Jan Rhodes, 'Private Devotion in England on the Eve of the Reformation' (University of Durham Ph.D. thesis, 1974), does not deal with primers, but is otherwise indispensable.

[7] Reprinted as vol. 262 of *English Recusant Literature, 1558–1640*, ed. D. M. Rogers (Menston, Yorks, 1975); I refer to it as *Primer III*.

includes a good deal of the history of Christian or Catholic religion as experienced, outside the 'religious' house, by laymen and -women from kings and queens down to the respectable tradesman and his family.

These prayer-books, as I shall call them, consist, especially before the mid-sixteenth century, of two kinds of thing. First, they contain pared-down versions of the divine office, notably the Office of Our Lady, with a good deal of related matter: Office for the Dead, penitential psalms, litany, and so on. Second, they have an assortment of petitionary prayers: some quasi-liturgical like the 'suffrages' to saints, others free-standing, first-person-singular, and usually long. In manuscript prayer-books the original deposit of these is often, perhaps normally, added to by the researches, inventions or commissions of the owner or owners. Since it is the latter which will most concern me now, I feel the need to say something about the first for a start.

The office consists, of course, mainly of the recitation of psalms, and I think it will be helpful to offer some kind of a description of the psalm as a form of prayer.[8] A psalm is a prayer, poem or hymn addressed to God by or on behalf of a believer, sometimes on behalf of a collectivity of believers, in some distress or tribulation. It is to be sung at or in connection with a sacrificial rite which, the believer hopes, will cause God to relieve him of his distress. It may be directly about the distress, or it may be in praise of God, his power, goodness or—perhaps especially—his justice. The distress or tribulation is caused either by the believer's own misdeeds or, more usually, by the evil machinations against him of his enemies; these are human and, if the prayer is individual, generally other believers. The praise is intended to bring God's favour, friendship and blessing and, where enemies are the problem, to persuade him to confound and if possible to exact vengeance upon them. Whatever the cause of the distress, the psalm will contribute to the removal of it and to the prosperity and general satisfaction of the pray-er.

This may seem a partial and tendentious account of a much venerated part of the Old Testament; I think it is both what a naive reader will infer from the texts, and reasonably supported by scholarship. I do not know to what degree it is relevant to the historic use of the psalms as Christian prayers or to their use in the monastic liturgy. There is a good deal of evidence that this was the general direction

---

[8] My guides to the psalms have been the article by P. Synave in *Dictionnaire de théologie catholique*, ed. A Vacant *et al.*, xiii (1936), 1094–1149; and the introduction to the psalms in the *Jerusalem Bible*. Both seem, to my uninformed judgement, over-pious. The main objections to my description would seem to be: (i) that the psalms are not to be taken literally; and (ii) that the praise in them is gratuitous not, as I suggest, instrumental, that is, intended to persuade God to effect the results prayed for.

of their use in the prayer-books of our period. Two characteristics of
the books may suggest this. In so far as individual input to them can
be discerned, they are generally about the tribulations of the owner;
and their view of tribulations is not that they are good for you and
should be endured with patience, as by Job, but that they are bad for
you and should, with the assistance of God and the saints, be got rid
of. They are also, and very distinctly, 'me'-prayer-books; usually in
the office, and universally in the non-liturgical additions, the prayers
are 'me'-prayers.

Repetition may have dulled the force of the 'Deus in adjutorium
meum intende/Domine ad adjuvandum me festina' with which each
of the hours begins. But I do not think it was lost on Blanche of
Burgundy, for whom one of the first well-known books of hours was
made about 1340. It contains, rather prominently, a 'prayer for
myself', 'memoire (memento) pour moy especial'. Under the picture
of herself, the prayer begins: 'Domine pater et deus vite mee, ne
derelinquas me in cogitatu maligno ...', which sounds like a prayer
against gossip. I doubt if it was lost on Mary of Burgundy, pictured
sitting in her closet in the middle of the political shambles bequeathed
to her by her father Charles the Bold. True, she looks *soignée* enough,
with her tall hat and her dog on her lap, holding her book open with
an elegant finger; the view at her window is not of soldiers but of
herself praying in a high chapel before Mary and Jesus. But in the
view her hands seem clenched and her expression nervous.[9] The me-
language of the psalms will often have been underlined by the figure
of David, which came to replace the figure of Christ the Judge at the
beginning of the penitential psalms: the identification will have been
particularly pressing when the pray-er was a king or male ruler.[10]

Hence the 'me'-prayers, in the prayer-books, are not necessarily
devotional prayers in the sense I mean. The penitential psalms, which
we can take to be generally devotional, are said with the litany, which
is certainly social. The extra petitionary prayers, by all accounts the
most popular items in the prayer-books, look devotional, but I doubt
if they really are so. They may be divided up into the standard and
the exotic, and I shall mention some of both. The most important
standard prayers were two long Latin prayers to Our Lady: *Obsecro
te* and *O intemerata*.[11] *Obsecro te* describes Mary's status and recites her
history as far as the Passion. In virtue of these it asks her to 'come and
hasten [veni et festina] to my aid and counsel, in all my prayers and

[9] Reinburg, in *Time Sanctified*, 39–40, and figs. 1 and 7.

[10] Wieck, *Time Sanctified*, 97–101.

[11] Reinburg, 'Popular Prayers', 111–126: text of *Obsecro te*, 376–380; Wieck, *Time Sanctified*, 94–96: texts of both, 163–4.

requests, and in all my jams [angustiis] and necessities; and in all those things I shall do, speak and think in all the days and nights, hours and moments of my life. And obtain for me, thy servant N., from thy Son, the fulness of all mercy and consolation, all counsel and aid, all blessing and holiness, all salvation, peace and prosperity, all joy and cheer, also the abundance of all spiritual and bodily goods.' The pray-er asks Mary to send him (or her) the gift of the Holy Spirit; a virtuous, orthodox and successful life ('vitam honestam et honorabilem'); and 'victory over all the adversities of this world'. He asks her to tell him the day and hour of his death. Like Blanche of Burgundy's prayer, this is a 'memento for myself'.

O intemerata is a version of this directed to Mary and John standing at the foot of the Cross, mother and son. The pray-er commends his body and soul to them as his guardians and intercessors; he affirms that their will is God's will, and that they can obtain without delay whatever they ask of Him for the 'deliverance of body and soul'; he asks them to persuade the Holy Ghost to purify them of vices and lead them to Paradise.

In my Elizabethan *Primer* these two prayers reappear, but fairly drastically recomposed: in *Obsecro te*, 'castam' has replaced 'hono-rabilem' and the 'adversities' have disappeared; in *O intemerata* the Holy Ghost, who in the original had been asked to 'help me to stand almost (*sic*) perfectly in God's favour', is now asked to 'cause me perfectly (*sic*) to stand ... in the love of God and my neighbour.'[12] I do not wish to say that the medieval versions are superstitious and the counter-reformation ones not. I do wish to say that the first are social prayers in a sense which has largely been removed in the second; and also to record the feeling, perhaps unfair, that in them the devotion has been put in as a bait to catch the social fish.

Now two exotic prayers. Both of them are famous, the first in this connection and the second in quite a different one. They have in common that they both appear as manuscript additions, and are therefore the result of personal choice or invention; they differ in that the first appears far and wide, the second only once.

The so-called 'Charlemagne prayer', whose history is naturally mainly French, is not really a prayer or prayers at all.[13] It is more a set of short invocations attached to a visual image or talisman which has a long legend as rubric. The image generally represents Christ's spear-wound from Longinus, specifying an exact proportion to the real life-size. The legend describes how the image was brought to

[12] *Primer III*, ff. 218v–220r; cf. Wieck, *op. cit.*, 164.
[13] Reinburg, 'Popular Prayers', 287–300; also discussed in Duffy, 'Prayer, Magic and Orthodoxy'.

Charlemagne by an angel when he was fighting the Muslims in the
Holy Land, or on some similar occasion. It was to keep him safe in
battle. Whoever looked at it, or wore it, would not die of sudden
death, fire, water or tempest, blow ('traict'), knife or sword. No enemy
could harm him, and no evil judge could judge against him if his
cause was good. A woman who did the same would be protected in
childbirth. The person is to add a set of self-blessings, which are
unremarkable; but manuscripts and printed versions add relevant
extracts from the psalms, notably Ps. 22:4 and 137:7. 'Nam et si
ambulavero . . .' 'For though I shall walk in the middle of the shadow
of death I shall fear no evil, for thou art with me.' 'For though I shall
walk in the midst of tribulation, thou shalt give me life; thou hast
stretched forth thy hand against the wrath of my enemies, and thy
right hand hath saved me. Amen.'[14]

This quite unallegorical shield was an extremely popular part of
what Dr Reinburg calls the 'devotional underground'. Dropped from
French printed prayer-books, though kept in those exported from
France to England, it was picked up and propagated in broadsheets
thereafter, and was apparently still being used by French soldiers in
the war of 1914. 'Underground' it may have been, or become, but it
was not unlearned. Eamon Duffy has found it in the prayer-book of
Lady Margaret Beaufort, joined to an extremely erudite exorcistic
prayer about the Names of God. The psalm-texts have not been added
to the prayer by clerical hands, and I should think that they had been
in the mind of the legend's public from an early date. I should also
think that the whole story is a version of the vision of the Emperor
Constantine at the Battle of the Milvian Bridge.

My second exotic prayer is from Richard III's prayer-book, and
dates from some time during his reign, probably later rather than
earlier.[15] It is extraordinarily long, theologically informed, and
unusually precise. It is not exactly repetitious, but comes back repeatedly with a sort of chorus to the same point—the jam in which Richard
is now situated—after a series of excursions into the history of human
salvation, of which the rescue of King Richard will be an example. It
is an elaborate version of *Obsecro te*, addressed not to Mary but to
Christ. It is not clear that we possess the original version of the
beginning of the prayer, but when we can be sure what is going on
we find the king motivating a prayer for peace by the history of
Christ's restoration of concord in the universe. Christ is asked to
remove the hatred of the king's enemies and to make peace between

[14] Reinburg, 'Popular Prayers', 296–299.
[15] Text in Pamela Tudor-Craig, *Richard III* (Ipswich/Totowa, N.J., 1973), 96–97;
the prayer-book described, 26–27.

them and him, according to the model (*sicut*) of his (?) making peace between Esau and his brother Jacob. After this there are two sequences of *libera me*, the first from jams and tribulations in general, the second from the snares of enemies, evil counsels and conspiracies in particular. The *sicut* for the first is the liberation of a string of people from Abraham to St Paul, including 'Susannam de falso crimine et testimonio' and Daniel from the lions' den; for the second the confounding of the counsel of Achitophel against King David. Then comes a litany of *per*s and *propter*s in which the particular events of Christ's history are brought into contact with Richard's needs. The sufferings of the Passion are detailed at length, the implication being that Christ has suffered from his enemies too, and will sympathise. The prayer ends with the evocation of Christ's triumph and judgement to come, and of all the benefits hitherto bestowed on the king; victory over his enemies is not explicitly prayed for, I assume on purpose. The omission is partly made up for by a petition for the assistance of the archangel Michael against the imitators of Achitophel.

Whether this prayer was written by Richard himself, or by a priest who had Richard looking over his shoulder, I am not competent to say. It has some special features, like its fertility in scriptural references and its description of Richard's tribulations in the present rather than in the future tense. But it is more a classic of an existing *genre* than an invention of Richard himself. We need not take it as evidence of his individual neuroses or persecution-mania, or indeed of his innocence or guilt, but of the general tradition of such prayers. Margaret Beaufort, who acquired the prayer-book, scratched out Richard's name, but otherwise left the prayer unchanged. If I were asked to encapsulate the tradition in a single text, I should offer the last verse of the first of the penitential psalms (Ps. 6:11):—'Erubescant et conturbentur vehementer omnes inimici mei: avertentur retrorsum, et erubescant valde velociter.' In the fifteenth-century English version published by Littlehales: 'Alle myn enemies be aschamed, and be disturbled greatly; be they turned together, and be they ashamed full swiftly.'[16]

This tradition is certainly not the only thing worth mentioning in the corpus of prayer-book piety of our period, but it does seem characteristic, and it does take up a good deal of space. I think we can make a few reliable observations about it which are relevant to Dix's implied description. It is individualistic, but it is social rather than devotional; it is also, in a quite defensible sense, liturgical. It has,

---

[16] *Primer II.* The second half of the verse seems to have been re-translated in the Clementine Vulgate of 1592, which has *convertantur* instead of *avertentur retrorsum;* hence *Primer III,* f. 174f, has 'let them be converted', where the Douai version has 'let them be turned back'. Both are found in medieval texts.

that is, evident liturgical sources: in the psalms, as mediated by the divine office or otherwise; in the Mass, notably in the memento for the living and votive masses deriving from it; and in the monastic *clamor* and in other aggressive or defensive rites to be found particularly in monastic missals.[17] The formulation of the prayers is often very similar to those which are found in the last two sources. My instinct is to think the monastic influence particularly strong, which is what one might expect from the character of the *genre*. Clearly, if all 'me'- prayers are taken by definition to be non-liturgical, these are not liturgical prayers; but the definition does not seem to stand up to historic practice.

I come finally to Dix's principal target, prayers *at* Mass: my general impression here, unlike his, is of a great diversity. If we are looking for a model of social prayer, in a sense rather wider than that so far used, we have a model in the *Lay Folk's Mass Book*. In discussing the Mass as a peace-ritual, I have already said what I have to say about this, and will say no more except that I find excessive J. J. Scarisbrick's remark that someone who was praying according to it would be praying *at* Mass, not praying *the* Mass. If people so praying were mistaken in what they thought the Mass was about, they were mistaken in the company of Innocent III, William Durandus and Gabriel Biel, not to mention that of Richard III.[18] My feeling is confirmed by a string of versions of the same kind of thing to be found in France at this time: vernacular prayer-sequences which stick equally close to the liturgy. I think in particular of a cycle which appears in various manuscript books of hours; its original owner seems to have been Philip the Bold, a man even more responsible for the government and peace of Christendom than the pray-er envisaged for the *Lay Folk's Mass Book*.[19]

At the devotional end of the spectrum we have 'Langford's', rather William Bonde's, *Meditations for Ghostly Exercise in the Time of Mass*,

---

[17] A. Franz, *Die Messe im deutschen Mittelalter* (Freiburg-im-Breisgau, 1902; repr. Darmstadt, 1963), 204–217; and J. Bossy, 'The Mass as a Social Institution, 1200–1700', *Past and Present*, no. 100 (1983), 41.

[18] *The Lay Folk's Mass Book*, ed. T. F. Simmons (E.E.T.S., no. 71; London, 1879); 'The Mass as a Social Institution', 54–55. J. J. Scarisbrick, *The Reformation and the English People* (Oxford, 1984), 43. For Richard III, Tudor-Craig, *Richard III*, 96: 'Et tu domine qui genus humanum cum patre in concordia restituisti ... et inter homines et angelos pacem fecisti, dignare inter me et inimicos meos stabilire et firmare concordiam ...', which seems an obvious echo of the expositions of the Mass. Rosalind and Christopher Brooke, *Popular Religion in the Middle Ages* (1984), accept the tradition that the *Lay Folk's Mass Book* was originally written in French, though in England, in the 12th century, but I should be surprised if it pre-dated Innocent III.

[19] Reinburg, 'Popular Prayers', 227 ff.

dating from the later 1520s.[20] It is, precisely, meditations, as Dix complained. The meditations are on the Passion: at the offertory one is to think of Christ withdrawing into the Garden of Gethsemane for prayer and contemplation; before the consecration, of the Last Supper; after the consecration, to follow in one's mind 'the whole process of the Passion'. This is another story both from the *Lay Folk's Mass Book* and from what we have seen in the prayer-books: here, prayer is on the whole an interior dialogue between the soul and its Saviour, embodying altruistic *pietà* on both sides and rather distracted by reference to the exterior world.

These are two very different responses to the sacrifice of the Mass, and I should like to end by trying to evoke the plurality they illustrate *à propos* of one of the great triggers of religious feeling, the elevation of the host. We all know what Erasmus and Cranmer had to say about this: people running from sacring to sacring, 'peeping, tooting and gazing'. We know about the elevation visions of Margery Kempe and others, the multiplied visual images of the Mass of St Gregory and the legends of bleeding hosts. But if we look at elevation prayers of the period we get, perhaps inevitably, a different impression. Or rather, we get several impressions, of which I record two.

The first is that it was possible for people to pray at the elevation in what seems to me a properly liturgical spirit. This is the elevation prayer in the *Lay Folk's Mass Book*:—

> Praised be thou, King,
> And blessed be thou, King,
> Of all thy giftes good;
> And thanked be thou, King,
> Jesu, all my joying,
> That for me spilt thy blood
> And died upon the Rood;
> Thou give me grace to sing
> The song of thy praising.

The worshipper is joining in the sacrifice of praise and thanksgiving as much as Cranmer would have wished, is he not? As Maynard Smith said, it is very nice.[21] There is a comparable French prayer which appears in 34 Ms. prayer-books, generally with an apocryphal indulgence of 2000 years supposedly given by Pope Boniface VI (*sic*)

---

[20] *Tracts on the Mass*, ed. J. Wickham Legg (Henry Bradshaw Society, xxvii, 1904), 19–29; Rhodes, 'Private Devotion in England', 337–341, and n. 97, for the authorship; she is not greatly impressed by the work.

[21] *Lay Folk's Mass Book*, 36 f; H. Maynard Smith, *Pre-Reformation England* (1938; London, 1965 edn), 100.

at the request of King Philip the Fair. The pray-er was to say it between the elevation and the *pax*:—

> Lord Jesus Christ, who assumed this your most holy flesh in the womb of the glorious virgin Mary, and shed your most precious blood on the tree of the Cross for our salvation, and in this glorious flesh rose from the dead and ascended into Heaven, and art to come in this flesh to judge both the living and the dead—
>
> deliver us by this your most Holy Body which now is held on your altar from all impurities of mind and body and from all evil and danger, now and for ever. Amen.'[22]

Like Bonde's meditator, this Mass-attender would have got his commemoration of the dead out of the way before the consecration; unlike him, he would remain in a liturgical mode, uniting his experience of the consecration to something like the Creed and something like the prayers of the priest from the *Libera me* onwards. He was, one must agree, not *doing* anything, but I find it hard to envisage what he might have been doing. What he was saying was at least quasi-liturgical; he was also generally saying it in Latin, since there are only three French versions out of the thirty-four.

My second impression is that it was possible to pray at the elevation in a non-liturgical spirit which was nevertheless of massive importance for the future of Catholicism. On the devotional side there was the prayer *Anima Christi*, much recommended to be said at this point. Of unknown early fourteenth-century authorship, and implausibly attributed to Pope John XXII who indulgenced it, it participated in the general climate by its concern with the Passion and with foes (here the Devil), but transcended it by a Roman concision and crispness. It was taken up by St Ignatius into the *Spiritual Exercises*, and was thenceforth a pillar of Catholic piety into the twentieth century.[23] On the social side, there was the hymn *O Salutaris hostia*, the last two verses of one of Aquinas's hymns for the office of Corpus Christi. It is found as an elevation hymn in fifteenth-century Germany, and was introduced into France by King Louis XII. At some point thereafter, I rather assume under the influence of the Wars of Religion, the combination of elevation and hymn developed into the separate service of Benediction. Here the salvation in question is still the salvation of soul and body, and the enemies are still real enemies.

---

[22] Reinburg, 'Popular Prayers', 235–239.

[23] O[xford] D[ictionary of the] C[hristian] C[hurch], 2nd edn. by F. L. Cross and E. A. Livingstone (1974), s.v. *Anima Christi*; Reinburg, 'Popular Prayers', 197, 225; *The Spiritual Exercises of St. Ignatius Loyola*, trans. T. Corbishley (Wheathampstead, Herts., 1973), 35, 54, 84 f.

Surprisingly to those who grew up with it, *O Salutaris* is a very social hymn.[24]

There was, I conclude, something in the elevation for everybody: for the mystic and the irretrievably mundane, the devout individualist and the communal fanatic. In its various incarnations it just about managed to keep the lid on the dense smog of self-centredness, malice and sanctified whingeing which comes off the prayer-books. It was surely rather ominous that sixteenth-century intellectuals should have found it a matter of complaint that it was so popular. In their vices as well as in their virtues, the prayers of Catholics from the fourteenth century to the sixteenth seem to me to testify to a thriving and various tradition. Liturgists and reformers rarely like it, but pluralism in prayer is one of the advantages of a relatively non-participatory rite.

NOTE ON JOHN BOSSY, 'PRAYERS'[25]

John Bossy rightly points out the importance of prayer within the social history of Christianity. He provides an interesting reflection on recent and forthcoming works by Eamon Duffy and myself, research which has explored the variety of devotions practised by clerics and lay people in late medieval and modern Europe.[26] These studies of the social history of prayer reveal the specific concerns, difficulties and hopes of ordinary men and women, as well as the distinctive modes of relationship they created with those to whom they prayed. We

[24] J. Bossy, *Christianity in the West, 1400–1700* (Oxford, 1985), 69; *O.D.C.C.*, s.v. *Benediction of the Blessed Sacrament*; *Die Musik in Geschichte und Gegenwart*, ed. F. Blume, ix (Kassel, etc., 1961), col. 176 & Figure 13; Reinburg, 'Popular Prayers', 196; Wieck, *Time Sanctified*, 107.

[25] Since this paper draws heavily on the work of Virginia Reinburg, it is appropriate to note that the views expressed are my own. Professor Reinburg's reactions are set out below.

[26] E. Duffy, 'Devotion to the Crucifix and Related Images in England on the Eve of the Reformation', in *Bilder und Bildersturm in Spätmittelalter und in der frühen Neuzeit*, ed. R. Scribner (Wiesbaden, 1990), 21–36. V. Reinburg, 'Prayer and the Book of Hours', in *Time Sanctified*, ed. R. Wieck (New York/Baltimore, 1988), 39–44; 'Les pèlerins de Notre-Dame du Puy', *Revue d'Histoire de l'Église de France* 75 (1989): 297–313; 'Praying to Saints in the Late Middle Ages', in *Sancta, Sanctus: Studies in Hagiography*, ed. S. Sticca (Binghamton, N.Y., forthcoming); 'Liturgy and the Laity in Late Medieval and Reformation France', *Sixteenth Century Journal* (forthcoming); 'Hearing Lay People's Prayer', in *Society, Sex, and the Sacred in Early Modern Europe*, ed. B. Diefendorf and C. Hesse (forthcoming); and a forthcoming book on the social history of prayer in fifteenth- and sixteenth-century France. See also the work of William Christian, Jr., which Bossy has not cited in his article: *Local Religion in Sixteenth-Century Spain* (Princeton, 1981); and *Person and God in a Spanish Valley* (New York, 1972) (the latter treats twentieth-century villagers).

can now see clearly how inadequate to describe popular religious experience are generalizations like those of Gregory Dix, who saw devotional life becoming gradually more 'individualistic', less 'corporate' and 'organic' by the eve of the Reformation. Professor Bossy's attempt to redraw our picture of the transformation of prayer practices is interesting and imaginative. However, his suggested categories of 'social', 'devotional' and 'me' prayers are misleading, and mask essential features of late medieval prayer. What is a prayer? It is most useful for social historians of religion to define prayer as a discourse, spoken or silent, expressed in the first person (singular or plural), which establishes a relationship with a person or persons believed to have supernatural power. For late medieval devotees these persons were God, the Virgin Mary and saints. Perhaps not surprisingly, the forms of discourse and relationship people used in prayer mirrored those they knew in the wider social world. All prayers speak about the self, the supernatural persons being prayed to, and the human community of which the praying self is part. Professor Bossy labels the long meditative prayers called 'Obsecro te' and 'O intemerata' as 'social', and suggests they are not truly devotional, even though he admits they appear to be so. Both prayers consist of a series of meditations on the Virgin Mary's experiences at her son's crucifixion, and conclude with a request for her assistance in earthly life and the hereafter. Even by Professor Bossy's own definitions, these prayers would seem to be both 'devotional' and 'social'; they speak about and to supernatural persons, and they express concerns and hopes about the visible world. In this case, as also with Blanche of Burgundy's 'memento for myself' and the Charlemagne prayer, dividing prayers into these exclusive categories hides their true social and devotional qualities.

A more serious difficulty is evident in Professor Bossy's discussion of what he calls 'me'-prayers. He cites here prayer texts composed for (probably not by) Blanche of Burgundy and Richard III, but adds that nearly all the prayers in books of hours can be called 'me'-prayers, presumably because they focus exclusively on the earthly desires of the person saying the prayer. True, most prayers in books of hours do address God or a saint on the devotee's behalf, and many of them do include petitions for personal assistance. Professor Bossy goes further, however, implying that such prayers are in some way selfish. His analysis of the portrait of Mary of Burgundy makes clear the shortcomings of his discussion of 'me' prayers. He sees Mary's hands as 'clenched,' her expression 'nervous'; perhaps she is thinking of the wars in her political domain, perhaps she is withdrawing into the chapel of her imagination in order to avoid seeing wars. Professor Bossy's language here is evocative rather than direct, but Mary of Burgundy's sincerity seems to fall short in his estimation. This late fifteenth-century Netherlandish painting is not a straightforward statement about prayer; like Professor Bossy, many have tried their hand at interpreting it. My own reading is that it represents a *visualization* of prayer. Reading her expression and gesture within the vocabulary of Netherlandish art, Mary appears to me meditative and serene, rather than 'nervous' and 'clenched'. As I have written elsewhere, the scene in the chapel can be interpreted as an expression of her understanding of the process of her own prayer.[27]

But my point here is not simply to dispute particulars of Professor Bossy's analysis. Rather, I question the validity of categories like 'social', 'devotional' and 'me'-prayers, which imply that prayers can or should be classified according to varying degrees of self-centredness and altruism, materialism and true devotion. We might well challenge Gregory Dix's argument that late medieval devotion had unfortunately devolved into individualism and ignorance. But the transformation of prayer by the eve of the Reformation is no better described as a movement toward increasingly materialistic, malicious, self-centred petitions. Relationships which human beings established in prayer with God and the saints most certainly underwent massive change from the fourteenth through the sixteenth century. However, we learn more about the qualitative features of this devotional revolution by reading it within the context of concomitant transformations in the social relations of kinship, patronage and lordship. It is that social world that provided the language and meaning of the petitions which Professor Bossy finds to be 'sanctified whingeing'.

[27] Reinburg, 'Prayer and the Book of Hours', 41, 44; and chapter 2 of my forthcoming book. I have received valuable suggestions about how to read this painting from Roger Wieck, and I have benefited more generally from the work of Anne van Buren, James Marrow, and Otto Pächt on Netherlandish art.

THE ENGLISH MONASTIC CATHEDRALS IN THE FIFTEENTH CENTURY

By Barrie Dobson

READ 15 SEPTEMBER 1990

IT might well appear an excessively abrupt change of pace to turn from Professor Bossy's topic to my own—to move from the most personal of all manifestations of individual Christian worship to the most formidably complex institutional corporations late medieval England has to offer for our contemplation. However, there is little about medieval monasticism, that ambivalent exercise in seeking one's own route to the divine but not in one's own company, which is quite what it seems. For perhaps no audiences in fifteenth-century England would have listened to Professor Bossy's lecture with greater fascination than the monastic communities of Canterbury, Durham, Ely, Norwich, Rochester, Winchester, and Worcester cathedrals. Not only did those Benedictine monks have an obligation to pray as assiduously as any religious in the country but they were also and *ipso facto* required to do so in the most public and exposed of all possible arenas, the formal prayer houses *par excellence* as well as the *ecclesiae matrices* of seven of late medieval England's nineteen dioceses. Precisely how those monks would have explained what they were doing when engaged in acts of communal and private prayer is no easy matter for a modern historian to surmise; but it seems certain that many of them must have been highly concerned about the purpose and quality of their devotions, not least because they could hardly have ignored the priority placed on the *oratorium* and *oratio* within the Rule of St Benedict, to chapters of which they listened more or less attentively every day of their professed lives. Admittedly it may well be that St Benedict himself placed the performance of prayers to the Lord at the centre of his ideal monastery's spiritual life without always making it absolutely clear what types of contemplation he implied by such *orationes*.[1] Not that such ambiguity must in any case detract at all from the much more fundamental issue that it was as a manual for monastic meditation and prayer rather than, as is now often assumed, as a blueprint

---

[1] The apparent ambiguities here are discussed in *R B 1980: The Rule of St. Benedict in Latin and English with Notes,* ed. T. M. Fry (Minnesota, 1980), 412–14.

for the successful organisation of a monastery that the influence of the Rule tended to be most highly regarded in late medieval England.[2]

For the increasingly large number of historians who are currently inclined to interpret the achievements of fifteenth-century cathedral monasteries in terms of qualified success rather than of qualified failure, it is perhaps to the seventy-three chapters of St Benedict's Rule that they should first and most obviously turn. After all, no more enduringly influential model for the defence of a human community against internal and external pressures, no more satisfactory a written programme for whatever a communal collective strategy might happen to be, has altogether emerged in the last fifteen hundred years of European history. So obvious, if important, a truism deserves at least some slight preliminary emphasis if only because this lecture is unlikely to mention either prayer or the Rule of St Benedict again. There are indeed some obvious hazards involved in neglecting those aspects of the religious life which most self-respecting cathedral monks of the fifteenth century might have thought most essential to themselves and indeed to posterity. But then historians, especially perhaps historians of the medieval Christian life, are inured to the necessity of dealing with the inessentials. Moreover, the monastic cathedral communities of late medieval England have perhaps even greater claims on our attention than those provided by their prayers and their obedience to the Rule. 'Little as we know about the monks of Durham, we are better informed as to their recruitment, their education, their employment, their ambitions and their interests than those of any comparable group of men' of the fifteenth century.[3] In the light of recent research among the records of the largest English monasteries, and in particular of Miss Barbara Harvey's recent exploration of monastic life at Westminster Abbey, that particular judgement no longer seems as secure in 1990 as it did in 1973. Nevertheless the case for a brief survey of pre-Reformation monastic cathedrals must rest most firmly on the fact that so extraordinarily much can be known

[2] B. Collett, 'The Civil Servant and Monastic Reform: Richard Fox's Translation of the Benedictine Rule for Women, 1517', *Monastic Studies: The Continuity of Tradition*, ed. J. Loades (Bangor, 1990), 211–28. As early as 1277 the statutes of the General Chapter of the English Black Monks in the province of Canterbury had required all novices to learn the Rule by heart: *Documents illustrating the activities of the General and Provincial Chapters of the English Black Monks, 1215–1540*, ed. W. A. Pantin (Camden Third Series, xlv, xlvii, liv, 1931–7), i, 73–4; cf. *ibid.*, i, 95, 111–12, 250; ii, 40, 70, 84. By the early fifteenth century English translations of the Rule were also readily accessible in monastic cathedral libraries: see, e.g., *Catalogi Veteres Librorum Ecclesiae Cathedralis Dunelm.*, ed. B. Botfield (Surtees Society, vii, 1838), 107.

[3] R. B. Dobson, *Durham Priory, 1400–1450* (Cambridge, 1973), 51.

about how their brethen lived and 'consorted together', if so very much less about what they thought and what they believed.[4]

Although never subjected to the full-scale comparative analysis they deserve, the abundance of the surviving records and manuscripts of England's later medieval monastic cathedrals needs no particular urging. Accordingly it might well seem all the more unfortunate that for the last century so many formidably critical minds have devoted themselves to twelfth-century monastic charters and so few to the as yet mysterious administrative revolution which in the thirteenth century gradually brought forth the most sophisticated private archives known to medieval England. During the third quarter of the thirteenth century, probably—in secular cathedrals too—one of the most critical periods in a long evolution, it had clearly become common for monastic cathedral communities to compile and preserve (amidst much else) those two most valuable instruments in their documentary armoury—obedientiary and other account rolls on the one hand and cartularies and registers (less happily perhaps termed letter-books by the late Mr W. A. Pantin) on the other.[5] Monastic registers, still the most important source for the official activities of cathedral priories during the fifteenth century, were naturally not confined to the latter; and in fact more cartularies and registers survive from Bury St Edmunds than from any monastic cathedral chapter. Nevertheless, it might be argued that cathedral monks had a more urgent need for such registers than their counterparts in other Benedictine religious houses, sometimes to record their own exercise of diocesan jurisdiction *sede vacante*, and certainly to preserve authenticated copies of their confirmations of their bishop's more formal *acta* and his appointments to office.[6] There are indeed some indications

---

[4] Although E. H. Pearce's *The Monks of Westminster* (Notes and Documents relating to Westminster Abbey, no. 5, Cambridge, 1916) still remains the only systematic attempt to publish a complete biographical register of a major medieval English monastery, that omission is at last in course of being rectified by Dr Joan Greatrex, Mr Alan Piper and other scholars. Cf. R. B. Dobson, 'Recent Prosopographical Research in Late Medieval English History: University Graduates, Durham Monks, and York Canons', *Medieval Lives and the Historian: Studies in Medieval Prosopography* (Kalamazoo, Michigan, 1986), 187–92.

[5] R. A. L. Smith, *Collected Essays* (1947), 23–73. The first surviving obedientiary account at the cathedral of Norwich is the *Camera Prioris* roll of 1265; and at Durham the earliest account is that of the bursar in 1278: H. W. Saunders, *An Introduction to the Obedientiary and Manor Rolls of Norwich Cathedral Priory* (1930), 18–21; Dean and Chapter of Durham Muniments, Bursar 1278–9; Cf. (for a fragment of a Winchester receiver's account of as early as 1280–1) *The Register of the Common Seal of the Priory of St. Swithun, Winchester, 1345–1497*, ed. J. Greatrex (Hampshire Record Series, ii, 1979), 268.

[6] *The Archives of the Abbey of Bury St Edmunds*, ed. R. M. Thomson (Suffolk Records Society, xxi, 1980), 4–5; W. A. Pantin, 'English Monastic Letter-Books', *Historical Essays in honour of James Tait*, ed. J. G. Edwards, V. H. Galbraith, and E. F. Jacob

that on occasion it was the Benedictine cathedral monasteries which pioneered important thirteenth-century monastic administrative and archival developments, notably if predictably at Christ Church in the case of the southern province and at Durham in the province of York.[7] By their very nature too, cathedral monasteries were always likely to produce more complex sequences of archives than most other religious houses. However, it was of course to the peaceful if somewhat haphazard transformation of England's eight major monastic cathedral communities into secular chapters between 1539 and 1542 that is due the survival of so many of these records. A much less happy archival as well as institutional fate was to befall those two unusual monastic 'semi-cathedrals', Bath and Coventry—to be excluded from consideration here as they were similarly excluded from discussion by Henry VIII in and after 1539. In the event neither Thomas Cromwell nor the king were at all responsive to Bishop Rowland Lee's eloquent plea for the 'continuance' of Coventry as a collegiate church 'for so much as it is my principal see and head church'.[8]

Despite such generally good fortune for the historian as well as for the last monks of every cathedral but Bath and Coventry, the present state of their archives still provides a classic object lesson in the selective vagaries of oblivion. The sources now available range from the chaotic abundance of Christ Church, Canterbury and the administrative wealth of Durham to the somewhat haphazard survivals at Worcester, the disappointments of Winchester and finally to a complete zero in the case of Henry I's unique foundation of a cathedral community of Augustinian canons at Carlisle.[9] The state of preservation of these records is similarly variable to a degree: to unwind one of fifteenth-century Norwich cathedral's long sequences of obedientiary account

(Manchester, 1933), 201–22. Several monastic cathedral registers are in fact more informative about diocesan affairs than the external and internal concerns of the convent; see, e.g., Canterbury Cathedral Library, Registers F, R, G, Q (*Sede Vacante* Registers, 1292–1502); *Register of Common Seal, passim.*

[7] A fully developed system of internal accounting is visible at Christ Church, Canterbury, by the early thirteenth century: see the *Assisa Scaccarii* rolls which survive there from as early as 1224. It was at a meeting of the Black Monk Chapter of the northern province at Durham in 1276 that Selby Abbey was instructed to introduce the then novel office of bursar 'to account for the receipts of that house': *Chapters of Black Monks*, i. 226, 238, 251; cf. R. A. L. Smith, 'The *Regimen Scaccarii* in English Monasteries', *Supra*, 4th ser. xxiv (1942), 73–94.

[8] *Letters to Cromwell and Others on the Suppression of the Monasteries*, ed. G. H. Cook (1965), 229–30. The 20 Benedictines who served the cathedral church of Coventry eventually surrendered their convent to the Crown in the very same month (January 1539) as did the 13 monks of Bath cathedral priory: D. Knowles and R. N. Hadcock, *Medieval Religious Houses, England and Wales* (2nd edn, 1971), 59, 63.

[9] R. B. Dobson, 'Cathedral Chapters and Cathedral Cities: York, Durham and Carlisle in the Fifteenth Century', *Northern History*, xix (1983), 24–5.

rolls is usually an unalloyed pleasure; but to try to do the same in the case of several Ely accounts of the same period (deposited in the Cambridge University Library since 1970) can sometimes involve the historian in seeing historical evidence vanish before his very eyes.[10] In other words, no fully comparative history of the eight English monastic cathedrals will ever be an attainable ideal. However, if the archives of monastic cathedrals have descended to us in highly assorted shapes and sizes, so too have those cathedrals themselves. Although nothing can be said on this occasion about the insights into the monastic life provided by the architectural remains still standing within all eight cathedral precincts, it is worth stressing that the fifteenth-century historian often suffers from the particular misfortune that it is usually the monastic buildings adapted and constructed in the 150 years before the Dissolution which were most seriously at risk immediately thereafter.[11] Architectural historians have sometimes regretted that medieval England never produced a Perpendicular cathedral, with the problematic exception of Bath; but for the historian it may be a matter for even more regret that only in a minority of cathedrals can he or she still observe the authentic fifteenth-century monastic environment.[12]

Not only is the evidence for the history of late medieval England's cathedral monasteries riddled with disparities: so too were the status, role and welfare of those eight cathedrals themselves. How indeed could it have been otherwise? The grafting of seven Benedictine (and one Augustinian) cathedral communities onto the already highly idiosyncratic diocesan map of the late Anglo-Saxon and early Norman *ecclesia Anglicana* was essentially a historical accident, the product of *ad hoc* decisions made by Lanfranc and others at a time of unique 'synthesis and change' when the older monastic orders were lords of the ascendant and when the secular canons were much less evidently so.[13] Not surprisingly, this Anglo-Norman experiment (only occasionally imitated elsewhere and then probably under English influence as at Coutances, Downpatrick and Palermo) created very uneven not to

[10] D. Owen, *The Library and Muniments of Ely Cathedral* (Dean and Chapter of Ely, 1973). To the approximately 1,500 surviving medieval obedientiary account rolls of Norwich cathedral priory the handlist available in the Norwich Record Office is a clearer guide than Saunders, *Rolls of Norwich*.

[11] For obvious reasons, chantry and other chapels, private chambers and the offices or 'checkers' of obedientiaries seem to have been especially vulnerable to destruction or alteration in the years after 1540: see, e.g., *The Rites of Durham*, ed. J. T. Fowler (Surtees Soc. cvii, 1903), 83–4, 99, 102–4, 283–4.

[12] A. Clifton-Taylor, *The Cathedrals of England* (1967), 195–6; J. Harvey, *The Perpendicular Style, 1330–1485* (1978), 215–33.

[13] R. W. Southern, *Saint Anselm, A Portrait in a Landscape* (Cambridge, 1990), 308–29; M. Chibnall, *Anglo-Norman England, 1066–1166* (Oxford, 1986), 41–3.

say erratic results.[14] Accordingly in terms of size and influence, the eight English monastic cathedrals of the fifteenth century were not only *sui generis* but also fell most readily into three main categories already visible in the twelfth century. By any standards, pride of place must go to the two colossi, the communities of St Thomas at Canterbury and of St Cuthbert of Durham. Quite apart from being the homes of the most influential thaumaturges in fifteenth-century England, quite apart from being the only two Benedictine monasteries with the resources and the corporate pride to maintain their own university colleges at Oxford, these two houses were without much doubt the largest cathedral communities in the country. Leaving on one side the complexities of monastic demography during this period (a subject which, thanks to Dr John Hatcher, Miss Barbara Harvey and Dr Joan Greatrex, has been much elucidated in recent years), it can be safely said that between 1400 and 1500 the Christ Church community usually oscillated at a size of around eighty.[15]

The Canterbury monks accordingly comprised the largest monastic fellowship in England, whereas the cathedral priory of Durham held more steadily at a figure of about 70, of whom however over twenty were usually serving its daughter houses.[16] No other monastic cathedral chapter had so many cells in its custody; and despite the legal and disciplinary problems often presented by these daughter houses in the fifteenth century, on balance they still probably did more to enhance than impair the prestige, influence and even the morale of the mother house.[17] If not quite the size of Durham and Christ Church, the second group of English monastic cathedrals (Ely,

[14] D. Knowles, *The Monastic Order In England* (2nd edn., Cambridge, 1963), 619. The cathedral chapter at Coutances was in fact reorganised on a secular basis before the end of the eleventh century: see *Gallia Christiana*, ed. D. de Sainte Marthe (Paris, 1870–), xi, *Instrumenta*, 220; K. Edwards, *The English Secular Cathedrals in the Middle Ages* (2nd. edn., Manchester, 1967), 8–17, 169.

[15] After an exceptionally severe demographic crisis in 1376, when only 46 Christ Church monks were present at Archbishop Simon Sudbury's visitation of that year, the extensive evidence suggests that the number of Canterbury Cathedral brethren never seems to have fallen below 70 during the course of the fifteenth century: see Canterbury Cathedral Library, Register G, fos. 229v, 235v–237, 285; D. Wilkins, *Concilia Magnae Britanniae et Hiberniae* (4 vols, London, 1737), iii, 110; E. F. Jacob, *Archbishop Henry Chichele* (1967), 20; R. A. L. Smith, *Canterbury Cathedral Priory, A Study in Monastic Administration* (Cambridge, 1943), 3–4.

[16] See, e.g., Dean and Chapter of Durham Muniments, 1.7. Pont., no. 17; Locellus XIII, no. 11; Register III, fos. 22–3, 213; *The Register of Thomas Langley, Bishop of Durham*, ed. R. L. Storey (Surtees Soc., 6 vols. 1956–70), i. 67–8; ii. 117–19.

[17] Dobson, *Durham Priory*, 297–341. However, these advantages, if such they were, were largely denied some of the other fifteenth-century monastic cathedrals, among whom only Norwich possessed as many as 5 daughter houses (all comparatively small) while Winchester held none at all (Knowles and Hadcock, 59, 61, 64–5, 72, 74, 80–1).

Norwich, Worcester and Winchester) were all impressively substantial religious communities by fifteenth-century standards: all four tended to house between thirty-five and fifty-five monks throughout the demographic vicissitudes of the century, the largest usually being Norwich and the smallest (somewhat surprisingly) Winchester.[18] As few as thirty St Swithun's monks were recorded as present at the election of Bishop Peter Courtenay in December 1486.[19]

Finally, and much the smallest monastic cathedral chapters in fifteenth-century England, were the two communities of Rochester and Carlisle. Like their respective bishops, these two convents were the most financially insecure members of the upper echelons of the country's ecclesiastical hierarchy. Only now and then is it possible to be certain how many Rochester monks and Carlisle regular canons constituted those two cathedral chapters in the post-Black Death period; but it seems probable that there were usually considerably more than twenty of the former but only rarely many more than twenty of the latter.[20]

Although highly impressionistic, these figures tend to reflect, predictably enough, the similarly very uneven comparative annual incomes of the monastic cathedrals in question. On the whole, and although the available evidence is usually uncomfortably indirect, it can be assumed that all eight chapters deliberately aimed at what Miss Harvey has called (in the case of Westminster Abbey) a numerical target. By the fifteenth century this target was less likely to be based on a traditional ideal complement of brethren than upon one related to the convent's estimate of its future yearly revenues in an age when new acquisitions of income-generating temporalities and spiritualities were no longer to be relied upon. In the words of the Durham monks in the late fourteenth century, only so many novices should be recruited into the community 'as its resources can support if they are well administered'.[21] Like, to take an implausible analogy,

---

[18] These provisional estimates will undoubtedly soon require refinement in the light of Dr Joan Greatrex's recent researches; but see, e.g., Cambridge University Library, Ely Cathedral Priory Muniments 5/3/1–2 (chamberlains' accounts), nos. 25, 26, 29, 33 (1404–46); 5/11 (feretrars' accounts), no. 3 (1423–4); Norfolk Record Office, DCN 1/5/95, nos. 94, 111 (chamberlains' accounts); Saunders, *Rolls of Norwich*, 160–2; Knowles and Hadcock, 64–5, 72, 81; J. C. Russell, 'The Clerical Population of Medieval England', *Traditio*, ii (1944), 189–90.

[19] *Register of Common Seal*, p. 151; cf. pp. 24, 100–1.

[20] Russell, 'Clerical Population', 190; Dobson, 'Cathedral Chapters', 24–5; R. N. Swanson, 'Sede Vacante Administration in the Medieval Diocese of Carlisle; the Accounts of the Vacancy of December 1395 to March 1396', *Trans. of Cumberland and Westmorland Antiq. and Archaeol. Soc.*, xc (1990), 190.

[21] *Visitations of the Diocese of Norwich, A.D. 1492–1532*, ed. A. Jessopp (Camden Society New Series, xliii, 1888), 73; *Literae Cantuarienses*, ed. J. B. Sheppard (Rolls ser. lxxxv, 1887–9), i. 24; Knowles and Hadcock, 81; R. B. Dobson, *'Mynistres of Saynt Cuthbert'*:

university admissions offices in the 1980s, the cathedral chapters of the fifteenth century by no means always met their targets absolutely; but by and large numerical stability, more or less exact self perpetuation indeed, seems to have been their deliberate aim. One rarely for instance encounters a fifteenth-century cathedral prior who was positively commended for increasing the size of his community, a far cry there from the heady expansionism of the twelfth and thirteenth centuries. Despite the late Dom David Knowles's occasional view to the contrary, it is in other words highly unlikely that the monastic cathedrals of this period 'were able to accept all who wished to come'.[22]

Such considerations were self-evidently common to all the major monasteries of fifteenth-century England; and the point need hardly be laboured that in many other ways the Christian life led within the walls of the monastic cathedrals was not at all dissimilar to that conducted in the other great Benedictine abbeys of the country, several of which were quite as wealthy and quite as large. Heavily localised recruitment; entry into the fraternity through the gateway of the convent's almonry or grammar school; gradually increasing exposure to university education; an elaborate round of liturgical observance made ever more elaborate by the multiplication of communal and private masses; a fully developed so-called obedientiary system; the separation of powers (and revenues) between the monastic prelate and his flock; an increasing tendency for the superior to acquire supreme control in financial matters, often by taking monastic obediences into his own hands; the growing distinction between choir monks and those who held administrative office: all these, and many other, central features of fifteenth-century English religious life may sometimes be best exemplified in the monastic cathedrals but they are hardly unique to them.[23] So clearly is this the case that the question naturally arises whether members of monastic cathedral chapters normally thought of themselves as particularly different from, or superior to, their fellows in prestigious non-cathedral Benedictine communities. It is difficult to be positive; but at the least they would have had to concede that for the dignity of serving a cathedral they had to suffer the not insignificant indignity of being ruled by a prior rather than an abbot. In practice however it probably affected them very little that cathedral priors failed to receive an individual

---

the Monks of Durham in the Fifteenth Century (Durham Cathedral Lecture, 1972), 10–11.
[22] D. Knowles, The Religious Orders in England (Cambridge, 1948–59), ii. 261.
[23] R. H. Snape, English Monastic Finances in the Later Middle Ages (Cambridge, 1926), passim. For an extreme example of a cathedral prior (William Fressel of Rochester in 1511) simultaneously occupying the offices of treasurer, cellarer, chamberlain, almoner, precentor and infirmarian, see Smith, Collected Essays, 53.

writ of summons to the upper house of late medieval English parliaments but could be represented in the Commons instead.[24] Much
more revealingly, the records of fifteenth-century Black Monk Chapters meeting every three years at Northampton leave an unmistakable
impression that cathedral priors enjoyed no inherent prestige superior
to that of, say, Abbot John Whethamstede of St Albans. Those records,
and those of the Augustinian Chapters in the case of Carlisle, are the
best evidence available that—except in the case of Christ Church,
Canterbury—those priors and their proctors showed no signs of
regarding themselves as *primi inter pares*: they were generally quite
content to associate themselves with other Benedictine abbeys in the
common purposes of their order.[25] It would no doubt be a mistake to
assume that the brethren of any one fifteenth-century English monastic cathedral knew as much about their fellows within the seven
others as we do; but they were at least likely, as in the case of Prior
John Wessington of Durham when investigating episcopal installation
practice within the southern province in 1439, to be aware of their
location and—even more—of their privileges.[26] Few issues, to take
only one example, ever provoked such rapid and alarmed response
from the monks of Christ Church as the news that in 1355 the prior
of Worcester had received papal licence to wear the mitre and other
pontificalia denied to their own prior.[27]

That the monastic cathedral chapters of fifteenth-century England,
their corporate memories often still scarred by wounds inflicted in
jurisdictional conflicts with their bishops not so long ago, were acutely
sensitive to their comparative status need occasion no surprise. More
problematic is their response to that more fundamental and perhaps
unanswerable question, particularly applicable to themselves and
never perhaps more cogently phrased than by St Jerome: 'But what
has a monk to do with cities, which are the homes not of solitaries but
of crowds?'[28] What indeed? The remainder of this paper will attempt
to consider, however briefly, that perennial question, first in terms of

[24] J. Enoch Powell and K. Wallis, *The House of Lords in the Middle Ages* (1968), 303–
4, 499, 536, 553; Knowles, *Religious Orders*, ii. 299–306; R. N. Swanson, *Church and
Society in Late Medieval England* (Oxford, 1989), 109–10.

[25] *Chapters of Black Monks*, ii. 95–223; *Chapters of the Augustinian Canons*, ed. H. E. Salter
(Oxford Historical Soc., lxxiv, 1920). The complete exemption of the monks of Christ
Church, Canterbury, from the authority of the English Black Monk chapters had been
confirmed by Urban VI in 1379: Canterbury Cathedral Library, Register G, fo. 213;
Wilkins, *Concilia*, iii, 126.

[26] Dean and Chapter of Durham Muniments, Reg. Parv. ii, fos. 111–12; Dobson,
Durham Priory, 229.

[27] *Lit. Cant.*, ii. 328–32; J. M. Wilson, *The Worcester Liber Albus* (1920), xiv.

[28] *Rule of St Benedict, 1980*, 313.

the contribution made by monastic cathedral chapters to the work of their bishops and to religious life in their dioceses, and secondly in terms of the impact of the monks' exposed situation upon their own life within their priory. One can be under no illusion that exactly the same results will emerge for each of the eight monastic cathedrals in question. Indeed in the case of communities as complex and well-documented as these it might well prove a mistake to hope for absolutely definitive or even dispassionate judgements at all. The time may well have come for historians to emulate the examples of recent archaeological, architectural and art historians in recognising that 'a great church is rather like a small universe, capable of absorbing any amount of study'.[29]

Not that future research on English monastic cathedrals will ever be likely to remove the traditional judgement that these were institutions which suffered if not from original sin at least from a serious genetic flaw. Even for Dom David Knowles, in a paper he published nearly sixty years ago, 'the golden age of patriarchal rule in the cathedral priories was of short duration'.[30] Thanks, in other words, to Archbishop Lanfranc and his contemporaries, bishop and monastery had been joined together in a marriage within which proper conjugal relations were unattainable but from which divorce (although several archbishops of Canterbury before 1240 tried hard to achieve it) had proved impossible.[31] To that particular problem no doubt the best, if not complete, solution would have been the elevation to the English episcopal bench of large numbers of monk bishops. However, between 1215 and the Dissolution, the only monastic cathedrals in England with a reasonable prospect of securing a monk or mendicant as their titular abbot were, predictably enough, the two poorest: eight bishops of Carlisle and seven bishops of Rochester were regulars in that period, only a minority of those being promoted from the ranks of the two cathedral communities themselves.[32] By contrast, the sees of Canterbury and Winchester were very rarely held by a monk or friar again after the thirteenth century.[33]

---

[29] R. Morris, *Cathedrals and Abbeys of England and Wales: The Building Church, 600–1540* (1979), 56.

[30] D. Knowles, 'The Cathedral Monasteries', *Downside Review*, li (1933), 88.

[31] As late as 1228 Gregory IX had been prepared to discuss the archbishop's proposals to replace the Christ Church monks as the cathedral clergy of the see of Canterbury by secular canons: *Royal and other Letters illustrative of the Reign of Henry III*, ed. W. W. Shirley (Rolls ser. xxvii, 1862–8), i. 339; M. Gibbs and J. Lang, *Bishops and Reform, 1215–1272* (1934), 78–9.

[32] John Le Neve, *Fasti Ecclesiae Anglicanae: 1066–1300*. ii (1971), 19–21, 76–8; *1300–1541*, iv (1963), 37–40; *1300–1541*, vi (1963), 97–9.

[33] Le Neve, *Fasti, 1066–1300*, ii. 6–8; *1300–1541*, iv. 4–5, 45. Henry Woodlock (elected bishop of Winchester in 1305 when prior of St Swithun's) was the only

Against that all too familiar background, it is therefore all the more surprising to discover that there was a period, at the very end of the fifteenth century in fact, which witnessed a brief if limited revival of the English monk bishop, a possible portent of things that were not in the event to come. Quite how one should interpret the promotion of monks and canons like Richard Bell to Carlisle (1478), William Senhouse to Carlisle and Durham (1495 and 1502), Richard Redman to St Asaph (1472), Exeter (1495) and Ely (1501), and Henry Deane to Canterbury (1501) is not entirely clear. However, the elevation of these predominantly northern religious to predominantly northern sees seems hardly likely to be an altogether random phenomenon.[34] Perhaps indeed the emergence of these last of all medieval English monk bishops should be associated, however marginally, with one of the more intriguing currents of religious opinion in the pre-Lutheran age. As is well known, for several early Tudor bishops, like John Longland of Lincoln and perhaps even Cardinal Wolsey himself, the long awaited *reformatio regni Angliae*, if it was ever to come at all, might well be generated from within as well as without the monastic precinct walls of the English church.[35] For not altogether dissimilar reasons must Bishop Richard Fox of Winchester not only have translated the Rule of St Benedict into English for the edification of nuns but also contemplated the foundation of a substantial academic college or *studium* at Oxford for eight of his own cathedral monks.[36] By a final irony, it seems probable that in the early sixteenth century more in the way of spiritual example and spiritual leadership was being expected of cathedral monastic communities than had been expected of their predecessors for the previous two centuries and more.[37]

---

member of the regular clergy ever to preside over the diocese of Winchester in the later middle ages. See H. Johnstone, 'Henry Woodlock of Winchester and his Register', *Church Quarterly Rev.* cxl (1945), 154–64.

[34] Richard of Gloucester's powerful influence undoubtedly helped to secure the promotion to high ecclesiastical office of Richard Redman and Richard Bell: C. Ross, *Richard III* (1981), 43, 156, 181; B. Dobson, 'Richard Bell, Prior of Durham (1464–78) and Bishop of Carlisle (1478–95)', *Trans. of Cumberland and Westmorland Antiq. and Archaeol. Soc.*, new ser. lxv (1965), 207–11, 215.

[35] For Wolsey's decisive role in ensuring the completion of the English Augustinian canons' academic college of St Mary's at Oxford, see *Chapters of the Augustinian Canons*, 129–30, 134–5; E. Evans, 'St. Mary's College in Oxford for Austin canons', *Oxfordshire Arch. Soc. Reports*, no. 26 (1931), 369–89. Cf. M. Bowker, *The Henrician Reformation: the Diocese of Lincoln under John Longland, 1521–1547* (Cambridge, 1981), 17–28; *Humanism, Reform and the Reformation, The Career of Bishop John Fisher*, ed. B. Bradshaw and E. Duffy (Cambridge, 1989), 73–4.

[36] Collett, 'Fox's Translation of Benedictine Rule', 214–24; J. G. Milne, *The Early History of Corpus Christi College, Oxford* (Oxford, 1946), 2; C. Harper-Bill, *The Pre-Reformation Church in England, 1400–1530* (1989), 43.

[37] Cf. C. Harper-Bill, 'Dean Colet's Convocation Sermon and the Pre-Reformation Church in England', *History*, lxxiii (1988), 195–6.

Whatever the reasons for that change of attitude, at least there are good grounds for believing that during the course of the fifteenth century the delicate relationship between bishops and their monastic chapters had been gradually drained of its most divisive and poisonous effects. The marriage remained potentially uneasy no doubt; and in most cases, as the late Professor Hamilton Thompson always liked to observe, it was episcopal absence rather than presence which tended to make the monastic heart grow fonder.[38] Much, too, naturally depended on the personality and other preoccupations of the prelates in question; and on the copious evidence available one must never underestimate the likelihood of occasional explosions of irritability, that not entirely unknown episcopal characteristic in any period, on the part of pontiffs who were debarred by protocol and convention from having much significant influence within the church which housed their own *cathedra*.[39] More serious still for the bishop of a monastic cathedral was the lack of prebendal patronage at his disposal as compared with an archbishop of York or bishop of London: this was a deficiency tolerable no doubt in the case of Canterbury or Winchester but at times genuinely disabling as at Rochester, and especially at Carlisle.[40] However, most monastic cathedral chapters were obliging enough to make available at least some of their own ecclesiastical and other patronage to their bishop; and for that and other reasons it could be argued that during the fifteenth century relations between the bishop and his monks had more or less assimilated themselves to contemporary patterns of secular 'good lordship'. In the pathetic words of one anonymous poem, almost certainly written by a monk of St Swithun's, to Bishop William Wayneflete shortly after 1450, 'Off all oure lordys that nowe ben trustyde beste/My lorde of Wynchestre men seyn that hitt ys he'.[41] However, if the characteristic stance of fifteenth-century prior and chapter towards their bishop was one of slightly nervous importunity, the latter for his part must have been only too aware that his cathedral community would provide him with those most precious of all blessings—the certain prospect of a permanent resting place in this world

---

[38] A. Hamilton Thompson, *The Cathedral Churches of England* (1925), 22–3, 165; *The English Clergy and their Organisation in the Later Middle Ages* (Oxford, 1947), 72–5.

[39] See, e,g, Dobson, *Durham Priory*, 227–9.

[40] At Rochester in the early sixteenth century it has been calculated that only 4% of the bishop's ecclesiastical patronage was derived from non-parochial sources: *Humanism, Reform and Reformation*, 72–3, 251–2. For the scarcity of episcopal clerical counsellors in the diocese of Carlisle, see Borthwick Institute of Historical Research, York, Reg. 18 (Henry Bowet, 1407–23), fos. 284–5.

[41] E. Wilson, 'A Poem presented to William Waynflete as Bishop of Winchester', *Middle English Studies presented to Norman Davis in honour of his seventieth birthday* (Oxford, 1983), 139. Cf. *Lit. Cant.*, iii. 274, 285, 287, 304, 333; Dobson, *Durham Priory*, 238.

as well as invaluable assistance (whether his chantry chapel was to be served by secular chaplains or the monks themselves) during his progress towards salvation in the next.[42]

For these and other reasons the constitutional history of the fifteenth-century cathedral monastery usually emerges as a harmonious if fascinating exercise in the successful containment of once notorious occasions for conflict with the titular abbot. Of those occasions, formal episcopal visitation undoubtedly remained the most likely cause for danger, not least because of its tendency to exacerbate rather than diminish personal tension and faction within the cloister. All the more unfortunate therefore that episcopal visitation records of cathedral monasteries after 1400 are usually so much less informative than those recently studied by Dr Greatrex for the immediately preceding period.[43] However, there can be little doubt that during the course of the fifteenth century not only did episcopal visitations become less frequent but also, and somewhat ironically, they increasingly became an instrument for securing episcopal approval of initiatives the prior and *sanior pars capituli* wished to make anyway. Post-visitation episcopal injunctions of cathedral churches were, in any case, by then often compiled with the active assistance and full co-operation of the prior, a circumstance which emerges especially clearly in the case of Bishop Robert Neville's exceptionally well documented visitation of Prior John Wessington and the Durham monks in July 1442.[44] To that extent the bishop's visitations of his cathedral chapter, like the triennial visitations conducted in the fifteenth century by commissioners of the Black Monk Chapters, had often been deprived of much of their capacity to alarm and indeed to reform.[45] All in all, the visitation records of the late medieval cathedral monastery are more likely to be an accurate guide to its own administrative priorities and sense of propriety rather than, as is often assumed, to the real moral shortcomings of its inmates.

[42] *Register of Common Seal*, 105–7, 113–14; G. L. Harriss, *Cardinal Beaufort, A Study of Lancastrian Ascendancy and Decline* (Oxford, 1988), 378–9; C. E. Woodruff and W. Danks, *Memorials of the Cathedral and Priory of Christ in Canterbury* (1912), 194–5.

[43] See, e.g., *Visitations of Norwich*, 7–8; *Kentish Visitations of Archbishop William Warham and his Deputies, 1511–12*, ed. K. L. Wood-Legh (Kent Records, xxiv, 1984), 1–6. Cf. J. Greatrex, 'Episcopal Relations with monastic chapters as reflected in 14th Century Visitation Records', *Sonderdruck aus Regulae Benedicti Studia, Annuarium Internationale* 14/15 (1988), 309–22; B. Harbottle, 'Bishop Hatfield's Visitation of Durham Priory in 1354', *Archaeologia Aeliana*, 4th ser. xxxvi (1958), 81–100; C. R. Cheney, 'Norwich Cathedral Priory in the Fourteenth Century', *Bull. of John Rylands Library*, xx (1936), 105–17.

[44] Dean and Chapter of Durham Muniments, 2.7. Pont. nos 8, 9; Dobson, 'Mynistres of Saynt Cuthbert', 22–38; cf. *Ely Chapters and Visitation Records, 1241–1515*, ed. S. J. A. Evans, in *Camden Miscellany*, xvii (Camden 3rd ser. lxiv, 1940), pp. xiv–xvi, 52–67.

[45] *Chapters of Black Monks*, ii. 162; iii. 82–4; Dobson, *Durham Priory*, 247–8.

Nor is it altogether easy to know how seriously to regard that feature of the fifteenth-century monastic cathedral which would have appealed to Kafka most—the titular abbot's right to appoint monks to certain obediences within a monastery of which he was not in reality the effective *abbas*. In this sphere variation of custom between the eight cathedrals was extreme, to say the least. At Durham, for example, by the terms of the agreement or *Convenit* made long ago with Bishop Richard Poore in 1229, the prior and chapter of St Cuthbert were in practice more or less completely free from episcopal intervention in making such appointments. By contrast, at Worcester the reluctance of successive bishops to surrender their authority over the cathedral's sacrist to the prior engendered conflicts which lasted for more than two centuries and could lead to allegations of 'simony, disobedience, dilapidation' and even incontinence and fornication.[46] It would be readily agreed that bishops tended to enjoy, and monastic chapters tended to abhor, such appointments to obediences, above all as a demonstration of the titular abbot's otherwise usually remote personal authority over his most immediate flock. But was the prelate's right to select an important obedientiary anything more than a symbol of that authority? The answer to that peculiarly difficult question also varied from cathedral to cathedral and from bishop to bishop; but in almost all cases it is hard to avoid the conclusion that this was a custom certainly not worth the trouble it took to preserve. At its worst, as in the no doubt exceptional case of the last priors of Canterbury College, Oxford, who were appointed by the archbishop, the practice may positively have encouraged disobedience to the cathedral prior and chapter.[47] Fortunately for both parties the much more important issue of the selection of cathedral prior seems to have been remarkably uncontentious, controlled as it was by the meticulous if cumbersome processes of free canonical election in chapter: the bishop in his turn could be certain that the detailed results of such elections would be communicated to him, usually in notarial form, for inspection and approval.[48] On the other hand, record rarely survives of a prelate letting it be known in advance which prior he would most like to emerge from the capitular processes of scrutiny, compromise or the *via Spiritus Sancti*. But were fifteenth-century bishops in practice quite so scrupulous, or so indifferent, in the case of such an important

---

[46] Dean and Chapter of Durham Muniments, 1.4. Pont. no. 4; J. Greatrex, 'Monastic or Episcopal Obedience: the Problems of the Sacrists of Worcester', *Worcestershire Historical Society, Occasional Publications*, 3 (1980), 1–16.

[47] *Canterbury College, Oxford*, ed. W. A. Pantin (Oxford Historical Society, vi–viii, xxx; 1947–50, 1985), iii. 148–55; *Letters and Papers, Henry VIII*, xiii (i), no. 527.

[48] E.g., Canterbury Cathedral Library, Reg. S, fos. 231, 249, 251–4; Dobson, *Durham Priory*, 84–8.

appointment as they were bound to appear in public? One may sometimes doubt it; and in the admittedly special case of the *prefectio* of a prior of Christ Church, archbishops were almost always very careful to be present at Canterbury itself for a day or two before their 'scrutiny' of the election in the chapter house of the cathedral.[49]

Throughout the fifteenth century a harmonious relationship between a bishop and his cathedral prior remained as critical to the welfare of the see as it had always been. For the former, his prior normally played a much more important role than that of personal deputy within the cathedral monastery. The two men can hardly not have known each other well; and the records relating to all eight monastic cathedrals and their dioceses are liberally adorned with references to personal encounters, to the mutual exchange of gifts and—by implication—to the discussion of difficult problems. From the time of Henry of Eastry onwards, the priors of Christ Church, Canterbury, present the best examples of the monastic superior as a sort of *éminence grise*.[50] However, the priors of Durham, to cite just another example, were often equally ready with advice to their bishop, sometimes inept as in their comments on how to contain the dangers presented by the Nevilles and Percys, sometimes astute as in their plans to protect the liberties of their church.[51] In this connection it is worth stressing that the preservation of a cathedral church's inherited franchises usually mattered a good deal more to a residentiary prior and chapter than it did to their much more peripatetic bishop. Indeed the latter, by contrast, often valued his prior's services most highly when they were exercised on a wider stage than the cathedral monastery itself. Several fifteenth-century priors, like their predecessors in the fourteenth century, would have startled St Benedict by being very ready to serve as episcopal vicars general and commissaries: admittedly they most often did so at the beginning of a bishop's term of office and before he had found time to select his personal team of high-level diocesan administrators.[52] The latter were themselves familiar figures in late medieval monastic cathedral churches, above all no doubt because so

[49] Stone's *Chronicle*, 21, 39, 46, 105–6, 116.

[50] Canterbury Cathedral Library, 'Eastry Correspondence'; *Lit. Cant.*, i. 221–43, iii. 70–2, 138–40; T. L. Hogan, 'The Memorandum Book of Henry of Eastry, Prior of Christ Church Canterbury' (Ph.D. thesis, University of London, 1966), i. *passim*.

[51] A. J. Pollard, 'St Cuthbert and the Hog: Richard III and the County Palatine of Durham, 1471–85', in *Kings and Nobles in the Later Middle Ages: A Tribute to Charles Ross*, ed. R. A. Griffiths and J. Sherborne (Gloucester, 1986), 118–19; Dobson, 'Richard Bell', 205–6.

[52] A. B. Emden, *A Biographical Register of the University of Oxford to A.D. 1500* (3 vols, 1957–9), ii. 783; Jacob, *Henry Chichele*, 90; I. J. Churchill, *Canterbury Administration* (2 vols, 1933), ii. 5–6.

many of those cathedrals housed one, more or all of the episcopal courts. The meeting places of the Official's consistory courts in particular seem to have become increasingly fixed during the course of the fifteenth century. They were not always located within the cathedral church itself, being as far away as Cambridge in the case of the diocese of Ely; but they were usually held in a comparatively quiet part of the cathedral, as under the north-western tower of Canterbury and in the Galilee Chapel at Durham.[53]

A more active, if unduly neglected, contribution of the cathedral monastic community as a whole to the spiritual welfare of its region concerned its participation in what Professor Roy Haines has recently called the 'penitential system at diocesan level'.[54] Senior brethren, and especially subpriors, within every one of the eight cathedral monasteries for which record survives were regularly commissioned by their bishop to act as penitentiaries; and there is indeed little doubt that within many late medieval cathedral cities these monks became the confessorial *corps d'élite*, with the natural exception of the bishops and suffragan bishops themselves. Once again, details of appointment and procedure varied from cathedral to cathedral; but in the not untypical case of Winchester the monk penitentiary was empowered to hear confession, to grant absolution and to impose penance not only on his fellow monks but also on all the other subjects of the bishop within the cathedral city and its diocese.[55] The effectiveness of this system of confession to diocesan penitentiaries, which remained intact to the Dissolution, more or less defies analysis; but it seems probable in this instance at least that monastic cathedrals had more assiduous confessors to offer the penitent than did their secular counterparts. More important still, nowhere else was the spiritual relationship between cathedral monk and members of lay society likely to be more literally close and personal.

Nevertheless it is tempting to suppose that it was as preachers rather than confessors that the cathedral monks of the fifteenth century exerted most influence outside their own community. The importance of trained preachers within a large abbey or cathedral priory of the fifteenth century was first made apparent in the late Mr W. A. Pantin's edition of material relating to the Chapters of the Black Monks; and what little work has been done on the subject since Pantin's death,

---

[53] D. M. Owen, *Ely Records: A Handlist of the Records of the Bishop and Archdeacon of Ely* (Cambridge, 1971), pp. vii–viii, 20–21; Woodruff and Danks, *Canterbury*, 274; *Rites of Durham*, 73, 252.

[54] R. M. Haines, *Ecclesia Anglicana: Studies in the English Church of the Later Middle Ages* (Toronto, 1989), 39–52.

[55] *Ibid.*, 46; cf. *Register of Henry Chichele, Archbishop of Canterbury, 1414–1443*, ed. E. F. Jacob (Canterbury and York Soc., 1937–47), iv. 150–2, 241–2.

for instance by Dr Harvey in the case of Westminster Abbey, makes it clear that the issue remains an important one.[56] As Pantin himself appreciated, one of the primary purposes of the late medieval monastic *studia* at Oxford and Cambridge was in fact to train the most intellectually able university monks in the *ars predicandi*. From 1444 onwards it was in fact compulsory for all Black Monk scholars at Gloucester College to preach at least four times a year in both Latin and English so that their course of sermons might be properly accomplished when the time came 'for them to be recalled to their monasteries'.[57] However, although sermons by monks regularly punctuated the routines of late medieval Oxford and Cambridge and of the Black Monk Chapters at Northampton, for obvious reasons no Benedictine could normally hope to find a larger audience than within his own monastic cathedral. Readers of John Stone's chronicle and of other fifteenth-century Christ Church biographical notices will need no reminding of the large number of sermons delivered in Canterbury cathedral every year by a multiplicity of preachers, nor of the particular enthusiasm displayed towards any member of the community itself who developed into an especially '*egregius predicator*'.[58] More significantly still, some members of monastic cathedrals, like John Langdon of Canterbury and Robert Rypon of Durham, gained outstanding national oratorical reputations. As in the case of mendicant preachers, the sermons produced by cathedral monks might have the capacity to say the unexpected: why else would Thomas Cromwell himself have commissioned Brother William Sandwyche of Christ Church to preach at St Paul's Cross in July 1537?.[59] But then, like the even more influential preaching of the friars, the sermons delivered by cathedral monks during the two or three generations before their sudden demise no doubt pointed in more than one direction. At this stage of research on the topic one can do little more than express the fairly safe conjecture that those directions were often more central to the Christian life in the later middle ages than is usually allowed.

A much more positive verdict seems possible, at least at first sight, in the case of the seriousness with which, as the fifteenth century

[56] W. A. Pantin, 'General and Provincial Chapters of the English Black Monks', *Supra*, 4th ser. x. (1927), 195–263; *Chapters of Black Monks*, iii. 400; B. Harvey, 'The Monks of Westminster and the University of Oxford', in *The Reign of Richard II*, ed. F. R. H. du Boulay and C. M. Barron (1971), 118–20.

[57] *Chapters of Black Monks*, ii. 214. For the university sermons regularly preached by the senior Black monk scholars at Oxford, see, e.g., Oxford University Archives, Reg. Eee, fos 362v, 366v, 392v.

[58] Stone's *Chronicle*, 24, 32–3, 188, 190, 193.

[59] *Ibid.*, 137; *BRUO*, ii. 1094; G. R. Owst, *Preaching in Medieval England* (Cambridge, 1926), 28–32, 181–6, 249–51; A. B. Emden, *A Biographical Register of the University of Oxford, A,D. 1501 to 1540* (Oxford, 1974), 504.

progressed, all eight monastic cathedral communities committed themselves more and more intensively to the cause of university education. In many ways, as once again the late Mr W. A. Pantin was the first to appreciate, the progressive exposure of increasing numbers of monks and regular canons to academic study was the single most important new departure in the late medieval religious life. Although now a familiar enough theme, not least because the university monks of the fifteenth century lend themselves so well to biographical and prosopographical investigation, it continues to be difficult to evaluate: in many ways what Pantin diagnosed long ago as 'a new monastic movement' still remains remarkably obscure.[60] One complicating issue is naturally that Christian monastic attitudes to academic learning have themselves rarely been other than ambivalent. Such ambiguities lay not very far below the surface of late medieval monastic and cathedral chapters, with the result that their enthusiasm for university education often tended to vary and oscillate from century to century and even from decade to decade. But although the evolution of the 'moine universitaire' is accordingly a highly complicated development, there is no doubt that cathedral monasteries played an important and, cumulatively speaking, perhaps a dominant role within that evolution. Because of their unique asset of controlling their own private monastic colleges at Oxford from the late fourteenth century onwards, the cathedral priories of Christ Church and Durham could hardly avoid becoming the homes of the largest conglomerations of university monks in the country. Although better documented than any other religious academic colleges within fifteenth-century England, at neither Canterbury nor Durham Colleges are the surviving administrative records at all complete. However, it seems certain that at least one in four of all Durham monks received some form of university education; and it would be surprising if future research did not eventually raise the comparative figure at Christ Church from the one in eight suggested by Pantin.[61] More interesting still is Dr Greatrex's recent calculation that at least one in seven Norwich cathedral monks must at one time or another have been university scholars, a figure reasonably comparable with her own estimate of one in nine at Worcester.[62] In the case of the other four monastic cathedrals the evidence from surviving obedientiary accounts is much less com-

---

[60] *Chapters of Black Monks*, iii. p. ix.

[61] *Some Durham College Rolls*, ed. H. E. D. Blakiston, in *Collectanea* iii (Oxford Historical Society, xxxii, 1896), 1–76; Dobson, *Durham Priory*, 351–3; *Canterbury College*, iv. 218–28.

[62] J. Greatrex, 'Monk Students from Norwich Cathedral Priory at Oxford and Cambridge: their attendance record and their impact on their community, c. 1300–1530' (*E.H.R.*, forthcoming).

prehensive, but perhaps not sufficiently so as to invalidate the general impression that, more than nearly all English monasteries, the eight cathedral priories were the homes of a genuine academic élite—if not necessarily the only élite—within their fraternity.

Precisely what difference exposure to university study actually made to the eight English monastic cathedrals of the fifteenth century is a more problematic and indeed controversial matter. Certain practical consequences there obviously were. Academic learning must imply books, and more and more specialised books at that: it usually tends to imply increasingly comprehensive, well organised and catalogued libraries too. Admittedly, in this sphere as throughout this lecture, there always seem to be exceptions to break every rule. The monks of Rochester may have had to wait until a legacy from Archbishop Thomas Rotherham as late as 1500 before they finally acquired a separate library building or room; and it seems even more surprising that the community of Ely cathedral priory—according to Dr Dorothy Owen—never possessed a custom-built common library building as such at all.[63] Elsewhere however, with Christ Church and Durham as the best documented examples, there is little doubt that the fifteenth-century cathedral monsteries, influenced by Oxford college practice and vice-versa, were in the vanguard of the first great library boom in English history.[64] Admittedly nothing can be harder to prove than that those who enter a library actually read much within it; but at least the avid appetite of all eight monastic cathedral communities for imported printed books during the last twenty years of the fifteenth century suggests that the scholarly atmosphere there may have some-times been permeated by currents of thought a little more impressive than the complete intellectual torpor and spiritual rusticity lamented by Dom David Knowles. Moreover, and as the *Rites of Durham* were so eloquently to remember, at least some of the resources of the cathedral libraries as well as the academic skills of the university-educated monks themselves were devoted to education within the cloister itself. In her Ford Lectures early last year Miss Harvey in-formed us that one of the last unresolved problems in the history of the medieval English religious orders is what monks actually did in the afternoons. Here again practice no doubt varied; but according to a chapter ordinance of 1448 what most of the younger monks

[63] W. H. Mackean, *Rochester Cathedral Library* (Rochester, 1953), 8; Owen, *Library and Muniments of Ely Cathedral*, 1–4.

[64] M. R. James, *The Ancient Libraries of Canterbury and Dover* (Cambridge, 1903), xxxv–lv; A. J. Piper, 'The libraries of the monks of Durham', in *Medieval Scribes, Manuscripts and Libraries: Essays presented to N. R. Ker*, ed. M. B. Parkes and A. G. Watson (1978), 213–49; J. Newman, 'Oxford Libraries before 1800', *Archaeological Journal*, cxxxv (1978), 248–50.

of Ely cathedral priory should have been doing between 1.30 and 3 o'clock precisely was receiving instruction in grammar and more advanced academic subjects.[65]

Accordingly the many ecclesiastical historians who in future may wish to defend rather than to denigrate the achievements of the late medieval monastic cathedral communities will not be without the means to do so. However, it would be idle to pretend that such a defence will ever be completely straightforward, above all no doubt because it must now seem that those communities did so much less than one might expect to defend themselves. In retrospect, not only the monks of Ely and Rochester but of Christ Church and Durham too appear—the arguments are admittedly largely *ex silentio*—to have suffered from a failure of self-projection in the public arena. Despite the unascertainable effect of all their sermons, despite the crowds of pilgrims and tourists who visited their shrines every day, the cathedral priors and chapters can rarely be said to have advanced a particularly vigorous case for their own way of life, whether their critic was Wyclif, Henry V or Erasmus.[66] Such disinclination to articulate one's own religious values, which reached so undeniable and disturbing a climax in the case of nearly all England's monastic superiors in the 1530s, no doubt has profound and complicated roots. This excessively general lecture should end by mentioning three of them. In the first place, and to return to a theme with which this survey began, it is not hard to appreciate that a monastic community, even a monastic cathedral community, will often suffer from a chronic and inherent incapacity when faced with the need to justify its existence in public, to defend before a sceptical world what is defensible only as an indirect rather than direct apostolate. Nor will English university teachers of the twentieth century need reminding that most members of institutional corporations tend—ironically enough—to be too preoccupied with office, too immersed in the burdens of detailed administrative and other responsibility, to be the ideal defenders of the wider interests of their corporation as a whole. Miss Harvey has recently concluded that at late medieval Westminster Abbey approximately 60% of the community held a time-consuming obedience. In most of England's eight late fifteenth-century cathedral monasteries that proportion seems to have been considerably more; and in a list of the fifty-nine monks of England's greatest cathedral on the very eve of its

---

[65] Cambridge University Library, EDR, G2/3, fo. 28; cf. *Rites of Durham*, 48.

[66] No comprehensive investigation of saints' cults and shrines at fifteenth-century cathedrals has yet been attempted; but see R. C. Finucane's discussion of 'new shrines and old saints' in *Miracles and Pilgrims: Popular Beliefs in Medieval England* (1977), 191–202.

suppression, no less than forty are recorded as holders of administrative office.[67]

Thirdly, finally, and perhaps most profoundly, both the strains of monastic administration and the effects of university education undoubtedly accelerated yet another development, a tendency towards what might be termed, for lack of a better phrase, enhanced individualism within the monastic and cathedral cloister. To use another word which may run the risk of being about to go out of fashion, the increasing 'privatisation' of the individual monk's personal religious life is obviously not easy to demonstrate; but the increasing privatisation of his economic position and of his environment is very easy to demonstrate indeed. By the early sixteenth century, private chambers and private offices (a particularly well-attested set at Ely, for example) were showing signs of becoming as important to senior cathedral monks as they are to us.[68] Or again, G. H. Rooke's short study of 'Dom William Ingram and His Account Book, 1504–1533' leaves no doubt at all of the way in which a Christ Church, Canterbury, obedientiary could readily establish what amounted to his own miniature household economy within the most elaborate estates and management structure in the country.[69]

Here and elsewhere in the intricate world of the fifteenth-century cathedral priory are we not at times likely to be observing an instance of somewhat paradoxical cause and effect? The larger and more publicly exposed the religious community, namely a cathedral monastery, the more possible perhaps it was for at least some of its inmates to retreat into metaphorical or real private fastnesses. Is the late medieval history of the major English religious houses, and of the eight monastic cathedrals above all, primarily an exercise in the gradual transformation of a unitary house of God into a divine mansion of many chambers? If so, one might also be tempted, although not all would, to judge this development as a source of greater strength rather than (necessarily) of weakness. Perhaps the last words on this issue might most appropriately go to a twentieth-century English churchman, now perhaps best remembered as the primary model for Paul Jago, the defeated candidate in C. P. Snow's *The Masters*, but also a celebrated canon who served one particular English cathedral chapter for several, not entirely happy, years. 'Ely Cathedral',

[67] *Canterbury College*, iii. 151–4; cf. *Compotus Rolls of the Obedientiaries of St Swithun's Priory, Winchester*, ed. G. W. Kitchin (Hampshire Record Society, vii, 1892), *passim*; Dobson, *Durham Priory*, 66–9.

[68] *The Monastic Setting of Ely*, ed, R. Holmes and G. Youell (Ely, 1974), 42–7; R. Gilyard-Beer, *Abbeys* (HMSO, 1958), 48.

[69] G. H. Rooke, 'Dom William Ingram and his Account-book, 1504–1533', *Journal of Ecclesiastical History*, vii (1956), 30–44.

exclaimed Canon Charles Raven at a moment of more than usual exasperation, 'Ely Cathedral is a great white elephant which feeds on the souls of men'.[70] Those in this audience who have spent part or all of their careers serving corporations may not be entirely irresponsive to such a *cri de coeur*. In the fifteenth century too, such dangers certainly existed; but to the credit of the English monastic cathedrals of the later middle ages it now seems more likely than not that they provided their brethren with greater opportunities for influence, material welfare and even individual fulfilment than has ever been properly allowed since their unique position within the medieval English church was brought to so arbitrary and unanticipated an end.

[70] F. W. Dillistone, *Charles Raven, Naturalist, Historian, Theologian* (1975), 189. I am most grateful to Dr David Smith, Dr Joan Greatex and Miss Barbara Harvey for their comments on the original version of this lecture.

PAROCHIAL CONFORMITY AND VOLUNTARY RELIGION IN LATE-MEDIEVAL ENGLAND

By Gervase Rosser

READ 15 SEPTEMBER 1990

MUCH evidence has been brought to light recently to demonstrate the vitality of religious life among the English laity on the eve of the Reformation. Attention has been drawn to the fact that, in the period before the advent of Protestantism, lay men and women evinced a high degree of commitment to their church.[1] The religious changes of the sixteenth century are as pressing a historical problem as ever; moreover, they provide a valuable litmus with which to test the qualities of the late-medieval church. Nevertheless, there is a danger that the fascination of the Reformation question, together with the bias of documentary sources on lay religion towards the latter end of the medieval period, may impoverish our appreciation of the ways in which, for a thousand years, Christians in Britain had been shaping their religious lives. To take a long view of religious voluntarism may help to put the developments of the fifteenth and sixteenth centuries in a proper perspective. There has also been a tendency, in discussion of lay religious life in the late middle ages, to accept the institutional framework as given. Yet in practice that framework was both adjustable and expressive of a wide range of lay initiatives in religion. That men and women were prepared to lend material support to a variety of religious institutions is apparent from any medieval collection of wills or set of churchwardens' accounts. But what, exactly, was expressed by such support? This is not an easy question to answer. Any assessment calls for an understanding of the medieval parish, not as a legal abstraction, nor yet as a supposedly 'natural' community of inhabitants, but as a more or less adaptable framework shaped by, and in turn shaping, the lives of its members. The evidence of religious activity, from processions to church-building, is, so far as it goes, not hard to find. But what of the parochial structure which gave meaning to these gestures, and which could in turn be modified by them?

The parish is so venerable an institution that it is in danger of

---

[1] E.g. J. J. Scarisbrick, *The Reformation and the English People* (Oxford, 1984); N. P. Tanner, *The Church in Late Medieval Norwich 1370–1532* (Pontifical Institute of Mediaeval Studies, Studies and Texts, 66, 1984); R. N. Swanson, *Church and Society in Late Medieval England* (Oxford, 1989), ch. 6; R. Morris, *Churches in the Landscape* (1989), ch. 9. For their very helpful comments on an earlier version of this paper I am grateful to Jane Garnett and Richard Morris.

being taken for granted. Even if we acknowledge that, as a formally constituted ecclesiastical body, the local parish is no older than the twelfth century, we might be beguiled by the canon lawyers of that period into believing that, by the thirteenth century, a complete parochial administration had been definitively imposed upon the English landscape, and that this was all-embracing and immutable. The clarity of the projected pattern, however, owes more to the contemporary legal imagination than it does to the realities of human behaviour. By 1300, it is true, every man and woman in the country had been assigned to a parish church, and was supposed to know which one. The attachment carried responsibilities, including regular attendance at Sunday services and the payment, towards the upkeep of the church and its ministers, of a tithe of produce.[2] These duties were underlined by the annual Rogationtide beating of parochial boundaries, a ritual which clarified the extent of influence of each parish church.[3] That lengths of those parish boundaries had in numerous cases already existed for many centuries before the twelfth as important territorial divisions seems only to strengthen the lawyers' view that, after 1300, the parochial system would be susceptible to strictly limited adjustment.[4] And indeed, it is the case that the bounds of most parishes and their approximate total number—somewhat above eight thousand—would remain unchanged between 1300 and the 1840s.[5] Yet the recognition of this outline is no more than the beginning of understanding. In practice the medieval parish always admitted a variety of concurrent patterns of religious activity. Within and around the parish, cross-cutting institutions and patterns of behaviour both fostered and gave expression to that independent impetus among the laity which has been observed in the immediately pre-Reformation will registers and churchwardens' accounts, and which should properly be traced back to the very beginnings of Christianity in Britain.

To understand this religious freedom within the late-medieval parish, it must be remembered that the number of parochial altars in the country was greatly exceeded by the quantity of officially

[2] For recent discussion of the development of parishes, see *Minsters and Parish Churches: The Local Church in Transition 950–1200*, ed. J. Blair (Oxford Univ. Committee for Archaeology Monographs, xvii, 1988).

[3] M. W. Beresford, 'A journey along boundaries', in his *History on the Ground* (2nd edn, 1971), 25–62.

[4] Parochial boundaries did not in all cases follow ancient territorial divisions; but that lengths of them did so in parts of Wessex is demonstrated by D. J. Bonney, 'Early boundaries in Wessex', in *Archaeology and the Landscape*, ed. P. J. Fowler (1972), 168–86.

[5] R. K. Morris, 'The church in the countryside: two lines of enquiry', in *Medieval Villages. A Review of Current Work*, ed. D. Hooke (Oxford Univ. Committee for Archaeology Monographs, v, 1985), 47–60, at 50–1 and table 5.1.

subordinate shrines and chapels, many of which formed part of the parish church itself, while numerous others were housed in separate buildings. In the later middle ages the provision of parish churches was widely perceived to be considerable: indeed, figures of forty-five to fifty thousand (six times the actual number) were on several occasions thought reasonable estimates.[6] Yet in many if not most counties the parish churches were outnumbered by separate, lay-supported chapels of various kinds. Lancashire before the Reformation supported 100 detached chapels in 59 parishes.[7] Cornwall may have been the county most densely scattered with non-parochial chapels, of which it has been estimated there were 700, in just 209 parishes.[8] Counties whose early density of population helped to establish a relatively greater concentration of parishes seem to have been less generously endowed with churches of other kinds, yet even here the numbers are impressive. Kent, with 500 parishes, boasted an estimated 300 chapels before the Black Death.[9] In Lincolnshire's approximately 600 parishes, 236 medieval chapels have been identified; and a subjective impression would suggest that the number of chapels in Norfolk, which comprised some 750 parishes, was, if no greater, not very much less.[10] Many of these detached chapels originated, as holy sites if not as fully-fledged churches, in the early Christian centuries; some, indeed, occupied the former *loci* of pre-Christian sanctuaries. Minor rural oratories already appear in the written record in the early seventh century;[11] and numbers of these would continue to be

[6] For the English government's acceptance of a figure of 45,000 in 1371, see O. Coleman, 'What figures? Some thoughts on the use of information by medieval governments', in *Trade, Government and Economy in Pre-Industrial England*, ed. D. C. Coleman and A. H. John (1976), 96–112, at 102–3, 107. A century later a Norfolk man, John Rennys, noted in his commonplace book that he believed 'the number of parish churches in England' to be 48,822. Oxford, Bodleian Library, MS Tanner 407, fo. 37v; W. M. Ormrod, 'An experiment in taxation: the English parish subsidy of 1371', *Speculum*, lxiii (1988), 59–82.

[7] G. Tupling, 'The pre-Reformation parishes and chapelries of Lancashire', *Transactions of the Lancashire and Cheshire Antiquarian Society*, lxvii (1957), 1–16.

[8] J. H. Adams, 'The mediaeval chapels of Cornwall', *Journal of the Royal Institution of Cornwall*, new ser., iii (1957), 48–65, at 48.

[9] A. Everitt, *Continuity and Colonization. The Evolution of Kentish Settlement* (Leicester, 1986), 184, 205–6.

[10] D. M. Owen, 'Medieval chapels in Lincolnshire', *Lincolnshire History and Archaeology*, x (1975), 15–22. Numbers of parishes in these counties in the early nineteenth century are given in S. Lewis, *Topographical Dictionary of England* (4 vols., 1840), iii. 77, 366. Further on the provision of chapels at the time of the Reformation, see C. Kitching, 'Church and chapelry in sixteenth-century England', *Studies in Church History*, xvi (1979), 279–90.

[11] *Bede's Ecclesiastical History of the English People*, ed. B. Colgrave and R. A. B. Mynors (Oxford, 1969), v. 12, p. 488 ('villulae oratorium').

maintained, apart from the developing stratum of churches of parochial status, during the ensuing generations.

I want to suggest where we should look for the well-spring of this fecundity within the parish. To begin with it will be helpful to indicate where that source should *not* be sought, in despite of the tendency of some recent research. It is widely recognised that the process of settlement of new lands at the margins of the occupied landscape, which had a long history before 1300, continued (although unevenly) thereafter. It is also acknowledged that these areas of colonised waste were often characterised by relatively lax lordship, in comparison with the older-settled lands. A further link has been proposed between the atmosphere of freedom which allegedly typified these marginal settlements and the drive to secure for them ecclesiastical provision in the form of dependent chapelries within their mother parishes. A distinguished proponent of this view, Alan Everitt, has developed the argument a stage further, hypothesising an evolution, from the chapels maintained by the free spirits of such frontier zones as the Kentish Weald, to later nonconformity.[12] The chapelry at the parochial margin is certainly an element in the picture of vitality within the medieval parish; but it is not a valid model for the understanding of the whole. The opportunities for lay involvement with and control of parochial institutions were not so simply determined; choice in religious activity was more widely available, and more readily expressed, than this. The proposed contrariety between authoritarian parish and voluntaristic chapelry does not do justice to the extensive voluntarism which shaped the parish itself. The common features of parochial structure which multiplied the available options in religious behaviour may be briefly illustrated.

In the first place, the locally-supported chapel at the margins may, as has been noted, be admitted as one demonstration of creativity in lay religion, provided it is recognised that the acquisition by a local community of such a chapel represented not wholesale secession from the parish but an increase in the range of choice. The East Anglian fens provide many examples. As the records of sewer commissions make very clear, the erection and maintenance of sea-dykes was a major undertaking which necessitated sustained collective action on the part of settlers in this aqueous zone.[13] The demand for the right

---

[12] Everitt, *Continuity and Colonization*, 220–2. A similar case was made specifically for the later period of nonconformity by the same author in *idem*, *The Pattern of Rural Dissent: The Nineteenth Century* (Leicester Univ. Department of English Local History Occasional Papers, 2nd ser., iv, 1972), 26.

[13] See *The Records of a Commission of Sewers for Wiggenhall 1319–1324*, ed. A. E. B. Owen (Norfolk Record Society, xlviii, 1981). Certain guilds of this region are known specifically to have undertaken the construction of dykes (e.g. Public Record Office,

to build local chapels came similarly from the new inhabitants as collectives. It was the community of inhabitants of the hamlet of Cowbit, in Spalding parish, who established their local chapel which was licensed by the bishop in 1363.[14] The village of Holbeach Hurn, in the parish of Holbeach, was twice daily separated from the mainland by the sea-tide; the right to maintain a local chapel was granted in 1399 to the occupants as a body.[15] Such a chapel congregation might be dependent for divine service upon the regular visits of the incumbent of the parish church; but it was common for funds to be raised locally to employ a permanent chaplain of the residents' own choice. At Fenne End, in the Norfolk parish of Tilney All Saints, the recipients of a chapel grant in 1481 explicitly undertook to employ their own priest.[16] On the other side of the country, in southeast Lancashire, a period of population growth and associated extension of agriculture and development of textile industries was similarly linked with a proliferation of chapel foundations: a score between 1500 and 1548; and here again, both buildings and clergy were largely funded by the communities of inhabitants.[17]

In the cases just cited a distinction may be drawn between primary and secondary settlements; the characteristic features of Everitt's Kentish upland chapels are found also in these Lincolnshire and Lancashire examples.[18] But human communications and settlement in the middle ages are not adequately described by this simple distinction between 'old' and 'new' lands. Individual mobility and shifting settlements exerted their own pressures for the proliferation of churches and services. The fifteenth-century moralising text *Dives and Pauper* recognised that it would be hard for 'messengers and pilgrims and wayfaring men' to attend regularly in their parish churches, but urged them to 'hear mass and matins if they can'.[19] The pastoral needs of

---

C47/46/475); and it is notable that no less than nine guilds are recorded in the four parishes of fourteenth-century Wiggenhall (PRO, C47/45/356–64).

[14] D. M. Owen, *Church and Society in Medieval Lincolnshire* (Society for Lincolnshire History and Archaeology, History of Lincolnshire, v, 1981), 6.

[15] Owen, 'Medieval chapels in Lincolnshire', 18; *Calendar of Entries in the Papal Registers relating to Great Britain and Ireland: Papal Letters* (1893–), vi. 131 (confirmation of 1408). In 1389, apparently before the chapel's construction, a guild of inhabitants of Holbeach Hurn had sustained lights in the parish church. PRO, C47/40/123.

[16] *Cal. Papal Letters*, xiii. 721–2.

[17] Tupling, 'Parishes and chapelries of Lancashire'.

[18] A similar pattern has been observed in the chapel foundations of the inland, Kesteven district of Lincolnshire. D. M. Owen, 'Chapelries and rural settlement. An examination of some of the Kesteven evidence', in *English Medieval Settlement*, ed. P. H. Sawyer (1979), 35–40.

[19] Cf. D. Rock, *The Church of Our Fathers* (4 vols., 1905), iv. 163; Owen, *Church and Society*, 17–18.

such travellers brought into being a number of fraternities which charged their priests with providing convenient masses, such as one at Northampton which in the late fourteenth century arranged a dawn service for those departing the town early and another at mid-morning for those arriving from elsewhere.[20] A similar guild at Thetford supported, again from common subscriptions, services in a chapel which was particularly frequented by visitors on market days or when law-courts were held there; from *c.* 1480 this chapel, with the appointment of two priests to serve it, was vested in the hands of the mayor and burgesses of the town.[21] Seasonal work created fluctuating demands for provision: on the sea-shore at Yarmouth in the twelfth century was a chapel in which, during the herring season only, divine service was offered for the benefit of the handful of fishermen who stayed there temporarily in beach-huts.[22]

The traditional view that settlement in medieval England was broadly divisible between primary and secondary sites—with which a hypothetical distinction between areas of less and greater religious independence might have been linked—is no longer tenable. As Christopher Taylor and others have demonstrated, since the late Iron Age, when the country was relatively densely populated, a pattern of dispersed settlement has been characteristic, not only of the 'wood-pasture' zones of upland England, but even of the arable countryside traditionally associated with centrally-placed, nucleated villages.[23] This scattered nature of settlement has meant that the demand for local churches has since the advent of Christianity been virtually ubiquitous. It was while examining what appeared to be isolated churches in Cornwall, for example, that Maurice Beresford realised that these were in fact linked with small, dispersed hamlets—and this in a landscape of open fields and shared ploughlands.[24] Such relatively remote churches would often find themselves, following the twelfth-century parochial organisation, dependent chapelries to mother-churches elsewhere; but they may not have been chronologically secondary. Indeed, the site of many a Cornish chapel hints at an ancient significance. The parish of Camborne, for instance, contained alto-

[20] PRO, C47/45/383; G. Rosser, 'Communities of parish and guild in the late middle ages', in *Parish, Church and People. Local Studies in Lay Religion 1350–1750*, ed. S. J. Wright (1988), 29–55, at 53 n. 86.

[21] PRO, C47/44/332; *Norfolk Archaeology*, xxix (1946), 205.

[22] *Norfolk Record Society*, xi (1939), 31–3.

[23] C. Taylor, *Village and Farmstead* (1983).

[24] M. W. Beresford, 'Dispersed and group settlement in medieval Cornwall', repr. in his *Time and Place: Collected Essays* (1984), 31–45. Similar evidence, again from a largely arable landscape, is discussed in *Royal Commission on Historical Monuments: Northamptonshire*, iv (1982), pp. xxxvii-xl.

gether seven chapels, of which several were evidently of Celtic origin, and excavation at that of St Ia at Troon has revealed a well and a tenth-century chapel within an enclosure. Such chapels were in the later middle ages regularly supported by guilds of local inhabitants, such as the fraternity of St Derwa's chapel at Menardarva, also in Camborne parish.[25] This scatter of holy sites across the landscape perpetuated a pattern of sub-parochial loyalties.

It has also been recently demonstrated that medieval settlement in most if not all areas had a tendency to drift, generally over short distances, once again provoking the regular review of ecclesiastical provision.[26] A shift in the parochial centre of gravity usually underlined or even extended the plurality of options available to parishioners. The site or remains of a demoted parish church would typically continue to be a focus of veneration and loyalty within its successor parish. When the church of Saltmarsh, on the Lincolnshire coast, had been destroyed by flooding of the sea in c. 1400, and been replaced as the parish church by another building further inland, strange visual effects ('wonders and shining lights at night') confirmed the enduring sanctity of the original place; and a new chapel was constructed, with provision for services, at this hallowed site.[27] It was probably the cultivation of new fields which caused the Oxfordshire village of Combe—whose first parish church was built at the valley bottom of the river Evenlode—to generate, probably by 1200, a secondary focus of settlement on a neighbouring ridge, half a mile to the north. Here a new church (the modern parish church) was constructed; and until the end of the middle ages the two churches of Combe parish appear to have operated in tandem. A thirteenth-century tomb slab found at the site of the earlier church records that its graveyard was still in use at that period: while the precise division of parochial functions in the medieval period is unrecorded, the crucial fact is the existence of dual centres of devotion within the parish.[28] Another late-medieval victim of the merciless sea was the parish church of Withernsea in Holderness, in the East Riding of Yorkshire: in the aftermath of destruction, the parishioners debated the relative claims respectively of a rebuilding of Withernsea church on a nearby hill and of the transferral of the status of parish church to an existing chapel at the hamlet of Hollym, which stood close to the geographical

---

[25] C. Thomas, *Christian Antiquities of Camborne* (1967), 64–71, 74–85; J. Mattingly, 'The medieval parish guilds of Cornwall', *Journal of the Royal Institution of Cornwall*, new series, x (1989), 290–329.

[26] Taylor, *passim*.

[27] *Cal. Papal Letters*, vi. 24–5.

[28] *The Victoria History of the County of Oxford*, xii (1990), 78–9, 92–4. Since the early sixteenth century the older church has disappeared.

centre of the parish. Once again, although the inhabitants disagreed as to which church was entitled to seniority, most expressed support for the continuance of both *loci* of worship. An inquiry held in the name of the archbishop in 1520 revealed that residents of Withernsea had assisted the enlargement of the church at Hollym, while those living at Hollym had conversely made offerings to the reconstruction at Withernsea: only both groups wished it to be understood that their contributions were spontaneous and voluntary—not alleged parochial duty but real concern for the two churches had guided their generosity.[29]

Furthermore, while it is clear that the nature of secular lordship must also have a bearing on the possible degree of independence of religious behaviour, over-simplification must again be avoided. Clearly, lands which were marginal to estate centres might be characterised by freedoms both of personal status and religious activity. The woodland society and economy of the Arden forest in Worcestershire and north Warwickshire, for example, produced locally-funded chapels to serve a relatively independent population: the chapel of Mosely in the parish of Bromsgrove, licensed in 1405, was one.[30] But scope for independence in religious behaviour by the lay population depended in the middle ages (as later) not merely on the institutional character of lordship, but on the way in which manorial control was exercised.[31] The contrasting experiences of two Thames-valley towns illustrate the point. Abingdon and Henley-upon-Thames were both manorial boroughs in the possession of ostensibly powerful lords. But whereas the monks of Abingdon Abbey, both resident and institutionally immortal, battened upon their town and constrained its expressions of corporate identity in both secular and religious spheres, the owners of Henley—at various times the Holland family and the crown—were perpetually both absentee and complaisant. The doomed battle of Abingdon's citizens to gain for themselves a cemetery independent of the Abbey church ended in disaster in 1392, when a funeral cortege bound for a new churchyard beside the town's parish church of St Helen was hijacked by the monks, and sixty-seven named individuals were disinterred from the illicit burial-ground to be re-

[29] York, Borthwick Institute of Historical Research, MS CP/G/117. I am most grateful to Dr John Thomson for drawing this dossier to my attention.

[30] *Cal. Papal Letters*, vi. 29; cf. T. Nash, *Collections for the History of Worcestershire* (2 vols., 1781–2), i. 164.

[31] For comparison with a later period, see also the comments on patterns of religious adherence recorded in the nineteenth century, and the impossibility of applying a rigid distinction between 'open' and 'closed' parishes, in *Church and Chapel in Oxfordshire 1851. The Return of the Census of Religious Worship*, ed. K. Tiller (Oxfordshire Record Society, lv, 1987), xxv ff.

buried at the monastery.[32] Meanwhile, at Henley, the townspeople collectively, through a guild, managed the local church as completely as did those urban corporations which after the Reformation acquired the impropriations of city churches. The 'communitas' of Henley determined all matters of ritual in their parish church, for example setting up a guild of Jesus in 1499 to sustain an additional priest when the rector defaulted on *his* responsibility.[33]

Still more significant for religious freedom was the fact that very few parishes coincided with single lordships. Most contained more than a single manor, or parts of several. Divided lordship meant that the parishioners enjoyed a certain freedom of manoeuvre, while the lords themselves might promote religious initiatives not wholly private in nature in order to compete with their peers and to recruit the support of the inhabitants. Upland parishes are the better known for this manorial diversity: four-fifths of Lancashire parishes contained upwards of three vills, and the vast parish of Whalley contained no less than thirty.[34] But in the Midlands zone of arable manors, lordship was commonly no less fragmented: not untypically, the village and parish of Harlestone in Northamptonshire were split amongst six lords. The necessity for the local inhabitants of such places to organise their collective interests in the common fields or, after enclosure, the common grazing lands, must—as is known to have occurred at Harlestone—have generated communal meetings, perhaps within the parish church.[35] Their deliberations may often, indeed, have been given a framework and coherence by the formation of a guild. An urban case is Boston, whose population, although divided between three lords, appears to have focussed its communal identity in the major guild of Our Lady, based in the church.[36]

Divided lordship and dispersed settlement within parishes sometimes also encouraged lords to advertise their status and recruit support by constructing additional chapels to which the local population would be admitted. Before the late twelfth century a chapel of ease was founded on their estate by the Lincolnshire family of Tateshall, with the aid of contributions from their tenants and other 'rustici' of the neighbourhood.[37] At Dene in St John's-in-Thanet in

[32] A. E. Preston, *Christ's Hospital Abingdon* (Oxford, 1930), 8–11, 75.

[33] *Henley Borough Records*, ed. P. M. Briers (Oxfordshire Record Society, xli, 1960), 91, 123 and *passim*.

[34] Tupling, 'Parishes and chapelries of Lancashire'; C. Haigh, *Reformation and Resistance in Tudor Lancashire* (Cambridge, 1975).

[35] J. Wake, 'Communitas villae', *English Historical Review*, xxxvii (1922), 406–13.

[36] S. H. Rigby, 'Boston and Grimsby in the middle ages: an administrative contrast', *Journal of Medieval History*, x (1984), 51–66, at 61–2.

[37] Owen, 'Medieval chapels in Lincolnshire', 16.

Kent, the original oratory was built by Sir Henry de Sandwich about 1230 for his own household, yet gradually 'not only the lord of that manor and his family, but the inhabitants of [the neighbouring hamlets of] Twenties, Vincents and Fleet likewise' resorted to it.[38] The chapel of Burnley in Whalley parish in Lancashire appears to have developed under the patronage of the Towneley family, yet by the early sixteenth century so many residents from a number of nearby vills were attending that the lord perforce shared his interest in the chapel with the community of inhabitants. An indenture of 1525 established a compromise between Sir John Towneley and the assembled villagers concerning their respective responsibilities for maintenance of the chapel.[39] Both the high degree of communal lay control over ecclesiastical affairs embodied in these various arrangements, and the extension of personal choice in religious behaviour which they facilitated, deserve emphasis. In 1428 the villagers of Piddington in Oxfordshire, following disputes with their mother parish of Ambrosden, gained parochial status for their local chapel. By the terms of the licence the people of Piddington were thenceforward to 'elect' their own priest, who would provide all divine services. On the other hand, even after this localist victory, Piddington residents would on occasion voluntarily attend services at Ambrosden church, where 'the Piddington seats' were evidently still used by them in the post-Reformation period.[40]

It is indeed important to stress that these various developments represented, not a fragmentation of the parish into wholly independent local units, but rather a diversification and enrichment of opportunities to exercise a degree of choice in religious behaviour. The acquisition of ecclesiastical provision by the inhabitants of a settlement at a distance from the site of the parish church was not tantamount to a unilateral declaration of independence, but represented rather an extension of available options, usually by the elevation in status of

[38] Everitt, *Continuity and Colonization*, 219. In a similar case, a private chapel having been founded within his house by Robert de Haldenby, who lived three miles from the parish church of Adlingfleet, Yorks., in 1403 he secured the right to a chaplain celebrating there regularly for the inhabitants of the neighbourhood. *Cal. Papal Letters*, v. 535–6.

[39] British Library, Additional MS 32104, fos. 301–2; T. D. Whitaker, *An History of the Original Parish of Whalley and Honor of Clitheroe*, 2 vols. (4th edn. 1872–6), ii. 158; W. Bennett, *The History of Burnley* (4 pts., Burnley, 1946–51), ii. 106–7; *The Victoria History of the County of Lancashire*, vi (1911), 450.

[40] 'Habeant dicti inhabitantes ... unum presbyterum in eadem villula de Pidington continue residentem ad ipsorum inhabitantium proprium arbitrium eligendum et nominandum atque praeficiendum.' White Kennett, *Parochial Antiquities* (2nd edn., 2 vols., Oxford, 1818), ii. 261–7, 282; *The Victoria History of the County of Oxford*, v (1957), 256.

some anciently venerated site. Thus at Ripon in the 1370s, a guild was formed to reconstruct an 'ancient' chapel of St Mary, then believed to date from the time of St Wilfrid, which had since become ruinous.[41] Many pre-Christian hallowed sites, marked by burial mounds or standing stones, lie on, or close to, early boundaries. Since stretches of such boundaries were commonly re-employed from the twelfth century as parish limits, numbers of pre-Christian holy spots were subsequently to be found at the parochial margins. This, rather than the chronology of settlement or variations of lordship, may sometimes be the explanation for the existence of liminal chapels, such as that 'old chapel of St James' on the boundary between the two parishes of Aughton and Bubwith, in the East Riding of Yorkshire, which the inhabitants on both sides undertook to renovate in 1427.[42] In Norfolk at the same period another chapel of St James was 're-established' by a guild constituted within the parish of Pulham: the guild transferred its focus from the parish church of St Mary to the old chapel, which after the Reformation was used as a school, a function for which its collective ownership and management by the late-medieval inhabitants had evidently prepared it.[43] Popular devotion to a shrine or chapel with miraculous associations might even, on occasion, lead the rector himself to transfer his attentions. When, in the late fourteenth century, the rector of South Tedworth in Hampshire erected in his parish an unauthorised chapel with an image, called 'St Catherine's Mount', and held services there rather than at the parish church, he was doubtless responding to a long history of local veneration of the site or the statue, or of both.[44] In the later middle ages very few detached chapels are recorded as being constructed de novo; much more common was the renovation of existing structures, many of which would have been ancient. Again, however, the effect in these various cases was not to destroy parochial unity but to underline the variety of lay-directed religious life which could be sustained within the parish.

In certain instances supplementary provision might be arranged at the very site of the mother-church and burial-ground. This could lead to the appearance of two or even more churches within a single churchyard, as occurred at several dozen sites in East Anglia. The parish church of Middleton stands in the midst of the churchyard; on the edge of the cemetery is the church of Fordley, whose name

[41] PRO, C47/46/452 (a).

[42] Cal. Papal Letters, vii. 521; cf. Bonney, 'Early boundaries'.

[43] P. C. Cowcher, 'The chapel of the gild of St. James and Pennoyer's School, Pulham', Norfolk Archaeology, xxx (1947–52), 65–74.

[44] The Register of William Edington Bishop of Winchester 1346–1366, ed. S. F. Hockey (2 vols., Hampshire Record Series, vii-viii 1986–7), ii. 62–3 (1365).

identifies it as a woodland clearing and probably a secondary settlement in the area; here it seems reasonable to envisage the latter church as secondary, although its independent parochial rights may indicate an early foundation. The inhabitants of such a place, desiring a church and burial-plot, might well feel a primary attraction to the hallowed site already occupied by the first church.[45] At Reepham no less than three churches (again, all of them parochial) share the same churchyard, probably for the same reason.[46] As is recorded in just such a case in Domesday Book, the supplementary churches are likely to have been provided by the collective enterprise of the expanding population.[47] By such means the parochial community could be sustained alongside a significant degree of sub-parochial localism: although in the examples just cited the secondary churches acquired parochial independence, elsewhere such foundations more commonly remained subordinate to the original parish. Independent chapels within the precinct of the parish church were more common in the middle ages than is apparent from the relatively few survivals.[48] At Wisbech in Cambridgeshire the chapel of a popular fraternity contrived to form part of the parish church, whose holy site it shared and whose very chancel it abutted, while at the same time stressing its distinct identity by having no door which communicated with the main building.[49] The same balance is expressed in those cases, such as that of Pakefield in Suffolk, where two churches, associated respectively with different parts of a parish, coexisted under the same roof. Pakefield church comprised two equal naves, divided by a (fourteenth-century) arcade: one was called All Saints' aisle, the other 'the aisle of the other half', being apparently dedicated to St Margaret. The church had already been in divided ownership in 1086, and the late-medieval manor was fragmented into several lordships. The structure of the church gave expression both to territorial localism within the parish (by the fourteenth century, when the church was rebuilt, the double nave could not be a reflection simply of lordship, which was more fragmented than this) and to a transcendent parochial unity.[50] Again, at Dickleburgh in Norfolk the single church was until 1454

[45] P. Warner, 'Shared churchyards, freemen church builders and the development of parishes in East Anglia', *Landscape History*, viii (1986), 39–52.

[46] *Ibid.*

[47] The case is Thorney in Suffolk; see *ibid.*

[48] Two Kentish examples, at Pembury and Eastry: E. Hasted, *The History and Topographical Survey of the County of Kent* (2nd edn., 12 vols., 1797–1801), v. 271, x. 117.

[49] *The Victoria History of the County of Cambridge and the Isle of Ely*, iv (1953), 248; A. Nicholas, *St Peter and St Paul, Wisbech* (Wisbech, 1988), 5.

[50] A. Suckling, *The History and Antiquities of the County of Suffolk* (2 vols., 1846–8), i. 282–7; B. P. W. S. Hunt, *Flinten History* (7th edn., 1953), 22–45.

divided into four separate portions, each served by a distinct rector: the Portion in the Marsh, the Portion in the Fields, Long Moor Portion, and Sea Mere Portion. In an arrangement whose origins would appear to lie in the pattern of centralised 'team ministries' which characterised the Saxon minster churches, the clergy seem to have taken services in turn.[51] The shared burial-ground was doubtless of critical importance in these cases. Often, of course, a separate churchyard was a desideratum of a settlement remote from or antagonistic to the mother-church, and where it was not felt to be enough that a body should have merely its 'last farewell' in the chapel before translation to the superior church.[52] Where the privilege was refused, defiance was far from unknown, as at Abingdon, or at the hamlet of Chimney in the Oxfordshire parish of Bampton, which is not recorded ever to have enjoyed the right of sepulture but where traces of medieval burials have been found.[53] But again, a local cemetery represented for inhabitants not a new monopoly but an increase of options. The chapel of St Clement at Brundall, in Norfolk, had evidently acquired the right of burial by 1368, when an inventory lists a bier and a manual with the office for the dead. Nevertheless, of the several wills of Brundall inhabitants extant from the fifteenth and early-sixteenth centuries, almost all record the testators' desire to be interred at the mother-church of Bradeston—where, naturally, their ancestors lay, and which partly for this reason must have possessed the greater prestige.[54]

Although, as has been noted earlier, subordinate chapels might rest on major religious sites, the powerful relics of a mother-church might exert an extra pull on the continuing loyalty of those parishioners who enjoyed in addition the use of a local chapel. In Cornwall the relics of St Piran, which were usually housed at the parish church of Peranzabuloe, were on Rogation days displayed at the daughter chapel of St Agnes, and additionally carried about the neighbouring countryside.[55] A similar action, no less expressive of differential status, was

[51] F. Blomefield, *An Essay towards a Topographical History of the County of Norfolk* (2nd edn., 11 vols, 1805–10), i. 191–2.

[52] This phrase was used in the chapelry of Dowdeswell in Whittington parish, Gloucs., in the early 15th century. *Cal. Papal Letters*, vi. 388.

[53] Abingdon: *supra*. Chimney: ex inf. Dr W. J. Blair. For a case-study of a legal struggle of this kind, see C. Lutgens, 'The case of Waghen vs. Sutton: conflict over burial rights in late medieval England', *Mediaeval Studies*, xxxviii (1976), 145–84.

[54] F. Johnson, 'The chapel of St. Clement at Brundall', *Norfolk Archaeology*, xxii (1924–5), 194–205; the inventory is printed in *Norfolk Record Society*, xix (1) (1947), 43–4. A similar case in a suburban parish of York: J. Solloway, *The Alien Benedictines of York* (Leeds, 1910), 254, 259.

[55] R. Whiting, *The Blind Devotion of the People. Popular Religion and the English Reformation* (Cambridge, 1989), 57–8.

that of the parish church of Croston in Lancashire, which possessed the skull of St Laurence, and which gave a part of this relic to a dependent chapel at Chorley.[56] A continuing attraction can also be observed in those former central or minster churches of the Saxon period which in various guises continued to exercise an element of pastoral care in the later medieval period. Many had been refounded in the tenth century as houses of Benedictine monks, or in the twelfth of Augustinian canons; but they typically continued to serve parochial functions, and to exert an enduring pull on the religious loyalties of laymen over large areas. The parochial naves of Tewkesbury, Thorney and Crowland abbeys are cases in point.[57] On occasion the separate chapelry might be the preferred focus of a drive for political independence and identity. Such a chapel might be literally an offshoot of the parish church, as was the case at Diss in Norfolk. Here the detached 'free chapel' of St Nicholas was the early fifteenth-century creation of the two town fraternities of St Nicholas and Corpus Christi, whose respective centres had previously been the north and south aisles of the parish church. Subsequently the guilds combined their resources to maintain both the chapel and a common guildhall for the town. At the same time however, guild funds continued to be allocated to the parish church.[58] Even in such instances, the special status of the mother church required that it not be ignored. The leading townsmen of Bridport in Dorset by the early fourteenth century formed a guild in order to promote the chapel of St Andrew in the town as the context for civic meetings; after the dissolution of the guild in 1547 the chapel was transformed into the guildhall. But the same civic rulers also kept their ceremonial mass within the nearby parish church of St Mary—not, indeed, at the high altar there but in a side-chapel, dedicated to St Catherine, which they directly controlled.[59] What is to be emphasised is not merely the number but the diversity of churches accessible to the individual parishioner, who would derive different kinds of satisfaction from each. This was true of both town and country. A city might support a high density of chapels (especially where, as for example at Winchester, a single mother church retained parochial rights over the entire town); yet

[56] Haigh, *Reformation and Resistance*, 67.

[57] Further discussion in G. Rosser, 'The cure of souls in English towns before 1000', in *Pastoral Care before the Parish*, ed. J. Blair and R. Sharpe (Leicester, forthcoming).

[58] Blomefield, *Norfolk*, i. 20, 32–3.

[59] Dorset County Record Office, MSS B3/CD/47–8, B3/CD/57–60, B3/M11, pp. 59–65, 158; J. Hutchins, *The History and Antiquities of the County of Dorset* (3rd edn., by W. Shipp and J. W. Hodson, 4 vols., 1861–70), ii, 22–4; and further discussion in G. Rosser, *English Medieval Guilds 900–1600* (forthcoming).

the distinction between urban and rural provision should not be drawn too sharply.

The internal arrangements of churchyards and parish churches reflected, in ways which merit further exploration, both social relations and the distribution of settlement within the parish: once more, they document a measure of the balance between the impulse within the parish community to splinter into fragments, and its ability periodically to realise, by collective action, at least a semblance of unity. Diversity was not subsumed in the gathering of the parish, but on the contrary it was manifested overtly, in ways which aspired to harmony but could be contentious. It appears to have been normal for different areas of a parish to bury their dead in different quarters of the churchyard: so much seems implied by orders on chapelries gaining cemeteries of their own to continue to keep up their accustomed sector of the graveyard at the parish church.[60] Within the church, the living disposed themselves variously according to trade, social status, and— not least— district of residence. So the discussion at Burnley in 1525 determined where, in the rebuilt church, the pews allocated respectively to the several hamlets should be located.[61] Sometimes a particular door into a parish church has been known by the name of a hamlet lying in the same direction, which may also indicate that parishioners assembled inside in territorial groups.[62] Guilds, too, sometimes represented different portions of the parish, as at Upwell in Norfolk where there existed in the fourteenth century two distinct guilds of the Purification of the Virgin Mary, one for 'the great dyke', the other for 'the little dyke'.[63] In the parish church of Knapton in the same county, candles ('plough-lights') were kept burning respectively by groups of inhabitants of the several quarters of Westgate, Woodgate, and Nethergate.[64] Certain pairs of guilds refounded in Queen Mary's reign in Cornish parishes were identified respectively with the

[60] E.g. a burial-ground to serve the hamlets of Shilton and Henley in the parish of Kirkby Mallory, Leics., was granted in 1415 on condition that the inhabitants should keep up both the southern part of the cemetery and the south half of the nave of the mother church. *The Register of Bishop Philip Repingdon 1405–1419*, ed. M. Archer (3 vols., Lincolnshire record Society, lvii, lviii, lxxiv, 1963–82), iii. 3–4. At Sourton, a chapelry of Bridestowe in Devon, the possessors of a new cemetery granted in 1451 were to continue to maintain that part of Bridestowe churchyard for which they had customarily been responsible. *Registrum Edmundi Lacy 1420–1455*, ed. G. R. Dunstan (5 vols., Canterbury and York Society, lx–lxiv, 1963–71), iii. 273–8. See also *ibid.*, iv. 314–18.

[61] See *supra*, n. 39.

[62] A. Hamilton Thompson, *The Historical Growth of the English Parish Church* (Cambridge, 1911), 68.

[63] PRO, C47/44/337–8.

[64] H. R. Loraine, *Knapton. Some Notes on the Church and the Manor* (North Waltham, 1952, repr. 1985), 6.

northern and southern halves of the parochial territory.[65] The evidence of church-building sometimes points in the same direction: a new stained-glass window for St Ives parish church in Cornwall was paid for in 1523 by 'the wives of the west part of the parish'.[66] On the other hand, where different parts of the church-work were undertaken by distinct groups of parishioners, the emphasis was more commonly on social than on regional identities: thus it was 'the young people' of Garboldisham in Norfolk who paid for the re-roofing of the church in c. 1450, while the parishioners in general covered the chancel.[67] Elsewhere particular fraternities erected their own chapels; and even where a guild lacked its distinct chapel, the members, at least on the feast days of the fraternity, would sit together within the body of the parish church.[68] If the roof were lifted from the parish church of Ludlow in the fifteenth century there would be revealed no less than eleven separate sub-groups of the parishioners at their several altars in the nave.[69] Such, in a market town parish, was the variety of linked social and religious associations, in several of which any individual might choose to participate in turn.

Within the broad framework of the medieval church, personal choice in the parish was not unrestricted, being in part determined by pressures of economic activity and social relations. However, the complexity and mobility of medieval society, combined with a relatively extensive measure of freedom from external interference at the level of local societies, encouraged the spontaneous development by the laity, within and around the parish, of complementary forms of religious life. Such were the numerous fraternities and chapelries, in which communities of lay inhabitants hired and fired at will priests recruited to supplement those, if any, endowed by the patron. Often a small chapel sustained by voluntary contributions stood close to the parish church, and its practical necessity would be questioned by the chantry commissioners of Edward VI's reign. But to their users such chapels represented a valued enhancement of the choice of religious adherence within the parish. When practical justification was demanded, as in 1548, they might (like certain examples at Doncaster, Richmond and Wakefield) be defended as 'plague chapels'—used alternatively by the sick or by the healthy in times of pestilence—yet they were undoubtedly more than this, and were in many cases of great antiquity, having undergone changes of particular use over the

---

[65] Mattingly, 'Parish guilds of Cornwall', 295–6.
[66] Ibid., 304; N. Pevsner, *The Building of England: Cornwall* (1951), 180.
[67] Blomefield, *Norfolk*, i. 268–9.
[68] E.g. PRO, C47/42/238 (the guild of the Ascension at Lynn).
[69] Plan in St Laurence's parish church, Ludlow.

course of the centuries.[70] The culling of allegedly supernumerary
chapels which was enabled by the royal statutes of the mid-sixteenth
century may indeed, as a modern commentator has observed in
defence of the legislation, have strengthened 'the parish as a unit for
enforcing social, moral and religious discipline'.[71] But for those who
lamented the suppressions of guild and other chapels, these had represented precisely a freedom, variety and focus of commitment in
religious life which the Reformation statutes, in this respect at least,
tended only to diminish.[72] It would be wrong to assume that the
chapel endowments of late-medieval guilds and chantries represented
an altogether novel diversity of religious provision, or that the Protestant Reformation, at any rate in its first phase, made possible an
enlarged scope for self-determination on the part of the laity. The
diversity was ancient. The network of parishes had been overlaid in
the twelfth and thirteenth centuries upon a landscape already dense
with holy sites. The parish had adapted itself to older patterns of
religious activity on the ground, and continued to do so in the changing social environment of the later middle ages. The fact that parishes
and other social and political structures tended to cut across one
another fostered an independence of religious behaviour, and a plurality of devotional allegiances, which characterised the fourteenth
century, and indeed the twelfth century, no less than the early
sixteenth, and which considerably exceeded that of the early years of
official Protestantism.

---

[70] *Yorkshire Chantries*, ed. W. Page (2 vols., Surtees Society, xci, xcii, 1892–3), ii. 142,
180–1, 315.

[71] Kitching, 'Church and chapelry', 289.

[72] Alarming rumours about the alleged intended suppression of chapels contributed
significantly to the Catholic rising in Lincolnshire in October 1536. See M. Bowker,
The Henrician Reformation. The Diocese of Lincoln under John Longland 1521–1547
(Cambridge, 1981), 153–5.

LOLLARDY AND LOCALITY

By Richard G. Davies

READ 15 SEPTEMBER 1990

THERE can now be no doubt of the intellectual substance and cohesion of early Wyclifitism as expressed in the writings of educated clerks in immediate contact with the man himself.[1] Most would accept, too, that this coherence was successfully transferred from Latin to English. However, although these Wyclifite scholars recognised the need for a corpus of literature to cater for a non-academic audience and provide the basis in ideas for a sustained movement, they had difficulty in supplying it.[2] This might seem to offer easy comfort to those who are already doubtful whether people called Lollards could or did grasp Wyclifitism; whether they just amputated the bits they liked, debased or perverted them, or really did not take anything on board at all. Even some less cynical would agree that the Church itself played a large part in shaping Lollardy's ideas and characteristics: such is so often the way in the birth of protest movements.[3] Indeed, to some hardliners 'Lollardy' seems little more than a scare-story invented by the Church in order to damn a large but motley crew of critics and dissenters. Or, if not the Church, then those historians in whom hope triumphs over experience.[4].

[1] This comment reflects, of course, the seminal work of Professor Ann Hudson, particularly in the field of Wyclifite literature; *Selections from English Wycliffite Writings* (Cambridge, 1978), esp. 8–13; *Lollards and their Books* (collected papers, 1985); *The Premature Reformation* (Oxford, 1988), esp. chapters 5–8. I make no apology for frequent reference to these now standard works.

[2] Hudson, *Premature Reformation*, esp. 103–10, 200–27, 385–9, where a more optimistic conclusion is, of course, formed.

[3] The presumed gulf between Wyclif and the Lollards, in terms both of intellect and social motivation, was argued most influentially, and to an extreme, by K. B. McFarlane, *John Wycliffe and the Beginnings of English Nonconformity* (1952). J. A. F. Thomson, *The Later Lollards, 1414–1520* (Oxford, 1965), a perceptive pioneering study, shared the same presumptions. See A. P. Hampshire and J. M. Beckford, 'Religious sects and the concept of deviance', *British J. of Sociology* 34 (1983), 208–29 on the interaction of orthodoxy and new deviance.

[4] For particularly sharp recent scepticism, see R. N. Swanson, *Church and Society in Late Medieval England* (Oxford, 1989), 329–47; D. Loades, 'Anabaptism and English sectarianism in the mid-sixteenth century', in D. Baker (ed.), *Studies in Church History: Subsidia 2* (Oxford, 1979), 63–4. This view tends to come from historians who emphasise the criterion of shared ideas as proof of cohesion and identity. For these, one basic objection is that the Wyclifites/Lollards had exclusive copyright at the time to very

Through the whole range of such views runs one, basic, assumption: namely, that one joins a movement such as Lollardy primarily because one likes its formal doctrines; and these are what hold a movement together. This is a time-honoured assumption in the history of religions, scarcely troubled by its regular failure to stand up to empirical test.[5] Just how far it permeates studies of Lollardy can be observed for example in both Professor Hudson's emphasis upon the quality of the sect-literature and her determination to demonstrate the understanding of it by its lay readership; and equally in the caustic observations of less sympathetic historians about the ventures of humbler so-called Lollards into theology, notably under cross-examination. The efforts of J. F. Davis and A. G. Dickens to associate Lollardy with Reformation Protestantism were likewise grounded principally upon demonstrating continuity of ideas.[6] Scepticism about Lollardy's very existence has been based similarly upon its supposed lack of a cohesive and characteristic body of doctrine. Then there are the ubiquitous numerical rankings of topics on which groups of suspects proved unsound.[7] The results have become familiar: objections to pilgrimages in first place, opposition to images runner-up, eucharistic deviation third, something rude about the clergy fourth, concern about confession a rather distant fifth, and then a long tail-off into all sorts of things attracting just one vote, most satisfying to those who do not rate Lollardy highly or even doubt its existence. Quite apart from the obvious methodological problems, notably the irregular composition of the group under review, the admixture of accusation and guilt, the nature of court processes and records, and the fact that the defendants were being asked about specific matters of potential controversy, rather than being invited to raise their own preferred (perhaps less offensive) themes, what do such tabulations prove? Case-studies in other sects, still open to first-hand analysis, permit that even very

---

few opinions and seem at odds amongst themselves. This is perhaps a misleading premise. See J. A. F. Thomson, 'Orthodox religion and the origins of Lollardy', *History* 74 (1989), 39–55, and Hudson, *Premature Reformation*, ch. 9, 'The context of vernacular Wycliffism'.

[5] E.g., D. A. Snow and R. Machalek, 'On the presumed fragility of unconventional beliefs', *Journal for the Scientific Study of Religion* 21 (1983), 15–26.

[6] J. F. Davis, 'Lollardy and the Reformation in England', *Archiv für Reformationsgeschichte* 78 (1982), 217–36; idem., *Heresy and Reformation in the South East of England, 1520–1559* (1983); A. G. Dickens, 'Heresy and the Origins of English Protestantism', in J. S. Bromley and E. H. Kossmann (eds.), *Britain and the Netherlands* II (Groningen, 1964), 47–66; idem., *Lollards and Protestants in the diocese of York* (1959), chs. 2, 3. See also M. Aston, 'Lollardy and the Reformation: survival or revival', *History* 49 (1964), 149–70 (reprinted in *Lollards and Reformers* (1984)).

[7] For an example from very reputable hands, *Heresy Trials in the Diocese of Norwich*, ed. N. P. Tanner (Camden Fourth Series, xx, 1977), 11.

committed Lollards might be not particularly virulent or even closely-informed about specific points of doctrine, or doctrine in general.[8] They still knew what the sect meant to them. William Thorpe's uniquely detailed account of his trial points up this gulf of perception. The experts kept cornering him on doctrinal points which he admitted he could not answer. Thorpe himself (and Archbishop Arundel) were much keener to talk about Lollards they had known and their moral and social attitudes. Thorpe, by the way, did not try to dissociate himself from any trait the Archbishop sketched out. He and the Archbishop could agree on a Lollard when they saw one.[9]

In extreme form, reconstruction and evaluation of Lollardy by its qualities as a formal belief-system suppose that a good book or a good sermon is all that is needed; the influence of personal contact and circumstances is more or less limited to that of determining what proportion of the theoretical total of potential recruits actually got the chance to hear the message. On the other hand, to suggest that the role of personal contact and circumstances was rather more important than this is not to relegate the function of ideology and religious belief to some nominal mark of willingness to conform with one's intimates.[10] Local studies do not have to be the preserve of the socio-economic determinists. In the earliest years, when Wyclifitism seemed even a fashionable option, it could attract overt sympathy and even active support from those who had plenty of other important interests in life. It did not require exclusive allegiance. For many, as society became more censorious, the attractions of adherence inevitably paled. Who

[8] See A. Hudson, 'The examination of Lollards', in *Lollards and their Books*, 125–40 for the formulation of a set list of questions; Tanner, *Norwich Heresy Trials*, 19–21 discusses the effect on responses in 1428–31. Cf. L. B. Brown and J. P. Forgan in *J. Sc. St. R.* (see note 5) 19 (1980), 423–5 for the differences between spontaneous and prompted statements of religious beliefs.

[9] 'Thorpe's memoir' is at present only printed in A. W. Pollard, *Fifteenth Century Prose and Verse* (Westminster, 1903), 97–174, from a sixteenth-century manuscript. Professor Hudson promises a modern edition from superior texts, and defends the authenticity of the source in 'William Thorpe and the question of authority', in G. R. Evans (ed.), *Church Authority: Essays in Honour of Henry Chadwick* (Oxford, 1988), 127–37.

[10] See R. Stark and W. S. Bainbridge, 'Networks of Faith: inter-personal bonds and recruitment to cults and sects', *American Journal of Sociology*, 85 (ii) (1980), 1376–85; D. A. Snow *et al.*, 'Social networks and social movements', *American Sociological Review* 45 (1980), 787–801, and note 14 below. As well as many useful local studies of Lollard groups, perceptive recent over-views have come from Hudson, *Premature Reformation*, ch. 3, 'Lollard Society'; A. Hope, 'Lollardy? the stone the builders rejected', in P. Lake and M. Dowling (eds.), *Protestantism and the National Church in Sixteenth Century England* (1987), 1–36; M. D. Lambert, *Medieval Heresy* (1977), 234–71. These leave far behind the unsubtle socio-economic determinism of some earlier commentators, such as those who eagerly canonised the tentative suggestions made in J. F. Davis, 'Lollard survival and the textile industry in the South-East of England', in D. Baker (ed.), *Studies in Church History* 3 (1965), 191–201.

then would not be daunted, but would carry the movement on; and how? Historians have picked up from sociologists the key role of the social marginal in the transmission of information—all those lovable tramps, peddlars, vagabonds, migrants and friars.[11] Less well-known is the other half of the theory, that this marginal figure is usually quite insufficient and uninfluential in securing the acceptance of that information, especially controversial information, by a stable social network. The stranger come to preach is no different. What he needs is the support and acceptance of his ideas by figures of substance and stability in the eyes of those around them; and because of *their* encouragement the adoption and support of the ideas in their society, along trusted, respected and preferably long-term and active personal ties. Can we see this already in the early years of Lollardy? As in the mayor of Leicester who protected Swinderby; in John Fox, mayor of Northampton, whose betrayer said he 'made the whole town Lollard'; in the so-called Lollard knights and Abbot Philip Repingdon who presented Lollard priests to their parishes—in the Chilterns, for example—and protected them?[12] It has often been remarked that most of the long-term Lollard strongholds started life early. Was it the case perhaps that the celebrated missionary efforts only really impressed where the locals were under heavy influence to be impressed?[13] In the long term, such close personal ties might eventually have emerged out of a common faith, especially when fellow-members lived under constant threat of detection and punishment and relied on each other's discretion, but it is at least as likely that they preceded the commitment to faith and accord with social norms, i.e., including degrees of deference and commitment within the group. It should not be demanded or expected that every Lollard should be identical to the next. Even in modern circumstances, where widespread anomie is supposed to have caused a boom in sect-membership amongst the alienated and rootless, a high incidence of pre-existent strong personal

[11] B. Geremek, 'Mouvements hérétiques et déracinement social au bas Moyen Age', *Annales E.S.C.* 37 (i) (1982), 186–92 (and previously in *The Church in a Changing Society* (Uppsala, 1978), 85–9) is a powerful and provocative evaluation of this time-worn theme.

[12] Hudson, *Premature Reformation*, 61, 75–9, 87–92; idem., 'Wycliffism in Oxford', in A. Kenny (ed.), *Wyclif in his Times* (Oxford, 1986), 75–7; McFarlane, *John Wycliffe*, 141–7; idem., *Lancastrian Kings and Lollard Knights* (Oxford, 1972), 192–6; A. H. J. Baines and S. A. P. Foxall, *The Life and Times of Thomas Harding* (Chesham, 1982), 8–16.

[13] Amongst the considerable literature on the diffusion of ideas and their acceptance along and within social networks, three essays might be singled out as particularly relevant here: M. Becker, 'Sociometric location and innovativeness', *American Sociological Review* 35 (1970), esp. 268–70; G. Weimann, 'On the importance of marginality', *ibid.* 47 (1982), 764–73; especially M. S. Granovetter, 'The strength of weak ties', *American Journal of Sociology* 78 (1973), 1360–80.

relationships between sect-members and recruits has been found.[14] William Thorpe spelled out how he had wanted personal example, not novel doctrine, when he sought out the Oxford Wyclifites, and sure enough that was what had moved him. Accordingly, personal loyalty, not doctrinal faith, was his last immovable line of defence at his trial.[15]

In emphasising the human touch, kinship of course turns up as the major conduit for the spread and maintenance of Lollardy. There are numerous well-known generational links in various groups: the Scriveners, Popes, and Hardings in Bucks., the Collins clan in Oxfordshire and Berkshire, Mother Agnes and her daughter (and probably god-daughters) in Coventry, and so on. New examples are being turned up all the time.[16] There are frequent tales of parents teaching children, most tragically the story of the Grevills of Benenden (Kent) in 1511, where father did the teaching but mother got sent to the fire.[17] In still more cases a defendant attributed his or her recruitment to a parent or grandparent, without giving dates but presumably again when young.[18] On each side there would be a predisposition to achieve agreement. Yet both Grevill boys said they had really only come to believe in the ideas of Lollardy on reaching adulthood and by talking to a group-leader.

Marriage similarly provided a well-known path for recruitment, with its priorities for harmony and security. Many couples were accused together and, more to the point, convicted. Various widows in the dock admitted that their husbands had been of the sect, or else the point was made by someone else.[19] Only very occasionally a spouse (usually the wife) cleared herself but let on about the unsavoury friends her husband brought home.[20] There were always far more

---

[14] A long-running debate: see note 9 and, e.g., *Review of Religious Research* 26 (1984), 146–57, 27 (1985), 32–48, 29 (1987–8), 44–56.

[15] 'Thorpe's memoir' (see note 9), esp. 113–7. His account of his own conversion deserves much closer attention, and reads fascinatingly in the context of work such as the much-discussed conversion model of J. Lofland and R. Stark, 'Becoming a World-saver; a theory of conversion to a deviant perspective', *Am. Sociol. R.* 30 (1965), 862–75.

[16] For the Buckinghamshire and Oxfordshire families, see J. Foxe, *Acts and Monuments*, ed. J. Pratt 4 (1877), 208–45 and below notes 27, 56, 58; also PRO CP40/946/93, 381, C85/115/10, 13 (for the Scriveners); for 'little Mother Agnes', see below note 81.

[17] Lambeth Palace Library: Reg[ister of William] Wareham [Archbishop of Canterbury] II, fos. 174v, 175v, 176r–7v.

[18] Hudson, *Premature Reformation*, 134–6 cites the best-known cases.

[19] E.g., Joan Austy in London, Joan Smith and Joan Washingby in Coventry (see note 23).

[20] Foxe 4, 221; Lichfield Joint Record Office: Ms. B/C/13, Court Book of Bishop Geoffrey Blythe, fos. 17r–v; Bishop Fitzjames's Court-book (see note 23) fo. 123, for Robert Bennett's wife being said to be quite unreceptive to his beliefs, and fo. 124 for Alice Wilkins' self-excusal.

men on trial or mentioned. In the outer rings of a group it might be much more possible for a wife to share her husband's views but still avoid detection, provided he kept mum. There is a widespread notion that women were unusually prominent and influential in Lollardy.[21] As likely, if they were not they just did not get indicted. Prominent women Lollards usually had equally prominent Lollard husbands. There were certainly some marriages explicitly between sect members. Joan and Thomas Washingby's, c.1492 in London, was even an arranged match between two people who had never met before. Joan supplied written references.[22] Some Lollard widows remarried to other Lollards.[23] Of note perhaps, this seems to have happened only amongst the core members in the sect. In court, some wives attributed their conversion to their husbands (presumably after their marriage, although this is rarely spelled out). The reverse could also be true, but much less often. In Coventry, John Cropwell's wife could not teach him herself, but knew someone who could.[24] Here indeed is a case of a recruit being persuaded into belief in order to please a close relation. A more splendid saga on such lines is the well-known, if slightly fishy, story of Robert Bartlett, the wealthy young farmer from Amersham.[25] First he was nagged into conversion by his new wife, who wore down his scepticism. Then he in turn twisted his brother Richard's even more reluctant arm. Then both of them worked on (or worked over?) their brother John and three sisters. One last dramatic example is that of Richard Ashford, who claimed that he

[21] M. Aston, 'Lollard Women Priests?', *Journal of Ecclesiastical History* 31 (1980), 441–61 (reprinted in *Lollards and Reformers*, 49–69); C. Cross, ' "Great Reasoners in Scripture": the activities of women Lollards, 1380–1530', in D. Baker (ed.), *Medieval Women* (Oxford, 1978), 359–80; characteristic caution by R. N. Swanson (note 4), 344–5. Well-known examples include Margery Baxter of Martham and Hawisia Mone of Loddon (*Norwich Heresy Trials* 41–51, 138–44), Alice Rowley of Coventry (see note 22, fo. 16), Alice Collins of Ginge, 'a famous woman among them' (Foxe 4, 238).

[22] Lichfield JRO, Ms. B/C/13, fo. 16. The Coventry group is discussed by Thomson, *Later Lollards*, 104–5, 108–16; J. Fines, 'Heresy trials in the diocese of Coventry and Lichfield, 1511–12', *J. Ecc. H.* 14 (1963), 160–74.

[23] In London alone, for example, Joan, wife of Thomas Austy, was the widow of John Redman; and the widow of Nicholas Saunders married (?William) Tilsworth: Trinity College, Dublin, Ms. D.3.4, Archbishop Ussher's transcripts of the Courtbook of Richard Fitzjames, bishop of London, fos. 123, 124v (folio numbers of the transcripts). I am grateful to Prof. J. A. F. Thomson for photocopies. Joan Smith is an example from Coventry; Ms. B/C/13 fo. 4.

[24] Ms. B/C/13 fo. 19.

[25] Foxe 4, 221–2, 223, 225, 228. The difficulty is that his late father was (according to Robert's brother, Richard) 'a better man than he was taken for' and named as suspect by more than one witness, their mother was a reluctant church-goer, and one of their sisters was already married to a Lollard. Robert was probably not the innocent he pretended to be.

only learned from his father-in-law (John Morden of Chesham) when the latter lay dying that he was about to become the head of an extended Lollard family.[26] Richard's subsequent learning-curve was as much an eye-opener to him as to us.

In and around every local group a picture of kinship and marriage ties builds up, albeit patently incomplete and frustrated by the medieval propensity to call in-laws 'brother' and 'cousin' in an unhelpfully generous way. One singular advantage with the Buckinghamshire groups is the wealth of additional material that exists to this end, for example in local manor court records, tax returns, legal cases and the many wills in the archdeacons' registers.[27] Not that this is unqualified good news. It makes it that much more obvious how little we know of the structure of other groups and how easy it is to misinterpret them from the church court records alone. It tempts historians to spend too much time on the well-rooted, well-documented rich and forget the still-obscure majority, whether the well-off deserve such prominence or not. It stretches the range of methodological skills required. It can make us choke on a surfeit of undigested anecdote.

There are examples of such other means of sect recruitment and bonding as lodging, apprenticeship and domestic service, confirmed by tales of anxiety not to say the wrong thing in front of those who were not sworn in. In the event, such close dependents almost never testified in court, but then Lollard trials rarely were based on the evidence of any but the sect-members themselves. Adult employees, tenants, business partners and next-door neighbours can also be found, although decisive evidence is more scarce.[28] Famously, Alice Saunders

---

[26] Foxe 4, 225, 227, 230–1; Hampshire CRO, Winchester: Reg. R. Fox IV fos. 18–19. This latter contains much hitherto under-discussed material about his Lollard contacts in Uxbridge and Walton-on-Thames. There is again some suspicion that Ashford was already more integrated than he made out (Foxe 4, 224–5, 230–2). For the Mordens, see note 58.

[27] Especially three publications of the Buckinghamshire Record Society: *The Courts of the Archdeaconry of Buckingham, 1483–1523*, ed. E. M. Elvey (19, 1975); *Subsidy Roll for the County of Buckingham Anno 1524*, ed. A. C. Chibnall and A. Vere Woodman (8, 1950); *The Certificate of Musters for Buckinghamshire in 1522*, ed. A. C. Chibnall (17, 1973); Bucks CRO, Aylesbury: Mss. We 2 etc., enrolled wills of the archdeaconry of Buckingham; the court rolls of Chesham and adjacent manors (in the possession of the Buckinghamshire Archaeological Society). Some tentative use of the material is made by D. Plumb, 'The social and economic spread of rural Lollardy: a reappraisal', in D. Wood (ed.), *Voluntary Religion* (Studies in Church History, 23, 1986), 111–29.

[28] There appear to be significant contacts with servants and employees in all groups, save possibly Kent, outweighing references to silence and care in their presence. The circumstantial evidence from Bucks. suggests that this sort of relationship might have been much more common than the evidence usually admits. Likewise, Isabel Tracher, a prosperous yeoman's wife from Chesham Bois, deliberately put her daughter into Alice Harding's service in order to further her Lollard education (Foxe 4, 227–8). Perhaps this too was a common practice.

told one back-sliding wretch that he risked never working in Amersham again.[29] Her husband Richard's taxable wealth (between five and ten times that of the second citizen of Amersham) showed she was not bluffing. Indeed, they had broken people before in that same town. Some of the most active local Lollards had directed business towards each other for at least forty years.[30]

It is not the fault of layfolk of this sort that they have been represented as the debased proletarian rump of some original, more exquisite, national movement and received little emphasis from historians until after 1414, save in connection with the Peasants' Revolt and Oldcastle's Rising. In truth, the first had nothing to do with them.[31] As for Oldcastle's Revolt, Henry V did everything he could to build it up for propaganda purposes. The King knew all about deviance amplification and was a great believer in it, but, as ever, the readership preferred media sensationalism to strike at least some faint chord with their own experience, and they knew that Lollardy really would not do as the enemy within. As a horror story, to pull the country together and make it feel good in its collective outrage, the Oldcastle Revolt really was an awful flop. Turning-point it was not.[32] Henry V had no real interest in rooting out Lollardy after 1414. Its only remaining usefulness to him was to illustrate his magnanimity and willingness to forgive. All that the noisy inquisitions after the revolt demonstrated was that no-one else was that bothered either.[33] Archbishop Arundel might have been, but he was dying and even, as it happened, unable to speak. His successor, Henry Chichele, had many qualities, but he was not appointed to Canterbury by Henry V

[29] Foxe 4, 231–2. Thomas Rowland reported her words: 'ye may see how Thomas Houre and others who laboured to have heretics detected before bishop Smith were brought to beggary; you may take example of them'. Houre confirmed his fate.

[30] See, e.g., *PRO, Calendar of Ancient Deeds* IV, 338 (A8636), 422 (A9419) and the references in note 84 below.

[31] See M. Aston, 'Lollardy and Sedition, 1381–1431', *Past & Present* 30 (1965), 3–7 (*Lollards and Reformers*, 1–5). The possibility of a connection between Wyclifite ideas and the 1381 revolt has recently been raised again by Hudson, *Premature Reformation*, 66–9, but not convincingly.

[32] See, however, for firmly contrary views, K. B. McFarlane, *John Wycliffe*, 183; M. D. Lambert, *Medieval Heresy*, 253; R. N. Swanson (note 4), 342; Thomas, *Later Lollards*, 5. J. I. Catto, 'Religious change under Henry V', in G.L. Harriss (ed.), *Henry V: the Practice of Kingship* (Oxford, 1985), 97–115, argued a much subtler line, that Henry V did take Lollardy seriously (at least at the élite level) and opposed it with positive orthodox reforms. T. B. Pugh, *Henry V and the Southampton Plot* (Gloucester, 1988), p. 51, as ever dismissive of Henry V's achievements, remarked that he 'was never in danger of overthrow by a small force of ill-equipped lower-class Lollards'.

[33] McFarlane, *ut supra*, 160–85 remains the standard account, for all his contempt for the insurgents. See also Thomson, *Later Lollards*, 5–19 and E. Powell, *Kingship, Law and Society* (Oxford, 1989), ch. 6, 'The Lollard Revolt' and pp. 132–3.

to be a great archbishop, and he did not let his patron down. All in all, 1414 had very little effect on Lollards for good or ill. Whatever place Wyclifitism as such might have had in the upper reaches of society had been worked out a while back. The important thing about the so-called 'Lollard knights', for example, was that they had been a solid clique, and cliques do not make many new friends.[34] Interconnected by blood, business and politics, their wills reflected the religious badge of affiliation that marked their clique-membership, with Bishop Repingdon a fully paid-up member.[35] They would never have recruited many of their social peers, and this because of themselves, not because of any supposed disrepute Lollardy had fallen into. They all died uncondemned and in their beds, still Wyclifite in thought and barely half-tamed in practice. Wyclifitism had intended a self-conscious personal morality which some aristocracy had already espoused. Merchants, gentry and academics would still read Wyclifite books, and a few approach even closer. It is not so much that they were now convinced that Lollardy was criminally disreputable. It was, rather, that their own social esteem and pattern of life kept them apart. Lollardy was not a great destroyer of social barriers.

Lollardy itself was left with its active practitioners outside the political élites, even though sympathisers in those circles remained. Nonetheless, phrases like 'discredited rump' or 'increasingly eccentric residue of half-baked ideas' sound a lot better from a distance than close to. Lollards were probably what they had always been. Thorpe's testimony shows that even someone with immediate and prolonged access to the academic origins of Wyclifitism found in it a sustaining personal faith, with evangelical overtones, rather than a series of doctrinal subtleties. His cannot be called a debased faith, or crude prejudice, or ignorant, or rumpish. What he found essential could also be sustained without the presence of the highly educated. Those who espoused Wyclifitism did so in the first place to reconcile themselves with their status quo. It was not a creed for the belligerent. A few marginal to the sect participated in Oldcastle's revolt. The core did not. The horizons of their faith were already those of their own environment.

Thus, post-1414 Lollardy was not 'fragmented' or 'dispersed' in any derogatory sense.[36] It had been built soundly, along the grain of English society: its strength lay in personally-linked clusters, not in

[34] McFarlane, *Lancastrian Kings and Lollard Knights*, esp. ch. 6; cf. M. Granovetter (note 13), esp. 1373–7.
[35] For Repingdon's curious will, see *Register of Henry Chichele, archbishop of Canterbury*, ed. E. F. Jacob II (Canterbury and York Society, 1937), 285–7.
[36] See, e.g., Swanson (note 4), 342; McFarlane, *John Wycliffe*, 183–5.

some countrywide enterprise with a national centre. Some supposed 'national defeat' of Lollardy, whether before or in 1414, was far from crippling to a sect made up essentially of such a series of micro-networks, interlinked but in which each part drew its identity from within itself rather than from its connections with the whole. At any time, effective prosecution needed to break up the personal structures within each group, not just chastise some teachers and members over their beliefs but leave the dynamics of the group in place. Sometimes bishops got this right, and burned or exiled the right people. What should one make, though, of the likes of Archbishop Wareham who in Kent in 1511 set about things keenly enough, but probably burned the wrong people and actually ordered others convicted to stay exactly where they were?[37] As the pathetic case of Joan Washingby of Coventry shows, some rank-and-file members had no sustenance or society outside of Lollardy.[38] Once abjured she was pretty well bound to go to the fire next time.

The geography of later Lollardy can never be fully established, but its main areas seem clear enough: all the counties abutting the Thames from source to estuary *via* London, with Bristol and Coventry as outriders. East Anglia's abrupt silence in the records after the 1428–31 prosecutions is suspicious, and Midlands towns such as Leicester and Northampton give off occasional hints of an enduring tradition of dissent. Did we but know, the picture probably remained fairly consistent from the early years. Allowing that local authorities would be looking harder in areas of notoriety, it is still the case that the chance leads and information they picked up led them back repeatedly to the same sort of places.

Historians' assumptions about the need for a strong national network as well as of one-directional faith-transmission have made far too much of the role of the travelling teacher—full-time or as a by-product of his occupational mobility—both in itself and as a measure of the cohesion and quality of the sect as a whole. There is no need to make a virtue out of a necessity on the Lollards' behalf when marking out the shift from early heavyweight missionary to later community-teaching.[39] As has been suggested, even the earliest, well-qualified as they were, needed a friendly audience to address. They had their shortcomings as populist writers. Some sermons may have been similarly rather heavy on the ear.[40] Which missionary was ever

---

[37] Lambeth Palace: Reg. Wareham fos. 166, 167r–v, 168–9v, 171v–2. Cf. the banishment for life from the entire Lincoln diocese of John Qwyrk 'on pain of relapse'; Lincoln DRO, Reg. John Chedworth fo. 60.

[38] Lichfield Ms. B/C/13 fo. 16, B/A/1/14 (i) [Register of Bishop Blyth] fo. 100.

[39] Hudson, *Premature Reformation*, 449–50 makes the point.

[40] This, of course, is not to deny the quality and quantity of the sermon literature

essential to a local group? Even William White, however influential, seems to have worked with an established East Anglian connection: not founded it. Even Hugh Pye, the influential local teacher, had been introduced to the Mone household group by John Pert, and heresy had supposedly been rife in the diocese for over twenty years.[41] White, being the catalyst for the inquisition, exercised a fascination over the court proceedings and the resulting record. The Coventry Lollards knew of other groups round the country but got all their nourishment from a resident corps. When these teachers were purged out in 1486, more stepped forward from the membership to teach and nurse the group back to health. In 1511 the local Lollards confronted Bishop Blythe as one of the most smartly-informed of all groups, perhaps because they did all draw on the same sources for their information and identity.[43] Apart from one secret five-day mission by an anonymous visitor, who was consulted furtively in his safe houses by the local leaders, they had done it all themselves.[44] They are also distinguished, incidentally, by the unusual enthusiasm with which they had been trying to recruit new members. They followed the Mormons' textbook to the letter: establish personal friendship first; then impress with names and social introductions; bring beliefs in only gently; lend the target a book if it seems interested.[45] Bishop Blythe sorted out goats and sheep rather well.

Several of the later migrant teachers were not intentional missionaries at all.[46] James Willis is a prime example.[47] He worked and taught in one group at a time until forced to move on. Bristol was home.

---

produced; see A. Hudson (ed.), *English Wycliffite Sermons* (Oxford 1983–), a four-volume project.

[41] Note the premise in the title of M. Aston, 'William White's Lollard followers', *Catholic Historical Review* 68 (1982), 469–97 (*Lollards and Reformers*, 71–100; for Pert and Pye see p. 82 n.43). For the supposed strength of dissent in the diocese as early as 1407, see Bodleian Library, Oxford: Ms. Arch. Seld. B.23 (Letterbook of William Swan) fos. 112v–3, 113v–4.

[42] Roger Laudesdale, Alice Rowley and Bartholomew Shugborough in particular, to give continuity and cohesion.

[43] This assertion rests on the premise that the marginal suspects and those only being wooed by group members can be identified and winnowed out from the true believers. For the 1486 teachers, see Lichfield JRO: Reg. John Hales fo. 166r–v.

[44] Lichfield JRO, Ms. B/C/13 fo. 20.

[45] E.G., ibid. fo. 18v, the case of Thomas Wrixham, who had lived for a long time in Coventry but not established firm roots. For all the local Lollards' efforts, he was still on the brink when the persecution came. Nonetheless, he had to abjure (Reg. Blythe fo. 99). Roger Dod of Burford seems a similar case (Foxe 4, 237–8)

[46] See note 39.

[47] Lincoln DRO: Reg. Chedworth fos. 57v–8v. Willis is discussed perceptively in Thomson, *Later Lollards*, esp. 68–71, although his influence in the Chilterns is perhaps over-stated.

Then to London, where he was goaled. Then to Henley-on-Thames. This was as near virgin soil as he ever dug. When he was caught again in 1462, his impact on Henley itself proved ephemeral in the extreme. Of those apprehended in his wake the more substantial actually lived at a distance, in the Chilterns. These admitted to pre-existent sentiments and local teachers there, and in fact owed very little to Willis. They were letting on to an established Lollard ring, which Bishop Chedworth followed up with only moderate rigour.[48] Here, as on other occasions, the prosecutor's terms of reference shape the inquisition records we have. In 1511 Thomas Man was credited with several hundred converts. Yet he himself (perhaps predictably) played down his role in Essex and said he chose to go to the Chilterns because it was known to contain sympathisers.[49] It has even been suggested recently that his own kin lived roundabouts.[50] Certainly Man became close to the Amersham high command that was broken up in 1511, but his name was not mentioned by many of those accused in 1521, for all the Lollards' supposed ploy of denouncing the dead when ordered to name names. John Hacker, the tireless long-distance water-carrier, was similarly a popular enough visitor around the Home Counties, but made his chief impression where he had kin or lived.[51] In short, it seems unnecessary and misplaced to measure the stamina of later Lollardy by its access to outside teachers. Whatever these did achieve was within the context of an existing local organization, and they did best when they settled into it.

This places a still greater burden upon the internal vigour of each area-group. The fact that *long-term* continuity of dissent has been argued for most of them is helpful. Nevertheless, sometimes the proof is a shade thin. Just because trials for heresy occurred in the district from time to time or, in addition, because the sentiments noted in those trials seem similar, is not really enough.[52] Not surprisingly, most historians prefer to look for a demonstrable person-to-person chain; even those who see Lollardy as the earliest mail-order book-club and argue its continuity on those grounds. Various studies of such inter-personal links have brought out that later Lollardy lived by far more than the chancy transmission of vague ideas between social marginals

---

[48] Reg. Chedworth fos. 60, 62r–v, 64v.

[49] Foxe 4, 210–14, 226, 228, 230, 234; Bishop Fitzjames's Courtbook (see note 23) fo. 124v.

[50] M. Aston, 'Iconoclasm at Rickmansworth, 1522', *J. Ecc. H.* 40 (1989), 543–6.

[51] I.E., in London, Colchester and the upper Thames Valley rather than in the Chilterns. For him, see Hudson, *Premature Reformation*, 464–5, 474–8; J. F. Davis, *Heresy and Reformation*, 57–8.

[52] E.G., A. G. Dickens, *The English Reformation* (2nd edn., 1989), 48–60; idem., *Lollards and Protestants*, chapters 2, 3.

and no-hopers, or in pockets cut off from the uniforming influences of parish discipline or manorial community. Such dissidents there were, and they may or may not have been Lollards. The Church at the time, and historians since, may have been less scrupulous, but Lollards at the time knew another Lollard when they saw one or at least took pains to find out. Much more important to them were those places where Lollardy had a stable home *and* a *modus vivendi* with the surrounding world. Not that this relationship was ever 'denominational', i.e. live and let live. Lollards were always wary of letting their orthodox neighbours know much, as witness-patterns in court indicate.

Nonetheless, the social position of each group helped to define the horizons within which they could operate. The Kent Lollards of 1511 (admittedly less well-reported than some others) appear to be of the least social substance by then and commensurately the most microcelled of all, with the personnel of each unit tightly defined, even based on a single household, and scarcely overlapping even locally, save by a very limited number of one-to-one conversations with a core teacher.[53] They were predictably the Lollard connection most given to urging secrecy upon each other, although possibly because they had been badly shaken by the purge of a key unit in Maidstone in 1495 (about which we knew very little).[54] Unfortunately, we only have a record of 1511 from Wareham's principal register, which naturally concentrates on those who were to die. It seems clear that none of these were group-leaders. The registrar concentrated on just the abjurations of the others convicted. Most of what they may have said about their local network was left in court working-papers which, like so many others, have not survived.[55]

In the Chilterns, where there were both some sympathisers on the edge and some key active members of greater wealth and standing, group activity was commensurately freer and wider-ranging.[56] Even then, though, it is possible to surmise variety of experience. Around Chesham itself, first Leicester Abbey's control of the advowson, and

[53] Lambeth: Reg. Wareham fos. 175v–6, 179, 180.

[54] It was mentioned by Joan Washingby, formerly and afterwards of Coventry, who had migrated there with her husband and been convicted in it; Lichfield JRO, Ms. B/C/13 fo. 16. John Brown of Ashford said in 1511 that he had abjured in Maidstone twelve years earlier; Reg. Wareham fo. 179v.

[55] Bishop Blythe's courtbook and general register at Lichfield provide an interesting contrast in choice and emphasis of material relating to the same persecution.

[56] See, for example, *Subsidy Roll, 1524* (note 27), 12–13 (Amersham), 15–16 (Chesham), and similar material in the *Certificates of Musters for 1522* and references in note 69 below. For the Durdaunts, see also PRO E179/141/115 and 131, STAC 2/32/106 (where Thomas was lord of the manor of Denham, like his ancestors before him).

then the local eminence of the durable but childless Sir John Cheyne gave Lollards scope until the 1460s.[57] Thereafter—with the Cheynes in some disarray, undergoing a long minority, living away and emerging Catholic—the sect's heartland shrank to the outlying hillside hamlet of Ashley Green where the deep-rooted but far less substantial Morden family could ensure its survival but provide only for a much-reduced circle of adherents.[58]

Yet by the same time the Lollards were in a much healthier position in Amersham, with an entry into the substantial citizenry of that town and, by the early sixteenth century, even a majority and an active one in the top dozen.[59] Especially, they had the sympathy of the pre-eminent Saunders family, living on the south side of the town at The Bury.[60] In a relatively small place like Amersham the Saunders, although not integrated with other Lollard families, still became too close and confident. They got stung when prosecution came. In Colchester leading citizens were just about ensnared on the margins where sympathy melded into active support.[61] In a bigger community still, Coventry for example, they might, like the mayoral families of Wygston and Pysford, get detected only vaguely as interested at a distance as reputed to own the enviable best of Wycliffite books.[62]

[57] Sir John Cheyne of Drayton Beauchamp (c. 1390–1468), heir male of his more notorious namesake of Beckford (d. 1414), and his brother, Thomas, were both imprisoned for involvement in the Oldcastle Rising (as was their father, Roger) and again in 1431 after 'Perkins' Revolt', although this latter arrest may well have been really a manoeuvre by their enemies in a serious local feud. I am completing a study of the family.

[58] Foxe 4, 225, 230–1; Winchester DRO: Reg. R. Fox IV, fos. 18–19. The Mordens appear in the court-rolls for Ashley Green and Blackwell Hall manors (Bucks. Archaeol. Soc., Box C2, items 49/184, 186, 188, 197), the Chesham Courtbook, 1461–1552 fos. 21v, 22, 26v (also held by the Society), and the cartulary of Great Missenden Abbey which held lands there (BL Sloane 747 fos. 30r–v, 31v–2). See PRO E150/17/5 for the inquisition *post mortem* on James Morden, who was burned on 15 Feb. 1522. John Morden's widow, Marion, made a blandly orthodox will on 13 May 1521, but was denounced as a heretic after her death, an example of a very common problem of evidence in this field; Elvey (see note 27), 327–8.

[59] See, e.g., PRO E101/107/27 (leading horseowners in Amersham, 1513) and compare with the records of the 1511 and 1521 persecutions and with the *Certificates of Musters for 1522* for the town (pp. 230–5). The same situation appears in Hughenden, but not in Chesham.

[60] Richard Saunders, who abjured in 1511, was assessed at a massive £300 in goods in Amersham in 1522 (*Musters*, 231), five times anyone else. He was not self-made: his father, William (d. 1488), had occupied the front pew in the church and been buried on that spot; PRO, Prerogative Court of Canterbury Wills, 14 Milles.

[61] L. M. A. Higgs, 'Lay piety in the borough of Colchester, 1485–1558', unpublished Ph.D. thesis, U. of Michigan, 1983, 291–7.

[62] Lichfield JRO, Ms. B/C/13 fos. 5, 18v; this is only the hearsay evidence of John Atkins and Thomas Wrixham, uncertain hangers-on to the Lollard group and dealing in gossip, but there are other indications that these two (related) families were indeed

In London they might have attended ultra-fashionable Whittington Hospital on Sundays with all the other *nouveaux riches* and challenged the resident preacher, Reginald Pecock, to prove at great and repeated length just why Wyclifite ideas were so wrong; and not by trotting out the tedious clichés of the established Church about tradition and authority but in terms of Wyclifite writings. They were not intimately involved with real live Lollards, so Pecock was only put to an old-fashioned wrestling match with the academically-inclined Wyclifite literature of yesteryear. Still, they had done their reading. They shouldn't have, but they could defy Pecock to indict them.[63]

From the Chilterns comes some of the best evidence that the active Lollard families of the early sixteenth century were not only far from poor and downcast but not even some old-guard at odds with all that was new in church and society and losing their place in the sun, as such better-born medieval heretics are often supposed to be.[64] The Saunders, Chase, Harding and Wydmer families were already well-set for their future social advance in Bucks., the Collins family likewise in Berks. and Oxon.[65] Someone may already know which of them grew out of sectarianism. At least the Chases did not, nor the yeomen Trachers either before or after the Cheyne family itself threw them off their land in 1539 for excess of Protestant zeal.[66] Christopher Hill's impression of the recurrence of nonconformity in the Chilterns between medieval and modern times was not predicated upon family descents, but W. H. Summers' assertions, based upon the formidable amount that he knew about these movements and the local population, deserve following up.[67]

---

sympathetic. See I. Luxton, 'The Lichfield Court Book: a postscript', *Bulletin of the Institute of Historical Research* 44 (1971), 120–5.

[63] From a big literature, particularly helpful here are E. F. Jacob, 'Reginald Pecock, bishop of Chichester', *PBA* 37 (1951), 1–34 (reprinted in his *Essays in Later Medieval History* (Manchester, 1968), 1–34); R. M. Haines, 'Reginald Pecock', in W. J. Sheils (ed.), *Persecution and Toleration* (Studies in Church History 21, 1984), 125–37; Hudson, *Premature Reformation*, 55–8, 189–91, 441–3.

[64] See e.g., R. I. Moore, *The Origins of European Dissent* (revised edn., Oxford, 1985), 267–8.

[65] See, e.g., the Amersham churchwardens' accounts for 1539–41, (badly) printed in *Records of Bucks* 7 (1897), 43–51; PRO E150/52/1, E179/78/125, P.C.C. 15 Coode (all for Thomas Saunders, son of Richard); J. W. Garrett-Pegge, 'Richard Bowle's Book', *Records of Bucks* 9 (1904–9), 329–48, 393–414, for the sensitive re-seating project in Chesham church in 1606, with descendants of Lollard suspects doing well. For the Durdaunts, see note 56 above and P.C.C. F.22 Dyngeley.

[66] PRO, SP1/136/ no. 27 pp. 34–5 (*Letters and Papers of Henry VIII*, ed. J. S. Brewer *et al.*, 13 (ii) no. 253 p. 101)).

[67] C. Hill, 'From Lollards to Levellers', latest version in his *Collected Papers Volume II: Religion and Politics in 17th Century England* (Brighton, 1986), 89–116; W. H. Summers, *The Lollards of the Chiltern Hills* (1906), 83–4, 106–8; idem., *Our Lollard Ancestors* (1904), 113–5.

Such well-shod sympathisers with Lollardy still did the right things in public. They went to church and sat as prominently as they should. They served as churchwardens and wardens of fraternities.[68] If such might be dismissed as merely prudent, testaments such as those from within the Bartlett and Saunders families spelled out arrangements appropriate to their social status with a thought and confidence suggesting they were not ashamed of it.[69] There is little to suggest discreet shame, any sense of having lived a lie, or alternatively any ambition to keep Catholic niceties to the minimum that discretion required. The trouble is that, whilst several testators, such as Richard and Alice Saunders, Isabel Bartlett and John Hill, had actually abjured in their time, we do not have the testament of anyone who emerges from the records of the sect-prosecutions as being amongst the *most* active and central in the local group. Given Bishops Smith and Longland's enthusiasm that such luminaries in life should depart in even more glowing a fashion, this is hardly a surprise. What we are left with are the perfectly sincere and reflective wills of people who had sympathy with Lollard ideas and connections with group activists, but found therein no crisis of conscience about upholding their own social status.

Physical geography played its part in the sect's life. The Buckinghamshire connection came from no further north than their main centres of Amersham, Chesham, the Missendens, and to a lesser extent Hughenden. All their tentacles, even marginal ones, spread along their respective roads south, following the Chess, Misbourne, Colne and Wye to the River Thames and so to London. Not one came from over the Chiltern crest. This simply reflects the social and economic division of Buckinghamshire since time began. Travellers pass the hills to east or west. The communities of the Chilterns and the Vale of Aylesbury turn their backs on each other; chalk and clay. If there were Lollards in both areas they did the same. Similarly, east-west

---

[68] *Courts of the Archdeaconry of Buckingham*, ed. Elvey, 208 (John Milsent, Churchwarden of Amersham, 1505), 289 (Robert Andrew the same, 1520); Lincoln Record Society 61 (1967), ed. M. Bowker, 139 (Thomas Copeland the same). Thomas Houre was holywater clerk in Amersham, but claimed to have been sacked through Lollard malice; and Henry Phip of Hughenden was keeper of the rood light in 1518 (Foxe 4, 231, 238). William Sweeting was holywater clerk in Colchester (see note 61). John Phipps and Henry Honor were wardens of the élite guild of St. Katherine's, Amersham, interesting in that neither of them lived there, whilst the guild attracted particular bequests from certain 'Lollard' testators (see note 59).

[69] P.C.C. F. 28 Bodfeld (Richard Saunders), F. 29 Spert (Alice Saunders), F.22 Dyngeley (Nicholas Durdaunt); Bucks CRO, Archdeaconry of Buckingham enrolled wills, We 2 fo. 3v (John Hill), fos. 30v, 92 (Katherine Bartlett), We 3 fo. 318 (John Fype), We 4 No. 5 (Emma Morden), We 7 no. 117 (Isabel Bartlett), We 154 no. 14 (Isabel Scrivener).

between the valleys of the Chess, the Misbourne (on which Amersham stands), and the Wye, the hills divide off the communities between. Chesham and Amersham had some overlap of catchment area, but the hinterland of High Wycombe, which included Hughenden, was quite distinct. Once more the Lollards in 1511 and 1521 reflected the geography. The Chesham Lollards had some reasonable contact with those in Amersham, much less with those in the Missendens and next to nothing with those in Hughendon. Even Thomas Africk in Amersham, a member of a prolific tribe, so rarely had contact with his in-laws in Hughenden that he had to ask someone whether they were alright and still keeping up the faith.[70] Their lives, though only six miles apart, were in a different world, and Lollardy roused in him no psychological urge or sectarian necessity to jog over the hill to share an epistle with them.

In 1521 Bishop Longland dealt with Bucks. and Oxfordshire in one sweep (picking up the Collins's additional colonies in Berkshire and pieces of Hertfordshire and Middlesex along the way). He has rather seduced historians ever since Foxe to deal in similar eclectic fashion with the resultant evidence. The Pope family, Lollard in both 1463 and 1511, had branches in both Amersham and West Hendred/Steventon (Berkshire). The two branches kept in touch, but in neither place were they influential in the sect, and it is not the case that the fugitive Robert Pope was an active link.[71] That apart, there was just Roger Dod of Burford, a gauche youth who passed along a chain of Lollard employers, and the inevitable John Hacker.[72] In fact, even the most active Chiltern Lollards were not much in touch with co-sectaries in places like Marlow, Henley and the villages in the deep south of their own county. To go to London they took the A413 and picked up the A40 at Uxbridge. The pattern of their Lollard contacts follows suit.

On the face of it, the Berkshire Lollards around the Hendreds and the Oxfordshire group around Witney and the Cotswold foothills seem better connected. In reality, though, the connection is largely the Collins family, pivotal within each group and often travelling to see each other, repositories of literature, possessors of formidable memories, wealthy, well-established and with a good sixteenth century ahead of them.[73] Similarly, the solid contact between the Chilterns and

---

[70] Foxe 4, 229.

[71] Lincoln DRO: Reg. Chedworth fo. 62; Foxe 4, 225–6, 229–30, 236–7, 239. Robert's brother and father stood their ground in Little Missenden. He denounced them when no-one else did and after the hunt seemed to have overlooked them and moved out of the district.

[72] Foxe 4, 237–8 (Dod); for Hacker, see note 51.

[73] Foxe 4, 234–40; Hudson, *Premature Reformation*, 463–5; see *Wills and Administrations:*

London before 1511 was founded upon a group of substantial families working in London but with property around Amersham and the Missendens, three even local by origin.[74] Bishops Smith and Fitzjames between them seriously undermined this coalition. At least one humbler survivor was heard sighing for those good old days.[75]

It is still wrong to describe these groups as 'isolated' or 'dispersed' in any desolated sense. Leaders of Lollard groups knew where each other were but did not go out of their way to meet each other. Items of literature were circulated, of course, but with what regularity and systematic intent is hard to recover from the abundant but necessarily anecdotal evidence.[76] All the established groups, however, appear to have had both their own stocks and access to fresh material if and when they wanted it. They are often reported to have been chatty and delighted with their latest acquisition, however old its composition. In personal terms, though, active inter-group contacts did not rise much above the natural parameters set by geography, economy and social convention. Because the more substantial tended to have the wider horizons, they were the *effective* links.[77] Certainly, in an emergency, leading Bucks. figures knew where to find safe houses in Hertfordshire, Essex, Kent and London, or vice versa. Even then, this may have been by transmission along a chain in the way that rank-and-file members of the Coventry group were passed through places like Northampton, London, Maidstone and Bristol.[78] Such links could have been dangerous when bishops began systematic prosecutions and passed information to each other. In 1428, when William White actually fled from Kent to Norfolk, it was a disaster for the East Anglian group, but he was the principal quarry in the chase and something of a special case. Otherwise, the inadvertent virtues of keeping such links indirect and known to few emerge as obvious.

The internal structuring of the groups in each area is of crucial

---

archdeaconry of Berkshire, 1508 to 1652, ed. W. P. W. Phillimore (British Record Soc., 1893), 41, and *Oxfordshire Probate Records, 1516–1732*, ed. E. Cheyne and D. M. Barratt 1 (B.R.S., 1981), 41. A proper tracing of the family would be valuable.

[74] A systematic collation of the evidence in Bishop Fitzjames's courtbook (see note 23) with the local evidence (especially that in Foxe (e.g., 4, 228 and BL Sloane 747, Missenden Abbey Cartulary) is required. For a John Tilsworth of Amersham as far back as 1393, see PRO E101/338/1 no. 9.

[75] Foxe 4, 228.

[76] M. Aston, 'Devotional Literacy' and 'Lollardy and Literacy', in *Lollards and Reformers*, 101–34, 193–218, and A. Hudson's studies (see note 1) now supersede all previous work.

[77] See, e.g., the wedding guest list at the Durdaunts' wedding at Iver-by-Staines (Foxe 4, 228) and the background to the 1511 leadership.

[78] Foxe 4, 228; Lichfield JRO: Ms. B/C/13 fos. 2v–3, 16.

importance, but poses problems of its own. When Thomas Holmes remarked after the 1511 inquisition in Amersham, 'The greatest cobs are yet behind', what did he mean?[79] Bishop Smith, after all, trapped the principal teachers and did not spare the social élite. Yet Holmes knew what was what: ten years later his desperate betrayals in court did not save himself but were the ruin of many others.[80] Not that being executed always meant one was important. In Norwich in 1428, Coventry in 1486, and Buckinghamshire in 1511 it did, to the extent that bishops moved primarily to purge out teachers. But when the bishops started to return a second time, the capital offenders were often small fry in the sect—followers, not leaders—women like Joan Washingby and Joan Grevill, men like Holmes and James Morden, who now fell into ruin solely because of their previous abjurations. It can hardly be called relapse: they were just involuntary life-members. Such people were additionally dangerous to the sect because, by marriage, kinship, and employment (and consequently incorrigible sympathy of belief) they were close to the heart of the local group yet without the calibre to lead, even known to be garrulous and indiscreet. On trial for their lives, they certainly were. Is it just coincidence that both Holmes and Morden were poorer than their immediate kin, in lesser employment, and, like Washingby, had to roam around for a living? In groups constructed by social and kinship co-ordinates, were such unavoidable discordancies of status a time-bomb?

Allowing that denunciation is not the same at all as guilt, that bishops even interrogated far fewer than were named, and convicted fewer still, and admitting all the problems we have with the court records, yet with care something of the internal subdivisions of each group can be recovered, and within each some patterns of behaviour and authority: who mixed with whom, who was influenced by whom, who taught whom, who just listened, who was loitering pale and uncertain on the edge. Usually, but not always, this is a matter of immediate neighbourhood. The Coventry group, for example, opens out amongst other things into a distinct sub-group in Birmingham, to a women's group under Mother Agnes and Alice Rowley, to an old people's group, and to an embryonic fraternity trying to set up shop amongst Coventry's young élite.[81] Similarly, in Earsham in Norfolk, the bishop may have interrupted a recruiting drive.[82] In Amersham in 1462 certain suspects admitted they had heard Lollard ideas, of

---

[79] Foxe 4, 227.

[80] Foxe 4, 245 commented sadly on his motivation.

[81] Reg. Blythe fo. 99v, B/C/13 fos. 10v–12, 16v–17.

[82] *Norwich Heresy Trials*, 206–16. Dr. Tanner suggests alternatively (p. 8) that there could have been a successful collective cover-up, based upon the quasi-autonomy of the village group.

which they liked some but not others.[83] There are hints in other evidence that they had business connections with the principal defendants.[84] They may have described their position very accurately in court. The East Anglian village-circles are said each to have had their own organiser and added their own distinctive gloss to what White and Pye taught them.[85] In Kent, groups came down in troubled times to single households and families and were particularly tightly sealed.[86]

Everywhere, there were lead-figures, both in teaching and in group organisation. These two sorts were not necessarily synonymous, but there was considerable overlap. The Collins family is one clear example: Alice Rowley in Coventry, the Tilsworths in London and Amersham, the Phippses in Hughenden, the Baxters in Martham are others. What with differentials of literacy, wealth, access to books, social independence, and economic horizons, it is perhaps no surprise that this degree of authority and influence was often matched by relative social eminence. However, the debate over the social standing of the later Lollards is now as bedevilled by anecdotal emphasis on the substantial as it has always been by harsh references to the numerical predominance of artisans and rustics. It is now appreciated, of course, that even some of these latter turn out to be rather more solid citizens than a first impression of their occupation suggests. Hence we run into J. F. Davis's 'middle-class' 'bricklayer', John Stacey; the fishmonger worth £30 in Colchester and forever mixed up in the town's government, Thomas Matthew; and our friend, the dyer worth £200 plus in Amersham, Richard Saunders.[87] More pertinently, though, we should be investigating the relationship of any sort of individual, whether ostensibly well-off, artisan and rustic, to the company he kept, and particularly to identifiable Lollard lead-figures. Lollardy was not some inchoate lumpen mass, the blind leading the blind.

This does not necessarily require the kind of treasure-trove of information there is for Buckinghamshire. There is growing perception in studies of the East Anglian heretics of 1428–31 (for whom it is said

[83] Lincoln DRO: Reg. Chedworth fos. 61v–4.

[84] See note 30; also PRO C1/100/38, 39, 43, 340/17, 218/30, 57/344; B.A.S. 618/40 (deed of 1506); *Cal. Inquisitions Post Mortem, Henry VII* 1 no. 544; Elvey (see note 27), 81, 88; see also *H.M.C. 15th Report* Appendix VII, 131, 132.

[85] Aston, 'William White', 95; Tanner in *Norwich Heresy Trials*, 27–8; Hudson, *Premature Reformation*, 137–9.

[86] See note 53.

[87] J. F. Davis, *Heresy and Reformation*, 55, 58 for Stacey (who is actually called a brick*maker* by Foxe 4, 236); for Saunders' citation as a dyer, PRO C1/133/22–3; for Colchester see note 61. Probably, in the Norwich diocese group, Thomas Mone, William Baxter and Richard Fletcher are also examples of men whose given occupation misleadingly undervalues their status to the unwary (*Norwich Heresy Trials*, 41–51, 84–9, 175–91).

that little supporting secular material exists) that when studies of the teachers and the confessed beliefs are coordinated with an equally close examination of the social network, a smoothly-functioning organisation comes into view, with beliefs, depth of knowledge, social contacts and degree of integration operating in concert.[88] Most importantly, there were just a few defendants in East Anglia who were particularly outlandish in their views. This supposed eccentric or lunatic fringe of Lollardy get quoted frequently, but can and should be swept away: they did not know the mainstream groups, nor these groups them; they did not even live in the main villages. They have little or nothing to do with Lollardy and their turns of phrase, however colourful, should cease littering textbooks and giving Lollardy a bad name. Likewise, it is high time to end the outrageous career of William Aylward, the Henley blacksmith and part-time warlock, who was picked up in the James Willis scandal of 1462 but quite clearly had no real connection at all with his fellow-suspects.[89] Freed of such local wild men, as well more importantly of the many other free-thinking but unconnected dissenters whose court-appearances have confused historians, the integrated sectarians everywhere emerge as well-informed and in concert, neither extreme nor vulgar: maybe sometimes not much to look at, but organised, instructed and with a stable core.

To evaluate Lollardy, every effort must be made to reconstruct its group-dynamics and align the expressed beliefs accordingly: central figures, rank-and-file, marginals, sympathisers. There should be no mudslinging of anecdotal evidence about the social standing of this or that member, still less predicating quality of belief upon it, without at least considering his or her role in the sect. We should not be reading too much into some undifferentiated index of taxable wealth or list of occupations. The hallmark of Lollards was their substantial local self-sufficiency, their strength that they were not trying to operate *against* the grain of local society. Theirs was not some salvage operation after the failure of a national movement, or some fading tradition, or some miscellaneous compost heap of dissent misconstrued as an environmental heritage garden by over-eager historians. It was their own appreciation of Wyclifite material as related to their own circumstances. They were not residual grumbling outcasts. They were households, kin, neighbours, employers, workmates and friends whose empathy and relationships could be identified in shared attitudes which might then be passed on to children, in-laws and anyone else they wanted to join the club. Lollardy has been written off by some

---

[88] Hudson, *Premature Reformation*, 137–9.
[89] Lincoln DRO: Reg. Chedworth fo. 61.

as just a series of attitudes; and as crude, diverse and discontinuous ones at that. This falls short on many counts. It has sucked in the comments of people who weren't Lollards and been undiscriminating amongst those who were. In terms of doctrinal beliefs, core Lollardy actually remained well-informed. Even if it had not been, such a write-off is based on a rarefied and unrealistic premise that would extinguish the congregation of just about any sect or church, including the Catholics of the time. Of course Lollardy was about attitudes, and Lollards drew both conviction and identity from sharing them with each other. For Lollardy was about personal contact and inter-dependence and drew therefrom its existence and life. If Wyclifitism was what you knew, Lollardy was whom you knew.

WOMEN AND IMAGES OF WOMEN IN THE SPANISH CIVIL WAR

By Frances Lannon

READ 12 OCTOBER 1990

AT the end of the Spanish Civil War in the spring of 1939, General Franco celebrated his victory by decreeing that full military honours be accorded to two statues of the Virgin Mary.[1] The first was Our Lady of Covadonga, patron of the first great reconquest of Spain through the expulsion of Islam in the middle ages. Now, after removal by her enemies 'the Reds' during the Civil War, she had been restored to her northern shrine in Asturias, marking the completion of what the decree described as the second reconquest. The other statue was of Our Lady of the Kings (de los Reyes) in Seville, invoked—so the decree ran—during the battle of Lepanto against the Turks in 1571 and the battle of Bailén against the French in 1808, and invoked once more in the first desperate days of the military rising in July 1936, when a victory for the 'Red hordes' in Seville might have changed the whole course of the war. In Covadonga and Seville, in the undefeated stronghold of the Virgin of the Pillar in Zaragoza, and across the length and breadth of the country, the Virgin Mary had saved Spain and deserved every honour and tribute. It was equally true that from far north to far south, Franco and his armies and his Nazi, Fascist, and Islamic allies had made Spain safe for the Virgin Mary. There would be no more desecrated churches, no more burned statues, no more banned processions, just as there would be no more socialists, anarchists, communists or democrats. Spain would be Catholic and authoritarian, and Spanish women could concentrate their energies on emulating Mary, and being good wives and mothers or nuns.

Many other possibilities were closed to them. During or just after the war, all of the emancipatory legislation passed in the first phase of the Second Republic from 1931–33 was repealed or became meaningless. Women had won the vote and there had been a few women deputies in the national parliament,[2] but the new regime was not

[1] *Legislación Española*, ed. L. Gabilán Plà and W. D. Alcahud (8 vols., San Sebastian, 1937–1940), vii. 6–7. The author would like to thank the British Academy for a grant to do research for this paper at the Hoover Institution, Stanford University.

[2] Clara Campoamor (Radical) and Victoria Kent (Left Republican) were elected to the Constituent Cortes in June 1931, followed by Margarita Nelken (Socialist) in

based on popular suffrage and representation. On 2 March 1938 all separation and divorce petitions were suspended, and on 12 March the law of 28 June 1932 which had introduced civil marriage was annulled. On 9 March the Labour Charter promised that the State 'will liberate married women from the workshop and the factory'. On 24 May the right given to women by the 1931 Constitution, to retain a nationality different from that of their husband, was removed. The following year, on 23 September 1939, the Divorce Law of 2 March 1932 was repealed, and divorces already granted under the law, that involved canonically-married people, were declared null and void.[3] The legalization of abortion by the Catalan Generalitat in December 1936 was swept away together with all vestiges of Catalan autonomy, abolished on 5 April 1938 as insurgent forces advanced on Catalonia.[4]

It was particularly evident in wartime legislation on education that the place of women was to be separate, subordinate, and domestic. This was in stark contrast to the contemporary campaign in Republican Catalonia for a 'unified school' for girls and boys in which both would be offered equal if not identical opportunities. As early as 4 September 1936 an order from the military Junta in insurgent Spain directed that when the new academic year began for secondary schools on 1 October, there must be no co-education. If a town had only one secondary school, then boys should come in the morning and girls in the afternoon, or vice versa. The ending of co-education was formalised a few days later in a decree signed by General Cabanellas, which also stipulated that all women teachers must teach in girls' schools, and that as soon as possible *only* women teachers should teach in girls' schools.[5] Given the paucity of women with a university degree, this virtually ensured that all girls in secondary schools would receive a less academic education than would be available to some boys, with the obvious consequences.

At primary level, not only was 'essentially immoral and anti-pedagogic' co-education to end wherever practicable, but girls' schools should be overseen by women inspectors who would not exercise similar responsibilities in boys' schools. The teachers in these girls' primary schools were enjoined to orientate all their work towards

---

December 1931. In the November 1933 general elections three female candidates were successful for the Socialist Party, Nelken, Matilde de la Torre, and María Lejarraga de Martínez Sierra. In the February 1936 elections, Nelken and de la Torre were joined by Julia Alvarez Resana for the Socialists, Dolores Ibárruri (Communist) and Victoria Kent (Left Republican).

[3] *Legislación Española,* iv. 24–5, 239–43, 26; viii. 136–7.
[4] *Legislación Española,* iv. 109–10.
[5] *Legislación Española,* i. part 2, 312–14, 320–1.

preparing their charges 'for their elevated function in the family and the home (hogar)' by developing sewing, gardening, and household skills. Inspectors were urged to establish local courses for women teachers, to help them prepare their pupils for their 'important maternal function'.[6] Those in power did not underestimate the difficulty of moulding education in this way, and it is not surprising that these measures ran alongside a massive ideological purge of the teaching profession at all levels in Spain, initiated in a decree signed by Franco on 8 November 1936, and applied province by province as the insurgents gained control of ever more territory.[7] Meanwhile, one female image was to be placed incessantly before all young Spaniards. In a circular of 9 April 1937, Enrique Suñer ordered every school to place a statue of the Virgin Mary in a prominent position, to hold daily prayers to Mary for the successful ending of the war, and to teach the children to greet teachers at the beginning and end of each day with the traditional words 'Ave Maria Purisima', to which they should reply, equally traditionally, 'conceived without sin'.[8]

It would be hard, and wrong, to evade the conclusion that one of the important issues at stake in the Spanish Civil War was the future position—legal, economic, and cultural—of women. By the summer of 1939 they found themselves, some with relief, others with repugnance, returned to the status that had obtained before the attempted New Deal of the early Republic of 1931–3. Those women who had been most active in resisting the reimposition of the traditional order had to face exile or imprisonment in appalling conditions and in many cases execution.[9] There was no honourable or safe place for them in the new dictatorship.

The very fact that this was a *civil war*, erupting from bitter ideological disagreements, made it inevitable that conflicting views about Spanish social structure, including the role of women, were at issue. On both sides there were powerful forces emphasising a contrary interpretation of the war as a defensive struggle against foreign invasion. This was the line taken and imposed by the Communist Party, seeking to rally the widest possible support for the protection

[6] *Legislación Española*, v. 563–6; vi. 131–4.

[7] *Legislación Española*, i. part 2, 294. For a study of this purge in one province, see J. Crespo Redondo, *Purga de maestros en la guerra civil (Burgos provincia)* (Valladolid, 1987).

[8] *Legislación Española*, i. part 2, 318–19.

[9] There is a substantial and growing prison and exile literature. For womens' prisons in Franco's Spain, see especially G. di Febo, *Resistencia y movimiento de mujeres en España 1936–1976* (Barcelona, 1979); on exile, see S. García Iglesias, *Exilio*, (Mexico, 1957), S. Mistral, *Exodo. Diario de una refugiada española* (Mexico, 1940), and T. Pamiès, *Records de guerra i d'exili* (Barcelona, 1976).

of the Republic against, in its view, international fascism.[10] Similarly Franco himself argued that he was protecting everything authentically Spanish from being overwhelmed by foreign bolshevism. As he travelled round Spain taking that curious symbol of *Hispanidad*, the preserved arm of St Teresa of Avila, with him, all those who opposed him were, indiscriminately, anti-Spanish 'Reds'.[11] But the invasion thesis, however strenuously promoted on either side, could not hide the fact that this was originally and in essence a civil war. The place of women in Spanish society was of central importance, albeit more often implicitly than explicitly, within the ideological aspirations that combatants were seeking to realize.

Wherever the military rising failed, and especially in the cities, it seemed that what women looked like and what women could do was being altered almost beyond recongition. Bourgeois dress disappeared because it was seen as incriminating and dangerous, and with it went hats. It took one American visitor, Dorothy Parker, a little while to work out why people laughed at her on the streets of Valencia eighteen months or so into the war, and she then removed the offending and conspicuous hat and all was well.[12] This compulsory sartorial proletarianisation applied equally to men, and dozens of commentators mentioned it.[13] The only permissible headgear was usually a police or military uniform cap. But because of the weight of religious and social convention governing women's head-dress, bourgeois women going bare-headed necessarily represented a new kind of gender self-presentation as well as class solidarity. This was much more apparent in the other immediate change in dress in the first days of the war. Some young women on the Republican side adopted unisex dungarees, the famous *mono*, in what was for Spain a startling break with tradition. It was practical, radical, and a protest simultaneously. A teenage Communist militant, Teresa Pamiès, reported that she never wore the blue *mono* because by the time she came from her village to Barcelona, probably in 1937, it was already out of favour, perhaps being too much associated for Communist taste with the Anarchists. But for the winter of 1937–8, she and her fellow-

[10] Dolores Ibárruri claimed with pride that the Communist Party had proposed this interpretation within days of the July 1936 rising; see her *Speeches and Articles 1936–38* (New York, 1938), 132–43, 232.

[11] For a thorough discussion of Franco's propagandist use of Teresa of Avila, see G. di Febo, *La santa de la raza. Un culto barroco en la españa franquista* (Barcelona, 1988).

[12] Parker's own account in *Among Friends* American International Brigade publication, Spring 1938, 4–5.

[13] Two contrasting accounts are given by George Orwell, *Homage to Catalonia* (1966 edn.), 8–9, who found it exciting, and Clara Campoamor, *La Révolution espagnole vue par une Républicaine* (Paris, 1937), 103, who found it sinister and threatening.

militant Lena Imbert decided it was of utmost importance to acquire culottes (falda-pantalón) for entirely practical reasons connected with getting on an off lorries, riding bicycles, doing agricultural work, or clearing up debris after air-raids. On cold winter days they could be worn with a blouse and sweater, sturdy shoes and socks.[14]

Both dungarees and culottes were directly connected, of course, with what women wanted to do. And the most antitraditional occupation imaginable was to bear arms and be a soldier. In both Madrid and Barcelona in the very first days of the war, some young women rushed along with men to the direct defence of the Republic against the military uprising by city garrisons. A few took part in storming the Montaña Barracks in Madrid and Atarazanas in Barcelona. They joined search parties stopping people on the streets, careered around waving their rifles with male companions in requisitioned lorries, and went off to help halt the enemy advance in the Guadarrama hills north of Madrid and elsewhere, in many cases at the cost of their lives. Probably the best-known female iconography of the war is of these young soldiers with their guns and dungarees. They were sketched in a famous collection by the artist Sim (pseudonym for Vila-Rey),[15] and they featured on dramatic Civil-War posters long after the phenomenon of women soldiers had virtually ceased to exist. An early casualty, Communist militant Lina Odena, was ambushed by insurgent troops in Almería and died before she was twenty, becoming a war icon. And the first British military casualty of the war was sculptress Felicia Browne, also a Communist who, already in Spain when the war began, joined the militia in Barcelona, and was shot in the head on 25 August 1936 at the front near Zaragoza.

It is tempting to contrast this brave action by militia-women at the front with the symbolic military role of the Virgin Mary, and to suggest that while one side on the war offered women a remarkable range of new activity, the other offered only symbolic public militancy and real domestic, cultural, and economic constriction, under a religious mantle. Conversely, some contemporaries argued that one side preserved and protected women in their traditional roles, while the other produced a quite new and disturbing kind of woman in the Republican cities who lacked every conventionally feminine attribute. As early as 25 July 1936 *The Times* carried a description of a man smashing a statue of a saint with a wooden mallet in the Church of Cor de María in Barcelona, while, more remarkably, 'women and

---

[14] T. Pamiès, *Cuando éramos capitanes* (Barcelona, 1974), 119–20.
[15] 'Sim', *Estampas de la revolución española 19 de julio 1936* (Barcelona, 1936). For a large collection of images of women during the war, see M. Nash, *Las mujeres en la guerra civil* (Salamanca, 1989).

girls stood about laughing'. A little later, *The Times* correspondent in Valencia reported with obvious alarm:

> Corps of milicianas [militia-women] have been organized, and women, armed and aggressive, take their place in the front line with men. All that womanhood traditionally stands for is rapidly disappearing. Women of the proletariat are not at all perturbed by the fact that in the region held by the government scarcely a church is open, scarcely a priest dares appear in public.[16]

Tradition on one side, a revolutionary new woman on the other; the polarised images have some truth in them, but they are of course misleading, and deconstructing them can tell us a good deal both about women in the Spanish Civil War and about the changing nature of the war itself.

It is undoubtedly true that some Republican women during the war acquired a status in public life at every level that was very different from pre-war experience. Much the most visible and audible woman on the Republican side was Dolores Ibárruri, universally known as La Pasionaria.[17] Before the war began she was already a member of the Central Committee of the rather small Spanish Communist Party, and had been a delegate to the Seventh Congress of the Third International in Moscow in 1935. She was also prominent in the international Popular Front organization Women Against War and Fascism, and was head of its Spanish section. In February 1936 she had been elected a deputy for Oviedo to the Spanish parliament. The war found her, then, an already very experienced and widely known politician. But her standing was transformed by her radio broadcast of 19 July 1936, when she appealed to the Spanish people to oppose the military rising and famously declared 'They shall not pass'.[18] Her ability to rouse crowds and to launch heroic slogans made her the public embodiment of Republican resistance. Her voice and her face were everywhere. Both inside Spain and abroad, she came to represent the Republic in a way that its President and successive Prime Ministers never did, and a woman in any equivalent propaganda role on the insurgent side would have been unthinkable.

None of the other women Cortes deputies of the pre-war period

---

[16] *The Times* 25 July 1936 and 4 August 1936. These are among the huge number of newspaper cuttings made for each day of the Civil War by the late Burnett Bolloten, and held in the Bolloten Collection at the Hoover Institution.

[17] There is an autobiography, *They Shall Not Pass* (1966). Among numerous accounts of her life based on interview material, see A. Carabantes and E. Cimorra, *Un mito llamado Pasionaria* (Barcelona, 1982). Cimorra was a long-standing colleague in the Spanish Communist Party and in exile.

[18] Text in *Speeches and Articles 1936–38*, 7–8.

attained anything like so high a profile. But the Anarchist leader Federica Montseny became the first female government minister in Spain, holding the post of Minister of Health in Largo Caballero's government (September 1936—May 1937). It is evident from recently-published memoirs, however, that at a lower level of political, propagandist, and union activity, the war propelled some young women into unprecedented and dizzying public responsibility. Hundreds of them joined political parties and youth groups, and plunged into organising food supplies and evening classes, writing articles, giving speeches, and maintaining communications with other groups and with the front. One of these, for whom the war—with all its agonies—was nonetheless a personal liberation, was Sara Berenguer.[19] She was a seventeen-year-old seamstress in Barcelona when the war began, having left school at twelve. She immediately offered her services to the local revolutionary committee of her *barrio*, and in an Anarchist milieu she briefly joined a Socialist union by mistake because she did not know the difference between the two. From this naive beginning, she became active in the Libertarian Youth movement and later the Anarchist-feminist *Mujeres Libres*. She learnt to type, became a secretary and administrator for the revolutionary committee, gave classes to children, kept accounts, gave public talks and took part in debates, and generally developed her own ideas, independence, and expertise. In the course of all this exhausting work, she also gained the kind of new freedom of movement often reported by women in belligerent countries in the first World War: she could go out alone, work closely with men, return home by herself very late at night without anyone thinking it at all strange.[20] For her, defence of the Republic was the defence of freedom and opportunity, and when the Republic fell she had no choice but to go into a lifetime of exile.

Not all those who would curtail a woman's freedom were enemies of the Republic, however. Sara was furious to see a group of young men laughing at a poster advertising a talk to be given by a representative of *Mujeres Libres* because it seemed so amusing to them that a woman should dare give a public lecture. She made sure she attended it, and intervened at the end to defend the speaker, Conchita Guillén, from the contemptuous criticism of men in the audience. And over and over again she discovered that her Anarchist male colleagues assumed that any woman talking about freedom must mean she was freely

[19] S. Berenguer, *Entre el sol y la tormenta: Treinta y dos meses de guerra (1936–1939)* Barcelona, 1988.
[20] Berenguer, *Entre el sol y la tormenta* 44–51.

sexually available for them.[21] Moreover she and Teresa Pamiès both give accounts of organised visits by young women militants to the front to take supplies, conversation, and entertainment to bored and frightened soldiers. And both discovered that the soldiers presumed they were coming to offer sex, and felt annoyed and cheated to learn differently.[22]

The women's secretariat of the POUM (the dissident, anti-Stalinist Communist Party), published in Barcelona a few, fortnightly issues of a newspaper from February 1937 until just after the May crisis of the same year that marked the eclipse of political forces in the Republic that were resistant to the dominance of the Spanish Communist Party and its allies. Appropriately enough, the paper was called *Emancipación*, and concerned itself with women's roles within the social revolution that POUM was determined to promote along with and as the essential component of the defence of the Republic. Various articles lamented the fact that men in the POUM who were revolutionary in their politics had not changed their understanding of family and sexual relations. Too many men had not yet 'made the revolution in their homes', and were 'little dictators' who still treated their wives as 'useful only for housework and bearing children'. Too many wives could not get involved in political work because their husbands insisted they had to be home to produce meals promptly at stated times, and could not be allowed out of the house at night.[23] Dolores Ibárruri made the same point later in the war when addressing a regional conference of the Spanish Communist Party, destroyers of the POUM, in Madrid:

> I have known many comrades who considered themselves great revolutionaries, but when I asked them, 'Why do you not get your wives to join the Party, why do you not see to it that your wives attend meetings?'—they would answer: 'My wife does not understand anything; she does not know anything; she has to look after the children.

Moreover, she pointed out that such men sometimes actively disapproved of their wives wanting to be involved in politics, which they themselves regarded as a male sphere.[24]

Emancipation often did not get very far. Where entry to the labour market was concerned, the experience of Spanish women on the Republican side replicated in many ways that of women elsewhere

[21] Berenguer, *Entre el sol y la tormenta* 114–15.
[22] Berenguer, *Entre el sol y la tormenta* 173–4; Pamiès, *Cuando éramos capitanes* 54–5.
[23] 'Militante comunista dentro y fuera del hogar', *Emancipación* 15 March 1937; 'El Comunismo y la familia', *Emancipación* 29 May 1937.
[24] *Speeches and Articles* 188–91.

during the First World War. Women moved into kinds of paid employment that were new to them, most notably in transport and munitions.
And the demand for them increased as Republican territory dwindled
and new sectors of the male population were mobilized for the front:
eventually, men from seventeen to fifty-five years old were conscripted.
It was not always clear, however, that women were being employed
in their own right. Preference was often given to the wives, daughters,
and sisters of the men who usually held the post, and in October 1937
a government regulation made this preference official.[25] While some
women argued that paid work was a right and not just a duty, and
saw it as necessary for progress to independence and equality, many
simply had to work in order to eat.[26] They were paid at lower rates
than men, and rarely enjoyed posts of responsibility except in clothing
industries, where women's work was long-established. Young, single
women predominated, as before, strengthening the impression that
paid work outside the home was essentially a temporary and con-
ditional occupation for women. And male trade unionists were notoriously hostile to the employment of women in erstwhile 'male' jobs,
and unconvinced that women could do 'equal' work and therefore
merit equal pay. Dolores Ibárruri criticized Communist trade union
leaders for seeing women in the workplace only as rivals, and one of
her perorations about women and work has the tone of a vision for a
different future rather than a projection of even partial present reality:

> Our women will be liberated from domestic slavery and seclusion,
> to which arab values and Christian mysticism have consigned them.
> They will become free citizens, with the opportunity in the factory,
> the workshop, the school and the laboratory, to work, study, and
> do research along with men, with the same rights and duties.[27]

Women were, however, encouraged to 'enlist in the work front' as
well as to help the war effort in more traditional ways ranging from
trying to relieve the enormous social problems created by the war to
knitting winter jerseys for soldiers. What they were emphatically not
encouraged to do after the first weeks of fighting was actually to
carry arms and go to the front. The Communist Fifth Regiment had
organized a women's battalion, but destined it for support work rather
than front line combat. More and more emphasis was placed on
getting women active at the home front, leaving the actual fighting

[25] J. Aróstegui (ed.), *Historia y Memoria de la Guerra Civil* (3 vols., Valladolid, 1988),
ii. 163.
[26] Aróstegui, *Historia y Memoria* 163–4; M. Nash, *Mujer y movimiento obrero en España
1931–1939* (Barcelona, 1981), 106–7.
[27] *Speeches and Articles* 234, where the text is abbreviated; full text published separately
under the title *Unión de todos los españoles* (Barcelona, no date), this quotation, 75.

to men. As the hastily-devised militias of the first stage of the war gradually gave way to more regular army discipline, women were edged out. Already in September 1936 Socialist Prime Minister Largo Caballero insisted that militia-women abandon the front. Much more dramatically than with admission to the modern labour force, women's participation in military action was seen as an emergency measure, a temporary expedient, which survived as a propagandist image of popular revolution well after it had virtually ceased to be social reality. Moverover, even the image was tarnished by the huge campaigns to alert soldiers to the dangers of venereal disease, many of which implied that women at the front were part of the problem.[28]

Even at the front itself, women found it difficult to escape traditional expectations. Militia-woman Leonor Benito described doing guard-duty at night equally with men, yet still being expected to do the washing for them.[29] Mika Etchebéhère had the exceptional experience of being a captain in a POUM column at Sigüenza, north-east of Madrid. Significantly, she was chosen by male comrades to replace her husband, killed in the very first days of battle there. On one early occasion the men refused to take turns sweeping out the sleeping quarters, arguing that the four militia-women in the company should do it. A little later two more women arrived saying—according to Mika—that they were tired of doing the washing-up and cleaning in their Communist Party column and had heard that the POUM organised things differently and would permit them to use a gun. In November, in a different section of the Madrid front, a soldier who had voluntarily done a general sock-wash in the trenches remarked to her, 'Now I've seen everything. A woman commands the company and men wash the socks. This really is a revolution'.[30] An eye-witness at the front in Somosierra recalled meeting a young woman called Carmen who had come originally to help wash and repair clothes, but seeing men fall all round her had grabbed a gun and become a soldier instead. At the same time a group of five militia-women there seemed always busy because they did all the chores as well as their military duties.[31] It seems often to have been the case that even when women were allowed to fight, they were expected to do a double shift, one with a gun, the other with a broom. Their removal back to the home front soon re-established the clear demarcation between what was a man's task and what a woman's.

[28] M. Nash, 'Milicianas and Home Front Heroines: Images of women in revolutionary Spain (1936–1939)', *Journal of the History of European Ideas* 1990.

[29] Aróstegui, *Historia y Memoria* ii. 159.

[30] M. Etchebéhère, *Ma guerre d'Espagne à moi* (Paris, 1976), 26, 58, 202.

[31] S. Blasco, *Peuple d'Espagne, Journal de Guerre de la 'Madrecita'* (Paris, 1938), 86–90, 125–6.

In the Republican rearguard, it was political groups most directly committed to a view of the Civil War as social revolution that produced women's organisations and publications determined to shape a new status for women in Spain. Neither the Spanish Communist Party nor the Spanish Socialist Party—nor even for that matter the Unified Socialist (and Communist) Party of Catalonia paid much attention to the question of what women, as women, might expect to gain from victory. The Communists wanted to mobilise women, but for the military and political aims of the Party and the Popular Front. Dolores Ibárruri was exceptional in these circles in calling for a new assessment of the place of women in Spain, but her energies were primarily absorbed in Party and Popular Front activities. The immediate task was to win the war against 'the fascists', not to reconstruct Spanish society. The Communist-dominated Organization of Women Against Fascism mobilized Communist, Socialist, and Republican women to help the war effort behind the lines, but as its title indicates, it postponed for another day all other issues.[32]

For this very reason, the Communist and Popular Front organisations were held in profound suspicion by Anarchist and POUM women for whom social revolution was not postponable. The contributors to POUM's *Emancipación* in its brief life distanced themselves both from bourgeois feminism, seen as trivial, and cross-class antifascism, seen as counter-revolutionary. They looked to a double emancipation, of the revolutinary proletariat from its capitalist enemies, and of women from gender subordination.[33]

A similar line was taken by the Anarchist-feminist *Mujeres Libres*, but with a very much greater feminist emphasis. Only women contributed to and produced the lively, stylish paper, that had a longer life and far greater circulation than *Emancipación*. And behind the paper there existed a large network of Mujeres Libres groups, propagandists, literacy classes, vocational courses, and other activities. From a feminist perspective, Mujeres Libres was the most innovative and clear-headed women's organization in existence during the Civil War, although not all of its members or even leaders counted themselves as feminists. It fostered radical views on sexual and family relations, campaigned against the exploitation of women in prostitution, worked hard to further working-class women's interests through training courses in everything from typing to electrical skills, encouraged women to join trade unions and engage in political activity, and generally promoted the image and reality of a new, independent, trained, working woman. It disagreed both with the view that Anarch-

[32] For Communist and Popular Front aims and organisations for women, see M. Nash, *Mujer y movimiento obrero* Chs 5 and 7.
[33] See especially various articles in *Emancipación* 29 May 1937.

ist women did not need an organisation separate from men, and with Popular Front women's movements that eschewed revolution.[34]

But before the Republic lost the war to Franco, the POUM and the Anarchists had lost their own struggle within the Communist-dominated anti-fascist alliance, and been suppressed. The longer the war continued, the less the Republic represented any revolution in gender roles. And some revolutionary women even found their aspirations cruelly ended, not first by insurgent victories but by incarceration in Communist prisons behind the Republican lines.[35]

It is nonetheless true that no sector on the Republican side shared the determination of the insurgents to return women to their traditional, domestic place. The Women's Section of the Spanish Fascist Party became, after Franco's forced unification of all political parties and movements in April 1937, the official women's movement of the emerging regime. Its leader Pilar Primo de Rivera had no doubt about a woman's place, which was in the family, as wife and mother. One might have expected that the women's section of a political movement that boasted of its revolutionary credentials would foster a more radical vision of a woman's place in the new order. But religious influences were always strong in the Women's Section, symbolized at the very beginning by the fact that its four founding members went off to a local church to recommend themselves and their new enterprise to Christ when launching the national women's movement at the end of 1934.[36] This religious spirit—very different from the at best indifference to orthodox Catholicism of many men in the Falange—was also apparent in the eighteen points chosen to guide the Women's Section after the unification of April 1937. Women were urged to lift their hearts to God each morning, to be obedient and disciplined, and to be content with lowly positions far from leadership.[37] More characteristically Falangist ideas and vocabulary also disappeared from the public rhetoric of the Women's Section as the war progressed. Pilar Primo de Rivera still referred to women having a place in unions and municipal life as well as in the family in a speech in Segovia in 1938,

[34] The essential work on Mujeres Libres and their publications is M. Nash, *Mujeres Libres* (Barcelona, 1976). See M. Ackelsberg, including 'Mujeres Libres: Individuality and Community. Organizing Women during the Spanish Civil War', *Radical America* xviii. no. 4, 1984, 'Women and the Politics of the Spanish Popular Front: Political Mobilization or Social Revolution', *International Labour and Working-Class History* no. 30, 1986, and *Free Women of Spain: Anarchism and the Struggle for the Emancipation of Women* (Bloomington, 1991).

[35] See for example K. Landau, *Le Stalinisme en Espagne. Témoignages de Militants Révolutionnaires sauvés des prisons staliniennes* (Paris, c. 1938).

[36] M. T. Gallego Méndez, *Mujer, Falange y Franquismo* (Madrid, 1983), 29.

[37] *Los 18 puntos de la mujer de F.E.T. y de las J.O.N.S.*, a single-sheet leaflet, in Hoover Institution Bolloten Collection, Box 53, Miscellaneous Documents vol. iv.

but by the end of the war her emphasis was entirely on women's work in the home, where 'we must ensure that the woman finds her whole life, and the man his rest and relaxation'.[38] Over and over again she insisted that women were subordinate to men, should never compete with them, and that men, not women were called to govern.[39] Moreover, since in the war soldiers, and Carlist and Falangist volunteers fought at the front while women did not, only they should have a say in decision-making.[40] At a rally of 11,000 members of the Women's Section at Medina del Campo in May 1939 to honour Franco and the victorious army, she put the whole argument into one simple statement, 'The only mission assigned to women in the nation's great enterprise (la tarea de la patria) is the home'.[41]

There was something inescapably paradoxical about a woman addressing thousands of people in great public gatherings, and taking as her constant theme the need for women to concentrate all their energies on husbands, home, and children. The paradox was especially obvious when, among her bizarre exhortations to women to teach children Christmas carols to sing around the crib, or regional dances from other parts of Spain to enhance national unity, she expressed her distaste for women who aspired to a public role, and for the 'detestable type of the female orator'.[42] Her own resolution of the paradox was to argue that only exceptional circumstances had brought women out of their homes to help rescue the country in its need. Peace would restore the priorities of domestic normality.[43]

But just as the radical images, and feminist aspirations and innovations released on the Republican side could not cancel out traditional gender relations,[44] so the rhetoric of traditionalism could not negate changes wrought by the war even on the victorious side. Pilar herself recognized in 1939 that 'customs have changed completely in Spain. Women now have much more liberty than they had before'.[45] Behind the insurgent lines too, women had been mobilised on a grand scale into war work, although mainly into medical, food, and other relief services. If the Women's Section of the Falange had opened the way here, the essential organisation was Auxilio Social, (Social Aid),

---

[38] P. Primo de Rivera, Escritos. Discursos, circulares, escritos (Madrid, c. 1943), 13, 26–7.
[39] E.g., Escritos 37.
[40] Escritos 15.
[41] Escritos 65.
[42] Escritos 36.
[43] Escritos 15.
[44] For a discussion of the reasons why wartime challenges to gender relations usually have very limited results, see S. Macdonald, 'Drawing the lines—gender, peace and war: an introduction', in S. Macdonald, P. Holden, and S. Ardener (eds.), Images of Women in Peace and War: Cross-cultural and Historical Perspectives (1987).
[45] Escritos 22. See also F. Farmborough, Life and People in National Spain (1938), 31.

founded in October 1936 by Mercedes Sanz Bachiller 'for the definite purpose of fighting hunger, cold and misery'.[46]

The patron of Social Aid was the Virgin of San Lorenzo, but it had a very dramatic emblem, a bare arm thrusting a dagger down the throat of a dragon that represented the raging ills it was designed to remedy. And its scale of operation was dramatic too. After beginning as a local variant on German Winter Aid, providing free meals for children in the Valladolid area in the winter of 1936–7, it expanded rapidly, helped by government backing. In February 1937 it was established in every liberated province and authorised to hold street collections in which the collectors were 'the young ladies affiliated to the Falange,'[47] as well as other fund-raising initiatives. Social Aid lorries followed troops into towns and villages won from the Republic, and the women ran food kitchens and centres to look after war orphans. Thousands of women participated, and a propaganda booklet claimed, probably accurately, that at the height of its wartime activity in late 1938, it dispensed about ten million meals per month to adults and children.[48]

There were numerous men directors of Social Aid, not least because Mercedes Sanz Bachiller wanted it to have the prestige virtually to constitute the Social Welfare system of the new state. But it retained close if sometimes uneasy ties with the Women's Section of the Falange, and acted as the agency of female mobilisation behind the insurgent lines. Franco defined in a decree of 7 October 1937, feast of Our Lady of the Rosary, the service women must offer to the country. Women aged 17 to 35 were to complete a period of six months' social service in the institutions run by Social Aid. It is worth noting that widows with at least one child still in their care were exempted, but that married women were exempted by that circumstance alone, regardless of whether they had children. And any woman eligible for service who did not complete it and gain a validating certificate, was debarred from entry into the professions or jobs in the state or local government bureaucracy.[49]

After the war, women's continuing social service was placed directly under the Women's Section of the Falange, which was given responsibility for the political and social formation of Spanish women.[50] In schools, colleges, orphanages, and training centres, the courses and propaganda of the Women's Section became an inescapable fact of

[46] *Auxilio Social. Social Help*, propaganda booklet in English, (Valladolid, c. Dec. 1938).

[47] *Legislación Española*, i. part 1, 244–6.

[48] *Auxilio Social. Social Help*.

[49] *Legislación Española*, iii. 22–4.

[50] M. T. Gallego Méndez, *Mujer, Falange y Franquismo*, 62–9.

life for a long generation of Spanish women. It is instructive to note that along with awareness of the stress on domesticity and mother-hood, many who experienced the training courses acknowledged that they also contained promotional elements, channeling energies and fostering leadership.[51] Mobilisation for service, for the home, and for political conformity was, nevertheless, mobilisation, and the whole immense system of Social Aid and the Women's Section bore the same kind of paradox exemplified in Pilar Primo de Rivera denouncing public power for women while exercising a form of it herself.

Behind the lines on both sides in the Spanish Civil War, more radical visions of what a woman might do were tamed: on Republican territory, Anarchist and POUM aspirations were swamped by the very different priorities of the Popular Front coalition from the spring of 1937 onwards; in Rebel Spain, what interest there was in a Fascist new woman succumbed to more widespread conservative values rooted in religious traditionalism.[52] In this way, the history of women's roles during the war replicates very accurately the political history in the two zones.

Moreover, it is possible to argue that where women were concerned, the antithesis between the two sides was far from complete. One of the Republican womens' organisations that aroused enormous scorn and anger in conservative circles in pro-Franco Spain was the Basque Nationalist Emakumes. Its members become involved in active propa-ganda as well as support services before and during the war, and it promoted women's politicisation and opposition to the military rising, but its fundamental inspiration was undoubtedly as much Catholic as Basque Nationalist or Republican.[53] Moreover, gender roles were on the whole not revolutionised behind Republican lines, and even triumphant traditionalism could not negate the new public duties, responsibilities and mobility experienced by so many women sup-porters of Franco. Indeed, there were extraordinary transpositions of value across the great divides of war and ideology, as for instance in the conviction held by POUM military captain Mika Etchebéhère that in order to earn the respect of her male revolutionary comrades at the front, she must observe a scrupulous chastity. She decided she had to be pure and tough, a woman not like other women, on a

---

[51] E.g., in L. Falcón's biographical prologue to C. Alcalde, *La mujer en la guerra civil española* (Madrid, 1976).

[52] See Pilar Primo de Rivera's speech to the women of the Basque Provinces and Navarre, defending the Sección Femenina from accusations by Carlist women—mar-garitas—that it was not properly Catholic and incorporated nothing from their Tra-ditionalism, *Escritos* 57–64.

[53] For a classic account see P. de Larrañaga, *Emakume Abertzale Batza. La mujer en el nacionalismo vasco* (3 vols., Donostia, 1978).

pedestal, and it is difficult to resist the comparison with the religious iconography of statues of the Virgin Mary.[54]

The differences, however, remained so fundamental, that the victory of the Rebel generals in the spring of 1939 necessarily settled the question for many, many years, of what women would be and would do in Spain. They should be wives and mothers, or nuns; they would be, officially at least, religious; their sphere would be domestic rather than public; and they would be subordinate. On both sides in the war there were mythologies of woman to be transformed into social convention, or—in the terminology of Roland Barthes—images that might transform contingent history into nature.[55] But to determine through law and language and imagery what should be perceived as natural, the battle of history had to be won first. The Spanish Civil War had a clear, unconditional victor.

---

[54] M. Etchebéhère, *Ma guerre d'Espagne à Moi*, 148–9, 176, 189, 218.
[55] R. Barthes, *Mythologies* (London, 1973), 129.

THE ORIGINS OF PUBLIC SECRECY IN BRITAIN

By David Vincent

READ 7 DECEMBER 1990

THE first modern crisis of public secrecy was set in motion in the Spring of 1844 when a little-known Italian exile began sending himself letters in which he had placed grains of sand, poppy seeds or fine hairs.[1] The discovery that the additional contents were disappearing in transit confirmed Joseph Mazzini's suspicions that his correspondence was being opened by Sir James Graham, the Home Secretary, at the request of the Austrian ambassador.[2] There then followed what Graham's first biographer described as a 'paroxysm of national anger'[3] as the extent of clandestine domestic espionage was exposed. A powerful coalition of working-class radicals and Parliamentary Liberals came together to protest at the use of 'the spy system of foreign states'.[4] 'The proceeding cannot be English,' thundered *The Times*, 'any more than masks, poisons, sword-sticks, secret signs and associations, and other such dark ventures. Public opinion is mighty and jealous, and does not brook to hear of public ends pursued by other than public means. It considers that treason against its public self.'[5]

Such violence of language reflected the depths of the prevailing uncertainty about the relationship between the post-Reform Act state and the newly reformed structures of mass communication. The previous Whig Government had committed itself to the support of elementary education, had legalised the political reading of the people by the reduction of the newspaper stamp, and in 1840, had made a bold attempt to liberalise the principal application of writing by the costly introduction of the Penny Post.[6] At the time of Mazzini's discovery, it seemed possible either that the new ventures were undermining both the finances and the internal security of the state, or that they were equippping governments with extra powers for

---

[1] J. Mazzini, *Life and Writings of Joseph Mazzini* (new ed., 1891), vol. III, 188.

[2] [J. Mazzini], 'Mazzini and the Ethics of Politicians', *Westminster Review*, LXXXII (Sept.–Dec. 1844), 242.

[3] T. M. Torrens, *The Life and Times of the Right Honourable Sir James R. G. Graham* (1863), vol. II, 348.

[4] *Hansard* 3rd Ser., LXXIV, June 4, 1844, col. 893.

[5] *Times*, 26 June, 1844, 6.

[6] D. Vincent, *Literacy and Popular Culture* (Cambridge, 1989), 32–49; 69–72; 233–6. Ironically, Mazzini's suspicions were alerted when, to save money, the Post Office used the Penny Post to forward to him an intercepted overseas letter.

frustrating the creation of a fully democratic society. Fears that the latter might be the case were intensified by Graham's disdainful refusal even to discuss, let alone discontinue, political surveillance.[7]

The concern here, however, is less with the detail of what was the major political event of 1844, than with its reverberations down the decades to 1914.[8] In one sense the controversy appears to mark an intermission in the history of state secrecy. Two months after Mazzini's protest had been brought to the House of Commons by the radical M.P. Thomas Duncombe, the Secret Department of the Post Office was abolished, and the official decypherer of foreign correspondence, Francis Willes, whose family had held the position since 1703, was pensioned off with secret service money.[9] Britain became the only major power bereft of the most effective weapon for spying on external enemies, and despite a public refusal to change its policy, it seems largely to have abandoned internal espionage. Once the crisis of 1848 had passed,[10] the state began a quarter of a century when for what may have been the first time in its history, and certainly was the last, it refrained from the surveillance of the thoughts and actions of its citizens.[11]

At the same time it may be argued that the Mazzini affair, and the debate which surrounded it, represented not the end but the beginning of a tradition of public secrecy whose effects were more pervasive and profound than the specific issue of interfering with the mails. An indication of the real direction in which the new liberal state was travelling was given by one of the many articles called forth by the controversy. 'Mazzini and the Ethics of Politicians', which appeared in the final 1844 edition of the *Westminster Review*, rehearsed the widespread complaints about the betrayal of 'official trust', and 'British honour', and about the widening gulf between public and individual morality. What gave the unsigned piece particular force

[7] Under pressure, he conceded the appointment of a select committee, but its proceedings were kept secret. See, *Report from the Select Committee on the Post Office* (1844), PP 1844, XIV.

[8] The fullest account of the event is to be found in, F. B. Smith, 'British Post Office Espionage 1844', *Historical Studies*, 4, (1970). See also, A. P. Donajgrodzki, 'Sir James Graham at the Home Office', *Historical Journal*, xx, 1, (1977); B. Porter, *Plots and Paranoia* (1989), 76–8; H. Robinson, *Britain's Post Office* (Cambridge, 1953), 47, 55, 91–2; E. Troup, *The Home Office* (2nd ed. 1926), 109–110; D. Vincent, 'Communications, Community and the State', in C. Emsley and J. Walvin (eds.), *Artisans, Peasants and Proletarians 1760–1860* (1985), 166–86.

[9] C. Andrew, *Secret Service: The Making of the British Intelligence Community* (1985), 3; Porter, *Plots and Paranoia*, 78.

[10] On the extent of surveillance during the final Chartist challenge, see J. Saville, *1848* (Cambridge, 1987), 125, 161–3, 185.

[11] B. Porter, *The Origins of the Vigilant State* (1987), 1–18.

was the fact that it was written by Mazzini himself,[12] but what endowed it with especial interest was the unexpected coda he added to his argument:

> This anxiety for secrecy on the part of public officers is a growing evil. In the Customs, in the Stamp office, in various Government departments, we hear now of common clerks sworn to secrecy, or told by their superiors that if they communicate to the public any information connected with the business of the office, they will be instantly dismissed ... Why, who are these men who treat as enemies their fellow subjects of the realm? Is it their business to prey upon the public or to serve it? Let diplomacy have its secrets, for diplomacy is but a refined mode of modern warfare, effecting its objects by tricks; but there needs no diplomacy between a servant and his employer. For public servants, we want responsibility; and responsibility cannot be obtained without publicity. Secrecy is but another word for fear.[13]

This was the earliest recognition of the emergence of a new ambition to control the flow of information between the rulers and the ruled. Mazzini's analysis raised a set of questions which were central to the development of public secrecy between the First Reform Act and the Official Secrets Act of 1911. Was the main arena of change administrative behaviour rather than political espionage? By what means and with what effect was the threat of external enemies confused with the danger of internal criticism? The 1911 Act, which, like the first Secrecy Act of 1889, yoked together treacherous spies and talkative civil servants, was notoriously forced through in the midst of a war panic, but the intermingling of national security and bureaucratic convenience had a longer and more complex history. In what sense was publicity integral to the growth of the nineteenth century state apparatus?[14] On the one hand we have an unprecedented outpouring of official information and political journalism, on the other an increasingly formal system not only of public secrecy, but of secrecy about secrecy. The outburst in 1844 was the first and also the last full-scale debate about the extent of such practices and their justification, until well into this century. Finally, if the motive force for the curtailment of official communication was fear, of what precisely was the state afraid?

---

[12] On the authorship of the article, see, J. W. Mario, *The Birth of Modern Italy* (1909), 81; H. Rudman, *Italian Nationalism and English Letters* (1940), 65.

[13] 'Mazzini and the Ethics of Politicians', 251.

[14] For a clear statement of its importance, first published a year before Mazzini's article, see, J. Bentham, 'Of Publicity', *The Works of J. Bentham* (1843), 310.

The participants in the debate of 1844 saw the pressures generated by the rapidly expanding practice of writing letters as at once the symptom and the cause of larger difficulties, and it is possible to take the same approach to the problem of administrative secrecy. At this time, most public officials spent most of their time on correspondence. The labour of opening, reading, docketing, drafting, writing, copying, filing and sending out letters occupied the relatively short working days of clerks throughout their frequently lengthy careers. The ebb and flow of business throughout the year was measured by the size of the postbag. Problems were initiated by incoming correspondence, they were considered by consulting past letters, and they were resolved by composing new despatches. The opportunity might be found for discussion with other officials and politicians, audiences might be granted to visitors, but the main channel of administration was through handwritten communication. In one sense the terminology of clerks and secretaries gives a misleading impression of the status, income and power of the bureaucrats who created and were created by the liberal state; in another it accurately reflects the bulk of their work.[15]

For this reason, the route taken by correspondence within a government office was virtually co-extensive with its entire organisation.[16] At no point in the period was one state bureaucracy typical of another, but all were exposed to two conflicting pressures. On the one hand there was a desire by those who ran them to maintain what was almost literally a 'hands-on' control of every item of business; on the other, there was a remorseless growth in the volume of letters which had to be processed. The form and timing of the stages of organisational reform through which every department passed depended on the evolving balance between preserving an effective oversight and achieving a basic efficiency as the correspondence continued to multiply.

The key characteristic of what the Northcote-Trevelyan report termed the 'great and continuing accumulation of public business'[17] was that it was both inescapable and inconsistent. The flow of paper-

---

[15] H. Parris, *Constitutional Bureaucracy* (1969), 106–111; J. Pellew, *The Home Office, 1848–1914* (1982), 7; N. Chester, *The English Administrative System 1780–1870* (Oxford, 1981), 282–3.

[16] Chester, *The English Administrative System*, 300. One of the few attempts to identify the technology of communication as an agent of administrative reform is to be found in, J. W. Cell, *British Colonial Administration in the Mid-Nineteenth Century* (New Haven, 1970), 43–6. Cell also draws attention to the later impact of the telegraph, which forced the involvement of junior clerks in dealing with incoming messages.

[17] *Northcote-Trevelyan Report* (1854), republished in *Public Administration* XXXII (Spring, 1954), 1.

work was everywhere growing, yet nowhere at the same rate. During the second quarter of the century, the correspondence dealt with in the Home Office multiplied fourfold, in the Foreign Office and Board of Trade threefold, in the Admiralty it nearly doubled, and in the Treasury and Colonial Office it increased by less than half.[18] Fittingly, the largest increase of official letters was recorded in the department in charge of private letters.[19] In each case the number of officials employed to read and reply to the correspondence grew more slowly. The permanent establishment of the Foreign Office, for instance, only expanded from thirty-five to forty between 1830 and 1849.[20] There was a shared perception that the pressure of work was intensifying and would continue to do so, but no atmosphere of general crisis. Instead separate departments were able to choose their own moment to embark on a common series of administrative changes.

There were two broad areas of reform which could be applied to the handling of correspondence. At the lower end of the bureaucracy, most departments, beginning with the Foreign Office in 1810,[21] established registries so that incoming mail at least could be listed and sorted before it was sent up to the senior officials, and a retrievable record made of their replies.[22] In the higher reaches of the service, it was becoming physically impossible for the Secretary of State to maintain the routine followed by Palmerston in the 1830s of personally dealing with every letter. Whilst the minister could be assisted by his parliamentary under-secretary, the increasing complexity of business demanded a more long-term engagement with the work of the department than could be provided by the more transient, political, appointments. Thus the permanent under-secretary began to become the focal point for processing the correspondence of the office.

The common factor in these developments was the emergence of a

[18] Report from the Select Committee on Official Salaries (1850), PP 1850, XV, 88, 204, 458; J. Barrow, An Auto-Biographical Memoir (1847), 418; A. P. Donajgrodzki, 'New roles for old: the Northcote-Trevelyan Report and the clerks of the Home Office 1822–48' in G. Sutherland (ed.), Studies in the growth of nineteenth-century government (1972), 93; Chester, The English Administrative System, 283; R. Jones, The nineteenth-century Foreign Office (1971), 13, 32; J. A. C. Tilley and S. Gaselee, The Foreign Office (1933), 66.

[19] PP 1850, XV, 505–6.

[20] Tilley and Gaselee, Foreign Office, 53, 65–7. For the early practice of the Colonial Office, see 'Regulation for Numbering and Docketing Despatches and Papers Sent to the Colonial Office', Jan. 1818, reprinted as Appendix IX of D. M. Young, The Colonial Office in the Early Nineteenth Century (1961).

[21] E. Herstlet, Recollections of the Old Foreign Office (1901), 29.

[22] By the 1840s, some departments were experimenting with separate grades of copying clerks. R. C. Snelling and T. J. Brown, 'The Colonial Office and its permanent officals 1801–1914', in Sutherland, Nineteenth-century government, 150; B. L. Blakeley, The Colonial Office 1868–1892 (Durham, N.C., 1972), 4–15. On the early reform of the Board of Trade see, R. Prouty, The Transformation of the Board of Trade 1830–1855 (1957), 100.

routine based on a nascent division of labour. However by mid-century, even in the most progressive ministries this fell far short of a full hierarchical specialisation of function. A Secretary of State would still see most of the department's mail, even if his permanent under-secretary first put it in order and then supervised the writing, copying and despatching of the replies. Amongst the established staff there was no effective device for filtering the flow of correspondence. At the Treasury, Trevelyan, the apostle of rational reform, personally wrote the immense body of correspondence generated by the Irish Famine.[23] His vision of a state bureaucracy consistently divided into intellectual and mechanical classes, each recruited by examination, was behind and ahead of its time.[24] Both the necessity and the terminology of reform had been clearly set forth nearly two decades earlier in Henry Taylor's *The Statesman* of 1836.[25] Most civil servants could see the course which change must take, and many had embarked on it; few, on the other hand, could see the justification for so crude and so precipitate a resolution to problems with which they had been living since the Reform Act state came into being.

If the report of 1854 had only a limited and inconsistent impact on the machinery of the civil service, it did at least clarify the issues surrounding reform. At the heart of the recommendations was the reciprocal relationship between selection and performance. The endless labour of processing correspondence was repelling potential entrants and destroying the minds of those who were recruited. As one of the Committees of Inquiry into Public Offices put it, 'If, after ten or fifteen years spent in incessant copying and other routine work, the spirit, the mental activity, and the wide extent of acquired knowledge necessary for vigorous intellectual exertion in the trans-action of business like that of the Colonial Office, are wanting, it is the fault of the system, and not of the individuals who have been placed in circumstances so unfavourable to them.'[26] A clear separation of function would enable the department to establish formal criteria for selection and identify and reward good performance.

The prospect of appointing two separate grades of clerks by exam-ination, and the associated intention finally to replace seniority by merit as the guide to advancement, brought into sharp focus the issue of the character of the British civil servant. As with every other aspect

---

[23] J. Hart, 'The genesis of the Northcote-Trevelyan Report', in Sutherland, *Nineteenth-century Government*, 102. See also the similar behaviour of the reforming James Stephen in Cell, *British Colonial Administration*, 7–11.

[24] *Northcote-Trevelyan Report*, 11; O, MacDonagh, *Early Victorian Government 1830–1870* (1977), 202–8.

[25] H. Taylor, *The Statesman* (New York, 1958 edn.), 109–12.

[26] *Reports of Committees of Inquiry into Public Offices* (1854), PP 1854 XXVII, 82.

of its affairs, the ethos of the state bureaucracy had been evolving in an unspoken and unco-ordinated fashion during the previous decades. Now both advocates and opponents of reform had to articulate what was required, and, perhaps more urgently, what was to be avoided in the personality and behaviour of the public official. During the debate it fell to Sir George Cornewall Lewis, then editing the *Edinburgh Review* prior to returning to Parliament in 1855 as political head of Treveleyan's Treasury, to identify the major danger:

> One of the first qualities required in the clerks of a public office is trustworthiness. In many public offices, papers containing information respecting pending questions of great importance, and of deep interest to private individuals, to companies and associations, to the public at large, and to the whole civilised world, necessarily pass through the hands of clerks in their successive stages of preparation. The honourable secrecy which has distinguished the clerks of our superior offices, and their abstinence from communicating information to interested parties or public journals, cannot be too highly commended. But this discrete reserve depends on qualities which cannot be made the subject of examination by a central board, or be expressed by marks upon a paper of written answers.[27]

The notion of 'honourable secrecy' was central both to Lewis's response and to the whole history of administrative confidentiality in the nineteenth century. In one sense it precisely inverted the arguments of 1844. Mazzini had claimed that if 'private gentlemen' had behaved like the government, they would have been punished 'with a horsepond or the treadmill.'[28] Yet it could also be seen as no more than a reformulation of an older attribute of the ruling class. Graham had been just as exercised as his opponents about a betrayal of honour. In his view, former ministers had broken their Privy Councillor's oath of secrecy by discussing the use of Home Office powers.[29] He could not respond in kind, neither would his own code of honour permit him to reveal his inner feelings. His nineteenth century biographer pictured him sitting in mute anguish in the Commons: 'Silently and

---

[27] *Papers on the Re-Organisation of the Civil Service* (1855), PP 1854–5, XX, p. 116. For a more extensive discussion of the 'high sense of honour' of the permanent civil service, and the inability of formal exams to identify this quality, see Earl Grey, *Parliamentary Government* (1858), 159–79.

[28] 'Mazzini and the Ethics of Politicians', 228.

[29] C. S. Parker, *Life and Letters of Sir James Graham* (1907), I, 426. On the Privy Councillor's Oath and cabinet secrecy, see, A. Todd, *On Parliamentary Government in England* (1869), 195; D. Leigh, *The Frontiers of Secrecy* (1980), 1.

secretly he suffered infinitely more than many of his accusers were capable of comprehending.'[30]

Whilst Graham was resisting assaults on his discrete reserve, attempts were being made to impose the same quality his civil servants. The gradual separation of the duties of the permanent and political heads of departments of state was accompanied by a division of communication. Over time, and with considerable friction, a deal was struck. The politicians accepted that within the department all lines of correspondence should flow through the permanent head, but demanded in return that civil servants should cease writing public letters and articles. Bureaucrats would forfeit the right to criticise their political masters, but in exchange could expect full protection from attacks levelled at them by an increasingly inquisitive Parliament and a decreasingly deferential press.[31]

The voluntary acceptance of anonymity by men of strong personality was gradually achieved by a re-working of their corporate ethos. The convention of the Privy Councillor's oath, that the advice of ministers became the possession of the monarch, was translated to the relationship between civil servants and their political masters. As at the higher constitutional level, the cloak of confidentiality both protected and obscured the distribution of power. Frustrated and rebellious as senior civil servants often were in this period of transition, they could now employ their secrecy as a shield and a banner. 'Silence has been my only defence', wrote Sir James Stephen of the Colonial Office in 1844, 'because any other vindication would have involved a breach of confidence.'[32] The refusal to respond to praise or criticism became a celebration of the civil servant's calling. Only men secure in their status could be expected to be so indifferent to their standing with the populace. The growth of anonymity both reinforced and depended on the emergence of a more sharply defined collective identity. Bereft of credit for what they did, officials demanded respect for who they were.

However, the more honour became interchangeable with secrecy, the more secrecy became vulnerable to the socially inferior. The personality which would observe and respect the conventions of discrete reserve could not be manufactured. Neither ambition nor application were any substitute for a good background and the right sort

---

[30] Torrens, *Life and Times of Graham*, II, 302. Also, A. B. Erickson, *The Public Career of Sir James Graham* (Oxford, 1952), 268–75; J. T. Ward, *Sir James Graham* (1967), 209–11, 306.

[31] G. Kitson Clark, ' "Statesmen in Disguise": Reflexions on the History of the Neutrality of the Civil Service', *Historical Journal*, III (1959), 21–38.

[32] E. Hughes, 'Sir James Stephen and the Anonymity of the Civil Servant', *Public Administration*, XXXVI (Spring, 1958), 30.

of education. In 1854 it was hoped to avoid the dangers posed by the lower status of the 'mechanical' clerks by adapting established patterns of remuneration and recruitment. The Treasury calculated that a salary of £200 to £300, which was roughly the bottom of the existing scale, would be 'sufficient to secure the services of persons of respectable character who are perfectly equal to the performance of all ordinary clerical duties.'[33] Lewis's doubts about 'marks upon a paper of written answers' were met by a general decision to use the new Civil Service Commission at most to qualify the traditional methods of personal nomination. In the short term, the main concern was not with those who came to be termed 'regulation II clerks' but on the staff known variously as 'temporary clerks, extra clerks, writing clerks, copyists, writers, law stationers' clerks, and Treasury extra clerks.'[34]

Departments had long been accustomed to hiring casual writers to cope with sharp fluctuations in correspondence which had to be written and copied. Many had been supplied by law stationers, but had stayed on and gained quasi-permanent status with implicit rights to promotion and even pensions.[35] They had no place in the new scheme, where such routine labour was to be the responsibility of the lower level of the established service. There were two solutions; either absorption into the ranks of the regulation II clerks or exile to the outer circle of the truly temporary. In 1871, the permanent under-secretary at the Treasury Ralph Lingen, worried about the varied background of such men and anxious to economise, chose the latter course. His repeal of all existing agreements and imposition of a uniform rate of tenpence an hour with no possibility of increments or tenure aroused a storm of protest amongst the more than two thousand writers, which could not be quelled by either a Select Committee in 1873,[36] or a concession to let recent recruits sit an exam for the permanent service.[37]

Retribution duly arrived in the form of Charles Marvin, a talented linguist of little means but a high estimation of his own importance. Having passed the now obligatory examination for civil service writers, he was sent by the Commission to the Foreign Office, from where, in 1878, he sold to the *Globe* the details of a secret treaty.[38]

[33] PP 1854, XXVII, 44.

[34] *Northcote-Trevelyan Report*, 11.

[35] For a concise history of the writer class, see, *Fourth Report of the Royal Commission on the Civil Service* [MacDonnell] (1914), PP 1914, XVI, 124–6.

[36] *Report from the Select Committee on Civil Service Writers* (1873), PP 1873, XI.

[37] *First Report of the Civil Service Inquiry Commission* [Playfair] (1875), PP 1875, XXIII, 6–12.

[38] Hertslet, *Recollections*, 191–2; Tilley and Gaselee, *The Foreign Office*, 139–40; D. Hooper, *Official Secrets* (1987), 19–21; J. Aitken, *Officially Secret* (1971), 7–15.

Viewed through his best-selling, self-dramatising memoir, Marvin appears little more than a solitary rogue. But set in the context of the preceding reforms, he represented the grievances of the writer class writ large, the fears of the permanent service made flesh. His resentment at the contradiction between the significance of his labour and the inadequacy of its reward echoed the complaints put to the 1873 inquiry. 'It was absurd', he protested, 'for the Foreign Office to employ a Writer to copy Cabinet secrets at tenpence an hour.'[39] And his account of how the new exams were being sat and passed by men of 'every degree of broken fortunes'[40] fulfilled all the warnings that had been made about this mode of selection. In the eyes of his outraged employers, his behaviour perfectly illustrated the dependence of character on income. 'I hope after this', observed Tenterden, the permanent under-secretary at the Foreign Office, to Lord Salisbury, 'we may have properly appointed Clerks for such work and not have to depend on this cheap and untrustworthy class of people.'[41]

Lingen's mistake in 1871 had been to incite indiscipline whilst sacrificing the most effective means of quelling it. With no prospects of advancement, and every opportunity of earning at least as much outside government, writers impelled by principle or avarice to communicate official information had little to lose. As Tenterden wrote of Marvin, 'The worst of these people is that there is no hold of them'.[42] Furthermore Marvin's subsequent acquittal indicated that the larceny laws provided no protection. In respect of the permanent civil service, with its proliferating clerks who did not come from the better families or schools, the prudent course was to amplify the status of their office whilst increasing the prospects of losing it. Following a leak concerning, as it happened, the salaries of letter carriers, Lingen issued a Treasury Minute in 1873 which spelled out with brutal clarity the consequences of the unauthorised communication of information: 'My Lords are of opinion that such breaches of official confidence are offences of the very gravest character which a public officer can commit, and they will not hesitate, in any case where they themselves possess the power of dismissal, to visit such an offence with this extreme penalty.'[43]

The phrase 'official confidence' had a double charge. It referred both to the confidentiality of the information, and to the faith the

---

[39] C. Marvin, *Our Public Offices* (2nd ed., 1880), 212.

[40] Marvin, *Our Public Offices*, 3.

[41] P.R.O., FO/363/3, Tenterden Papers. Tenterden to Salisbury, June 15, 1878.

[42] P.R.O., FO/363/3, Tenterden Papers. Tenterden to Salisbury, June 21, 1878.

[43] *Premature Publication of Official Documents. Treasury Minute* (13 March, 1884), PP 1884, LXII, Appendix No. 1, Minute of 1873, 356. Also, K. G. Robertson, *Public Secrets* (1982), 52–4.

public vested in the discretion of officials. The civil service's 'character for fidelity and honour'[44] was at once the victim of such practices and the most effective means of preventing their occurrence. The focus of the Minute, and of the two that followed it in 1875 and 1884, was not on the identifiable damage caused to particular state activities, but on the more diffuse and abstract harm done to the honourable secrecy of the civil service. It was the fact of improper communication, rather than the communication of improper facts which invoked sanctions. The distinction was firmly drawn in the third Minute, prepared following 'cases of the premature publication in the newspapers of official documents about to be circulated to Members of Parliament'.[45] It was stated that, 'in all these cases, *the publication without authority, of official information* constitutes the offence; and that the danger, to which all Governments are equally exposed by it, cannot be adequately guarded against if distinctions are allowed to be drawn between one kind of unauthorised publication and another.'[46] Although the wording changed, this blanket definition of secrecy survived intact through the later Acts of 1889 and 1911.

Between the First and Third Reform Acts the conception of official secrecy had been clearly defined, and devices for imposing it had been put in place. All that remained for the rest of Victorian and Edwardian Britain was the search for more effective means of achieving established ends. One route lay through the mechanisation of writing. It is no accident that crude copying presses were introduced at the same time that Lingen was trying to regulate the copyists.[47] Orders in Council and patent devices were both ways of trying to reduce the involvement of low level writers in high level affairs. A decade later, typewriters were beginning to make their appearance.[48] But if such inventions reduced the need for inferior male staff, they also multiplied the possibilities of unauthorised disclosure. The easier it was to make copies, the more difficult it became to limit their circulation. Marvin had had to commit the secret treaty to memory in order to leak it; future malcontents might not require such mental feats.

The second route lay through the law. In March 1887, exactly three years after the final Treasury Minute, the Government was forced to accept that internal regulation was failing to achieve its objective. The publication of secret instructions to the Naval Intel-

---

[44] PP 1884, LXII, 356.

[45] *Hansard*, 3rd Ser., CCLXXXV, 3 March, 1884, col. 361.

[46] PP 1884, LXII, 355. Emphasis in the original.

[47] PP 1873, XI, 37.

[48] *Second Report of the Royal Commission appointed to inquire into the Civil Establishments of the different Offices of State at Home and Abroad* [Ridley] (1888), PP 1888, XXVII, 36; Tilley and Gaselee, *The Foreign Office*, 154.

ligence Department, followed a week later by the dismissal of a draughtsman in Chatham Dockyard 'for betraying the trust reposed in him by selling information acquired by him in his official capacity',[49] exposed the First Lord of the Admiralty to an embarassing interrogation in Parliament. The key questions were put by the Tory M.P. Robert Hanbury:

> What classes of officials or workmen engaged at Chatham or other public Dockyards are employed in positions of confidence and secrecy; who are permitted to possess information of a confidential nature which has a money value; what precautions are taken as to character, or by means of an oath or some other binding engagement, to guard against a breach of trust; and, what are the lowest salaries or wages paid to such persons.[50]

The dockyards presented an extreme form of concern about secrecy not only because their business was so vital to national defence, but also because they employed so large a proportion of the lower white-collar and manual workers in the civil service. The reluctant answer to Hanbury's final query was five shillings a day. The First Lord had to admit that such men could not be excluded from confidential matters, and that there were increasing doubts whether appeals to their honour or threats to their jobs were sufficient security against breaches of trust. At the end of the debate, an undertaking was given to introduce legislation.[51]

This was a momentous step. For the first time since the Mazzini affair, the state's conception and enforcement of public secrecy would have to be openly defined and debated. Lingen's first Minute had remained unpublished for fifteen years, and in 1887 it was stated that further changes to internal rules would not be brought to the House, 'because the publicity thus occasioned might defeat their object'.[52] Legislation, on the other hand, could not be conducted in private. In his advice to young statesmen in 1836, Henry Taylor had observed that, 'a secret may be sometimes best kept by keeping the secret of its being secret',[53] and this had been the ruling maxim of governments ever since. Now the state had to reconsider whether secrecy about secrecy was a desirable practice, how it might be maintained in the face of Parliamentary scrutiny.

At first sight, the instinctive refusal to discuss any aspect of domestic security was at best unnecessary, and at worst counterproductive.

---

[49] *Hansard* 3rd Ser., CCCXI, 10 March, 1887, col. 1745.
[50] *Hansard* 3rd Ser., CCCXII, 11 March, 1887, col. 20.
[51] *Hansard* 3rd Ser., CCCXIII, 5 April, 1887, col. 488.
[52] *Hansard* 3rd Ser., CCCXIII, 5 April, 1887, col. 488.
[53] Taylor, *Statesman*, 89.

In the early 1880s, for instance, postal espionage was raised in the Commons once more, as the Home Office began opening the mail of Fenians. All questions were met with a blank refusal to confirm or deny the practice, which, as in 1844, merely inflamed the suspicions of complaining M.P.s. However in about 1890, a secret paper was prepared in the Home Office, giving precisely the detail which Parliament had been demanding in vain.[54] Aside from the Irish surveillance, of which the victims, as ever, were well aware, there was nothing in the record to embarrass the government. The public would scarcely have complained about interceptions designed to identify the accomplices of a 'noted procuress', or to establish the guilt of a master suspected of scuttling his ship. The Home Office had much to gain from revealing the action it had taken against the sender of threats to the Queen and Princess Beatrice and much to lose from the mistrust which its silence engendered.

Nevertheless the desire to preserve freedom of action in an uncertain world always appeared a more persuasive consideration. The attraction of the wall of confidentiality which Graham had fought to preserve was that it permitted maximum flexibility with minimum publicity. If dangers could appear without warning, so also could counter-measures be taken without notice. Although there was always a risk of exposure, the process of espionage was becoming safer as more attention was paid to telegrams, copies of which were kept by the Post Office for three months after transmission.[55] Postal espionage could be quietly combined with the first Official Secrets Act, as first happened in 1899.[56] A few months later, the Intelligence Office of the War Office was able to employ the G.P.O. to open all letters addressed to the officers of the South African Republic and the Orange Free State.[57] When war threatened in Europe in 1911, Captain Kell of the newly created Secret Service Bureau was allowed to add the weapon of postal interception to his armoury.[58] Powers which had been most recently used in the hunt for Crippen and Le Neve were unobtrusively turned over to the pursuit of German spies, helped by Churchill's

[54] P.R.O., HO45/9752/A59329, 'Production of Telegrams and Post Letters on the Warrant of the Secretary of State'. The paper is dated 19 February 1886, but contains material up to 1890. Comparison with the contemporary Home Office Minute Books confirms the accuracy of the report.

[55] The first warrant for the interception of a telegram was issued in 1875. P.R.O., HO151/1.

[56] P.R.O., HO151/8. Warrant of 29 Sept. 1899.

[57] P.R.O., HO151/8. Warrants of 13 Jan. and 19 Jan. 1900.

[58] P.R.O., HO151/9. Warrant of 15 Sept. 1911. See also N. Hiley, 'The Failure of British Counter-Espionage against Germany, 1907–1914', Historical Journal, XXVIII, 4 (1985), 857.

unannounced decision to issue general as well as individual warrants.[59] The following March, Special Branch, which had been set up with a similar absence of formal regulation,[60] began opening the letters of suffragettes.[61]

Rapidity of response was valued for its own sake; one of the major reasons for the introduction of the second Official Secrets Act was the conviction that the machinery of arrest embodied in its predecessor was too cumbersome.[62] But the commitment to tactical mobility was itself part of a broader strategy. The freedom to capture enemies of the state depended on a licence to escape the state's principal democratic structures.[63] 1844 had taught governments a lesson which they never forgot, that official secrecy was an explosive substance when exposed to the oxygen of public debate. The ingrained apprehension of Parliamentary scrutiny was laid bare by the confidential discussions surrounding the proposed Post Office (Obscene Matter) Acts of 1897 and 1898.

The bulk of the Home Office sponsored espionage during the last decade of the nineteenth century and the early years of the twentieth was directed against not foreign spies but overseas pornographers. As so often the objective was to defend the moral integrity of the ruling class, or rather, in this case, its sons. Following complaints from the headmasters of Eton and Winchester about the volume of obscene literature being obtained from abroad by their pupils, the Home Secretary began issuing warrants to intercept suspected packages.[64] The Post Office complained that its surveillance system was being severely stretched and requested a clarification of the law, arguing, 'that unless this is done at some time or other there is great danger of strong popular feeling against the exercise of the present undefined power by the Secretary of State, and that it would be much better that the power should be defined and rest on distinct statutory authority.'[65]

---

[59] W. S. Churchill, *The World Crisis 1911–1914* (2nd ed., 1923), I, 52; Andrew, *Secret Service*, 60.

[60] B. Porter, *The Origins of the Vigilant State* (1987), 67–78.

[61] P.R.O., HO151/9. Warrant of 23 March, 1912.

[62] P.R.O., HO45/10629/199699, 41; P.R.O., CAB16/8, *Proceedings of a Sub-Committee of the Committee of Imperial Defence Appointed by the Prime Minister to Consider the Question of Foreign Espionage in the United Kingdom* (1909), 8.

[63] *Pace* K. G. Robertson, who in *Public Secrets* argues that official secrecy 'was one of the mechanisms used to enhance control of elected representatives over unelected administrators.' (42).

[64] P.R.O., HO45/9752/A59329/2. The complaint from Eton College was received in 1890, and from Winchester College 'and other places' in 1894. The first warrants were issued in 1891.

[65] P.R.O., HO45/9752/A59329/2. Memorandum from Ridley to Walpole, 28 Jan. 1898.

The Home Office was sympathetic to its problems but anxious to confine legislation to obscenity. Whereas public opinion might be quiescent on this narrow topic, wrote the permanent under-secretary, 'it is much more likely that at some time or another there may be a row about the exercise of the power as regards crimes or suspected crimes of other kinds—especially at times of political excitement.'[66] The pervasive fear of 'strong popular feeling' produced an impasse. As it was to do again prior to the first World War, the Post Office fiercely rejected any attempt to transfer to its officials the authority to initiate espionage, on the grounds that, 'public sentiment is very strong in the support of the supposed inviolability of letters passing through the post.'[67] Unable to divest itself of even part of its responsibilities, the Home Office permitted the drafting of two successive bills on obscene publications, but then withdrew its support altogether when advised by the law officers that it would not be able to limit discussion to the specific issue: 'questions might arise as to the existing powers of the Secretary of State, which it is undesirable to discuss.'[68] It was impossible to unravel the blanket of secrecy row by row.

To describe the desire to avoid debate is not, however, to explain how it was achieved. Two generations on from 1844, the electorate was larger and the press more independent. Yet where legislation could not be shelved indefinitely, it proved possible to get it through both Houses with a minimum of controversy. The Act of 1911 is notorious for the brevity of its passage, but the debate which took place in half an hour on a Friday afternoon generated more discussion than accompanied the first Act of 1889. Part of the answer lies in the abiding caution of successive governments. Once the decision to legislate was taken in 1887, scarcely a year passed when one or more bills were not at some stage of drafting in the Home Office or elsewhere. Two attempts were made at the first Official Secrecy Bill before it was tabled in 1889, and the search for the opportunity to introduce an amendment began following comments by the judge during the first prosecution under the Act in 1892.[69] Into the waste-paper basket containing the abandoned obscenity acts were thrown

[66] P.R.O., HO45/9752/A59329/2, Digby to Sir Spencer Walpole, Secretary of the Post Office, 29 Oct. 1897. Also, R. M. Kamm, 'The Home Office, public order and civil liberties, 1870–1914' Unpublished Ph.D thesis, Cambridge University, 1987, 274–5.

[67] P.R.O., HO45/9752/A59329/2. See also the observations of Sydney Buxton, the then Postmaster General, to the 1909 Imperial Defence Sub-Committee. P.R.O., CAB16/8, 9.

[68] P.R.O., HO45/9752/A59329/2. Report of Law Officers, dated 5 April, 1898.

[69] P.R.O., WO32/6347, papers relating to the trial of Robert Holden; *Times*, 11 April, 1892, 6.

secrecy bills of 1896, 1908, and 1912, a series of bills from 1905 onwards to enforce press censorship in an emergency, and two aliens acts in 1911 which were due to be attached to the Secrets Act of that year.[70] It was not the absence of Parliamentary time or a potential majority which determined the fate of these bills, but the danger of their provoking any discussion at all. In most cases, prudence dictated inaction; occasionally, as in 1908, a misjudgment was made, and a bill was introduced only to be hurriedly withdrawn following press criticism.[71]

Despite the combination of scrupulous preparation and quite unscrupulous tactics inside Parliament once the plunge had been taken, the silent passage of a bill still came as a relief to the Ministers involved. 'It was open to anyone of all the members of the House of Commons to get up and say that no bill had ever yet passed through all its stages in one day without a word of explanation from the ministry in charge', wrote Colonel Seely of the 1911 Act, '... But to the eternal honour of those members, to whom I now offer, on behalf of that and all succeeding governments, my most grateful thanks, not one man seriously opposed.'[72] The appeal to honour was addressed to each of the players in the modern state. The code of the British gentleman had been reformulated to engineer the discretion of the bureaucrat, the deference of the legislator and the indifference of the elector. By 1911 it represented a powerful and complex set of definitions about both a specific social ethos and a particular political nation.

In the first case, the outcome of the attempts to reform the civil service had been the incorporation rather than the victory of the professional ideal. To the zealots of the 1850s, the qualities of efficiency, rationality and meritocratic endeavour had appeared destructive of the idle and amateurish ways of those appointed and protected by patronage. The newly emerging professions supplied both a model for reform and a wealth of innovatory policy. In practice however, there was room for compromise. The basis for negotiation was a shared interest in the restriction of information. If the modern professional was the product of a book-based, exam-tested course of learning, he was also the beneficiary of a legally enforced closure upon it. The Medical Registration Act for instance, passed just four years after the Northcote-Trevelyan Report, sought to enhance the income

---

[70] P.R.O., CAB17/91; HO45/10629/199699, 3, 9.

[71] For the campaign organised by the Newspaper Proprietors' Association, see *Times*, 27 April, 1908, 11; 4 May, 1908, 3; 7 May, 1908, p. 11. Also, *Hansard*, 4th Ser., CLXXXVIII, 11 May, 1908, cols. 673–4; CXC, 23 June, 1908, cols. 1476–8.

[72] J. E. B. Seely, *Adventure* (1930), 145.

and status of doctors by denying their rivals and clients the training they had received.[73] They rested their authority on an exclusive access to a body of knowledge and a right to determine the form and circumstance of its dissemination. Whilst the new professions sought the trappings of gentility, the old administrators desired the clothing of regulation. The process of employing formal examinations and rules of conduct to transform their increasingly inquisitive public into deferential patients had every attraction for beleaguered government departments. By the last quarter of the century, the civil service was becoming more professional in its recruitment practices, but in turn imposing the culture of public secrecy on the professionals it employed.[74]

At the same time the notion of Britain and the freedoms which it embodied was also redefined by a process of inclusion rather than rejection. In 1844 the critics of domestic secrecy had charged the government with manipulating its unwritten powers to support a foreign tyrant. The outcome of the controversy was a defeat for Mazzini's case, but a victory for his cause. Young Italy became a focus of Liberal enthusiasm and a model for other liberation campaigns.[75] All were based on an unshakeable assumption that freedom of communication was both a measure of the superiority of the British system and a vital weapon in the fight against repressive regimes abroad. As *The Times* observed in 1858, 'Any defence of so important a department of the liberty of the press as the right to criticise foreign Governments is happily a work of supererogation'.[76] During the succeeding decades, the frame of reference became more ambiguous. The tradition of defining British liberties against foreign tyranny survived—in the argument over the abortive 1908 Secrecy Act *The Times* could protest that 'We are asked to graft upon British laws some of the worst features of Continental bureaucracy'[77]—and was to burst forth in all its glory when Germany invaded Belgium in 1914. However as the need to impose formal restrictions on the flow of information increased, so there developed a greater respect for the constitutional arrangements of neighbouring countries.

By the final quarter of the nineteenth century, there was a growing sense that rather than representing a beacon of hope in a dark world,

---

[73] I. Waddington, *The Medical Profession in the Industrial Revolution* (Dublin, 1984), 96–132; N. Parry and J. Parry, *The Rise of the Medical Profession* (1976), 124–6; Vincent, *Literacy and Popular Culture*, 167.

[74] R. Macleod (ed.), *Government and Expertise* (Cambridge. 1988), 15–17.

[75] On the impact of the 1844 controversy on the cause of Italian Nationalism in Britain, see Smith, 'British Post Office Espionage', 202.

[76] *Times*, 7 May, 1908, 11.

[77] *Times*, 6 December, 1858.

Britain was merely one amongst a number of modernising states facing common problems requiring similar solutions. As part of the careful preparation for the first Official Secrecy Act, the Foreign Office was asked to supply detailed summaries of the machinery which had been established to prevent the disclosure of information in France, Germany, Italy and Austria-Hungary.[78] Ironically, the one continental statute which was specifically cited as a model for sections of the 1889 Act had been passed in 1875 by the country to whose creation Mazzini had devoted his life.[79] By the second Act, ministers had become well versed in the twin appeal to the strength of foreign secrecy regulations and the superiority of domestic constitutional safeguards. Virtually the only argument set forth by Seely in the brief debate on the 1911 Bill was that, 'Every other country has legislation of this kind I understand, and in no case would the powers be used to infringe any of the liberties of His Majesty's subjects.'[80] In most other countries, the powers were much more sharply defined, but it was the glory of the British constitution to leave as much as possible unwritten.

The state's capacity to generate both complacency and anxiety by reference to overseas rivals was apparent in its campaign to quieten the newspapers' opposition to further secrecy legislation. On the one hand fears about the possible misuse of extra power were met with the assurance that if editors behaved as gentlemen should, then the British tradition of liberty would be security enough. As the Lord Chancellor put it in 1908, 'it should be clear that anyone in the Press conducting his duties honourably would be quite safe.'[81] On the other it was urged with ever-increasing stridency that the failure to observe the discretion expected of gentlemen was imperilling the safety of the nation.

The vulnerability of the press to this double appeal stemmed from the equivocal nature of its own position. This was nowhere better illustrated than in the affair of 'Defenceless Dover'. In March 1908, the *Morning Post* published an article which began with the provocative claim that 'Dover is a fortress as strong as Nature can make it and as weak as the present Government can leave it.'[82] The Admiralty, already irritated by a series of unauthorised disclosures, was outraged by the detailed discussion of the disposition of the batteries around the port, and successfully pressed the Government to introduce its long prepared Bill to expose newspapers to prosecution for publishing

[78] P.R.O., T1/8308B/16646.
[79] P.R.O., WO32/6347. MS note on drafting secrecy legislation, 24 December, 1887.
[80] *Hansard* 5th ser., XXIX, 18 Aug., 1911, col. 2252.
[81] *Hansard* 4th ser., CLXXXVIII, 11 May, 1908, col. 674.
[82] *Morning Post*, 21 March, 1908.

official information.[83] This in turn provoked a spirted and temporarily effective defence by the newly formed Newspaper Proprietors' Association. However the *Post* article was itself merely the latest instalment in the 'invasion scare' campaign in which most of Fleet Street was vigorously participating.[84] The Government's business managers knew that it was only a matter of time before the press so magnified the threat of Germany that it would be wholly unable to oppose the loss of civil liberties required to protect Britain. That moment arrived with the Agadir crisis of 1911, and the newspapers' articulate insubordination of three years earlier was duly replaced by a deferential silence.[85] A year later the N.P.A. tamely participated in the creation of the D-Notice system.[86]

More generally, the failure of the dogs to bark was a consequence of their assumption that they would continue to be fed. The issue of official secrecy in Victorian and Edwardian Britain was about the control rather than the volume of public communication.[87] From the 1873 Treasury Minute onwards, the state's principal concern was not with what was disclosed, but who disclosed it. Whilst a prolonged campaign was conducted against attempts by journalists to suborn junior civil servants, senior officials were permitted to maintain a steady stream of information on and off the record.[88] Over the years, as governments became more defensive and newspapers more enterprising, there was a breakdown of trust that the rules would be voluntarily observed, but little questioning of the game itself. Editors and their now fequently honoured proprietors were open to persuasion that the blanket clauses of the two Official Secrecy Acts would not destroy the gentlemanly relations they enjoyed with upper reaches of the establishment.

Honourable men sought to maintain official secrecy in order to preserve a deferential political culture. In a sense, Mazzini's questions were both apposite and misleading. The threat of foreign espionage was merely a special form of the broader challenge to a particular conception of the British state. It is no accident that in the spy stories

[83] P.R.O., ADM1/8030.

[84] D. French, 'Spy Fever in Britain, 1900–1915', *Historical Journal*, XXI, 2 (1978), 356–62.

[85] The most trenchant account of the Government's manoeuvring between 1908 and 1911 is to be found in *Report of the Departmental Committee on Section 2 of the Official Secrets Act of 1911* (Franks Committee), Cmnd 5104 (1972), I, 23–5.

[86] Hooper, *Official Secrets*, 223.

[87] P. Birkinshaw, *Freedom of Information* (1988), 70.

[88] Z. Steiner, 'The Last Years of the Old Foreign Office, 1898–1905', *Historical Journal*, VI, 1, (1963), 66; J. D. Gregory, *On the Edge of Diplomacy* (London, 1929), 265; S. Koss, *The Rise and Fall of the Political Press in Britian. Vol. 1: The Nineteenth Century* (1981), 219–22, 412.

of Le Queux, the heroes were always of aristocratic demeanour, and the villains drawn from the lower orders.[89] The essence of the invasion scare was a mistrust of the domestic population in whose ranks were thought to be hidden an ever larger fifth column. The challenge posed by the Irish, always excluded from this definition of Britain and from the protection of her liberties, and later by anarchists, Germans and suffragettes, were particular instances of an older dilemma. The fear to which Mazzini referred was not of this organisation or of that power, but of all those outside the traditional order. By the middle of the nineteenth century, it was evident that the lower reaches of the middle class and those beneath them could not forever be denied either the vote or employment in the bureaucracy of the new state. The proliferating flow of political communication had created the problem; the task now was to impose control over it in the name of the better born and better educated. If official information could become the property of the state, then the state would be safer for the holders of property.

A solution was found as Armaggedon approached. Edward Shils noted on a later occasion that there is a particular type of secret which is always more persuasive than any other: 'It is a secret with an aura of fatefulness. It is a secret in which the apocalypse dwells.'[90] But this was a destination which Mazzini had already reached. 'Secrecy is but another word for fear', his article concluded: 'MYSTERY was the name of the beast in the revelations. The great monster by which was typified all the civil and ecclesiastical corruptions of the earth, had on its forehead a name written, and that name was MYSTERY, BABYLON THE MOTHER OF HARLOTS.'[91]

---

[89] D. A. T. Stafford, 'Spies and Gentlemen: the Birth of the British Spy Novel 1893–1914', *Victorian Studies*, 24 (Summer, 1981), 491.

[90] E. A. Shils, *The Torment of Secrecy* (1956), 27. Also, S. Bok, *Secrets* (Oxford, 1984), 191–200.

[91] 'Mazzini and the Ethics of Politicians', 251. The passage is a misquotation from *Revelation* 17, v. 5.

THE ROYAL HISTORICAL SOCIETY
REPORT OF COUNCIL, SESSION 1990–1991

THE Council of the Royal Historical Society has the honour to present the following report to the Anniversary Meeting.

During the year Council has again kept a close eye on government reforms which affect the study of history in Britain. It welcomed the Secretary of State's Draft Order for History in the National Curriculum, which incorporated many points recommended by the Society. However, Council deplored the decision to make the study of history optional for pupils aged 14–16. After a debate on the National Curriculum in the House of Lords, initiated by Professor Russell, Council welcomed the proposal for a regular review of the curriculum and the suggestion that there should be a moving twenty year cut-off point for the study of recent history in schools.

Council was also much concerned with the proposals for reforming the Public Record Office. It broadly welcomed the report of the Scrutiny Committee, which rejected the case for privatisation. It expressed reservations about the proposal to move the records at Chancery Lane to Kew, unless specific additional accommodation was provided at Kew. After the House of Lords debate on the P.R.O., Council welcomed the Lord Chancellor's decisions not to change the name of the archive and not to introduce charges in the immediate future.

Council has continued its past practice of maintaining close links with other organisations concerned with the study of history. The Society continued to give financial support to the Historical Association's Young Historian Scheme and assisted Cadbury-Schweppes in awarding its prize for innovative History Teaching in Higher Education. Grants were also made to the British Association for Local History; the History Links Group; and the British National Committee of the International Historical Congress. Income from the Robinson Bequest was again given to Dulwich Picture Gallery to cover part of the cost of its special exhibitions. The Society has also provided further financial support for its major project, *The Bibliographies of British History*. The General Editor reported good progress during the year.

Council approved a number of changes designed to enhance the efficiency and appeal of the Society. The office has been equipped with a Fax machine and a laser printer. Council has agreed to establish a new committee to scrutinise Fellowship applications. It hopes to increase membership significantly in the future. Councillors will now be more directly involved in the selection of speakers and papers. It is hoped that attendance at paper readings may be increased if a Respondent comments briefly on each paper. A summary of the Respondent's comments and the subsequent discussion will be published with the paper, in the Society's *Transactions*.

Council is desirous that the Society should operate, as much as possible, as a genuinely national organisation. In pursuit of this objective, two Council meetings and paper readings will be held outside London in every session. They will be followed by receptions to which Fellows living in the region will be invited. The History Departments of several universities have invited the Society to visit them. The first provincial meetings will be held at Durham University (in December, 1991) and Newham College, Cambridge (in February, 1992).

An evening party was held for members and guests in the Upper Hall at University College London on Wednesday, 4 July 1990. 178 acceptances to invitations were received, and it was well-attended.

The Whitfield Prize for 1990 was awarded to Dr Duncan Tanner for his book *Political change and the Labour Party, 1900–1918* (Cambridge University Press). Two other volumes, Jacqueline Eales, *Puritans and Roundheads: The Harleys of Brampton Bryan and the Outbreak of the English Civil War* (Cambridge University Press), and Simon Walker, *The Lancastrian Affinity, 1361–1399* (Oxford University Press), received special commendation from the assessors.

The representation of the Society upon various bodies was as follows: Professor G. W. S. Barrow, Mr M. Roper and Professor P. H. Sawyer on the Joint Committee of the Society and the British Academy established to prepare an edition of Anglo-Saxon charters; Professor H. R. Loyn on a committee to promote the publication of photographic records of the more significant collections of British Coins; Professor P. E. Lasko on the Advisory Council of the reviewing committee on the Export of Works of Art; Professor G. H. Martin on the Council of the British Records Association; Mr M. R. D. Foot on the Committee to advise the publishers of *The Annual Register;* Professor K. Cameron on the Trust for Lincolnshire Archaeology; Professor W. Doyle on the History at the Universities Defence Group and the Court at the University of Exeter; Professor A. G. Watson on the Anthony Panizzi Foundation; Professor N. McCord on the Council of the British Association for Local History; and Dr Alice Prochaska on the National Council on Archives; Professor W. A. Speck on the Advisory Board of the Computers in Teaching Initiative Centre for History; and Professor Glanmor Williams on the Court of Governors of the

University College of Swansea. Council received reports from its representatives.

Professor E. B. Fryde represents the Society on a committee to regulate British co-operation in the preparation of a new repertory of medieval sources to replace Potthast's *Bibliotheca Historica Medii Aevi;* Professor A. L. Brown on the University of Stirling Conference; Professor C. N. L. Brooke on the British Sub-Commission of the Commission International d'Histoire Ecclésiastique Comparée; and Miss V. Cromwell and Professor N. Hampson on the British National Committee of the International Historical Congress. During the year, Dr. E. James agreed to succeed Professor K. Cameron as the Society's representative on The Trust for Lincolnshire Archaeology; Dr R. C. Mettam agreed to succeed Professor W. Doyle on the History at the Universities Defence Group: Mr C. P. Wormald agreed to succeed Professor G. W. S. Barrow on the Joint Committee of the Society and the British Academy established to prepare an edition of Anglo-Saxon charters; Professor M. C. Cross agreed to succeed Professor N. McCord on the Council of the British Association for Local History. The Society also accepted an invitation to be represented on the Court at the University of Birmingham, and Professor W. Davies agreed to accept Council's nomination.

Professor R. R. Davies accepted Council's invitation to succeed Professor F. M. L. Thompson, as President of the Society, in November 1992.

At the Anniversary Meeting on 16 November 1990, Dr R. E. Quinault was elected to succeed Professor A. N. Porter as Honorary Secretary and Dr M. C. E. Jones was elected to succeed Dr A. B. Worden as Literary Director. The remaining Officers of the Society were re-elected.

Professor D. Sugarman accepted Council's invitation to act as the Society's Honorary Legal Adviser.

The Vice-Presidents retiring under By-law XVII were Miss Barbara Harvey and Professor W. R. Ward. Professor J. Gooch and Professor C. J. Holdsworth were elected to replace them. The members of Council retiring under By-law XX were Professor Olive Anderson, Professor H. T. Dickinson, Professor N. McCord and Professor D. M. Palliser. Following a ballot of Fellows, Professor E. P. Hennock, Dr R. D. McKitterick, Dr R. C. Mettam and Dr A. G. R. Smith were elected in their place.

Messrs Davies, Watson and Co., were appointed auditors for the year 1990–91 under By-law XXXIX.

Publications and Papers read

Guide to the Local Administrative Units of England, Volume II, ed. F. A. Youngs (Guides and Handbooks, No. 17), *Transactions, Sixth Series*, Volume 1, *The Diary of George Canning, 1793–1795*, ed. P. Jupp (Camden, Fourth Series, Volume 41) and *Sir John Hayward's 'The Life and Reigne of Henry IIII (1599)*, ed. J. Manning, (Camden, Fourth Series, Volume 42), went to press during the session and are due to be published in late-1991.

The following 2 volumes in the STUDIES IN HISTORY series were published during the session: *Freewill or Predestination*, Andrew Penny (Volume 61) and *Amphibious Warfare in the 18th Century*, Richard Harding (Volume 62).

The *Annual Bibliography of British and Irish History, Publications of 1989*, was published by Oxford University Press.

A second edition of the *Memoirs of Sir John Reresby*, ed. A. Browning, with a new preface and notes by M. K. Geiter and W. A. Speck, went to press during the session.

At the ordinary meetings of the Society the following papers were read:

'The Continuity of the English Revolution' by Lord Dacre of Glanton (4 July 1990: Prothero lecture).

'Women and Images of Woman in the Spanish Civil War, 1936–1939' by Dr Frances Lannon (12 October 1990).

'The Origins of Public Secrecy in Britain' by Dr David Vincent (7 December 1990).

'Charles I, the Privy Council and the Parliament of 1628' by Dr Richard Cust (25 January 1991).

'Nazi Genocide in the Warthegau' by Professor Ian Kershaw (1 March 1991).

'Westminster and the Victorian Constitution' by Dr Roland Quinault (19 April 1991).

At the Anniversary Meeting on 16 November 1990, the President, Professor F. M. L. Thompson, delivered an address on 'English Landed Society in the Twentieth Century: II, New Poor and New Rich'.

A one day conference entitled 'Christian Life in the Later Middle Ages, was held in the British Local History Room at the Institute of Historical Research on 15 September 1990 at which the following papers were read:

'Prayers' by Professor John Bossy;

'The Cathedral Monasteries in the Fifteenth Century' by Professor Barrie Dobson;

'The Parish in Pre-Reformation English Society' by Dr Gervase Rosser;
and
'Lollardy and Locality' by Dr Richard Davies.

The Alexander Prize for 1991 was awarded to Dr David L. Smith for his essay *Catholic, Anglican or Puritan? Edward Sackville, Fourth Earl of Dorset, and the Ambiguities of Religion in Early Stuart England*, which was read to the Society on 17 May 1991.

Membership

Council records with regret the deaths of 29 Fellows and 2 Associates. They included Professor R. H. C. Davis, a former member of Council, and Professor C. D. Chandaman.

The resignations of 8 Fellows, 3 Associates and 13 Subscribing Libraries were received. 71 Fellows and 4 Associates were elected and 9 Libraries were admitted. 56 Fellows transferred to the category of Retired Fellow. The membership of the Society on 30 June 1991 comprised 1853 Fellows (including 51 Life Fellows and 272 Retired Fellows), 40 Corresponding Fellows, 146 Associates and 678 Subscribing Libraries (1811, 37, 149 and 682 respectively on 30 June 1990). The Society exchanged publications with 14 Societies, British and foreign.

Finance

The Society's surplus for the year 1990/91 had fallen to £8,290 as a result of increased costs of publications, yet the balance carried forward has increased owing to a surplus on sale of investments. The Society's finances continue to be in a satisfactory position and the level of subscriptions may accordingly be held at the existing rate for a further year.

The Society continues to pursue its policy of introducing new initiatives, and in the course of the year has instituted:

Bursaries to holders of ORS awards
Training bursaries
Funding towards research in archives outside the United Kingdom and
A workshop fund.

The Society continues to be grateful to its benefactors and during the year the new edition of Professor Browning's *Memoirs of Sir John Reresby* has been published as a mark of the Society's gratitude to Professor Browning, and as an indication of the continued excellence of his scholarship.

Benefactors of the Royal Historical Society:

Mr L. C. Alexander
The Reverend David Berry
Professor Andrew Browning
Professor C. D. Chandaman
Professor G. Donaldson
Mrs W. M. Frampton
Sir George Prothero
Professor T. G. Reddaway
Miss E. M. Robinson
Professor A. S. Whitfield

ROYAL HISTORICAL SOCIETY

Balance Sheet as at 30th June 1991

	Notes	1991 £	1991 £	1990 £	1990 £
Fixed Assets	2		764		1,993
Investments	3		818,140		730,897
Current Assets					
Stocks	1(c)	6,350		5,756	
Debtors	4	14,306		13,542	
Cash at Bank and in Hand	5	41,265		18,349	
		61,921		37,647	
Creditors: Amounts falling due within one year	6	70,739		44,050	
Net Current Liabilities			(8,818)		(6,403)
Net Total Assets			810,086		726,487
Represented by:					
General Fund			764,540		680,671
Miss E. M. Robinson Bequest			22,968		23,684
A. S. Whitfield Prize Fund			15,353		13,235
Studies in History			7,225		8,897
			810,086		726,487

ROYAL HISTORICAL SOCIETY

Income and Expenditure Account for the Year Ended 30th June 1991

GENERAL FUND

	Notes	1991		1990	
		£	£	£	£
INCOME					
Subscriptions.	7		60,790		56,49
Investment income			78,068		77,90
Royalties and reproduction fees.			8,195		2,63
Donations and sundry income			1,832		2,84
			148,885		139,88
EXPENDITURE					
SECRETARIAL AND ADMINISTRATIVE					
Salaries, pensions and national insurance		19,062		16,357	
Printing and stationery		4,629		8,920	
Postage and telephone		1,261		1,658	
Bank charges		1,507		1,196	
Audit and accountancy		2,632		1,783	
Insurance		447		471	
Meetings and travel.		5,931		4,697	
Repairs and renewals		703		552	
Depreciation	1(b)	1,345		1,316	
			37,517		36,95
PUBLICATIONS					
Literary director's expenses		94		363	
Publishing costs for the year.	8(a)	37,504		30,803	
Provisions for publications in progress.	8(b)	49,000		31,000	
Other publication costs	8(c)	2,287		1,273	
Sales of publications.		(176)		(463)	
			88,709		62,97
LIBRARY AND ARCHIVES	1(d)				
Purchase of books and publications		–		305	
Binding		1,414		1,715	
			1,414		2,02
			127,640		101,94
OTHER CHARGES					
Centenary Fellowship		4,863		6,075	
Alexander prize.		297		100	
Prothero lecture		260		286	
Grants		1,885		375	
Donations and sundry expenses		1,150		1,987	
A level prizes		500		500	
Young Historian		1,000		2,000	
British Bibliography.		3,000		1,096	
			12,955		12,41
			140,595		114,36
(Deficit)/Surplus for year			8,290		25,52
Surplus on sale of investments			75,579		43,74
			83,869		69,26
Balance brought forward at 1.7.90			680,671		611,40
Balance carried forward at 30.6.91			764,540		680,67

Income and Expenditure Account for the Year Ended 30th June 1991

SPECIAL FUNDS

	1991		1990	
	£	£	£	£
MISS E. M. ROBINSON BEQUEST				
INCOME				
Investment income		1,284		963
EXPENDITURE				
Grant to Dulwich Picture Gallery. . . .	2,000		1,000	
Other expenses.	—		2,727	
		2,000		3,727
(Deficit) for the year		(716)		(2,764)
Balance brought forward at 30.7.90 . . .		23,684		26,448
Balance carried forward at 30.6.90 . . .		22,968		23,684
A. S. WHITFIELD PRIZE FUND				
INCOME				
Investment income		1,650		1,367
EXPENDITURE				
Prize awarded	1,000		1,000	
Advertisement	—		309	
Other expenses	—		347	
		1,000		1,656
(Deficit)/Surplus for year.		650		(289)
Surplus on disposal of investments		1,468		—
		2,118		(289)
Balance brought forward at 1.7.90 . . .		13,235		13,524
Balance carried forward at 30.6.91 . . .		15,353		13,235
STUDIES IN HISTORY				
INCOME				
Royalties		1,375		3,843
Investment income		1,254		1,214
		2,629		5,057
EXPENDITURE				
Honorarium	3,500		3,313	
Editor's expenses	789		791	
Ex gratia royalties and sundry expenses . .	—		404	
Bank charges	12		—	
		4,301		4,508
(Deficit)/Surplus for the year		(1,672)		549
Balance brought forward		8,897		8,348
Balance carried forward		7,225		8,897

ROYAL HISTORICAL SOCIETY

STATEMENT OF SOURCE AND APPLICATION OF FUNDS FOR THE YEAR ENDED 30TH JUNE 1991

	1991 £	1991 £	1990 £	1990 £
SOURCE OF FUNDS				
Excess of income over expenditure for the year				
General fund		83,869		69,263
Miss E. M. Robinson Bequest		(716)		(2,764
A. S. Whitfield prize fund		2,118		(289
Studies in History fund		(1,672)		549
		83,599		66,759
Adjustment for items not involving the movement of funds				
Depreciation	1,345		1,316	
Surplus on sale of investments	(77,047)		(43,741)	
		(75,702)		(42,425
Total generated from operations		7,897		24,334
Funds from other sources				
Sale of investments		146,150		138,950
		154,047		163,284
APPLICATION OF FUNDS				
Purchase of fixed assets	116		609	
Net increase/(decrease) in Iceberg investments	2,515		29,025	
Purchase of investments	153,833		130,870	
		156,464		160,504
		(2,417)		2,780
INCREASE/(DECREASE) IN WORKING CAPITAL				
Stocks		594		(251
Debtors		1,536		(927
Creditors		(27,463)		(145
Liquid funds		22,916		4,103
		(2,417)		2,780

ROYAL HISTORICAL SOCIETY

NOTES TO THE FINANCIAL STATEMENTS FOR THE YEAR ENDED 30TH JUNE 1991

1. ACCOUNTING POLICIES
   (a) *Basis of accounting*
       These financial statements have been prepared under the historical cost convention.
   (b) *Depreciation*
       Depreciation is calculated by reference to the cost of fixed assets using a straight line basis at rates considered appropriate having regard to the expected lives of the fixed assets.
       The annual rates of depreciation in use are:
       Furniture and equipment   10%
       Computer equipment   25%

       Prior to 1st July 1987 the full cost of fixed assets was written off to General Fund in the year of purchase.
   (c) *Stocks*
       Stock is valued at the lower of cost and net realisable value.
   (d) *Library and archives*
       The cost of additions to the library and archives is written off in the year of purchase.

2. FIXED ASSETS

	Computer Equipment	Furniture and Equipment	Total
	£	£	£
Cost:			
At 1 July 1990	5,016	620	5,636
Additions during year.	116	—	116
At 30th June 1991	5,132	620	5,752
Depreciation:			
Opening depreciation.	3,457	186	3,643
Charge for year.	1,283	62	1,345
At 30th June 1991	4,740	248	4,988
Net book value:			
At 30th June 1991	392	372	764
At 30th June 1990	1,559	434	1,993

The cost of additions to the library and archives is written off in the year of purchase.
Prior to 1st July 1987 the cost of furniture and equipment was written off in the year of purchase. Items acquired before that date are not reflected in the above figures.

3. INVESTMENTS	1991 £	1990 £
Quoted securities at cost	699,255	614,527
(market value £1,389,494; 1990 £1,417,243)		
Money at call	118,885	116,370
	818,140	730,897

4. DEBTORS		
Sundry debtors	11,348	10,896
Prepayments	2,958	2,646
	14,306	13,542

5. CASH AT BANK AND IN HAND		
Deposit accounts.	38,015	15,242
Current accounts.	3,201	3,058
Cash in hand	49	49
	41,265	18,349

	1991 £	1990 £
6. CREDITORS		
Sundry creditors .	1,000	1,040
Subscriptions received in advance .	16,915	9,997
Accruals	3,824	2,013
Provision for publications in progress	49,000	31,000
	70,739	44,050
7. SUBSCRIPTIONS		
Current subscriptions .	56,188	53,569
Subscriptions arrears received .	2,769	1,365
Income tax on covenants .	1,833	1,565
	60,790	56,499

8. PUBLICATIONS

(a) Publishing costs for the year

	1991	1990
Transactions, fifth series Vol. 39	—	15,30
Camden, fourth series Vol 38 .	—	15,43
Camden, fourth series Vol 39 .	—	25,37
Guides and Handbooks No 16 .	10,145	3,69
Guides and Handbooks No 17 .	10,375	—
Handbook of Dates .	2,430	—
Transactions, fifth series Vol 40	19,110	—
Camden, fourth series Vol 40 .	15,738	—
Index to Authors	971	—
Reresby	2,881	—
Indirect costs, paper storage & usage & insurance .	6,854	
	68,504	59,803
Less: Provision brought forward .	31,000	29,000
	37,504	30,803

(b) Provision for publications in progress

	1991	1990
Transactions, fifth series Vol. 40 .	—	11,000
Camden, fourth series Vol 40 .	—	10,000
Guides and Handbooks No. 16 .	—	10,000
Guides and Handbooks No. 17 .	14,500	—
Reresby .	1,500	—
Transactions, sixth series Vol. 1 .	15,000	—
Camden, fourth series Vol. 41 .	16,000	—
List of Fellows .	2,000	—
	49,000	31,000

(c) Other publication costs

	1991	1990
Annual Bibliography .	2,450	2,633
Less: royalties received .	(163)	(1,360
	2,287	1,273

F. M. L. THOMPSON, *President*
M. J. DAUNTON, *Treaurer*

We have audited the financial statements on pages 7 to 12 in accordance with Auditing Standards.
In our opinion the financial statements give a true and fair view of the Society's affairs at 30th June 1991 and of its surplus and source and application of funds for the year then ended.

118, SOUTH STREET, DORKING
13th September, 1991

DAVIES, WATSON & CO.
Chartered Accountants

THE DAVID BERRY ESSAY TRUST

BALANCE SHEET AS AT 30TH JUNE 1991

	1991 £	1991 £	1990 £	1990 £
INVESTMENTS				
1117.63 units in the Charities Official Investment Fund		1,530		1,530
(Market Value £5,871: 1990 £5,746)				
CURRENT ASSETS				
Bank Deposit Account.	8,051		7,391	
	8,051		7,391	
CURRENT LIABILITIES				
CREDITORS: Amounts falling due within one year .	3,842		3,842	
	3,842		3,842	
NET CURRENT ASSETS		4,209		3,549
NET TOTAL ASSETS		5,739		5,079
Represented by:				
Capital fund		1,000		1,000
Accumulated Income account		4,739		4,079
		5,739		5,079

261

INCOME AND EXPENDITURE ACCOUNT FOR THE YEAR ENDED 30TH JUNE 1991

	1991		1990	
	£	£	£	£
INCOME				
Dividends		321		67.
Bank Interest Receivable		339		44.
		660		1,11.
EXPENDITURE		—		—
Excess of income over expenditure for the year		660		1,11.
Balance brought forward		4,079		2,96.
Balance carried forward		4,739		4,07.

The late David Berry, by his Will dated 23 April 1926, left £1,000 to provide in every three years a gold meda. and prize money for the best essay on the Earl of Bothwell or, at the discretion of the Trustees, on Scottish History of the James Stuarts I to VI, in memory of his father the late Rev. David Berry.

The Trust is regulated by a scheme sanctioned by the Chancery Division of the High Court of Justice dated 23 January 1930, and made in action 1927 A 1233 David Anderson Berry deceased, Hunter and Another v Robertson and Another and since modified by an order of the Charity Commissioners made on 11 January 1978 removing the necessity to provide a medal.

The Royal Historical Society is now the Trustee. The investment consists of 1117.63 Charities Official Investment Fund Income units.

The Trustee will in every second year of the three year period advertise, inviting essays.

We have audited the accounts on pages 13 and 14 in accordance with approved Auditing Standards.

In our opinion the accounts, which have been prepared under the historical cost convention, give a true and fair view of the Trust's affairs at 30th June 1991 and of its surplus for the year then ended and comply with the provisions of the Trust deed.

118, SOUTH STREET, DORKING
13th September, 1991

DAVIES, WATSON & CO
Chartered Accountants

ALEXANDER PRIZE

The Alexander Prize was established in 1897 by L. C. Alexander, F.R.Hist.S. The prize is awarded annually for an essay on a historical subject, which has been previously approved by the Literary Director. The essay must be a genuine work of original research, not hitherto published, and not previously awarded any other prize. It must not exceed 8,000 words, including footnotes, and must be sent in by 1 November. Further details may be obtained from the Executive Secretary. Candidates must *either* be under the age of 35 *or* be registered for a higher degree *or* have been registered for a higher degree within the last three years. The winner of the prize is awarded a silver medal and £250.

1991 PRIZE WINNER
David L. Smith, MA, PhD
'Catholic, Anglican or Puritan? Edward Sackville, Fourth Earl of Dorset, and the Ambiguities of Religion in Early Stuart England'

DAVID BERRY PRIZE

The David Berry Prize was established in 1929 by David Anderson-Berry in memory of his father, the Reverend David Berry. The prize is awarded every three years for an essay on Scottish history, within the reigns of James I to James VI inclusive. The subject of each essay must be submitted in advance and approved by the Council of The Royal Historical Society. The essay must be a genuine work of original research, not hitherto published, which has not been awarded any other prize. The essay should be between 6,000 and 10,000 words excluding footnotes and appendices. Further details may be obtained from the Executive Secretary.

1988 PRIZE WINNER
J. Goodare
'Parliamentary Taxation in Scotland, 1560–1603'

WHITFIELD PRIZE

The Whitfield Prize was established by Council in 1976 as a money prize out of the bequest of the late Professor Archibald Stenton Whitfield. Until 1982 the prize was awarded annually to the STUDIES IN HISTORY series. From 1983–1990 the prize was awarded annually to the best work of English or Welsh history by an author under 40 years of age, published in the United Kingdom. From 1991 the prize will be awarded to the best work on a subject within a field of British history published in the United Kingdom. It must be its author's first solely written history book and an original and scholarly work of historical research. Authors or publishers should send three copies (non-returnable) of a book eligible for the competition to the Executive Secretary before the end of the year in which the book was published. The award will be made by Council and announced at the Society's annual reception in the following July. The current value of the prize is £1,000.

1990 PRIZE WINNER
Duncan M. Tanner, BA, PhD
'Political change and the Labour Party, 1900–1918'

The nature and causes of change in Liberal and Labour politics between 1900 and 1918 is a much argued question. This book attempts to provide a new, integrated and coherent explanation of this process.

Much of the book concerns the pattern and explanation of the electoral changes. By examining pre-war elections (municipal and parliamentary), the First World War, and the 1918 parliamentary election, the book reveals where, how and why the Labour party replaced the Liberals. A series of chapters on industrial areas and other regions examine the electoral and organisational strengths and weaknesses of the Liberal and Labour parties in England and Wales before 1914. This is combined with an analysis of how Labour's electoral and political alliance with the Liberals worked.

The ideological and political similarities between the two parties, and the electoral, organisational and financial realities, prevented Labour from emerging as a serious contender to the Liberal party. Structural explanations, such as the limited nature of the franchise, are largely discounted. More emphasis is placed on the nature of the Liberals' political appeal and the inability of Labour to generate an attractive alternative. The Liberal party had created a powerful political coalition. Organisational change ideological radicalisation, a political image which could express a variety of local circumstances, and an ability to merge this with still popular 'traditional' Liberal rallying cries, ensured that Labour made comparatively little headway before 1914. There was not the electoral and organisational expansion, nor the trade union support, to make an assault on the Liberals a desirable or practical proposition.

Nonetheless, the Labour party was not identical to the Liberal party. It had a core of committed support, and in some areas it was making more pronounced progress. While the Liberals were handicapped by political events during the First World War, Labour pushed slightly ahead. Nonetheless, the Liberals were not eradicated. Labour needed years of campaigning and political restructuring before they were defeated. There was no single and inevitable onward march of Labour, but advance by stages and through a growing political credibility.

The nature and functioning of the two parties at local and national level is also examined. Trade unions are seen as a less significant political influence at this stage in Labour's development than is often recognised, and a critical look is taken at the role and ideas of the Labour left. The structural weaknesses of both organisations as means of initiating and developing radical policies are emphasised. The conclusion surveys events between 1918 and 1931.

In this, and other respects, the book goes beyond a narrow concern with the debate over the 'rise of Labour'. It is concerned with the role of social class in political change, the nature of political parties and the forces which have governed the evolution of the Labour party as a political machine.